ANTONY AND
CLEOPATRA

ANTONY AND CLEOPATRA

Adrian Goldsworthy

Yale
UNIVERSITY PRESS
New Haven & London

First published 2010 in the United States by Yale University Press
and in Great Britain by Weidenfeld & Nicolson

Yale University Press books may be purchased in quantity
for educational, business, or promotional use. For information,
please e-mail sales.press@yale.edu (U.S. office) or
sales@yaleup.co.uk (U.K. office).

Typeset by Input Data Services Ltd, Bridgwater, Somerset.
Printed in the United States of America.

Library of Congress Control Number: 2010929122
ISBN 978-0-300-16534-0 (hardcover : alk. paper)

A catalogue record for this book is available from the British Library.

This paper meets the requirements of ANSI/NISO Z39.48-1992
(Permanence of Paper).

10 9 8 7 6 5 4 3 2 1

CONTENTS

ACKNOWLEDGEMENTS

Like all my books, this one has been greatly improved by the generosity of friends and family who have taken the time to read drafts of the manuscript or listen to my ideas as they developed. All contributed to making this a much better book, and added to the great pleasure of writing it. There are too many to name them all, but particular mention should go to Ian Hughes and Philip Matyszak, both of whom took time off from their own writing to comment on the chapters of *Antony and Cleopatra*. Kevin Powell also read the entire manuscript and provided many insightful comments and criticisms. Of those who were patient enough to talk through the various ideas at length, I must single out Dorothy King for special thanks. Her knowledge and enthusiasm were always very helpful – and in addition she provided me with pearls for some modest experiments in an effort to replicate Cleopatra's famous wager with Antony!

In addition, I must once again thank my editor, Keith Lowe, and the other staff at Orion, as well as Ileene Smith and the team at Yale University Press, for seeing the book through to production and making such a fine job of it. Finally, thanks must go to my agent, Georgina Capel, for once again arranging for me to have the time and opportunity to do the subject justice.

MAP LIST

INTRODUCTION

Antony and Cleopatra are famous. With just a handful of others, including Caesar, Alexander the Great, Nero, Plato and Aristotle, they remain household names more than two thousand years after their spectacular suicides. Cleopatra is the only woman in the list, which in itself is interesting and a testament to her enduring fascination. Yet most often Antony and Cleopatra are remembered as a couple, and as lovers – perhaps the most famous lovers from history. Shakespeare's play helped them to grow into fictional characters as well, and so their story can now be numbered alongside other tales of passionate, but doomed romance, as tragic as the finale of *Romeo and Juliet*. It is unsurprising that the tale has been reinvented time after time in print, on stage and, more recently, on screen. Since they both had strongly theatrical streaks, this enduring fame would no doubt have pleased them, although since neither was inclined to modesty it would probably not have surprised them or seemed less than their due.

The story is intensely dramatic, and I cannot remember a time when I had not heard of Antony and Cleopatra. As young boys, my brother and I discovered a small box containing coins collected by our grandfather, a man who had died long before either of us was born. A friend spotted one of them as Roman, and it proved to be a silver denarius, minted by Mark Antony to pay his soldiers in 31 BC for a campaign partly funded by Cleopatra – the same coin shown in the photograph section in this book. Already interested in the ancient world, the discovery added to my enthusiasm for all things Roman. It seemed a connection not only with a grandparent, but also with Marcus Antonius the Triumvir, whose name circles the face of the coin with its picture of a warship. We do not know where our grandfather acquired this and the other coins – an eclectic mixture, several of which are from the Middle East. He may have picked them up in Egypt, where he served with the Royal Field Artillery during the First World War. It is certainly nice to think that.

So in some ways, Antony and Cleopatra have always had a special place in my interest in the ancient past, and yet the desire to write about them is fairly recent. A lot has been written, most especially about the queen, and it seemed unlikely that there could be much more worth saying. Then, a few years ago, I fulfilled a long-held ambition by working on *Caesar: The Life of a Colossus*, which amongst other things involved looking in far more detail at his affair with Cleopatra, as well as Antony's political association with him. Some of what I found surprised me, and – though this was less unexpected – there were vast differences to the popular impression of the story. If it was valuable to look at Caesar's career with a straightforward chronology, and to emphasise the human element in his own behaviour and that of his associates and opponents, it soon became clear that most other aspects of the period would benefit from the same approach.

For all their fame, Antony and Cleopatra receive little attention in formal study of the first century BC. Engaged in a power struggle, they were beaten and so had little real impact on later events. Academic history has long since developed a deep aversion to focusing on individuals, no matter how charismatic their personalities, instead searching for 'more profound' underlying trends and explanations of events. As a student I took courses on the Fall of the Roman Republic and the creation of the Principate, and later on as a lecturer I would devise and teach similar courses myself. Teaching and studying time is always limited, and as a result it was natural to focus on Caesar and his dictatorship, before skipping ahead to look at Octavian/Augustus and the creation of the imperial system. The years from 44–31 BC, when Antony's power was at its greatest, rarely receive anything like such detailed treatment. Ptolemaic Egypt is usually a more specialised field, but, even when it is included in a course, the reign of its last queen – poorly documented and anyway in the last days of long decline – is seldom treated in any detail. The fame of Cleopatra may attract students to the subject, but courses are, quite reasonably and largely unconsciously, structured to stress more 'serious' topics, and shy away from personalities.

Antony and Cleopatra did not change the world in any profound way, unlike Caesar and to an even greater extent Augustus. One ancient writer claimed that Caesar's campaigns caused the death of one million people and the enslavement of as many more. Whatever the provocation, he led his army to seize Rome by force, winning supreme power through civil war, and supplanted the Republic's democratically elected leaders. Against this, Caesar was famous for his clemency. Throughout his career he championed social reform and aid to the poor in Rome, as well as trying to protect the rights of people in the provinces. Although he made himself dictator, his rule was generally benevolent, and his measures sensible, dealing with long-neglected problems. The path to power of his adopted son, Augustus, was considerably more vicious, replacing clemency with revenge. Augustus' power was won in civil war and maintained by force, and yet he also ruled well. The Senate's political freedom was virtually extinguished and popular elections rendered unimportant. At the same time he gave Rome a peace it had not known in almost a century of political violence and created a system of government that benefited a far wider section of society than the old Republic.[1]

Antony and Cleopatra proved themselves just as capable of savagery and ruthlessness, but the losers in a civil war do not get the chance to shape the future directly. Apart from that, there is no real trace of any long-held beliefs or causes on Antony's part, no indication that he struggled for prominence for anything other than his own glory and profit. Some like to see Cleopatra as deeply committed to the prosperity and welfare of her subjects, but this is largely wishful thinking. There is no actual evidence to suggest that her concerns went any further than ensuring a steady flow of taxation into her own hands, to cement her hold on power. For only a small part of her reign was she secure on the throne, at the head of a kingdom utterly dependent on Roman goodwill, and it would probably be unreasonable to expect her to have done more than this.

Julius Caesar was highly successful. He was also highly talented across a remarkable range of activities. Even those who dislike the man and what he did can readily admire his gifts. Augustus is an even harder figure to like, especially as a youth, and yet no one would fail to acknowledge his truly remarkable political skill. Caesar and his adopted son were both very clever, even if their characters were different. Mark Antony had none of their subtlety, and little trace of profound intelligence. He tends to be liked in direct proportion to how much someone dislikes Octavian/Augustus, but there is little about him to admire. Instead, fictional portrayals have reinforced the propaganda of the 30s BC, contrasting Antony, the bluff, passionate and simple soldier, with Octavian, seen as a cold-blooded, cowardly and scheming political operator. Neither portrait is true, but they continue to shape even scholarly accounts of these years.

Cleopatra was clever and well-educated, but unlike Caesar and Augustus the nature of her intelligence remains elusive, and it is very hard to see how her mind worked or fairly assess her intellect. It is the nature of biography that the author comes to develop a strong, and largely emotional, attitude towards his or her subject after spending several years studying them. Almost every modern author to come to the subject wants to admire, and often to like, Cleopatra. Some of this is a healthy reaction to the rabid hostility of Augustan sources. Much has to do with her sex, for as we noted at the start, it is a rare thing to be able to study in detail any woman from the Greco-Roman world. Novelty alone encourages sympathy – often reinforced by the same distaste for Augustus that fuels affection for Antony. In itself sympathy need not matter, as long as it does not encourage a distortion of the evidence to idealise the queen. There is much we simply do not know about both Antony and Cleopatra – and indeed most other figures from this period. The gaps should not be filled by confident assertions drawn from the author's own mental picture of Cleopatra as she ought to have been.

By the time I had finished *Caesar*, I knew that I wanted to take a break from the first century BC and look at the decline of the Roman Empire and its collapse in the West. As much as anything this was because none of the books on that period seemed to explain events in a way I found satisfactory. The same sense that there was nothing that really did justice to the story of Antony and Cleopatra made me just as convinced that this book must come next.

To have real value, the study of history must be a quest for the truth. The whole truth is no doubt unobtainable even for comparatively recent events. For the ancient past, there will inevitably be many more gaps in our evidence as well as all the problems of understanding the actions of people from very different cultures to our own. That absolute success is impossible does not make the attempt to achieve it any less worthwhile. Similarly, although no historian can hope to be wholly objective, it still remains of fundamental importance to strive for this. If we always seek for the truth in history, whether or not it fits with our preconceptions or what we would like to believe, then we are far better placed to look for the truth in our own day and age.

This, then, is an attempt to tell the story of Antony and Cleopatra as objectively and dispassionately as possible, for there is passion enough in it without the author adding too much of his own personality. My aims are also to reveal as much of the true events as is possible, while making plain what we do not know, and bring the couple and their contemporaries alive as flesh-and-blood human beings. Getting to the facts is a lot less easy than it might seem, for even serious scholars so often want to see something else when they look at these two extraordinary lives.

THE PROBLEM

It begins with the question of just what Cleopatra was. Cleopatra was the queen of Egypt, and for the last few centuries Ancient Egypt has fascinated the modern world. At first interest came mainly from a desire to understand the Old Testament better, but rapidly moved far beyond that. Egypt is perceived as the most ancient of civilisations and its monuments are amongst the most spectacular. Some, such as the pyramids, sphinx and the great temples, are awe-inspiringly massive. Others are more intimate, such as the mummified animals and people, and the models of everyday things left in the tombs of the dead. Tutankhamen's lavish death mask is immediately recognisable and conjures up images of ancient mystery and massive wealth. Hieroglyphics, with their mixture of symbols and pictures, or the flattened figures of people walking in the strange posture of wall paintings and reliefs are again both instantly recognisable as Egyptian. They are dramatic and at the same time alien.

Such imagery has time and again proven itself irresistible to film-makers depicting Cleopatra. Her palace, court and indeed her own clothes are invariably inspired more by a caricatured version of New Kingdom Egypt than the reality of the first century BC. This is the chronological equivalent of presenting Elizabeth I as Queen Boudica of the Iceni, yet it has the dramatic virtue of making Cleopatra and Egypt utterly different and visually distinct from the Romans who form such a major part of her story. The Cleopatra of stories has to be exotic, and the images of an Egypt that was ancient even to her are a powerful part of this.

The exotic is almost always reinforced by the intensely erotic. Cleopatra has become one of the ultimate femmes fatales, the woman who seduced the two most powerful men of her day. Beautiful, sensual, almost irresistible and utterly unscrupulous, she distracted Julius Caesar, and perhaps filled his head with dreams of eastern monarchy. She then dominated Antony and brought him low. This Cleopatra can be seen as a danger – the last great danger – to the *Pax Romana* Augustus would bring to the Roman world. Fashions change, so that empires are no longer seen as admirable, and the Augustan system viewed with a more sceptical eye. These days many want to tell the story differently, turning the sinister seductress into a strong and independent woman struggling as best she could to protect her country.

For all that the title of Shakespeare's play makes it natural to speak of Antony and Cleopatra, the glamour associated with the queen readily overshadows her lover. She had anyway already had an affair with Caesar – the scene where she is delivered to him hidden in a rolled carpet is one of the best-known images of the queen, even if it does not quite fit the ancient source. Caesar was first, and history has on the whole relegated Mark Antony to the second place and the role of Caesar's lieutenant. A 'good second-in-command' or a 'follower rather than a leader' have been common verdicts on Antony, both politically and militarily. He is also seen as the man who ought to have won, but failed, and this again feeds an impression of a flawed character – talent without genius. Some would blame Cleopatra for unmanning the tough Roman soldier, a tradition encouraged by his ancient biographer, Plutarch. Others would prefer to see Antony as simply not good enough to match her ambitions. For one historian, Cleopatra was 'a charismatic personality of the first order, a born leader and vaultingly ambitious monarch, who deserved better than suicide with that *louche* lump of a self-indulgent Roman, with his bull neck, Herculean vulgarities, and fits of mindless introspection'.[2]

Cleopatra readily provokes an emotional response. In addition, myth and romance surround Antony and Cleopatra and make the truth elusive. Both of them consciously worked to shape their public images during their lifetime – as strong rulers, as godlike, as lovers of life and luxury. Simultaneously, political opponents sought to damn them. The orator Cicero directed his *Philippics* against Antony, producing some of the most effective character assassination of all time. Far more thoroughly, Caesar's adopted son Octavian – the man who would become Rome's first emperor and take the name Augustus – defeated Antony and Cleopatra. They died and he survived, holding supreme power for more than forty years. It gave him plenty of time to shape the historical record to best suit his new regime. His strongly hostile view of both Antony and Cleopatra influenced our fullest sources for their lives, all of which were written under the rule of Augustus' successors.

Cleopatra continues to attract plenty of biographers. A few of these books also study Antony's life in detail, but biographies devoted exclusively to him remain rare. He now tends to be an accessory to the life of his lover. Anyone looking at the period will be quick to point out the problems caused by Augustan propaganda; often it is difficult to know whether an incident happened, and it would be tempting to reject any negative story. Unfortunately, however, there are well-attested incidents in which both Antony and Cleopatra behaved in ways that seem irrational or at best politically unwise.[3]

The young Octavian is difficult to like. He was unscrupulous, could be vicious and at times was a physical coward. The Principate, the system by which Rome was ruled by emperors for the next two and a half centuries, was his creation and attitudes to this often do much to shape views of Antony and Cleopatra. Admirers of the Augustan system will pardon the brutality of his path to power and see his enemies as delaying – even endangering – Rome's great legacy to the world. Critics will praise them for resisting an extremely unpleasant tyrant, and some will claim that the pair offered a far better alternative, although they cannot usually be too specific about what this was.[4]

Cleopatra was a strong and independent woman in an ancient world that was dominated by men. She had power in her own right as queen, unlike Roman women who were more likely to have influence as the wives or mothers of great men. For most modern authors this is extremely attractive and encourages a generous treatment. Serious accounts of Cleopatra's life never let this mood slip into eulogy, but sympathy for the queen all too readily combines with the glamour of her fictional portrayals to distort our view of her times. There are two very basic truths about her, which conflict so strongly with the legend that it takes a conscious and determined effort to maintain them.

The first of these is at least usually noted. All recent biographers will begin by pointing out that Cleopatra was Greek and not Egyptian. Greek was her first language, and it was in Greek literature and culture that she was educated. Although represented on Egyptian temples and in some statuary clad in the traditional headgear and robes of the pharaohs' wives, it is unlikely that she actually dressed this way save perhaps occasionally to perform certain rites. Instead, she wore the headband and robes of a Greek monarch. Cleopatra proclaimed herself the 'New Isis', and yet her worship of the goddess betrayed a strongly Hellenised version of the cult. She was no more Egyptian culturally or ethnically than most residents of modern-day Arizona are Apaches.

Noting the essential Greek-ness of Cleopatra is one thing. It is much harder to resist the lure of truly ancient Egypt – both the popular imagery and the actual reality. Egypt is exotic, and it is also to Westerners decidedly eastern. In the past, a sensual Egyptian

Cleopatra could be an alluring, almost irresistible threat to stern Roman virtue and the advance of Rome's empire and civilisation. Even if she was Greek, then she was a representative of Hellenic culture, which had decayed through contact with eastern decadence. Such views have not been fashionable for a long time, and often the pendulum has swung to the opposite extreme. Empires are now automatically bad things, imperialists brutal and exploitative, and European culture itself is often seen by many Westerners today in a negative light. Thus it is common to emphasise the savagery of Rome's rise to empire, and Cleopatra is admired for resisting the onslaught. Occasionally this is as a Greek, but the attraction of the orient is strong, and usually she once again becomes a representative of the east.

This is not really helped by the tradition of separating the period following the rise of Philip II and his son Alexander the Great from earlier Greek history. In the nineteenth century this later period was dubbed Hellenistic – not Greek or Hellenic, but 'Greek-like'. Classical Greece had been dominated by city states, of which the greatest were Athens and Sparta. Athens produced art, literature and philosophy, which have profoundly influenced the world to this day; Sparta became famous for the formidable prowess of its soldiers at the cost of creating a particularly repellent society. Athens took the idea of democracy further than any other ancient state, and was exceptionally aggressive and ruthless in its foreign policy.[5]

Eventually, the promise of this democracy faded, as did Athens' power. Kings appeared again and so did tyrants, while those cities who retained any vestige of democracy reduced the electorate to ever smaller sections of society. By the later fourth century BC the kings of Macedonia dominated all of Greece. In this different political climate the cultural spark appeared to fade. To modern eyes – and indeed to many people at the time – no more drama or literature was being created to match the heights reached in the past.

Scholarly attitudes have changed somewhat and many would now dispute any inherent inferiority of the Hellenistic Age – at least in terms of government and society. They still employ the term, for convenience if nothing else. The tradition also remains of dating the end of this period to the death of Cleopatra. That makes her the end of an era beginning with Alexander and his conquests. This connection is there in the best modern biographies, but it often struggles to compete with the romance of the much older Egyptian past. That several recent biographers have been Egyptologists has only made it harder for them to maintain an essentially Greek Cleopatra. Yet that was the reality, whether we like it or not. Her world was not the same as the fifth century BC and the height of Athenian achievement, but it was thoroughly Greek none the less. So if there was a great struggle in Cleopatra's lifetime it was not between east and west, but Greek and Roman.[6]

The second uncomfortable fact about Cleopatra is universally ignored by her modern biographers. These routinely lament that our sources focus almost exclusively on Cleopatra's affairs with Caesar and Antony. The rest of her life, including the years she spent ruling Egypt on her own, receive scant mention. Unfortunately, documents on papyrus that give details of official decrees, the workings of government, and private business and affairs are rare for the first century BC in general and Cleopatra's reign in particular. The vast bulk of these texts date to much earlier in the rule of Egypt by her family. A papyrus discovered relatively recently consisted of a decree issued by the queen and may well end with a single Greek word written in her own hand. This is exciting, but scarcely sufficient to do more than give us the slightest glimpse of her government in action. Significantly, it also grants a concession to a prominent Roman.[7]

The literary sources were all written either by Romans or by Greeks writing under the Roman Empire at least a century after Cleopatra's death. A good deal of information and personal anecdote comes from Plutarch's *Life of Mark Antony*. This is the only biography of him to survive from the ancient world. There is no surviving ancient biography of Cleopatra. A familiar complaint is that the story is not simply told by the victors, but always from the Roman viewpoint – in some cases that this is a male Roman viewpoint may be emphasised even more.[8]

There is a reason why this is so. Whether we like it or not, Cleopatra was not really that important. Her world was one utterly dominated by Rome, in which her kingdom had at best a precarious independence. She was a queen, and controlled an Egypt that was wealthy and by ancient standards densely populated. Yet it was a Roman client kingdom and never fully independent. Egypt was the largest, and in many ways the most important, of Rome's subordinate allies, but it was always subordinate, and its power was dwarfed by that of the Roman Republic. Cleopatra only became queen because her father was placed back in power by a Roman army. Even after that, she would have been dead or exiled by her early twenties were it not for Caesar's intervention.

Cleopatra only had importance in the wider world through her Roman lovers. Television documentaries and popular books often repeat the claim that the Romans only ever feared two people – Hannibal and Cleopatra, but people usually ignore the fact that this sweeping statement was made in the 1930s. It rests on no ancient evidence, and does not make any real sense. Much as Augustan propaganda demonised the queen, no one could seriously have believed that she had the power to overthrow Rome. It was simply far more convenient to hate a foreign, female enemy, than to face the fact that Octavian's great war and subsequent triumph was over a distinguished Roman. For all her glamour, Antony was of far greater power and significance than Cleopatra.[9]

None of this means that Cleopatra is any less fascinating. We need to understand the reality of the first century BC if we are to understand her. In many ways this makes her career all the more spectacular because it was unexpected. Her achievements were remarkable: she not only survived in power for almost two decades, but also for a while expanded her realm almost to the extent of her most successful ancestors. That she did this through harnessing Roman power to her own benefit does not detract from the scale of her success. It is vital to step beyond the myth and the wishful thinking and seek the reality of Cleopatra and her place in the world.

Just as importantly, we need to understand Antony as a Roman senator, not simply relegate him to the supporting role of Caesar's subordinate and Cleopatra's lover. On closer inspection, many of the familiar assumptions about him prove to be mistaken. Plutarch and others painted him as very much the military man, a bluff and coarse soldier brought low by a woman. It is debatable how far Antony ever let Cleopatra determine his policy. What is clear is that he actually had very little military service by Roman standards, and most of his experience came in civil wars. He was not an especially good general, although at times he was a popular leader. There was much that was traditional about Antony and this goes a long way to explaining his importance and his ambitions. It was certainly not inevitable that he was defeated by Octavian. If the latter's rise to power was spectacular for such a young man, Antony's own career also owed a great deal to good fortune and the unusual opportunities presented by a Roman Republic rent by civil wars.

Both Antony and Cleopatra need to be understood within the context of their culture and times. Yet this book cannot hope to cover this turbulent era in every detail. Its concern is always with them, on where they were and what they were doing. Events elsewhere will be treated briefly, and only as far as is necessary to understand their story. Therefore, Caesar's career is treated very quickly, and only in greater depth when it also involved Antony and Cleopatra. Similarly, the rise of Octavian is both remarkable and fascinating, but cannot be dealt with at any length. Other important figures, notably Cicero, Pompey and his son Sextus, are treated even more briefly. This is not a reflection of their importance, but a question of focus.

Politics will be at the forefront of the story, because Antony and Cleopatra were first and foremost political animals. So was Caesar, the queen's first lover and father of her oldest child. None of them ever acted without at least a degree of political calculation. In spite of a few unconvincing accusations of debauchery, the evidence strongly suggests that Cleopatra only took two lovers and each was the most important man in the Roman Republic at that time. None of this need mean that there was not also strong and genuine attraction involved on both sides. Indeed, it is hard to understand this story in any other way. It is vital in studying any history to remember that the characters were flesh and blood human beings much like us, however different the times and their cultures may have been. The romance must be there because it was real. One of the reasons for the enduring appeal of Antony and Cleopatra's story is that all of us can understand the power of passion from our own lives.

The story of Antony and Cleopatra is one of love, but also one of politics, war and ambition. The actual events were intensely dramatic – hence the appeal to novelists, dramatists and screen-writers. Looking at the facts as far as we know or can confidently guess them only reinforces the drama. So does the acknowledgement of what we do not know, for many of the mysteries remain fascinating in themselves. A closer look at the truth exposes an episode in human history more remarkable than any invention. It may not be the story we expect, or even perhaps would like to believe, but it is one of lives lived intensely at a time when the world was changing profoundly.

[1]

THE TWO LANDS

Egypt was already ancient long before Cleopatra was born in 69 BC. Almost four hundred years earlier Herodotus – the first man to write a prose history in any western language – assured his fellow Greeks that they must have learnt much of their own religion and knowledge from the Egyptians. Like much of his work, Herodotus' account of Egypt is a curious mixture of myth, fantasy and confusion, occasionally leavened with accurate information. Greeks tended to idealise Egypt as the home of ancient wisdom, while at the same time despising a people who worshipped sacred animals and practised circumcision. They were also awed by the sheer scale of the pyramids at Giza and included them amongst the Seven Wonders of the World.

It is sobering to remember that Cleopatra lived closer to us in time than she did to the builders of the great pyramids. The largest pyramid of all was built for the Pharaoh Khufu, who died in 2528 BC, some twenty-five centuries before the queen took her own life. That is the same distance of time separating us from Herodotus himself, from the Persian invasions of Greece and the early days of the Roman Republic.

Khufu was not the first pharaoh, but belonged to what is known as the Fourth Dynasty. The organisation of rulers into dynasties was done by a priest scholar working for Cleopatra's family, and the scheme he devised is still largely followed today. There were no fewer than thirty dynasties before her family came to power at the end of the fourth century BC. The first pharaoh ruled from around 2920 BC – it is difficult to be precise at such an early period. That was not the beginning of civilisation in Egypt – there were organised communities farming on the banks of the Nile long before then, and in time two major kingdoms had emerged, which eventually combined. The pharaohs were the lords of 'two lands', Upper and Lower Egypt, and wore a crown symbolising this union. Upper Egypt lay to the south with its capital at Thebes. Lower Egypt was to the north, reaching to the Mediterranean coast and with Memphis as its centre. (This arrangement of upper and lower only seems strange to us because we are so accustomed to maps and globes showing north at the top.)[1]

The Nile made everything possible. Each summer it flooded its banks and then receded – a natural cycle only ended by the building of the Aswan Dam in the second half of the twentieth century. The annual inundation left behind a rich deposit of dark alluvial silt, and with it moisture to make the land wonderfully fertile. All of the earliest civilisations rested on the ability of farmers to produce a surplus. They grew because communities were better able to develop large-scale irrigation systems than individuals. In Egypt the problems of dealing with and exploiting the bounty offered by the inundation were greater, and did even more to encourage the growth of central authority.

People lived only where there was water. Egypt's population was very large by ancient standards, but was overwhelmingly concentrated in just two areas. In the north was the Delta, where the river split into many separate channels to flow into the Mediterranean, irrigating a wide stretch of land as it did so. South of this was the Nile Valley as far as the first cataract. The inundation did not spread far, producing a very densely populated strip of land some 500 miles long and never wider than a dozen miles. The lands beyond were desert. A few communities survived around the rare oases, but mainly there was nothing.[2]

Egyptians saw themselves as the centre of the world and the one true civilisation. Outside there were chaos and hostile barbaric peoples. Even inside there were threats to order – the Nile inundation was unpredictable in its scale. Too much water could be as disastrous as too little, producing very poor harvests – the years of plenty and years of famine of pharaoh's dream in Genesis. There were supernatural threats to add to the natural ones and the human enemies, for the struggle between order and chaos was reflected in the divine world as well. The pharaohs stood between gods and men and communicated with both, ensuring that order and justice – embraced by the term 'Maat' – prevailed over chaos.[3]

They were also the heads of a rich and powerful nation, but there were other powers in the world and conflict was not uncommon. At times Egypt was strong, and pharaohs extended their rule further south along the Nile at the expense of the Kingdom of Meroe, or eastwards into Syria and Palestine. Sometimes the balance of power favoured their neighbours and they lost territory. In the second millennium BC a foreign people known as the Hyksos overran much of Egypt and ruled for nearly a century before they were expelled and the New Kingdom created. Nor was Egypt free from internal rebellion and civil war. At times the two kingdoms were divided and rival dynasties ruled simultaneously.

Egyptian culture was never entirely static or immune to change, but it was remarkably conservative. At its heart was the annual agricultural cycle centred around the inundation, and farming methods changed hardly at all in thousands of years. Surrounding this and all aspects of life were the rituals and beliefs that secured the order of seasons, the growth of crops and every aspect of life itself. Outside Egypt the power of the pharaohs stretched far afield or shrank as other empires rose and fell. In the last millennium BC the Assyrians, Babylonians and Persians in turn dominated the middle east. For some of this time Egypt was itself powerful, controlling substantial territories in Asia, but its strength declined and for over a century from 525 to 404 BC the Persians ruled Egypt. Finally, the Egyptians rebelled and expelled them, and for the next sixty-one years were ruled again by native pharaohs. Yet the Persian Empire remained strong and in 343 BC it again conquered Egypt. This occupation seems to have been especially brutal, and was certainly bitterly resented.

Less than a decade later, the world changed suddenly and drastically with the arrival of Alexander the Great. Persia fell, and all of its territories came under the control of the new conqueror.

THE KING OF MACEDON

It would be difficult to exaggerate the impact of Alexander. Impact is the right word, for there was something intensely physical about his career, and we need to keep reminding ourselves of the speed and sheer scale of what he did. Alexander was not quite thirty-three when he died at Babylon on 10 June 323 BC and had been king for just twelve and a half years. He inherited from his father, Philip II, a Macedonia that was internally strong, possessed a superb army and already dominated Greece. The preparations had also already begun for an expedition against Persia, but although Alexander inherited the idea from his father, it was his own restless energy and insatiable lust to excel that drove the wars that followed.

Alexander and his soldiers marched or rode more than 20,000 miles. By the fifth year the Persian king was dead and his royal city reduced to ashes. Alexander was now head of the largest empire in the known world, but saw no reason to stop. He kept on eastwards, until he controlled all the lands from the Balkans to what is now Pakistan. When Julius Caesar was thirty he saw a bust of Alexander and is supposed to have wept because his own life seemed so paltry by comparison.[4]

Alexander left Macedon in 334 BC and never returned. The same was true of many Macedonians and Greeks who accompanied him. What Alexander hoped ultimately to achieve is now impossible to say. It may well be that he had not yet made up his own mind how he wanted his new empire to function. Alexander was clever, subtle, ruthless, suspicious, at times appallingly savage, and at others merciful and generous. His army was powerful, but far too small to have held down the empire by force. He founded cities populated by settlers – often veteran soldiers – in many places, but these remained a tiny minority of the overall population. Greek language and culture was spread far more widely as a result of Alexander's conquests, but it was also spread thinly.

Alexander's empire was too vast to be ruled simply as a collection of provinces of Macedonia. As the years went on he made more and more use of Persian noblemen as governors and administrators, as well as Persian soldiers. There were not enough Macedonians and Greeks with the linguistic skills and experience to fulfil every role. It was far more practical to enlist local men, and this had the important benefit of giving his new subjects a stake in his empire. Aspects of court ceremony and the king's role changed from a traditional Macedonian pattern to a hybrid monarchy including Persian elements as well as new innovations. Alexander took honours and symbols that were at least semi-divine, and may even have wanted to go further and be worshipped as a living god. Yet once again we must remember the time factor. In little more than a decade there was very little chance for any aspect of the new regime to bed itself in.[5]

All of the various territories were tied directly to Alexander, with nothing else to unite them. This might not have mattered if there had been a clear and viable heir when Alexander died. He had a half-brother, Arrhidaeus, who had only been allowed to live because he was considered to be a half-wit. In spite of this, he was now named as king. Alexander's latest wife Roxanne, the daughter of a Bactrian chieftain (and thus from what is now Afghanistan), was pregnant when he died. Some months later in 322 she gave birth to a boy who was named Alexander IV and promptly made joint king. The empire now had two monarchs ruling jointly, but one was an infant and the other incapable. Real power was exercised by the group of senior officers and officials, most of whom were in Babylon during these months.

A general named Perdiccas was appointed as regent – Alexander was supposed to have handed him his signet ring in his last moments. The dying conqueror was also supposed to have replied that his empire should go 'to the strongest', and that 'his foremost friends would hold a great funeral contest over him'. If he actually uttered these words, it may have reflected a yearning for the heroic age of a man who slept with a copy of Homer's epic, the *Iliad*, under his pillow, or a realistic understanding of the inevitable. It is doubtful that even if he had chosen an adult heir at this late date his empire would have held together.[6]

At first the others co-operated with Perdiccas, as they sought to build up personal power bases amidst a climate of growing suspicion and fear. The most important men were appointed as satraps, regional governors who were in theory loyal to and controlled by the monarchs and the regent. Ptolemy, a distant relative of Alexander and now in his early forties, was made satrap of Egypt at his own request. Soon it became apparent that Perdiccas could only control the satraps by force and he and his army could not be everywhere at the same time. In 321 he marched against Ptolemy, but the campaign ended in disaster with a botched attempt to cross the Nile. Perdiccas' senior officers murdered their leader. They offered command to Ptolemy, but when he cautiously refused the bulk of the army marched away.

That was just one episode in a long and convoluted series of wars fought between Alexander's generals as they tore his empire apart in a struggle for personal power. Ptolemy was one of the more cautious players, determined not to risk losing what he already controlled. The 'funeral games' lasted for almost fifty years, and almost all of the main protagonists died violently. Arrhidaeus was murdered in 317 BC, and Alexander IV and his mother in 311 BC. They were not replaced, and at no point did any of the rival generals have a realistic chance of reuniting the whole empire under his own control. The prospect of any one man gaining supremacy invariably prompted the others to forget their differences for the moment and combine in opposition. Yet for years the satraps continued to style themselves as governors serving monarchs who no longer existed. In Babylon and Egypt official documents were even dated according to fictional years in the reign of the murdered boy king Alexander IV.[7]

It was not until 305–304 BC that Ptolemy and the other satraps threw off the pretence and declared themselves to be kings. He was Cleopatra's ancestor and for nine generations his family would rule the empire he created during the struggle with Alexander's other former generals. Ptolemy was a Macedonian, and Cleopatra herself was the first of the family able to speak the Egyptian language – only one of nine languages in which she was said to be fluent. The Ptolemies spoke Greek, and for centuries it was a mark of prestige at their court to be able to speak the peculiar Macedonian dialect of the language. As we shall see, they were kings who controlled Egypt, but they were not primarily kings of Egypt. Yet it was always the wealthiest of their possessions, and the last one to fall.[8]

THE HOUSE OF LAGUS

There were Greeks in Egypt long before Alexander arrived. Some came as merchants and many more as mercenaries. In the last centuries of an independent Egypt the pharaohs relied heavily on foreign professional soldiers, who were used against both foreign and domestic opponents. These soldiers with their alien religions were not always popular with the Egyptians. Alexander himself came to Egypt late in 332 BC. Although he had won two battles against the Persians, and taken Tyre and Gaza, the struggle with the Persian King Darius was still far from over. The Persians did not defend Egypt, and the Egyptians, who had no love for the Persians, seem to have welcomed Alexander as a liberator. They were anyway in no position to resist him, but there may have been genuine enthusiasm when he was named as pharaoh. Alexander spent several months in Egypt, and some have seen this as longer than the strategic situation warranted, giving time for Darius to regroup.

Mystery surrounds the long march he made into the western desert to reach the oasis at Siwah with its temple of the god Ammon, equated by the Greeks with Zeus. The shrine was famous for its oracle, and it was widely believed that the priest who acted as the god's mouthpiece welcomed the conqueror as Ammon's son. One tradition claimed this was a slip of the tongue. Less controversially, Alexander laid out and began the construction of Alexandria. It was not the only city founded by him and bearing his own name, but it would prove by far the most important. A man named Cleomenes, who came from the Greek community in Egypt, was appointed to govern when Alexander left in the spring of 331 BC. He never returned to Egypt during his lifetime.[9]

Soon after Ptolemy came to Egypt in 323 BC as satrap he had Cleomenes dismissed and executed. In 321 BC his men intercepted Alexander the Great's funeral cortège on its way to Macedonia, and instead brought his mummified body to Egypt. It was eventually installed in a specially built tomb in Alexandria. Ptolemy himself wrote a detailed history of Alexander's campaigns, helping to shape the myth of the conqueror in a way favourable to his own ambitions.

Ptolemy began with relatively few soldiers. He and his successors encouraged immigrants from Greece and Macedonia to settle in Egypt. From the beginning Alexandria was to be an overtly Greek city, with its own laws inspired by those of Athens. Mercenaries serving only for pay were not fully reliable and inclined to change sides if the campaign went against them. Therefore the Ptolemies granted their soldiers plots of land known as cleruchies to give them a stake in the new regime. It was not a new idea, but was done quickly and on a generous scale. Officers received more than ordinary soldiers, cavalry more than infantry. The produce of these farms was taxed, but the main obligation of the settlers or cleruchs was to serve in the king's army. On at least one occasion when some of Ptolemy's soldiers were captured by a rival leader, they preferred to remain as prisoners in the hope of eventually returning to Egypt rather than defect. This was extremely unusual.[10]

In the third century Egypt may have had a population as big as 7 million. Probably half a million lived in Alexandria. A few other cities, such as Memphis, may have had populations a tenth of that size, but most were smaller. The Ptolemies were less enthusiastic about founding cities than others of the Successors, and most people lived in villages, better suited to housing an agricultural workforce. The Delta and the Nile Valley continued to be densely occupied. The Ptolemies also developed the Fayum to the west, creating irrigation systems around Lake Moeris and elsewhere to make farming possible. Many cleruchies were established here, as were large estates leased to prominent and wealthy Greeks. It added a third highly populated area to the country. The development of this area had the advantage of increasing the scale of the harvest, which the king could tax. At the same time he rewarded his soldiers and followers without having to evict large numbers of Egyptians from their land.[11]

Egypt's population remained overwhelmingly rural under the Ptolemies; it was also overwhelmingly Egyptian. Even in the cleruchies, the bulk of the actual labouring was done by Egyptians; there were very few slaves outside Alexandria. In many cases the cleruchs leased some or all of their land to tenant farmers. Military duty took the cleruchs themselves away, but over time many became absentee landlords living off rents.

Greeks remained a small minority throughout the rule of the Ptolemies. It was clearly impossible for the two communities to live in complete isolation. Yet scarcely any Egyptian words passed into Greek and it is striking how separate the two cultures remained over the course of the centuries. There were separate Greek and Egyptian law codes with their own judges and courts. At times individuals from one group chose to have particular aspects of their life regulated under the other law code if this seemed advantageous. Egyptian law granted considerably more rights to women and was often employed by Greek families wishing daughters to inherit property. One papyrus surviving from the early first century BC (and so more than two hundred years after Ptolemy I took control of Egypt) is the will of an Egyptian soldier in the service of the Ptolemies. It is written in Demotic – the form of the Egyptian language written in an alphabet rather than hieroglyphics – but the layout and style are Greek in every respect. In most cases Greek law was dominant, and there was never any attempt to merge the two legal systems.[12]

There were many wealthy and influential Egyptians. Just as Alexander had done, the Ptolemies assumed the religious role of the pharaohs. In name – and sometimes even in person – they performed the rites necessary to ensure that order prevailed over chaos and the natural cycle continued. The family spent heavily on temple building, and many of the most spectacular temple sites visible in Egypt today were either heavily restored or constructed by the Ptolemies. Large estates were granted to particular temples to support the cults. Priests were men of considerable importance, and acted as judges in cases involving Egyptian law.

Other Egyptians served in the royal bureaucracy. This was large and complex, and had as its principal role the collection of taxation: there were levies of a share of the harvest and taxes paid in money. Even the produce taken from land dedicated to one of the temple cults passed through the hands of the royal bureaucracy. There were never enough Greeks to have provided all the necessary clerks and officials and, in particular, there were never enough of them capable of speaking the native language. As a result there were always large numbers of Egyptians at all levels of the administration and over time in the army as well. Many could read and write in Greek as well as their own language and they often adopted Greek names for certain aspects of their life, while retaining their own names in other contexts.

An example of this is Menches or Asklepiades, a village clerk at the end of the second century BC. An official at this level of the administration needed to be fluent in both languages. In his official capacity he is always called Menches, perhaps because most of the time he dealt with Egyptians. However, he proudly styled himself a 'Greek born in this land' in one text. Ethnically, he seems to have been predominantly – perhaps wholly – Egyptian, but knowledge of Greek gave him and his family a distinct status. It was in many respects a question of class as much as race.[13]

There were some poor Greeks in Ptolemaic Egypt and considerably more well-off Egyptians. Most of the latter adopted some aspects of Greek culture and certainly employed the language, at least when performing their public roles. The majority of Egyptians, however, were not especially wealthy and worked on the land. Some owned or leased fields, but most were labourers paid in kind. This had been true throughout Egypt's history. There is no great indication that the Ptolemies exploited the workforce more brutally than earlier governments. At first they may have done it more efficiently, and certainly significantly expanded the area under cultivation.

Some individuals moved in both communities and over the years there was some intermarriage. Yet in spite of this the separateness of the Greek and Egyptian communities endured. The Greeks were dominant, but they could not have governed or profited from Egypt without the compliance and assistance of large numbers of Egyptians, who themselves benefited from the regime. The Egyptian religion required a pharaoh to help preserve Maat. The Persian kings had nominally fulfilled this role during the years of occupation and now the Ptolemies took over. They supported the temples, whose priests performed all the necessary rituals to hold back the forces of chaos.

Yet the Ptolemies were first and foremost Greek kings, who always had ambitions for territory outside Egypt from the old empire of Alexander. There is no indication that they ever thought of themselves as anything other than Greek, and specifically Macedonian. Three centuries of ruling Egypt did not change this.

THE 'SHE-WOLF': ROME'S REPUBLIC

In 273 BC King Ptolemy II sent ambassadors to Rome. It was the first formal contact between the two states. The Romans had recently defeated the Greek city of Tarentum in southern Italy and now controlled all of Italy south of the River Po. Tarentum had been aided by King Pyrrhus of Epirus, one of the ablest military commanders to emerge during the wars fought by Alexander's Successors. He had beaten the Romans in a series of battles, but in the process suffered such heavy losses that that he could not continue the struggle – the origin of the expression 'a pyrrhic victory'. Pyrrhus had at one time been a protégé of Ptolemy I, but alliances were apt to change quickly during Alexander's 'funeral games'. It was satisfying for the king to see a potential rival beaten, especially by such a distant people as the Romans.

The ambassadors were welcomed and friendly relations established. Trade was also encouraged. The Romans had not as yet made any attempt to expand beyond Italy. From the perspective of the eastern Mediterranean, they were a distant and rather minor power, but successful enough to warrant notice. The Ptolemies were usually on good terms with Syracuse, the most powerful Greek city in Sicily, and also with Carthage, the wealthy trading power whose fleets dominated the western Mediterranean.[1]

Rome had been founded in the eighth century BC – according to myth this was done by Romulus in 753 BC. The Romans did not start to write history until the late third century BC and had little certain knowledge of the distant past. Greek writers showed little interest in them until gradually the Romans forced their way onto the world stage. In 264 the Romans sent an army to Sicily. It was the first time the legions had gone outside the Italian Peninsula. The

Carthaginians resented this intervention in an area they considered wholly within their own sphere of influence. The result was the First Punic War, fought for more than two decades and at massive cost to both sides. The Romans proved consistently more aggressive and more stubborn in prosecuting the war, and finally the Carthaginians gave in.

Roman arrogance left many Carthaginians feeling deeply bitter and in 218 BC a second war was fought. This time Hannibal led an army from Spain, over the Alps and into Italy itself, where he proceeded to inflict a series of staggering defeats on the Romans. In three years almost a quarter of Rome's adult male population and more than a third of her aristocracy were killed. Alexander conquered Persia in three major battles and a couple of sieges, and yet Rome refused even to negotiate with Hannibal after this string of appalling defeats. The Roman Republic had huge resources and again proved willing to devote them to waging war with truly remarkable stubbornness and determination. The Carthaginians were defeated in Sicily and Spain, and eventually a Roman invasion of North Africa forced the recall of Hannibal from Italy. When he was defeated at Zama in 202 BC, Carthage once again capitulated.

The two great wars with Carthage set Rome on the path to world empire. In the First Punic War the Romans created a navy and managed to defeat Carthage, with its long maritime tradition. In the Second Punic War the Romans became used to massive levels of mobilisation, sending armies simultaneously to several distant theatres of operation and maintaining them there. In the process they acquired their first overseas provinces – Sicily, Sardinia and Corsica, Spain and Illyria – which needed to be governed and garrisoned.

The Ptolemies watched the struggle between Rome and Carthage, but carefully avoided being sucked in. During the First Punic War the Carthaginians asked them for a substantial loan to fund their war effort, but the request was denied because of the alliance with Rome. However, in 210, during the height of the Second Punic War, the Romans sent an embassy to Alexandria asking to purchase grain and Ptolemy IV agreed to supply this. Neutrality was preserved, but there does seem to have been more sympathy for

Rome, quite possibly because Carthage was seen as a greater potential threat.[2]

The Kingdom of Macedonia did not judge the situation so well. Concerned about the growing Roman presence on his western borders in Illyria, King Philip V of Macedon scented an opportunity when Hannibal overran Italy. He allied with the Carthaginians and declared war on Rome. The Romans were outraged at what they saw as an unprovoked stab in the back and sent an army to Macedonia. Eventually, having lost their local allies and needing all their resources to cope with Carthage, the Romans accepted a negotiated peace with Macedon, which the Ptolemies helped to arrange. The outrage remained, and almost as soon as the Second Punic War was won, the Romans declared war on Philip V. Macedonia was defeated in just a few years.[3]

Two major rivals to the Ptolemies had emerged from the wars between Alexander's Successors. Macedonia was one, and the other was the Seleucid Empire of Syria. The Seleucids intervened in Greece after the defeat of Philip V, but their expedition was savaged by the Romans. Not content with this, a Roman army was despatched to Asia Minor. Philip V supported the Romans' campaign, proving his loyalty to them and at the same time hurting a rival. The Seleucid army was smashed at Magnesia in 189 BC. Throughout these conflicts, the Ptolemies maintained their close alliance with Rome and watched as their two rivals were successively hammered.

Philip V's son Perseus also fought against Rome and with no more success than his father. He was taken prisoner and the kingdom broken up. A later rebellion finally persuaded the Romans to turn Macedonia into a province. The Romans fought their third and final war with Carthage around the same time. In 146 BC Carthage was stormed by a Roman army and the city razed to the ground; it ceased to exist as a political entity. In the same year the Romans demonstrated their dominance of Greece when they sacked the famous city of Corinth. The Kingdom of Macedonia was gone and the Seleucid Empire greatly weakened, yet the Ptolemies had not come into conflict with Rome. Nevertheless, the minor Italian power they had allied with back in 273 BC had now become the overwhelmingly dominant force in the Mediterranean.

THE REPUBLIC

The rise of Rome surprised many Greeks and prompted the historian Polybius to write a *Universal History* explaining just how this had happened. Sent as a hostage to Rome, he had gone with the staff of the Roman commander who sacked Carthage. In the introduction to his work he wondered: 'who is so worthless and indolent as not to wish to know by what means and under what system of polity the Romans in less than fifty-three years have succeeded in subjecting nearly the whole inhabited world to their sole government'.[4]

Following a long-established tradition in Greek political thought, Polybius believed that Rome's political system gave it a stability and strength lacking in other states. Rome had originally been ruled by kings, but the last of these had been expelled at the end of the sixth century BC – the traditional date was 509 BC – and the city became a republic. It did not have a formal constitution, but instead over the centuries a mixture of law, convention and precedent shaped its governance. The most important principle underlying this system was the refusal to let any one group or individual have permanent supreme power.

There were three elements to government. Executive authority lay with magistrates, all of whom were elected. In almost every case they served only for a single year and could not seek re-election to the same post until a decade had passed. In every case they served with one or more colleagues who had equal power. The most important magistrates were the two consuls. Civil and military power was not separated at Rome, and the consuls led Rome's armies in the most important campaigns and also framed law and carried out other peaceful tasks at Rome.

The magistrates had considerable power, but no permanence. Continuity was provided by the Senate, an advisory council consisting of former magistrates and other distinguished men. There were some three hundred senators, and all had to be freeborn and possess considerable wealth. The Senate could not pass law, but it issued decrees that were normally respected. Laws could only be passed by a vote of the Popular Assemblies. These also elected magistrates and approved the declaration of war or peace. The Assemblies could not introduce or debate an issue, or modify a bill in any way. They could only vote yes or no to a proposal, and in the case of elections choose candidates from a list.

Greek city states proved desperately prone to internal revolution, but in contrast Rome managed to avoid this for centuries. Where the rule of monarchs or tyrants became common in the Hellenic world from the fourth century onwards, this did not happen at Rome. The few Greek democracies to survive reduced the number of citizens eligible to vote, restricting this to the wealthy, while in contrast the Republic displayed a unique ability to expand and absorb others. Greek cities had always been extremely jealous of citizenship, especially at the height of Athens' democracy. At Rome, freed slaves gained citizenship, with only a few restrictions on their rights, something that would have been unimaginable in most Greek communities, and their children were full citizens in every respect. Defeated enemy communities throughout Italy over time received the franchise en masse. By Mark Antony's day the free inhabitants of all of Italy south of the Po had become Roman.

There were millions of Roman citizens, a number dwarfing the citizen body of even the largest Greek city states in their heyday. Roman manpower made possible the defeats of Pyrrhus and Hannibal. The legions were recruited from all those citizens wealthy enough to afford the necessary equipment. Therefore the richest, who could afford horses, served as cavalrymen. Those of more middling income – the vast majority of them farmers – fought as heavy infantrymen, while the poor and the young needed only the modest gear of skirmishers. Romans identified strongly with the Republic. They were willing to answer the state's call for military service, subjecting themselves to the army's harsh, even brutal discipline. No other state could have absorbed the appalling death toll inflicted by Hannibal and continued to muster new armies.

At the end of a conflict the legions were discharged and each man returned home. Military service was a duty to the Republic and not a career. During the Punic Wars some men found themselves serving with the army for a decade or more. As Rome expanded and acquired more and more overseas provinces, such long spells of military service became normal. Garrison duty in the Spanish provinces or on the borders of Macedonia offered little glory or plunder, with a good chance of death by disease or in some nameless skirmish. It was a considerable burden and meant that many discharged soldiers returned to find their families had been unable to maintain their farms. During the second century BC many Romans believed the class of farmer soldiers who were the backbone of the legions was shrinking under the pressure of excessively long periods of service. Inevitably, this only made the problem worse, as a dwindling number of men found themselves more often called up by the state, and even more fell into ruin. Once a duty willingly – often enthusiastically – accepted, military service changed into a crushing burden.[5]

Overseas expansion brought massive profits, but the benefits were not evenly shared. Magistrates who led an army to victory grew fabulously rich on the spoils of war, especially if the enemy was one of the wealthy states from the Greek world. Apart from plunder, hundreds of thousands of people were taken prisoner and sold as slaves. The generals took the lion's share of the money, but there were also considerable opportunities for private companies who handled the sales. The Republic possessed almost no bureaucracy. Magistrates sent to govern a province did so with a tiny staff, supplemented by their private household. Taxes were collected by private companies who bid for the contract to perform the tax. They were called the *publicani* – hence the publicans of the Authorised Bible – because they undertook public contracts. Their interest was in making money and thus they had to collect more from the provincials than they passed on to the Republic. There were other business opportunities in the empire, and simply being Roman and connected with the new great power was a huge advantage.[6]

Wealth flooded back to Italy and the gap between the rich and poor widened. Senators were not supposed to indulge in business ventures apart from landholding, although many covertly ignored this rule. Many of the fortunes made overseas were used to buy up grand rural estates, worked by a force of slave labourers. Slaves became cheap as the captives of frequent wars flooded the market. As importantly, they could not be called up for military service unlike labourers or tenants who were citizens. There were good steady profits to be made from farming, and sometimes conditions created even greater opportunities. It was always easier for the owners of big estates to exploit such situations. During the late second and first centuries there was an almost insatiable demand for Italian wine from the communities in Gaul. It is estimated that some 40 million wine amphorae from Italy were sent north of the Alps in the first century BC alone.[7]

Times were good for the wealthy and the big landowners, but difficult for the small-scale farmer. In 133 BC an ambitious senator named Tiberius Sempronius Gracchus claimed that:

> The wild beasts that roam over Italy have their dens and holes to lurk in, but the men who fight and die for our country enjoy the common air and light and nothing else. ... they fight and die to protect the luxury of others. They are called the masters of the world, but they do not possess a single clod of earth which is truly their own.[8]

Gracchus exaggerated – this speech was part of a successful electoral campaign, and men seeking office in any age rarely understate their case. Some farmers survived and even did well in the new conditions, but significant numbers failed. The minimum property qualification for military service had to be lowered several times in the course of the second century to find sufficient recruits. Ultimately, the tradition of men of property fighting in the army ended. By the first century the legions were recruited mainly from the poor, for whom military service provided a steady income and even a career.

FIRST AND BEST

Roman public life was fiercely competitive. There were more junior magistracies than senior posts, and so simple arithmetic meant that it was harder to attain the consulship. Many senators never held any magistracy. Members of a small group of well-established families provided a disproportionately high number of consuls. These families had good reputations and voters tended to prefer names they recognised; they also had the wealth to advertise themselves.

Winning the consulship was a great achievement, bringing the chance to present legislation, and enhancing the reputation of the holder and his family. Former consuls were men of status, whose opinion would normally be sought in any meeting of the Senate. A consul's descendants were from then on counted as nobles (*nobiles*). The consulship might also bring the opportunity for a provincial command and control of an army in a major war – a successful military campaign could be highly profitable.

Even governing a province in peacetime offered plenty of opportunities for enrichment. The *publicani* and other Roman businessmen were likely to be generous to any governor who helped them. The locals themselves were also usually eager to buy the favour of the Roman governor with generous gifts. When Antony's contemporary, the poet Catullus, came back from serving on the staff of a provincial governor he claimed that the first thing a friend asked him was 'How much did you make?' Some governors were put on trial after they returned for extorting money and other misbehaviour in the provinces. One Roman governor was supposed to have said that three years were needed in a post: in the first year a man stole enough to pay off his debts; in the second he made himself wealthy; the third was reserved for making enough money to bribe the judge and jury for the inevitable trial when he returned.[9]

Yet in the end there was nothing to compare with the glory associated with fighting a successful war. Ideally, this was completed by the Senate voting the commander the right to celebrate a triumph. This ceremony celebrated the general's achievements. It was the only occasion when formed and armed bodies of soldiers were allowed to march through the centre of Rome itself, along the Via Sacra ('Sacred Way') through the Forum and to the Capitoline Hill. Columns of prisoners and wagons carrying the spoils of war and pictures of scenes from the campaign processed with the troops. The general rode in a chariot, dressed up like the statues of Rome's most important god, Jupiter Optimus Maximus – 'Best' and

'Greatest'. His face was painted red, because the oldest statues of the god had been made of terracotta. For that day he was honoured almost as if he was a god. Tradition dictated that a slave stood behind him, holding the laurel wreath of the victor above his head and whispering reminders that he was only mortal.[10]

Men who had triumphed had laurel wreaths carved on the porches of their houses as a permanent reminder of their achievement. Each year there was a new batch of magistrates and new wars would be fought. The urge to win glory and make a fortune in the short term of office was a major factor in driving Roman imperialism. The Senate introduced a rule that at least five thousand enemies needed to be killed in battle before a general was eligible for a triumph. It is doubtful that they had any way of ensuring an accurate count. Plenty of men enjoyed triumphs, which meant that the competition was to have a bigger and more spectacular victory over a famous enemy.

Reputation mattered. If a senator was felt to be important, then people would come to him for favours and would respect his opinion. Reputation, past magistracies, victories won and other achievements all gave reputation. Wealth helped to advertise all this and could generate prestige on its own. The most important men lived physically closer to the heart of the city, in the grand and very ancient houses on the slopes of the Palatine Hill fronting onto the Via Sacra. Another sign of wealth was the possession of grand country estates worked by huge gangs of slave labourers. The splendour of houses, country villas and gardens offered more visible proof of importance. Art treasures from the Greek world were brought back as plunder or bought to decorate the homes of Rome's elite.

A man could stand for the consulship at forty-two. This meant that after he had held this supreme office he could reasonably expect to continue in public life for decades afterwards. A lucky few might win a second consulship ten years later, and a tiny handful might even manage a third consulship after another decade. Occasionally a man won a second triumph. Competition was always there. Men struggled to win office against other candidates who often also had wealth, reputation, ability and good family connections. If they managed to win, then they tried to ensure they got the most important and attractive duties and provincial commands. On their return, they competed to make best use of the glory and wealth they had won.

There were no political parties at Rome as we would understand them. Politics was an individual business because no one could share a magistracy or an honour. Families co-operated, and so at times did groups of friends, but such alliances were fluid and impermanent. Men seeking office rarely stood for any specific policies. Voters chose candidates on the basis of their character and ability rather than their ideals. Annual elections meant that the balance of power constantly shifted. Magistrates, especially consuls, were of huge importance in their year of office – the year was officially named after them. Afterwards they might have influence, but new consuls held actual power. All of this reinforced the constitutional ideal that no one should come to possess permanent power and so dominate the state.

Competition was always fierce, but until 133 BC it remained peaceful. In that year Tiberius Gracchus died during a political riot. His head was smashed in with a broken chair leg wielded by another senator, who was also his cousin. His opponents accused Tiberius of wanting to stay permanently in power – even of wanting to be king. Just over a decade later Tiberius' younger brother Caius was killed in another bout of political violence, this time much more organised and larger in scale. In 100 BC another politician and his followers were massacred after large-scale and violent rioting in the Forum. Worse was to follow. In 88 BC a Roman consul turned his legions on Rome itself, seizing power and executing his opponents. Mark Antony was born while the civil war that followed this act still raged.

There were many reasons why Polybius' vision of a well-balanced and stable Roman constitution fell to pieces in the late second century, and we shall consider these later in more detail. For the moment it is worth simply emphasising that Mark Antony was born and lived in a Republic already fractured by mob violence, discord and civil war. He never knew a time when the Republic was stable in the way it had been in Polybius' day and before. Then, no one could have imagined senators killing each other or winning power through direct military force. For Mark Antony and his contemporaries, such things were ever-present threats, which quite often turned into reality.

[III]

THE PTOLEMIES

The kingdom of the Ptolemies was at its height in the third century BC, helped by the longevity of the first three monarchs. Ptolemy I was well into his eighties when he died in 282 BC, and had ruled Egypt as satrap and then king for forty-one years. To last so long and die a peaceful death was no mean achievement for one of the main protagonists in Alexander the Great's funeral games. He had already made one of his sons co-ruler several years before, and the succession was smooth and unchallenged. Ptolemy II ruled until 246 BC, when he was in turn succeeded by his son, Ptolemy III, who ruled until 221 BC.

It was more than chance — still less lack of imagination — that all the kings of Ptolemy's line were also named Ptolemy. Alexander's generals had carved up his empire and made themselves kings, but the new kingdoms they created lacked any obvious legitimacy or natural coherency. Egypt was well established as a kingdom, although the Ptolemies had no particular claim to it. They also added Cyrenaica to the west, and for much of the third century controlled Palestine, substantial parts of Asia Minor and Syria, as well as Cyprus and other Aegean islands. There was nothing apart from their rule to unite these regions, and there were plenty of competitors to challenge this. Apart from Macedonia, Alexander the Great's empire was 'spear-won' land — the prize of conquest. This was effectively true of the new kingdoms, and the Successor kings ruled ultimately by right of conquest. Yet land taken in war could just as easily be lost in war, especially in wars fought against enemies who spoke the same language and came from the same culture. There was nothing obvious to unite the peoples of the Ptolemies' realm against the Seleucid or Macedonian kings.[1]

Ptolemy was distantly related to the Macedonian royal family, but the connection was scarcely close enough to justify his rule. A rumour was spread – perhaps encouraged by the king – claiming that Philip II had seduced Ptolemy's mother and was his real father. More emphasis was placed on the tradition that his family was descended from Hercules, just like the Macedonian royal family. None of this made him in any way a more legitimate heir to Alexander the Great than any of the other Successors. In the end it was up to Ptolemy and his heirs to make their own legitimacy.[2]

There were always two distinct aspects to his kingship. In Egypt he and his successors were pharaohs. Ptolemy II was crowned in an elaborate ceremony at the old capital of Memphis to reinforce this point, as were the later Ptolemies. The temple cults were generously supported and the rites and rituals they oversaw treated with respect. Plunder taken from the temples during the Persian occupation was recaptured and piously returned by the Ptolemies. Yet it is very hard to know how far any of the kings played an active role in the religious rites themselves. Much was simply done in their name – and at their expense – to preserve order and justice against chaos. Egyptians needed a pharaoh and, since there was no realistic alternative, the Ptolemies fulfilled this role, even though they and their court resided in the overtly Greek city of Alexandria.[3]

Greeks in a Greek city – well into the Roman period it was referred to as 'Alexandria by Egypt' not 'in Egypt' – from the very beginning the Ptolemies were far more concerned with winning recognition from the Hellenistic world. Like the other Successors they drew heavily on philosophical ideals of kingship, of monarchs as law-givers and generous benefactors. Ptolemy I was also inspired by Alexander's example, but did not blindly follow it. Like almost all of the latter's generals, he quickly repudiated the Persian wife he had taken in the mass wedding organised by the conqueror. The regime Ptolemy created was purely Hellenic, not a merging of cultures. Some images of Egypt were promoted to lend grandeur and antiquity to the new regime, but these were more the product of Greek stereotypes than the reality of Egyptian culture. Unlike Alexander, Ptolemy did have the advantage of decades of rule to establish his kingdom, and the process continued under his son and grandson. Founder of a new dynasty, there was much emphasis on the exceptional virtue of Ptolemy himself. Like Alexander, he received honours that were at least semi-divine and moved towards full divinity. He took the name Soter ('Saviour'), having been proclaimed in this way by the Rhodians for aiding them in a war with one of the rival Successors.[4]

Culture was important to the public image of the Ptolemies. Ptolemy I's history of Alexander was highly respected as a work of literature. The creation of the Museum and Library in Alexandria was intended to place them at the heart of the Greek intellectual world, and by extension the political world as well. The Museum – the name means literally, 'shrine/temple to the muses' – provided lavish accommodation and facilities to leading philosophers, who came from all over the Greek world. The Library was intended to collect all of Greek literature to ensure its preservation and purity – scholars worked on establishing the most accurate text of classics such as Homer's epics. Ptolemy II was a particularly aggressive collector of books. The king paid Athens a massive surety to persuade them to loan him the original manuscripts of the great writers of the stage: Aeschylus, Euripides and Sophocles. In the event, he kept the originals and sent back copies, preferring to give up his money. One of the later Ptolemies is supposed to have ordered that books be confiscated from any ship entering Alexandria. They were copied, and the copies returned to their owners while the originals remained in the Library.[5]

Ptolemy I created a new kingdom, and emphasised his power, wealth and beneficence as proof that he deserved to rule. Naming his son and heir Ptolemy reinforced the regal associations of the name. Ptolemy II honoured his father by founding a festival called the Ptolemaieia, modelled on the Olympic Games and held in Alexandria. A decree from Samos agreeing to take part explained that 'Ptolemy Soter has been responsible for many great blessings to the islanders and the other Greeks, having liberated the cities, restored their laws, re-established to all their ancestral constitution, and remitted their taxes' and that his son 'continues to show the same goodwill'. The festival helped to confirm alliances, but more generally reinforced the grandeur of the name of Ptolemy. It was not the kingdom of Egypt – or indeed of any set region – but the kingdom of the Ptolemies. The name itself became effectively a title. Ptolemy II did much to shape the divine cult surrounding his family.[6]

The kings of Macedon tended to have more than one wife, mainly for political reasons. Existing wives were not usually divorced, but they and their children might lose favour and prominence. Philip II's marriage to a younger wife – coincidentally called Cleopatra – precipitated his murder and the accession of Alexander. The Ptolemies continued this practice, and Ptolemy II was not born until 308 and was neither the oldest son, nor the product of the earliest marriage. He in turn married twice. Both women were confusingly called Arsinoe, but what shocked opinion at the time was that his second wife was also his full sister. There was no precedent for such an incestuous union in Macedonian or Greek culture. At the time people may have believed that the pharaohs of Egypt offered a few examples of this, but there is little evidence that this inspired Ptolemy II's decision.

Arsinoe II was a truly remarkable individual in an age of spectacular ambition. Her first husband was Lysimachus, one of Alexander's generals and a contemporary of her father and some forty-five years her senior. It was believed that she encouraged him to execute his oldest son by an earlier marriage, but her plans to advance her own children's claims were thwarted when her husband was killed in battle shortly afterwards. Arsinoe then married her own half-brother Ptolemy Ceraunos or 'thunderbolt'. The latter was estranged from their father, and was making a particularly murderous career for himself in Macedonia. He seems to have seen her and her children as dangerous rivals. Ceraunos married Arsinoe and promptly killed two of her children. She managed to escape, and a year later Ceraunos was killed in battle fighting against an invading army of Gauls.

Eventually Arsinoe made her way to Egypt and a few years later married Ptolemy II, who was her junior by some eight years. He exiled his first wife, the other Arsinoe, although her children remained in favour – the future Ptolemy III was one of them. Propaganda celebrated the union of brother and sister. They appeared together on coins, making Arsinoe the first female member of the family to be depicted on a coin in her lifetime. She was given the name Philadelphus ('brother-loving'). There were comparisons to Zeus and his sister and wife Hera, and for the benefit of Egyptians to the siblings Isis and Osiris. All of this added to the growing divinity of the Ptolemies. They were special, not bound by the same rules or restrictions as ordinary mortals.

There is no doubt that Arsinoe was fascinating, ambitious and politically experienced, and actively and capably assisted her brother until she died in 270 BC. Images on coins and statuary depict her as attractive, perhaps even beautiful. It is hard to believe that the idea of marriage did not originate with her, or equally that her brother did not feel a genuine passion for her. Perhaps it was even mutual. It is worth remembering that until her arrival in Egypt they had seen little of each other. There were also political advantages in the union. The emphasis on the special nature and majesty of the Ptolemies was reinforced by claims that only one of their own blood was worthy to become husband or wife. More practically, it prevented any other ambitious family from gaining a claim to the throne.[7]

This last concern may not have been foremost in the minds of either Ptolemy II or Arsinoe II. Ptolemy III married outside the family, but his son Ptolemy IV married his sister Arsinoe III. From then onwards it became the exception to marry outside the royal family. Brothers married sisters, nephews married aunts, and uncles married nieces, making the family tree of the Ptolemies remarkably complicated. The initial shock of the marriage between Ptolemy II and Arsinoe II faded, and later they were celebrated in the royal cult as the 'sibling gods' (*Theoi Adelphoi*). None of the other major Hellenistic dynasties copied the practice to anything like the same degree, but there seems to have been a general acceptance that this was simply what the Ptolemies did. Similarly, although the other dynasties tended to choose from a small selection of names, no other line called all of their kings by the same name.

INTRIGUE AND REBELLION

Ptolemy IV was named Philopator ('father-loving'), but clearly his attitude to his family varied. When his father died in 221 BC, Ptolemy IV had one of his brothers killed, along with his supporters, and promptly married his sister. Polybius accused the young king of drunkenness and being fonder of luxury than he was of administration. The results were defeats abroad and internal plots against him. This picture is not entirely fair, for Ptolemy IV had his successes – most notably defeating the Seleucids at the Battle of Raphia in 217 BC. Yet there were substantial losses of territory, while in Alexandria his court became dominated by favourites, and he left the kingdom weaker than he found it when he was murdered in 204 BC by some of his senior courtiers. His son Ptolemy V was a child of six and there followed an extremely savage contest to control the child and become regent. The boy's mother Arsinoe III was just one of the victims. A succession of powerful ministers seized control briefly before falling to their enemies or the wrath of the Alexandrian mob.[8]

We know of a short-lived Egyptian rebellion soon after the accession of Ptolemy III, but far more substantial risings began to break out during his son's reign. Large numbers of Egyptians had been recruited to fight in the Raphia campaign, serving for the first time in the infantry phalanx, the most important part of the army. Polybius claimed that these men returned home with a new sense of their own strength. The details of the rebellions that followed are unclear, but there does seem to have been a nationalistic element to them. There was a revolt in the Delta region, but by far the most successful rising was in Upper Egypt, where two Egyptian pharaohs were proclaimed and held power for some twenty years. It was not until 186 BC that they were finally defeated by Ptolemy V's troops.[9]

The famous Rosetta Stone, discovered in 1799 and now in the British Museum, carries a decree issued at Memphis in 196 BC by an assembly of Egyptian priests. The text is repeated in hieroglyphics, Demotic and Greek, and it was from this that Champollion and others were able to decipher the second and make substantial progress in understanding the first. The decree mentions that Ptolemy V punished men who had rebelled against his father, and refers to rebels as 'impious', while stating that a statue of the king was to be placed in every temple. Although there would never again be other Egyptian pharaohs, rebellions continued to occur every generation or so.[10]

The problems in Egypt were compounded by threats from outside, as the Macedonians, Seleucids and other lesser powers were quick to profit from the Ptolemies' weakness. The Ptolemaic fleet ceased to dominate the eastern Mediterranean. Palestine was lost, along with most of Asia Minor and many of the islands. At one point the Macedonian and Seleucid kings formed a secret pact to carve up Ptolemaic territory between them, but mutual suspicion and the growing power of Rome stopped this from being altogether fulfilled. The Seleucid Antiochus III threatened Egypt and imposed a treaty by which Ptolemy V was married to his rival's daughter.[11]

Her name was Cleopatra, the first member of the Ptolemaic royal house to have the name, although it was relatively common amongst Macedonian women. Apart from Philip II's last bride, Alexander the Great had also had a sister called Cleopatra. (For all its exotic sound and associations, there was absolutely nothing Egyptian about the name.) The Romans had not been informed of this treaty until some time after it had been agreed and were more than a little suspicious of the new alliance. Yet for a while it kept the peace and Cleopatra I proved an able queen, ruling jointly with her infant son Ptolemy VI after her husband died in 180 BC, aged only twenty-eight and amidst rumours of poison. The new king received the name Philometor ('mother-loving'). On her death in 176 BC he was married to her daughter and his full sister Cleopatra II (for a detailed family tree of the Ptolemies of this period see page 399). Both king and queen were children, and real power rested with whichever courtier could control them.

Once again the Ptolemaic kingdom seemed vulnerable. The Seleucid Antiochus IV invaded and seemed determined on adding Egypt to his own realm. That the Romans were busy fighting the Third Macedonian War no doubt made the opportunity even more

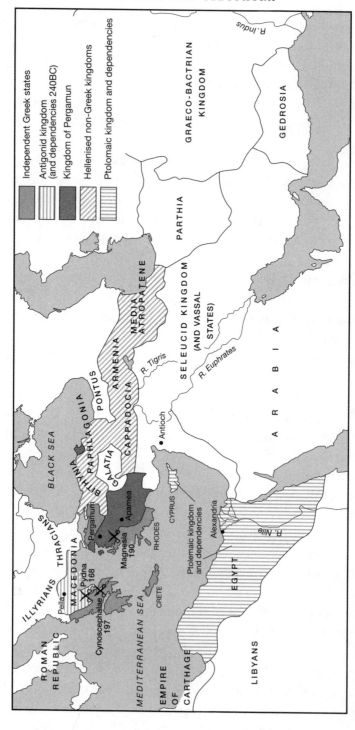

Independent Greek states

Antigonid kingdom
(and dependencies 240BC)

Kingdom of Pergamum

Hellenised non-Greek kingdoms

Ptolemaic kingdom and dependencies

R. Indus

GRAECO-BACTRIAN
KINGDOM

GEDROSIA

PARTHIA

SELEUCID KINGDOM
(AND VASSAL
STATES)

R. Tigris

R. Euphrates

MEDIA
ATROPATENE

ARMENIA

CAPPADOCIA

PONTUS

PAPHLAGONIA

GALATIA

BITHYNIA

BLACK SEA

THRACIANS

ILLYRIANS

ROMAN
REPUBLIC

MACEDONIA

Pella

Pydna
168

Cynoscephalae
197

Pergamum

Apamea

Magnesia
190

RHODES

CRETE

CYPRUS

Antioch

A R A B I A

Ptolemaic kingdom
and dependencies

Alexandria

R. Nile

EGYPT

LIBYANS

MEDITERRANEAN SEA

EMPIRE
OF
CARTHAGE

The Hellenistic world in 185 BC

44

attractive. Unfortunately for Antiochus, the Romans defeated the Macedonians, and this knowledge put their ambassadors in bullish mood. When they reached Antiochus' army and were presented to the king, he graciously offered a hand in greeting to the leader of the delegation, Caius Popillius Laenas. Instead of shaking it, the Roman brusquely gave him a scroll containing Rome's demands. Shocked, the king said that he must consider these with his advisers before giving a response. Laenas used his staff to draw a circle in the earth surrounding Antiochus. He then demanded that the king answer before he stepped out of the circle. Antiochus backed down and gave in to all of the Roman demands. He withdrew and left Ptolemy VI to his kingdom.[12]

The confrontation between Antiochus and Popillius Laenas quickly became famous – not least because Laenas and his family publicised it enthusiastically. The story also appealed to the senators' belief that they were at least the equals of any king, and reinforced all Romans' sense of their power. Here was a king at the head of a powerful army, being treated like a naughty child by ambassadors with not a single soldier to back them. In truth, the threat of Rome's military might – distant perhaps, but no longer committed to war with Macedon – was what forced the Seleucid king to accept both the behaviour and the demands of the Roman embassy. In the course of the second century BC the balance of power shifted steadily, and eventually overwhelmingly, in Rome's favour. Macedonia was broken up and later turned into a Roman province. The Seleucids lost more and more territory, their empire fragmenting as smaller kingdoms flourished. Most were themselves essentially Greek states, although in Judaea the Maccabees led an overtly nationalist and religious rebellion against the Hellenisation policy of Antiochus. After a bitter struggle the Seleucids were defeated and an independent Jewish kingdom created.

The Ptolemies clung on to Cyprus and Cyrenaica as well as Egypt itself, but lost most of the rest of their other territory. They avoided direct confrontation with Rome and so did not suffer the consequences of defeat. Yet the contrast to the stability of the third century BC could not have been greater. Ptolemy IV had been weak and too readily dominated by advisers. His son and grandson both came to the throne as infants. For decades the royal court became a place of intrigue as its members plotted, manoeuvred and killed for power. Ptolemy VI for a while ruled jointly with both his sister/wife and his younger brother Ptolemy (who is known as Ptolemy VIII for reasons that will be explained below). Behind each of the brothers was a faction of courtiers, who saw their own interests as best served by gaining more power – ideally, exclusive power – for the one they could dominate. This vicious internal struggle was going on when Antiochus invaded and Popillius Laenas bludgeoned him into withdrawing.

In 164 Ptolemy VI fled to Rome, fearing that his brother would kill him. The Roman Senate took little decisive action to reinstate him and so after a while he went to Cyprus and set up court there. By this time his brother was unpopular in Alexandria and he in turn went to Rome to seek help. Several years of politicking and occasional violence followed, both men seeking Roman backing and trying to arrange a partition of the kingdom in their own favour. Ptolemy VI eventually captured his brother when the latter tried to invade Cyprus, but pardoned him and betrothed him to his daughter, Cleopatra III, although the marriage did not take place at this stage. The last years of his reign were more secure, until he opportunistically led an army to intervene in a Seleucid civil war and was killed.[13]

Ptolemy VI's son was sixteen and swiftly proclaimed as Ptolemy VII Neos Philopator ('new, father-loving'), joint ruler with his mother. However, his father's younger brother was lurking in Cyrenaica to the west and through agents managed to incite the mob in Alexandria to call for his return. On his arrival he married Cleopatra II and had Ptolemy VII murdered during the wedding celebrations. The boy's name was removed from all official documents for a generation. The new king took the name Euergetes ('Benefactor'), like Ptolemy III, so that he is usually referred to by scholars as Ptolemy VIII Euergetes II. The population of Alexandria were a good deal less formal and would always show a fondness for nick-naming their rulers. To them he was Physcon ('Fatty'), or the punning Kakergetēs, which meant 'Malefactor'. He executed some of his opponents and drove many more into exile. Even his supporters were not safe, and accounts of his reign stress seemingly random acts of violence.

The marriage to his sister and his brother's widow produced a son. However, Physcon was not satisfied and he had an affair with his wife's daughter and his niece, Cleopatra III. They married and he fathered several children by her. To distinguish the two Cleopatras, inscriptions often list the daughter as 'Cleopatra the Wife' and the mother as 'Cleopatra the Sister'. For a while the trio ruled Egypt together, but in 131 or 130 BC there was an outbreak of furious rioting in Alexandria, the crowd favouring Cleopatra II. Physcon and Cleopatra III fled to Cyprus, leaving the older Cleopatra in fragile control of Egypt. She proclaimed her son by Physcon as co-ruler. The boy was only twelve and was not with her. He fell into his father's hands, who not only killed the lad, but also had his corpse chopped into pieces and sent to his mother.

Civil war followed when Physcon invaded Egypt and a desperate Cleopatra II summoned help from the Seleucid Demetrius II, who was married to one of her daughters with Ptolemy VI. He soon pulled back to Syria to face problems of his own and Cleopatra fled to join him. However, Demetrius was defeated and killed by a pretender to the throne whose spurious claim was backed by Physcon. Cleopatra II returned to Alexandria in 124 BC and, in public anyway, was reconciled to her brother/husband and daughter. Physcon died in 116 BC, survived by both of his wives. There was very quickly a fresh round of intrigue and murder as his family squabbled for power.[14]

CHANGING WORLDS

Physcon had been especially hostile to the Greek elite and the Jewish community of Alexandria, since these were most inclined to support Cleopatra II. The Museum was virtually closed and the philosophers fled abroad, ensuring that his name was roundly damned in intel-lectual circles. In contrast, he was supported by large sections of the Egyptian priesthood. Greeks like Polybius believed he favoured the Egyptians over Greeks, but this was a considerable exaggeration.

Over time the number of Egyptians serving in the royal bureaucracy had increased. Large numbers had also served in the army and been settled in cleruchies, although it is notable that on average they received significantly smaller plots of land than 'Greek' soldiers. Yet as we have seen the cultural mixing of Greek and Egyptian was extremely limited. Roman and Greek observers alike were inclined to speak of the intermingling of Macedonians and Greeks with natives. For them this was a sign of decline, explaining the decay of the Ptolemaic kingdom and such judgements need to be treated with caution. As overseas possessions were lost, the Ptolemies became kings who controlled Egypt and little more, but remained in culture, language and education utterly Greek. Even Ptolemy Physcon wrote a work studying Homer.[15]

The Egyptian priesthood accepted the Ptolemies as necessary, and they were generous in their support of the temple cults. Some Greek-speaking Egyptians entered royal service and did well. As time passed the numbers who did this increased and a few reached more senior posts. None seems ever to have been employed to govern territory outside Egypt and the vast majority of senior officials were always of Macedonian or Greek stock. For the bulk of Egyptians life continued to be a round of toil working the fields – hard labour for modest reward, just as it had been for their ancestors and would be for their descendants. The Greek community remained distinct. Very few Egyptians showed any interest in such quintessentially Greek institutions as the gymnasia and none saw any reason to see Greek culture as anything other than inferior to their own traditions. Acceptance of the occupying power did not mean that they developed any affection or admiration for it.

At least some were actively hostile. Periodic rebellions continued till the end of Ptolemaic rule. We also know of prophecies – ironically enough preserved in Greek versions – foretelling the destruction of the 'impious' Greeks and especially their vice-ridden and corrupt city of Alexandria, which will be 'abandoned like my kiln because of the crimes, which they have committed in Egypt'. An Egyptian pharaoh would return and usher in a better age of prosperity, health and righteousness, 'when the Nile will run its proper course'. It is more than likely that such works – one is known as the Potter's

Oracle – were written by members of the priesthood. Yet in the end this resentment came to little. Rebellions were always limited, while the Egyptian population was divided by region and social class and there was nothing to unite them in concerted opposition. The Greek minority and the Egyptian majority had little choice but to tolerate each other. Their lives were not entirely separate, but the communities remained distinct.[16]

The Greeks had always associated Egypt with great wealth. They also expected kings to be rich and generous. All of the Successors of Alexander the Great paraded their prosperity and power. It was an age obsessed with size and spectacle. Lists of the Seven Wonders of the World were popular at the time and all of the monuments were invariably massive in size. Cities were built in grand, monumental style, with clear and wide grid-patterned roads. Ships – especially warships – were built to be gigantic, sometimes at the expense of practicality. Sheer scale impressed.

The Ptolemies embraced this obsession with as little restraint as they displayed for intrigue. As well as warships, they built massive pleasure boats. The Pharos lighthouse had a practical purpose in guiding ships to Alexandria's harbour, but was also designed to be spectacularly huge. A description survives of a grand parade held by Ptolemy II in Alexandria, which had abundance as its main theme. Dionysus, the god of wine and plenty, was honoured, and revellers wearing gold crowns feasted as his followers were supposed to do. There were exotic animals, statues and gold in abundance. A huge wineskin made from leopard pelts contained 300,000 gallons of wine, which was allowed to dribble out along the procession's route. Other floats had fountains of wine and milk, and on another was a huge mechanical statue. It is striking that much of the ingenuity of the philosophers in the Museum was devoted to clever displays such as this or the steam engine that moved under its own power. Few of the ideas were transferred into any significant practical use. There were also big versions of objects, such as a lance made of silver and some 90 feet in length. Even more bizarre, at least to modern eyes, was a gold phallus 180 feet long and 9 feet in circumference, painted and decorated with more gold. After the procession was a great feast held in a specially built and lavishly decorated pavilion.[17]

The splendour, even the excess, surrounding kings reinforced the sense that they were special. They were givers of law and justice, more than ordinary men and close to the gods in life, and after death deified. Luxury was celebrated as symbolic of a strong king and a prosperous kingdom. Ptolemy VIII was mocked as 'fatty' by the Alexandrians, but was himself proud of his massive weight. To show off this sign of plenty, he was inclined to wear light, almost transparent clothing. Polybius accompanied a Roman embassy to the king's court in about 140 BC and shared the Romans' disgust when Physcon greeted them at the harbour. To them Ptolemy was grotesque, and they made him accompany them on foot from their ship to the palace, their leader later joking that the Alexandrians were in his debt because now 'they had seen their king walk'. They were far more impressed by the overall sense of Egypt's wealth and productivity, deciding that it could be very powerful if ever it found decent rulers.[18]

Unrestrained luxury, weakness abroad and murderous competition for royal power characterised the career of Ptolemy VIII. The kingdom founded by Ptolemy I two centuries earlier had become far less stable and efficient. It is true that no serious challenger for the throne appeared from outside the Ptolemaic family. To that extent the celebration of the family, and the frequency of incestuous marriage, ensured that only blood relations were seen as capable of attaining the monarchy. Yet in spite of the incest, and the generally high rate of infant mortality in the ancient world, the Ptolemies remained numerous, their numbers thinned more by homicidal ambition than anything else. In spite of its best efforts, the family failed to wipe itself out, and the battles for power continued.

The shadow of Rome grew stronger as the second century progressed. The Romans did not want the wealth of Egypt to be taken over by any other power, but had limited interest in the family squabbles of the Ptolemies and, as yet, no desire to turn it into a province of their own. Both Ptolemy VI and Physcon at different times fled to Rome and tried to gain support. Foreign assistance was preferable to letting a rival win, as Cleopatra II also showed when she sought Seleucid help. The Hellenistic kingdoms decayed, spending their strength in struggles with each other or smashed by the

Roman military machine. The Ptolemies survived, in spite of a succession of weak kings and bitter family in-fighting.

Cleopatra was born into the ruling house of a decaying kingdom in a world dominated by Rome. For generations her family had married and slaughtered each other as they struggled for power. None doubted their absolute right to rule, or questioned that luxury and excess were not admirable in themselves. To be born a Ptolemy brought unique expectations and dangers. Ambition, ruthlessness and an utterly self-centred attitude mingled with the ever-present fear of death at the hands of courtiers and family.

[IV]

THE ORATOR, THE SPENDTHRIFT
AND THE PIRATES

On 14 January 83 BC friends and relatives of Mark Antony's parents were called to their house. The aristocratic families of Rome liked witnesses to the arrival of a new member and his mother Julia had gone into labour. Only women attended the birth itself, unless things went badly wrong and a male doctor was summoned. Usually, the mother was attended by a midwife and some female relations and slaves. The father and guests waited elsewhere in the house.

Infant mortality was very high in the ancient world, as indeed it was until comparatively modern times. Many children were stillborn or died hours, days or months later. Some Roman tombstones are very precise in the age of the little boys or girls they commemorate. It was also a very dangerous time for the mother and many women died during or soon after childbirth. The Roman aristocracy used marriage to cement political alliances, so women like Julia were usually young – quite often in their mid teens – for their first pregnancy.

In this case everything seems to have gone smoothly. A boy was born and when the midwife laid the infant down for inspection there was no sign of deformity or unusual weakness. Julia would produce two more sons in fairly rapid succession and all grew into healthy adults, and she would herself enjoy a long life. Some children were rejected by their parents, but in well-off families this was usually only the case if they had serious defects or seemed far too weak to survive. There was no question of that in this case and once Antony's father was shown his son, he and Julia quickly accepted the child.[1]

Ritual was everywhere in Roman society and marked every stage of an individual's life. Fires were lit on the family altars in the house. The witnesses would also make offerings when they returned to their own homes. On the night of 21/22 January, the family held a vigil and performed a series of rituals as part of a purification ceremony (*lustratio*). The next morning priests observed the flight of birds to predict what the future held for the boy. He was also presented with a talisman or charm called the *bulla*. This was normally of gold and was placed in a leather bag around the boy's neck. He would wear this until he became an adult.

On the day of the purification the boy was formally named as Marcus Antonius and soon afterwards this was registered officially. 'Antonius' was the family or clan name – in Latin, the *nomen*. Most Roman aristocrats had three names, the *tria nomina* and the *nomen* were followed by a *cognomen* peculiar to that section of the wider family or clan. Julia's father was called Lucius Julius Caesar. The Julii were a large and very ancient group, and the more specific 'Caesar', which first appeared at the turn of the third and second centuries BC, helped to differentiate the various branches of the line. Some families, including the Antonii, never felt this necessary, probably because there were not many branches of the line.[2]

'Marcus' was the *praenomen* equivalent to our first name (or in Britain, still habitually, the Christian name). Although it was not an absolutely fixed system, aristocratic families tended to employ the same names in the same order for each generation. Antony's father was also called Marcus Antonius, as was his father. In due course his two brothers were named Caius and Lucius. In formal documents each would also be listed as 'son of Marcus'.

It was important in Roman public life to identify a man very specifically. The same was not true of women, who could not vote or stand for office. Girls received only a single name, their father's *nomen* in the feminine form. Therefore Antony's mother was Julia because her father was a Julius. Any daughter born to an Antonius was named Antonia and if more than one daughter was born these were simply numbered – at least for official purposes. Families tended to employ nicknames to avoid confusion.

Julia was a patrician, but her husband's family was plebeian and so were her children. The patricians were Rome's oldest aristocracy and in the early days of the Republic only they could hold the consulship. Over time many wealthy plebeian families forced their way into politics and were able to demand a greater share of power. It was eventually established that one of the two consuls each year must be plebeian, and as time passed it became reasonably common for neither to be a patrician. Some patrician lines dwindled in wealth and influence, and others died out altogether. By the first century BC the overwhelming majority of senators were plebeian. There were a number of plebeian families who could boast of having been at the centre of public life for centuries. Simply being patrician was no guarantee of political success.

The Antonii were not the greatest of the plebeian lines, but they were very well established as members of the Senate and had done particularly well in the last two generations. Antony's grandfather Marcus Antonius was famous as one of the greatest orators ever produced by Rome. Cicero claimed that along with one of his contemporaries, Antonius took Latin eloquence to

a level comparable to the glory of Greece. ... His memory was perfect, there was no suggestion of previous rehearsal; he always gave the appearance of coming forward to speak without preparation. ... In the matter of choosing words (and choosing them more for weight than for charm), in placing them and tying them into compact sentences, Antonius controlled everything by purpose and by some-thing like deliberate art. ... In all these respects Antonius was great, and combined them with a delivery of peculiar excellence.[3]

In 113 BC Antonius was elected quaestor, a junior magistracy with mainly financial responsibilities, and was sent to assist the governor of the province of Asia (modern-day western Turkey). A man became eligible for the quaestorship at thirty. En route to the province Antonius found himself caught up in scandal when he was accused of having an affair with a Vestal Virgin. Rome's only female priesthood, the Vestals took a vow to remain chaste for thirty years and tended the temple and sacred flame of the goddess Vesta. For a man to seduce a Vestal was a dreadful impurity, which threatened Rome's special relationship with the gods. If found guilty, a man's career would be over and he might suffer even worse punishment. The penalty for the Vestals was far more ghastly, for they were entombed alive to bury the impurity.

Trials of Vestals and their alleged lovers tended to occur following some disaster when people were nervous and wanted someone to blame. Three Vestals were accused of breaking their vow in 114 BC, and when only one was condemned the issue was raised again in the next year and a new round of trials begun in a special tribunal presided over by an eminent and stern former consul.

As a magistrate serving on public business, Antonius was exempt from prosecution, but won general admiration when he voluntarily returned to Rome to answer the charge. This did nothing to dampen the enthusiasm of judge and prosecution in pressing for a conviction. Although Antonius staunchly denied the charge, his accusers sensed that a young slave who carried a lantern for his master at night could be coerced into incriminating him. Roman law only accepted the testimony of slaves if they were questioned under torture, since it was assumed that otherwise they would always support their owners. The boy is supposed to have assured Antonius that nothing could persuade him to speak against his master, regardless of the pain. 'Lacerated with many stripes, put on the rack, and burned with hot plates, he guarded the defendant's safety and destroyed all the force of the prosecution.' Antonius was acquitted. It is not recorded whether he rewarded the slave. Our source for the story blamed fortune for such a great spirit being 'enclosed in the body of a slave'. Two Vestals – it is not clear whether one was the woman with whom he was accused of having an affair – were less fortunate and were condemned to death.[4]

Oratory was very important in a political career, but the success of Marcus Antonius suggests that he also had considerable military and administrative ability. In 102 BC he went to govern the nearby province of Cilicia as praetor. His command was extended for a further two years by the Senate and he led a tough and ultimately successful campaign against the pirates infesting that area. He celebrated a triumph, which no doubt helped him to win election to the consulship for 99 BC. Two years later he was censor, one of the two magistrates who oversaw the census of Roman citizens completed every five years. Only one in five consuls could hope to reach the censorship and it was an office of tremendous prestige.

THE ORATOR AND THE DICTATOR

Marcus Antonius was one of the leading senators of his day, but prominence would prove to be a dangerous thing in the first century BC. In 91 BC a politician pressing for the extension of Roman citizenship to the allies of Italy was assassinated. Many of the Italian communities chose to rebel and the result was the Social War – the name comes from the Latin *socii*, meaning 'allies' – which was fought at high cost in lives and with great savagery. Roman victory had as much to do with their willingness to grant citizenship to all those who remained loyal, and many more who capitulated quickly, as it did with military skill. It was a conflict that accustomed many soldiers to fighting against enemies very much like themselves.

By 88 BC the rebellion was substantially over and the consul Lucius Cornelius Sulla was given command in the war against King Mithridates VI of Pontus. The latter was exploiting the crumbling of the Seleucid Empire and Roman preoccupation to expand from his heartland on the southern coast of the Black Sea. A campaign in the Hellenistic east offered a Roman general all the glory and plunder he could desire, and Sulla left Rome to recruit and train his army. In his absence a radical politician campaigned to have the command transferred to Marius, the great military hero of the last generation, but now in his late sixties.[5]

Consul for the first time in 107, Marius had won a victory in Numidia, but was then voted into an unprecedented succession of consulships every year from 104 to 101 BC. This violated precedent and law, which stipulated that ten years should elapse between each consulship. At the time, the Italian Peninsula was menaced by migrating northern tribes who had already slaughtered every army sent against them and there was clearly a strong feeling that the crisis required an extraordinary solution. Marius dealt with the barbarians, smashing them in a final battle in 101 BC. He celebrated a triumph

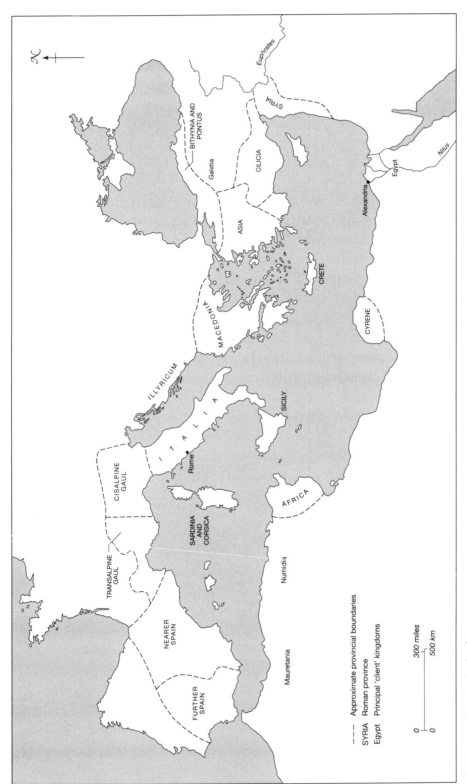

The Roman Empire in the first century BC

and was rewarded by being voted a sixth consulship by a grateful Rome.

It was a spectacular career, especially since Marius was the first of his family to embark on a public career and enter the Senate. He was what the Romans called a 'new man' (*novus homo*), who had had to make a name for himself rather than rely on the fame of his family. Marius revelled in popular acclaim and seems to have struggled to cope when this began to fade. He played a relatively modest part in the Social War and may well have suffered from poor health. Yet in spite of his advanced age he decided that he wanted the command against Mithridates and the Popular Assembly was willing to pass a law transferring it to him. In every respect this was a break with tradition, even if it was not actually illegal. Yet in the past Marius had broken other traditions and gone on to win.[6]

This time it was different. Sulla was a patrician, but came from a family that had long since fallen away from the centre of public life. He had come to politics at a late age, determined to rise to the top and had secured the plum command against Mithridates. He refused to let this be taken from him, and his soldiers were equally unwilling to lose the chance of the rich plunder likely in an eastern war. The senior officers were less keen and only one man of senatorial rank accompanied Sulla as he led his legions to Rome. Marius and his opponents had no organised force to meet them and could not hope to defend the city successfully. Many were killed, although Marius escaped. Sulla stayed only for a short time before taking his troops off to fight Mithridates and did not return for five years.

Marius came back first, raising his own army and seizing Rome in 87 BC. This time the attack was more violent and the executions that followed more numerous and brutal. Marcus Antonius was one of the victims, although whether because of a long-standing grudge or recent opposition to Marius is uncertain. At first the orator went into hiding and was sheltered in the house of one of his clients, a man attached to him by long-standing obligation or favour. His protector was not especially wealthy, but wanted to entertain his guest in a manner appropriate for such a distinguished senator. He sent a slave out to buy some high-quality wine. The owner of the tavern was surprised at this unusual purchase and, chatting to the slave, discovered what was happening. He then promptly took the story to a delighted Marius, who was at dinner. Our sources claim that he had to be persuaded by his friends not to go and kill Antonius himself.

Instead, he sent a military tribune called Annius with a party of soldiers. The officer seems to have been reluctant to get his hands dirty and sent his men inside the house to perform the execution. He waited, but when the soldiers did not return Annius grew suspicious and followed them. To his amazement his men were listening to the great orator speak, entranced by his words so that some could not bear to meet his gaze and even wept. In one version of the story the men actually left without harming the senator. Annius was less easily enthralled. He stabbed Antonius to death and then decapitated him, taking the head as trophy to Marius.[7]

The story of the famous orator holding his would-be killers spellbound is repeated by all our main sources for this incident. It may be true or simply a good story and what Romans wanted to believe. Whether or not things happened this way, the basic truth was that a distinguished senator was brutally killed and beheaded on the whim of another man who had seized control of the state by force. Antonius' head went to join those of other victims of Marius' purge and was displayed in the Forum. Before that Marius had exulted over the death and

> held the severed head of Marcus Antonius for some time between his exultant hands at dinner, in gross insolence of mind and words, and allowed the rites of the table to be polluted with the blood of an illustrious citizen and orator. And he even took to his bosom Publius Annius, who had brought it, bespattered as he was with the marks of recent slaughter.[8]

Mark Antony was born four years later.[9] We do not know whether his father was in Rome during Marius' occupation of the city. Perhaps he was elsewhere or, as a young man in his middle twenties, not considered worth killing. Marius' wife was also a Julia, although from a different branch of the family to Antony's mother, making it unlikely that this on its own would have been sufficient protection. Marius fell ill and died within weeks of storming Rome and taking up a seventh consulship, and this more than anything else brought a halt to the violence. His supporters continued to dominate the Republic, but had now established themselves and hoped for the return of something like normality.

By Roman reckoning, Mark Antony was born in the six hundred and seventy-first year 'from the foundation of the city' (*ab urbe condita*). More usually, they referred to the year by the names of the two consuls to hold office, in this case Lucius Cornelius Scipio Asiaticus and Caius Norbanus. Yet it was Sulla who dominated everyone's thoughts at the time. Mithridates' army had been beaten and a peace treaty imposed on him. Sulla and his army were free to return. They landed in southern Italy late in the spring, when Antony was just a few months old.

Marius' allies had had years to prepare and the fighting now was on a massive scale. In November 82 BC Sulla won a great battle outside Rome and took control of the city. Fighting continued for some time – one of the Marian commanders would continue the struggle in Spain for another decade. Both of the consuls of 82 BC, who included Marius' son, were killed, but Sulla did not replace them. Instead, he was made dictator by a law passed in the Popular Assembly.

The dictatorship was an ancient emergency measure that gave one man supreme executive power. The office lasted for just six months and could not be renewed, so in this way the principle of preventing any individual from gaining supreme permanent power was preserved. A dictator was appointed rather than elected and, unlike a consul, he did not have a colleague but a subordinate known as the Master of Horse (*Magister Equitum*). The commonest reason to name a dictator was to supervise consular elections when no consul was available. Once these were complete, the dictator resigned his office, often after only having held office for a few days. On a few occasions – for instance at times of crisis during the Punic Wars – a dictator had been appointed to take command in the field. The last occasion was in 216 BC.

Sulla used the old title, but added new powers that would last for as long as he chose to retain them, hence the need for a specific law. He was *dictator legibus scribundis et rei publicae constituendae* – dictator to make laws and restore the Republic. At the same time he presided over mass executions that were both bloodier and far more organised than Marius' purge. Lists of names were posted and anyone included on them lost all legal rights. They could be killed with impunity and their murderers granted a share in their property as a reward. We do not know how many men – and it was only men – were proscribed in this way. Some senators perished and many more equestrians, who had fought against Sulla or were associated in some way with his enemies. Others were killed so that their wealth could be confiscated and many of Sulla's subordinates were believed to have added names to the lists for their own profit. One wealthy equestrian is supposed to have greeted the news that he was on a proscription list with the dry comment that his Alban estates wanted him dead.[10]

Once again Roman slaughtered Roman, bodies floated in the Tiber and heads were nailed up to the speaker's platform in the Forum. Alongside the massacres went reform. Sulla tried to legislate to prevent any provincial governor from leading his army outside of his province – in a sense to stop anyone copying his own example. He also severely restricted the powers of the tribunes of the plebs, the office used by the Gracchi and more recently by Marius' allies to secure him the command against Mithridates.

Sulla's reforms shifted the balance of power in favour of the Senate and senior magistrates. Yet more important than the legislation was the Senate itself, which was supposed to guide the state. The proscriptions removed a number of senators, and still more had been killed by one side or the other during the civil war. Many new members were enrolled by the dictator, doubling the size of the Senate to around six hundred. With his enemies removed and the council packed with his own sympathisers, in 79 BC Sulla gave up the dictatorship and retired to private life. His health was poor and, in spite of a rapid marriage to a lively young widow, he died a year later. His self-composed epitaph was that no one had ever been a better friend or worse enemy.[11]

CRETICUS

Antony's father was part of Sulla's Senate. We do not know whether he had played an active part on the dictator's side in the civil war, but the murder of his father clearly made him unfriendly to the Marians. As a member of an established family with a highly distinguished father, he was an important man and stood out from the hundreds of recently enrolled senators. Civil war and proscriptions had also severely thinned the ranks of the former consuls and other prominent men. Sulla's Senate was larger, but far less balanced than in the past, presenting opportunities for the best connected and ambitious to rise far faster than would normally have been the case. In 78 BC one of the consuls, Marcus Aemilius Lepidus, launched a coup and was only defeated by military force. He and his leading supporters were executed.

Marcus Antonius again passed unscathed through an outbreak of civil war. There is no indication that he had inherited his father's gift for oratory or, indeed, was notably talented in any direction. Plutarch claims that he was respected as a decent man, but other sources are far less complimentary about both his ability and character. As his father's son and a member of the Antonii, he did not need to be especially capable to enjoy a reasonably successful career. He was elected as one of the eight praetors for 74 BC. This office could not be held until a man was thirty-nine. It was a point of pride for men from good families to hold office at the first opportunity – the expression was 'in his year' (*suo anno*) – and it is most likely that Antonius managed this.

The family was not especially wealthy by the standards of the Roman aristocracy, and campaigning for office was expensive. Marcus Antonius was heavily in debt, not helped by a tendency to live beyond his means. His generosity was famous – Plutarch tells a story of a time when a friend asked to borrow money. Antonius did not have any to give, so instead summoned a slave to bring water in a particular silver bowl. He then poured out the water and gave the bowl to his friend. Only when Julia began questioning the household slaves about the vessel, threatening them with torture to extract the truth, did her husband meekly confess. Sallust, the historian and senator who knew and disliked Mark Antony, claimed that Antonius was 'born to squander money, and never cared until he had to'.[12]

As praetor, Antonius was given a special military command to deal with piracy throughout the Mediterranean. This was a serious problem and his father's victory had been both temporary and local. In earlier times, the Ptolemies, Seleucids and island states like Rhodes had done much to police the eastern Mediterranean, but now their navies were little more than a memory. Piracy flourished, encouraged still further by Mithridates, who once again came into conflict with Rome. Attacks on ships became common, disrupting trade and making travel dangerous. The young Julius Caesar was taken hostage and ransomed during these years.

Dealing with the problem was a major task, which would normally have been given to a consul. However, the war with Mithridates was a more attractive opportunity and both consuls arranged to be sent to provinces where they could hope to confront the king. There was considerable intrigue surrounding these appointments and that of Antonius. All three men were given larger than normal responsibilities. Antonius was authorised to act all around the Mediterranean and his authority stretched for up to 50 miles inland and would be equal to that of the governor of each specific province. In most cases provincial commands were initially allocated for twelve months and then could be extended by the Senate year by year. Antonius was given three years in his post from the beginning.

One reason why Antonius was able to get such a grand command was his name. The Romans strongly believed that talent was passed on through a family, and since his father had triumphed over pirates it seemed reasonable that his son would also be victorious. On its own this would not have been enough. Antonius was supported by Quintus Lutatius Catulus, a former consul who was very prominent in the Senate during the 70s and 60s BC. Catulus' father had committed suicide rather than be killed by Marius' men, and the son was subsequently an important supporter of Sulla. Fellow feeling may have encouraged him to favour Antonius, but more importantly Catulus generally favoured men from established families.

Sulla's enlarged Senate contained many men who were unlikely ever to be asked their opinion during a debate, yet they could still vote. Since this was done by physically moving to stand near the man proposing a measure, such back-bench senators were nicknamed 'walkers' (*pedarii*). With hundreds of men who had been in the House for less than ten years, patterns of voting and loyalty were not easily predictable. Anyone able to manipulate and persuade significant numbers of *pedarii* to vote a certain way gained influence. The slickest operator during these years was Publius Cornelius Cethegus, who never held any of the senior magistracies and was content to remain behind the scenes. Lucullus, one of the consuls for 74 BC, secured his eastern command by lavishing attention and gifts on Praecia, a famous courtesan who was Cethegus' mistress. It is not known whether Antonius did the same, but he was supported by Lucullus' colleague, the consul Cotta.[13]

The command against the pirates was a huge responsibility and gave Antonius considerable power. One later source hints that it was more readily given to him because he was not thought capable enough to be a threat to the state. A successful war against the pirates would bring glory, which every Roman senator craved, and potentially vast profit from the sale of captives and plunder. If he was fortunate, Antonius could hope to both pay off his massive debts and make himself truly rich.[14]

All that relied on victory, and victory was not going to be easy. It is possible that the Senate did not give him sufficient resources. There were certainly complaints from commanders fighting in Spain around this time that they were not being adequately supplied by the state. On the other hand, Antonius may have lacked ability and certainly had no experience of conducting large-scale operations.

At first he focused on the western Mediterranean, but achieved little. Critics claimed that his enthusiastic requisitioning caused more devastation than the pirates. A levy of grain in Sicily was commuted to one of money. However, Antonius fixed the price far higher than the current rate at which wheat was selling, since it was just after harvest time and there was glut on the market. Although he certainly needed money to pay, equip and supply his fleets and men, it is hard to avoid the conclusion that one of his main preoccupations was restoring his own fortune.

By 72 BC, Antonius transferred his attentions eastwards and attacked the pirates on Crete. Whether through incompetence or bad luck, the enemy thrashed the Roman fleet in a naval battle. The campaign fizzled out and Antonius negotiated a peace treaty that was very favourable to the pirates and rejected out of hand at Rome. He died soon afterwards without returning home. The Romans sarcastically named him Creticus — successful commanders were often given a name to commemorate the people they defeated or the place they conquered.[15]

Antony was eight when Antonius left to take up his command and eleven when his father died. Nominally at least, Antony was now head of the family. With that responsibility came his father's huge debts. One estate was so heavily mortgaged that the family chose not to claim it, something that the Romans always saw as especially shameful. His father was survived by a younger brother, Caius Antonius, but after a while Julia married Publius Cornelius Lentulus Sura and Antony spent the rest of his youth in his stepfather's house. Lentulus was a rough contemporary of Marcus Antonius and would win the consulship in 71 BC. Julia's family probably considered it a good match. She was most likely only in her late twenties and it was unusual for aristocratic widows to remain single unless they were substantially older.

Cicero later insulted Antony for being 'bankrupt while still a boy'. Lentulus may have been a father figure for the teenager, but marriage to Julia did not mean that he had to meet Antonius' debts, and these remained. Mark Antony was an Antonius, heir to his father, grandfather and the rest of the line. He inherited the expectation that simply as a member of his family he deserved to play a distinguished role in public life. Rome was the greatest power in the world, senators led Rome and a small number of families including the Antonii led the Senate. Bankrupt or not, Antony imbibed this supreme self-confidence from his earliest days.[16]

[v]

THE OBOE PLAYER

Cleopatra was probably born in 69 BC, or perhaps a little earlier in 70 BC (for Cleopatra's detailed family tree see page 400). We cannot be more precise as to the year, and have no idea at all of the month or day. It would seem most likely that her mother gave birth in one of the extensive and grand royal palaces in Alexandria, but again we do not know. For Mark Antony we at least have a fair idea of the rituals and customs surrounding a birth in one of Rome's aristocratic families and can assume these were followed. How the Ptolemies did things is unknown.

Alexandria had a well-established reputation for the skill and knowledge of its physicians – in part because the earlier Ptolemies seem to have permitted vivisection. Cleopatra's mother is likely to have had access to the finest medical assistance available in the Greek and Roman world. For generation after generation, the Ptolemies and their wives kept producing plenty of children who survived the perils of birth and infancy. The prospects of babies born into the family were probably as good or better than those of any other children in the ancient world, at least as far as natural perils were concerned.[1]

Not knowing precisely when or under what circumstances someone from the ancient world was born is nothing unusual. Rather more frustrating are the many other things we do not know about her. Cleopatra means 'distinguished in her ancestry', but the name had become a common one for the Ptolemies, and it is doubtful that the choice was seen as especially significant in her case. However, it does seem ironic given the difficulty of working out her family tree. We do not know who her mother was, because this is not mentioned by any of our sources. Again, this is not unique for even major figures from this period. We do not know who Cleopatra's father's mother was either, leaving two possible gaps in her immediate ancestry. The Ptolemies tended to be far more concerned about the paternity of members of the royal family, and this is reflected in both the surviving official documents and the literary sources about the family. Added to this, the confusingly narrow selection of names and the frequency of incest and successive marriages make it even harder to piece together the family tree.

Cleopatra's acknowledged father was Ptolemy XII, the last adult male from the family to rule as king of Egypt. He already had one, perhaps two, other daughters, and would in due course have another before finally fathering two sons. Of the five certain children, none was to die of natural causes and four of the deaths occurred as part of rivalry within the family. Cleopatra herself outlived all the others, disposing of three of them herself. Only the sixth child, a possible older sister who was also called Cleopatra, escaped a violent death – assuming she existed at all.

The evidence for this and so many other details of the family is extremely limited and confusing. Were it not for the subsequent fame of our Cleopatra, it is unlikely that it would ever have become of more than academic interest. Yet the appearance of Cleopatra has often fascinated, even obsessed, historians and the wider public. More recently this controversy sometimes assumes a racial element, making discussion even more heated. It is worth reminding ourselves that this had never been much of an issue for the vast majority of other men and women from the ancient world, and is part of the special mystique of Cleopatra.

Later we shall consider the evidence and see if any tentative conclusions can be reached. For the moment it is worth considering her father, whose career was truly remarkable. Ptolemy XII was often vilified and ridiculed in his lifetime, by his subjects and the Romans alike. Yet he was a survivor who was king for three decades and managed the very rare achievement of dying of old age. His reign tells us much about the kingdom Cleopatra would inherit.

BROTHER AGAINST BROTHER

Ptolemy VIII Euergetes II, or Ptolemy 'Fatty', died on 28 June 116 BC – for once we have the precise date from a building inscription – after a reign lasting fifty-four years, albeit with a number of inter-ruptions. He was in his late sixties and was survived by both Cleo-patra II and Cleopatra III. The daughter would play the dominant role for the next decade and more, but initially one of Physcon's sons ruled jointly with the two Cleopatras, until the mother died some months later. The new king was Ptolemy IX, also named Soter (Saviour) II, and is usually assumed to be a child of Cleopatra III, although it has been suggested that he was in fact the child of Cleopatra II.[2]

A brother of the new king – or perhaps half-brother since Cleo-patra III was definitely his mother – controlled Cyprus. He was Ptolemy X Alexander I, who in 107 BC managed to supplant his sibling and take control of Alexandria. The positions were reversed and Ptolemy IX fled to Cyprus and eventually captured the island. In Egypt Cleopatra III dominated her son. Her name always appeared first in official documents as she ruled jointly with her son. She became the senior priest of the cult of Alexander, a post never before held by a woman, and was simultaneously venerated as a goddess herself.

Cleopatra III's remarkable career finally ended when she died in 101 BC. There were rumours that her son had poisoned her. Ptolemy X now jointly ruled with his wife, Cleopatra Berenice. In 88 BC internal unrest expelled the king and queen from Alexandria. Ptolemy IX led an army back to Egypt from Cyprus and defeated his brother, who was eventually killed. Order had broken down in much of Egypt, especially in the south, and it took some time and heavy fighting for him to regain control. The last Egyptian to claim the title of pharaoh emerged in these years, but was not widely recognised and was simply one rebel leader amongst many.[3]

Ptolemy IX died late in 81 or early in 80 BC. He had two sons, but in 103 BC these, along with a child of Ptolemy X and a good deal of treasure, had been sent to Cos by Cleopatra III. It may be that she wanted them somewhere under her control as security against her son, but in the event the boys and the treasure were all captured by Mithridates of Pontus. For a short while Berenice, widow of Ptolemy X, ruled alone from Alexandria. However, the son of Ptolemy X by an earlier marriage had managed to escape to the Romans and the dictator Sulla sent him to Egypt to become king.

Ptolemy XI had not been to Alexandria or Egypt for more than twenty years and felt no love for his stepmother, whom he cannot have really known. Within a matter of days he had her murdered. Berenice had been popular with many Alexandrians. This, quite possibly combined with other mistakes, prompted a mob to storm the palace some weeks later. Ptolemy XI was dragged to the gymnasium and in this quintessentially Hellenic location was torn to pieces. Official records soon pretended his brief reign had not occurred and the rule of Ptolemy XII was counted as if it had begun immediately on the death of his father, Ptolemy IX. The new king was one of the two boys sent to Cos. Mithridates had betrothed both to a couple of his daughters, but by now the pair had been released and had quickly repudiated these marriages. The older brother was installed as king in Alexandria, while the younger boy ruled Cyprus.

Ptolemy XII styled himself the 'New Dionysus' and was also 'father-loving' and 'brother-loving'. As usual, the Alexandrians were less complimentary. Some called him 'Auletes', the flute, or better, oboe player, because of his enthusiasm for and skill in playing the instrument. This was not proper behaviour for a king. Others simply called him Nothos (bastard). It is usually assumed that this meant that his mother was not Ptolemy IX's wife, but an unknown concubine. His father had married in turn two of his sisters, Cleopatra IV and Cleopatra Selene. The first marriage occurred when both siblings were young, and Ptolemy was made to divorce his wife soon after becoming king. No other Ptolemy married his full sister before he was king, and it is possible that the first marriage was not approved by the wider family, and in particular by the domineering Cleopatra III. Marrying his sister was effectively an assumption of kingship and divine status, and so also a rebellion.[4]

If the first marriage was never considered legal and proper by the rest of the family, then Auletes may have been a bastard because of this. A fragment of a speech by Cicero is usually taken to mean that Auletes was still a 'boy', and so no more than sixteen, when he came to power. If so, then he cannot have been the child of Cleopatra IV, since she had gone off and married a Seleucid and then been murdered at the behest of another sister married to yet another Seleucid in 112 BC. This would also mean that he cannot have been one of the princes sent to Cos in 103 BC since he would not yet have been born. If so, then there must have been two more children of Ptolemy IX who were sent to the island and subsequently captured by Mithridates, and yet who subsequently disappear from the record. However, it is perfectly possible that the boy mentioned by Cicero is not Auletes at all, in which case we have no idea of his age.[5]

Auletes may have been in his twenties when he became king in 81 BC, and his mother may have been Cleopatra IV, but he was the product of a marriage not seen as valid, making him illegitimate. On the other hand, scholars may be right to assume that Ptolemy IX fathered him on a mistress at some point. If this is the case, then we have no idea at all about her identity. It does seem most probable that he and his younger brother were two of the princes sent to Cos. On the whole, the suggestion that Cleopatra IV was his mother fits the evidence marginally better than any other theory, but the simple truth is that we do not know. It is important to remember this.

The Romans were not directly involved in the appointment of Ptolemy XII and his brother as kings. Sulla does not seem to have taken any action in response to the murder of his nominee, Ptolemy XI. Active Roman intervention in Egypt was rare. During his war with Mithridates, Sulla had sent a subordinate to Alexandria to request military aid, and in particular warships. Ptolemy IX ensured that the Roman envoy was lavishly entertained, but sent him away empty-handed, perhaps because he was not sure whether Sulla's authority was legal or because his sons were held hostage by Mithridates. The Romans were unwilling or unable to insist on the king's support.[6]

Roman visitors to Egypt were becoming more common in the

late second and first centuries. Some were there on business, others in a more official capacity. There seems to have been a fairly well-established programme of lavish entertainment for more distinguished guests such as senators. These were taken along the Nile to see the sights, including watching the sacred crocodiles at the Temple of Petesuchos being fed and a visit to the pyramid temple at Hawara. The Romans were interested in Egypt, drawn most of all by its wealth, but for a very long time this interest was largely passive. Instead, it was members of the royal family who continually appealed for Roman backing in their disputes with each other.[7]

One way of strengthening their position was to bequeath their kingdom to the Roman Republic. The aim was to gain immediate support and it is not at all clear how much they were concerned with what happened after their deaths. In 96 BC the Ptolemy ruling Cyrene bequeathed this to Rome. Ptolemy Physcon had already made a similar provision in his will if he died without an heir. Ptolemy X went further and willed the entire realm he claimed – both Egypt and Cyprus – to the Republic.[8]

The Roman response to these bequests was cautious. They accepted the royal estates in Cyrene, but declared the communities of the region self-governing. Only later, in either 74 or 73 BC did the Senate decree that the region was to be annexed as a province. There does not seem to have been any formal response to Ptolemy X's will. The Romans were an aggressive imperial power, but that did not mean that they took every opportunity to gain more territory. Expansion occurred in fits and starts, and there was still considerable reluctance to create new provinces. Some of this came from fear that rivals within the Senate would gain too much wealth and prestige if they were in charge of the annexation process. More important was a reluctance to commit the Republic's resources to new provinces unless this was necessary. There were plenty of opportunities and commitments elsewhere. Egypt and the Ptolemies were simply not central to Roman concerns, especially since they did not pose any threat.

As usual, it was the Ptolemies who tried to interest the Roman Senate in the affairs of their kingdom. In 75 BC two rival claimants to the throne arrived in Rome. They were the sons of Cleopatra

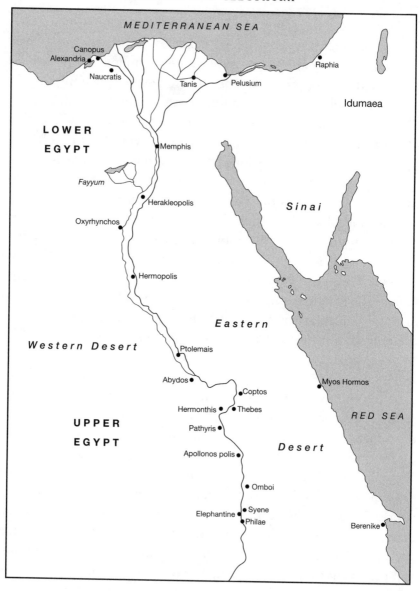

Ptolemaic Egypt

Selene. They were not sons of Ptolemy IX, but came from a later marriage to a Seleucid. The basis of their claim was through their mother, who actively supported them. The Senate was unimpressed, and probably none too enthusiastic about the possibility of a union between Egypt and Syria, so it refused to intervene. To add insult to injury, on his way home one of the princes was even mistreated by the Roman governor of Sicily.[9]

Rejecting this appeal did not mean that the Romans actively supported the rule of Ptolemy XII. There was the real danger that the princes would try again or some other challenger would emerge. As a result Auletes worked steadily to win formal recognition by Rome, spending lavishly to cultivate influential senators. At the same time he put a lot of effort and money into pleasing his subjects, embarking on a grand building programme. Auletes was especially generous to the Egyptian cults and their temples. The costs were substantial at a time when the inundation produced a number of very poor harvests. Added to that was the impact of decades of sporadic civil war and internal tension throughout the two king-doms. Royal officials needed to squeeze harder than ever to raise sufficient revenue. The recent upheavals had done little to promote efficiency within the bureaucracy and at the same time fostered corruption. There were more outbreaks of unrest amongst the hard-pressed peasantry, even if the priestly aristocracy were generally loyal.[10]

THE ROMAN ALEXANDER

Pompey – fully, Cnaeus Pompeius – was a maverick general who first came to prominence when he raised an army at his own expense and led them to join Sulla in 83 BC. He was just twenty-three, had never held office and thus had no right to command. The fact of the existence of his loyal army, raised mainly from his family estates, meant that this did not for the moment matter. Sulla employed him, and he repeatedly hammered the older Roman generals he faced in Italy, Sicily and North Africa. Pompey was young and fancied himself a new Alexander, aping the Macedonian's hairstyle and mannerisms. Sulla named him Magnus (the Great), although he may have intended it ironically. Others called him 'the young butcher' because of his alleged enthusiasm for executions.[11]

When the dictator retired, the Senate he had created also chose to employ Pompey rather than try to force him into a more conventional and legal career. He was sent to Spain to fight a bitter war against Marian supporters who refused to surrender. For the first time Pompey was formally voted the power to command (*imperium*), although this was a special dispensation since he had still not held any elected office and was not even a senator. In 71 BC Pompey returned victorious from Spain and demanded the right to begin his political career and seek election to the consulship for the next year. He was too young, but his popularity – and the fact that his army was camped not far from Rome waiting to celebrate his triumph – ensured that he was granted this special privilege.

Pompey was elected consul for 70 BC, with Marcus Licinius Crassus as his colleague. The latter had just defeated the slave rebellion led by the gladiator Spartacus, and similarly had an army near the city. Both of them were Sulla's men and had done well out of the proscriptions, but there was little love lost between the consular colleagues. Crassus was some ten years older and had resented the praise and rewards received by Pompey during the civil war. The situation was not improved when Pompey destroyed a band of slaves fleeing from Crassus and tried to claim the glory for ending the war.

The pair were rivals and disliked each other intensely. They were also for the next decade and more by far the most influential and wealthiest men in the Republic. Crassus worked hard at politics, as he did in his business activities, steadily increasing his fortune. He owned property and maintained a large group of slave craftsmen to repair and construct buildings. Others acted as firemen at a time when there was no fire service in Rome. Crassus was wont to buy up property in the path of a blaze at a bargain price and then send in his slaves to control the fire, usually by demolishing buildings to create a firebreak. Later these could be rebuilt by his craftsmen. Crassus was a shrewd businessman, but did not simply use his money to make more money. He was generous in giving loans to other senators, and was equally generous with his time, often acting as an advocate in the courts. In this way a large proportion of senators were placed under obligation to him. Strikingly, Crassus was considered too dangerous for anyone else to prosecute.[12]

Pompey had spent most of his life on campaign and did not know how to play the political game anywhere near as well. He relied far more on the glory of his victories. When these began to fade in the public consciousness, he decided that he needed new ones. In 67 BC he was given an extraordinary command to deal with the pirate problem, which had grown even worse since the failure of Mark Antony's father. Pompey received massively greater resources than Antonius. He was also a good deal more competent, with a true genius for organisation. In a matter of months, he and his subordinates swept the Mediterranean clear of pirates. Looking for a long-term solution, many of the pirates were resettled on land where they could support themselves and their families without resorting to crime.[13]

Pompey's success was spectacular, but he wanted far more and in 66 BC was granted another extraordinary command to deal with Mithridates of Pontus. Once again there was more than a hint of poaching the glory of others, because the war had already almost been won by Lucullus, one of the consuls of 74 BC. Pompey used the pretext of the war with Mithridates and his ally, King Tiridates of Armenia, to launch a series of eastern expeditions against various opponents. He expanded Roman territory and then systematically reorganised the eastern provinces. In the process he abolished the last rump of the Seleucid Empire. The Ptolemies were left as the only survivor of the three great Successor kingdoms.[14]

Pompey did not visit Egypt, but Auletes took care to provide aid to his army, including the supplies necessary to support 8,000 cavalrymen. In addition, he sent lavish gifts, including a gold crown, to the commander himself. In the meantime, Crassus held the censorship in 65 BC and began agitating to have Egypt declared Roman public land, which could then be distributed. He clearly hoped to be placed in charge of the process and so make a substantial profit, as well as placing large numbers of citizens in his debt. Julius Caesar – still only in his thirties, but extremely ambitious – was also involved, although it is not clear whether he supported Crassus or wanted to take charge of the process himself. Crassus was very influential and extremely rich – probably only Pompey could match his wealth – yet other senators had some wealth and some influence, and if enough of them combined to block a measure then there was no means of forcing it through. All proposals about Egypt made at this time were blocked.[15]

The move to annex Egypt failed, and Crassus and Caesar both passed on to other schemes. It is vital to remember that Egypt was not at the centre of Roman public life. Occasionally it became an issue, usually as part of the personal ambitions of a leading senator, as each struggled to rise to the top. In late 64 BC a law was proposed to make a widespread distribution of publicly owned land to poorer citizens. Egypt was wholly or partly to be included within this, but once again the measure was defeated and public life moved on to other concerns.[16]

Pompey also discovered that there were limits to his real power when he returned to Rome in December 62 BC. His prestige was colossal, his popularity huge and the triumph he celebrated shortly afterwards more spectacular than any ever seen before. Yet for all that he failed to gain the Senate's approval for eastern settlement or secure land for the soldiers due for discharge from his army. Time and again attempts to secure these things were blocked. Other senators, including Crassus and the supplanted Lucullus, were eager to cut the great general down to size. None wanted to see the Republic dominated by Pompey, and at the same time thwarting him helped to build up their own influence and reputation. The issues were almost irrelevant. Pompey's eastern settlement was sensible and thorough, the desire to reward his soldiers reasonable. This did not in any way restrain other senators from blocking them and Pompey was not a skilful enough politician to find a way round.[17]

It may have been Julius Caesar who came up with the idea of bringing Pompey and Crassus together in a secret alliance known to scholars (although not at the time) as the 'first triumvirate'. On their own, neither Crassus nor Pompey could get what they wanted. Working together, and with Caesar as consul for 59 BC, all three men were far harder to resist. That did not prevent rival senators – including Caesar's consular colleague Bibulus – from trying to block them every step of the way. Both sides in turn escalated the conflict, and there was intimidation and violence that stopped just short of serious bloodshed. Pompey's settlement was ratified and his veterans given land, while Crassus won a favourable deal for the *publicani* with many of whom he had close connections. Caesar forced through a law redistributing public-owned land in Italy to poor citizens and secured himself an extraordinary military command for five years.[18]

Auletes had cultivated Pompey for some time and the king scented an opportunity now that the latter and his allies were so strong at Rome. At last Ptolemy XII gained formal recognition, being named as king and a 'friend and ally of the Roman people' by a law passed by Caesar in 59 BC. The price tag was enormous. Auletes promised to pay 6,000 talents – somewhere between half and all the annual revenue of Egypt. The bulk of this went to Pompey and Caesar, although Crassus may also have profited. Ptolemy's representatives borrowed on a huge scale from Roman bankers to make the initial down payment.[19]

Auletes' younger brother in Cyprus was unable to afford the cost of similar recognition. In 58 BC an ambitious Roman senator persuaded the People's Assembly to pass a law granting a free dole of grain to every citizen in Rome. To meet the cost of this, the law authorised the seizure of Cyprus – or at least royal property there – by the Republic in accordance with Ptolemy X's will. The king was offered comfortable retirement, but chose suicide instead when all his protests were unavailing.[20]

The Alexandrians seem to have welcomed the formal recognition of Auletes by Rome, but the annexation of Cyprus provoked deep resentment and a sense of humiliation. Auletes had done nothing to save his brother or resist the seizure of one of the oldest parts of the Ptolemaic Empire. At the same time the royal bureaucracy was especially aggressive in its collection of revenue, since the king needed to pay his debt to the triumvirate. Resentment festered. Romans became unpopular – we hear of one member of a delegation being lynched after accidentally killing a cat. Cats were sacred in Egypt (and this is one respect where elements of the Greek population had taken on existing beliefs), but the outburst was probably as much anti-Roman as anything else.[21]

MOTHERS AND DAUGHTERS

The king himself was seen as weak because he fawned to the Romans, and repressive because of his efforts to pay them. There may well have been other factors at work, and ambitious members of the court scented an opportunity for personal advantage. Late in 58 BC, Ptolemy XII Auletes left Alexandria and travelled to Rome, where he claimed that he had been driven out. Certainly, it was some years – and only by force – before he returned. His eldest daughter, Berenice IV, was proclaimed as queen in his absence and clearly against his will. We do not know how old she was, or whether she or her senior advisers were the prime movers in this coup. She was unmarried and took as co-ruler another member of the family called Cleopatra.[22]

This was definitely not our Cleopatra, who was only eleven at the time. Auletes married his sister Cleopatra V Tryphaena soon after he became king. She may have been his half-sister, especially if he was in fact the son of Cleopatra IV, which would suggest he was some twenty years older than her. In that case, her mother could well have been an unknown concubine. Solving one problem with the Ptolemaic family tree often seems only to create different questions.[23]

Cleopatra V Tryphaena was certainly the mother of Berenice IV, but ceased to be named in official documents late in 69 BC. From November of that year only Ptolemy himself is mentioned and it has often been assumed that the queen must have died. Reliefs on the temple at Edfu bearing her name seem to have been deliberately covered up at about the same time. This would seem odd if the queen had died and hints that she was withdrawn from public life, either in disgrace or for reasons of health. For whatever reason, Auletes did not marry again. If Cleopatra V Tryphaena was still alive in 58 BC then Berenice may have ruled jointly with her mother.[24]

The Geographer Strabo, writing at the end of the first century BC, mentions casually that Ptolemy Auletes had 'three daughters, of whom one, the eldest, was legitimate'. The eldest was Berenice, and this implies that she was the only child the king had with his wife.

Our Cleopatra was born before Cleopatra Tryphaena disappeared and therefore it is chronologically possible that the latter was her mother, even if she died soon afterwards. Many slurs and insults were hurled at Cleopatra during and after her lifetime, but it is significant that no other source claims that she was illegitimate – in marked contrast to her father Auletes. It is very hard to believe that something of that sort would not have been used against her.

So there are two main possibilities. One is that Strabo's throwaway comment was correct, even though the point is never mentioned anywhere else. This would make Cleopatra, her younger sister Arsinoe and their two brothers the offspring of a liaison between Auletes and one or more concubines. If Cleopatra Tryphaena was still alive after the end of 69 BC, then she was either incapable of producing more children or the king was disinclined to have them with her. There is no positive evidence for the existence of a royal mistress or mistresses. Since we do not even know whether this woman or women existed, it is important to emphasise that we have no idea at all about their identity. The suggestion made by some that she was an Egyptian from one of the priestly families is pure conjecture.

Alternatively, if Cleopatra Tryphaena survived after 69 BC, but was in disgrace, it is not impossible that she was the mother of some or all of Auletes' children. This would mean that our Cleopatra's parents were full brother and sister, which would in turn mean that she had only two grandparents. If Tryphaena was no longer officially queen, then that might just explain Strabo's statement that only Berenice was legitimate. We simply do not know and should not pretend otherwise.[25]

A Cleopatra ruled jointly with Berenice IV. If it was not her mother, then the only real alternative is that there was another sister, Cleopatra VI, between Berenice and our Cleopatra. In this case Strabo would have been wrong to say that Auletes had three daughters. Once again, we simply do not know. Our Cleopatra is known as Cleopatra VII, but opinion is divided over whether or not there really was a Cleopatra VI. Whether mother or sister, Berenice IV's co-ruler died within a year or so.

★

Mystery surrounds almost every aspect of Cleopatra's family and birth. Our sources are equally blank about her early life. At least until 58 BC, she was probably raised in Alexandria. Tutors for the Ptolemies were often drawn from the scholars of the Museum. In later life Cleopatra would display formidable intellect and erudition. By this period, the royal family gave girls as full and thorough an education as boys. Her first language was Greek, but Plutarch says that she was also able to converse in the languages of the Medes, Parthians, Jews, Ethiopians, Trogodytae, Arabs and Syrians – all peoples living relatively near to her kingdom. Latin is notably absent from the list. Significantly, she was the first of her family to speak Egyptian.

When Ptolemy Auletes left Alexandria, we do not know what happened to the eleven-year-old Cleopatra. She may have remained behind and because of her youth played no part in the new regime. A vague and undated inscription set up in Athens has been interpreted as showing that she went with her father. There is nothing inherently impossible about this. If Ptolemy was suspicious of the loyalty of some senior courtiers and his eldest daughter, he might have preferred to keep some or all of his children with him. That something is not impossible does not mean that it happened.[26]

Yet there is something intriguing about the idea that the little girl accompanied Ptolemy, for the king would now go to Rome.

[VI]

ADOLESCENT

Very little is known about Mark Antony's mother. Plutarch called her 'as noble and virtuous a woman as any of her day'. Aristocratic women at Rome tended to be married young, usually to older men. If they survived the perils of childbirth, then there was a good chance that they would outlive their husbands. Politicians rarely became too prominent during their father's lifetime, but many had living mothers and some of these had a powerful influence on their sons. Julia could still change her son's mind when Antony was in his forties.[1]

The Romans celebrated mothers who disciplined their sons, trained them in virtue and drove them on to excel. The ideal was more stern than soft and forgiving – although that may simply be because the latter was taken for granted. One of the most famous was Cornelia, wife of a man who was twice consul and censor, and the mother of Tiberius and Caius Gracchus. The brothers had spectacular careers, but each was killed in succession – the first acts in the violence that dominated the last century of the Republic. By that time she had long since been widowed and was said to have turned down a proposal of marriage from Ptolemy VIII. Julius Caesar's mother Aurelia was held in similarly high regard.[2]

Julia was fifth cousin to Julius Caesar. The two branches of the family had diverged several generations earlier, to the extent that they were now members of different voting tribes in the Popular Assembly. Her own brother was Lucius Julius Caesar, who was consul in 64 BC and a distinguished member of the Senate. Their father had also reached the consulship, but he and his brother were both victims of the massacre carried out by Marius' supporters in 87 BC. In spite of his failures against the pirates, it is highly likely that her husband, Marcus Antonius, would have reached the consulship had he not died before returning to Rome. Julia's second husband was consul in 71 BC.

Women could not vote or stand for political office, but senators' daughters were raised to be proud of their family. Unable to have a career of their own, many did their utmost to promote the career of their husband and sons. On marriage, Julia did not take her husband's name. She remained Julia, the daughter of Lucius Julius Caesar, and one of the Julii and a patrician. This was reinforced because her property remained her own and so was not eaten away by her first husband's debts. Her own father dead, Julia enjoyed a remarkable degree of independence even though she married again.

Aristocratic women rarely breastfed their children, and the amount of time they chose to spend with them when they were infants varied considerably – as indeed it does today, especially amongst the more affluent. We know nothing at all of how Julia felt about or treated her three sons – in the same way that we know nothing about her emotions towards either of her husbands. The mother's role was important in supervising the upbringing of her children, even if this was sometimes done at a distance and their day-to-day care left to nurses, who would usually be slaves. These would also be selected by the mother. Yet, ideally, many Romans seem to have believed that the mother should be more directly involved. Writing at the end of the first century AD, the senator Tacitus claimed that:

> In the good old days, every man's son, born in wedlock, was brought up not in the chamber of some hireling nurse, but in his mother's lap, and at her knee. And that mother could have no higher praise than that she managed the house and gave herself to her children. ... In the presence of such a one no base word could be uttered without grave offence, and no wrong deed done. Religiously and with the utmost diligence she regulated not only the serious tasks of her youthful charges, but their recreations also and their games.[3]

Education was carried out at home in aristocratic families. Only the less well-off, but still moderately wealthy, sent their children to fee-paying primary schools. The poor had little or no access to education and many were probably illiterate. In contrast, the aristocracy were raised to be bilingual, fluent in Greek as well as Latin. A slave from the Hellenic east would act as the child's attendant (*paedagogus*) to begin teaching him Greek (or her – by this period senators' daughters were usually as well educated as their sons). Along with numeracy and literacy, children were taught about history, and in particular the part in it played by their family. As Cicero put it, 'For what is the life of a man, if it is not interwoven with the life of former generations by a sense of history?'[4]

Julia would have made sure that Antony and his brothers knew they were heirs both to the Antonii and Julii. Personal virtue was emphasised. Rome had grown to be the greatest power in the world because of its special respect for the gods, and the courage, constancy and proper behaviour of the Romans, especially the aristocracy and most of all the boys' ancestors. From his earliest years Antony would have been surrounded by expectation that he would live up to – or better still surpass – the achievements of previous generations. Rome was the greatest state in the world and it had been led to that greatness by its aristocratic leaders. Being born into a senatorial family made a child special, particularly if his family was one of the handful at the centre of public life. Rome had no monarch and senators considered themselves greater than the kings of other countries. Antony will never have doubted that being born to his parents meant that he would be one of the most prominent men of his generation. He was born to distinction and glory.

From about the age of seven he began a practical preparation for this, accompanying his father as he went about his daily business. Senators' lives were lived very much in public. Apart from meetings of the Senate, there was a daily round of receiving the greetings of clients – people attached to the family, usually as a result of past favours – and meetings with other senators. Boys were supposed to observe and copy the proper way of doing things. They were not admitted to the Senate's meetings themselves, but were allowed to sit outside the open doors and hear what they could of the procedure and debates. Clustered there were the other boys of aristocratic families, so that from very early on there was a close association with the men with whom a boy would later compete for office.[5]

Antony can only have spent a few years following his father in this way, before Antonius went off to fight the pirates. After this he may have learned about the conduct of politics by accompanying one of his uncles – either his father's brother Caius Antonius Hybrida or Julia's brother Lucius Julius Caesar. We do not know how soon Julia remarried, although at least a year was a common period of mourning, not least because it made clear the paternity of any child. After this Antony may have learned from Lentulus. We simply do not know.

Formal education continued alongside the hours spent observing public life, with the emphasis now on what the Romans called *grammatica*. This included detailed study of the classics of Latin and Greek literature, as well as written and spoken exercises in rhetoric. Pupils were expected to memorise large chunks of literature and also learnt by rote such things as the Twelve Tables, Rome's oldest collection of laws. The ability to speak, and in particular to deliver a coherent and convincing argument, was vital for any man entering public life. Although Mark Antony never gained as great a reputation for oratory as his grandfather, he was certainly a capable speaker.[6]

As usual, senators' sons were expected to learn as much by observing as doing. Public life was carried on in a very public way, with speeches made from the Rostra in the Forum to crowds gathered before an assembly met or on other important occasions. Criminal trials were also conducted in the open air on platforms in the Forum and regularly attracted a wide audience. Many famous orators published their speeches, although Antony's grandfather refused to do so, saying that it risked something he said in one case being used against him in another. In spite of this he had written a study of oratory. In 92 BC the Senate had decreed the closure of schools teaching rhetoric in Latin. The ostensible reason was the superiority of such teaching in Greek, although it may also have been intended to restrict formal training to the very wealthy alone.[7]

As a man Mark Antony was very proud of his physique. Like other Roman boys his education included a strong thread of physical exercise and specialised training. The purpose was practical, so that alongside simple exercise in running, swimming and lifting weights,

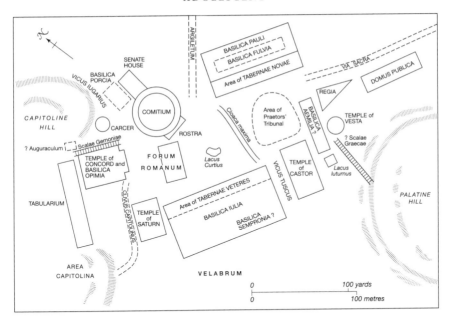

The City of Rome – central area, Forum etc. Some details are conjectural.

aristocratic boys learned to fence with swords, handle a shield and throw a javelin. They also learned how to ride, probably both bareback and with the four-horned saddle used by the Romans in an age before the stirrup. Ideally the boy was to be taught these things by a male relative – many senators prided themselves on their skill at arms. The ideal general was supposed to be able to control his army as well as he handled his personal weapons. Again, a good deal of a boy's training occurred in public view on the Campus Martius – the Field of Mars to the west of the Tiber where once the army had mustered. Just as they saw each other waiting outside the Senate's meetings, boys trained and competed with their peers as a prelude to the competition of public life.[8]

Julia raised Mark Antony and his brothers to be leaders of the Republic. It is quite possible that her brother-in-law Caius Antonius and her second husband helped to fulfil the role normally played by the boy's father. In 70 BC, when Antony was just thirteen, their capacity to do so was severely limited. The censors of that year proved far more rigorous than usual and expelled no fewer than sixty-four senators – just over 10 per cent of the house. These men were condemned as unfit, chiefly for their morals and general character as much as any specific crimes. Both Caius Antonius and Lentulus had their names struck off the senatorial role and had to begin climbing the political ladder almost from scratch.[9]

WILD YOUTH

As a boy Mark Antony wore the *toga praetexta*. This had a purple border and was otherwise only worn by serving magistrates. When his family decided, he would lay this aside in a ceremony that marked his formally becoming a man. There was no set age for this, and although somewhere between fourteen and sixteen was usual, some boys became men as young as twelve. The death of his father may have encouraged the family to do things earlier than would normally have been the case. There was not a fixed time of year for the ceremony, although many chose to celebrate it on 17 March, during the Liberalia festival. Tradition dictated that the boy was given a shorter, adult hairstyle, and was shaved for the first time, although in most cases there can have been little for the barber to do. The *bulla* charm was also removed and never worn again. On the day of the ceremony, Antony donned the plain *toga virilis* for the first time and was taken through the Forum by relatives and led up to the Capitoline Hill where he would make a sacrifice to Iuventus, the god of youth.[10]

Although now formally a man, and the *paterfamilias*, or head of the household, with authority over his younger brothers, Antony continued to live with his mother and stepfather. Not until their late teens was it common for aristocratic youths to move out from the home, usually renting an apartment rather than a house. There was still much for them to learn about public life and the duties of a senator, and they were supposed to keep following relatives or family friends about their daily tasks, as well as watching events in the Forum. At the same time, there was a generally indulgent feeling towards youths of this age. A little enjoyment of the pleasures offered by the greatest city in the world was pardonable, as long as it was not taken to excess and a man eventually grew through this phase.[11]

Restraint was never a prominent feature in Antony's character, and this was an age when there were plenty of temptations for the young. Empire brought wealth on a massive scale and there were soon plenty of people eager to sell luxuries of all kinds to those willing to buy. Older senators and equestrians invested in lavish country villas and estates – Cicero continually complained about ex-consuls more interested in their exotic fish than the affairs of state. The young usually wanted quicker thrills.

One of Antony's contemporaries, himself hounded out of politics on charges of corruption, later railed against the mood of their generation:

> As soon as riches came to be held in honour, when glory, dominion, and power followed in their train, virtue began to lose its lustre, poverty to be considered a disgrace, blamelessness to be termed malevolence. Therefore ... riches, luxury and greed, united with insolence, took possession of our young manhood. They pillaged, squandered; set little value on their own, coveted the goods of others; they disregarded modesty, chastity, everything human and divine; in short they were utterly thoughtless and reckless.[12]

As well as indulgence and pleasure, there was also competition, for even the riotous youths remained Roman aristocrats. The young Julius Caesar marked himself out as different by wearing a tunic with long sleeves and so loosely belted that it fell down past his knees. It was a style soon aped by other senators' sons who wanted to be unconventional. Cicero mocked the young men 'you see with their carefully combed hair, dripping with oil, some smooth as girls, others with shaggy beards, with tunics down to their ankles and wrists, and wearing frocks not togas'. Antony had his own way of standing out. As he grew into manhood he cultivated a neater, thicker beard, and instead of letting his tunic hang low he was fond of girding it up unusually high to show his well-muscled legs. Encouraged by a story that the Antonii were descended from Hercules, he sometimes added a rough, animal-skin cloak, wore a sword and revelled in exuberant, even vulgar displays. Such myths were not uncommon. The Julii claimed the goddess Venus as an ancestor.[13]

The young aristocrats were determined to enjoy themselves, but men like Antony never lost the utter assurance that in due course it would also be their right to lead the Republic. He soon became the closest of friends with a man of similar temperament, Caius Scribonius Curio, whose father was consul in 76 BC. Plutarch claims that it was Curio who really introduced Antony to heavy drinking, the pursuit of women and an extravagant lifestyle. If this is true, then he was certainly an eager pupil and would remain devoted to all these things for the rest of his life.[14]

Sex was readily available in Rome's slave-owning society. Slaves were property and their owners could sell, punish or kill them as they wished. They had no right to refuse any treatment. There were also plenty of brothels, from the cheap and squalid to the lavish and expensive. More important for a young aristocrat were the higher-class courtesans, whose favours were less easy to secure. These had to be cultivated more carefully, lavished with gifts and money to pay for their own slaves and an apartment in which to live. Some were famous — like Praecia, the mistress of Cethegus, who had helped influence the commands in 74 BC — and passed from one famous lover to the next. A story is told of Pompey ending an affair with one courtesan to clear the path of a friend and so place the latter in his debt.[15]

Courtesans offered far more than just sex. Most were well educated, witty and elegant. They offered companionship and the thrill of an affair. There was an even greater thrill to be had in the pursuit of aristocratic women. Senators' daughters were too valuable as a means of cementing political alliances to be left unmarried for long. There were almost no young, single and aristocratic women in Rome. Yet many had husbands far older than themselves, whose political career took them off to the provinces for years on end. In an era where girls were as well educated as their brothers, most women were fluent in Greek as well as Latin, had an extensive knowledge of literature of all kinds and especially poetry, as well perhaps as philosophy and music.[16]

All of these attributes could be seen as virtues, but could also leave a woman bored with the task of raising children and running a household. Just like the men of their generation, many aristocratic women refused to obey traditional conventions and sought more immediate pleasure. The historian Sallust left a full, if jaundiced, description of Sempronia, well known to Julia's second husband Lentulus, and the mother of Decimus Junius Brutus, a contemporary of Antony's:

> This woman was well blessed by fortune in her birth and physical beauty, as well as her husband and children; well read in Greek and Latin literature, she played the lyre, danced more artfully than any honest woman should, and had many other gifts which fostered a luxurious life. Yet there was never anything she prized so little as her honour and chastity; it was hard to say whether she was less free with her money or her virtue; her lusts were so fierce that she more often pursued men than was pursued by them. . . . She had often broken her word, failed to pay her debts, been party to murder; her lack of money but addiction to luxury set her on a wild course. Even so, she was a remarkable woman; able to write poetry, crack a joke, and converse modestly, tenderly or wantonly; all in all she had great gifts and a good many charms.[17]

Aristocratic women were exciting, challenging lovers, and gossip suggested that extramarital affairs were common in these years. Julius Caesar was notorious for his seduction of other men's wives – he slept with the wives of both Pompey and Crassus, and maintained a long-term affair with Servilia, the mother of the Brutus who would lead the conspiracy against him and the half-sister of Marcus Cato, his bitterest opponent. The poet Catullus wrote of the joys of love with Lesbia, a married woman from a prestigious patrician family, and the bitterness of subsequent rejection.[18]

We know nothing of Antony's earliest love affairs, other than that he had them. Cicero claimed that he also let men make love to him, dubbing him little more than a prostitute, until Curio came along and offered him a 'stable marriage'. This was part of a speech vilifying every aspect of Antony's character and needs to be treated with caution. Roman politicians habitually threw the most scurrilous abuse at each other – elsewhere, Cicero accused another prominent senator of incest with his sister. The truth is impossible to know, but it was probably just gossip.[19]

Yet Curio and Antony were certainly extremely close. They spent a lot of time in each other's company, throwing themselves into a round of wild parties. It was not a cheap lifestyle. Antony inherited heavy debts from his father, but was soon running up new ones of his own. There were plenty of people willing to loan him money, both on the basis of his remaining property and also gambling on Antony having a successful career. If he did well enough then he would be in a position to repay the loan and interest, or alternatively do the lender a favour in future. Even so his debts rose to staggering levels.

Curio stuck by his friend, and personally went surety for the sum of 6 million sesterces. (A senator needed property of at least 1 million, while a soldier had a gross annual salary of just 500 sesterces.) Curio's father was not impressed and barred Antony from coming to their house. Cicero claims that the undeterred Antony climbed onto the roof and was let down through a hole in the tiles. The orator also says that both the father and son came to see him, the latter imploring him to convince Curio senior to make good on the pledge. He did, but would not permit his son to take on any more of his friend's debts.[20]

SAVIOUR OF THE REPUBLIC

Antony was not alone in running up massive debts. Julius Caesar was just one example, but there were many more. The creditors were usually willing to wait as long as the debtor continued to be successful. Serious political failure risked an immediate demand for payment, which could only end in utter ruin. Both Lentulus and Caius Antonius had to spend heavily to get back into the Senate and public life, seeking offices they had already held in the past. They made steady progress and were elected praetor and consul respectively for 63 BC.

Marcus Tullius Cicero was Antonius' colleague in the consulship. He was a 'new man', whose fame rested on his great talent as an orator – in fact, he claimed to have learned much from listening to Antony's grandfather. Defying one of Sulla's more brutal minions in a court case, he quickly made a name for himself and continued to play a conspicuous role in some of the most notorious cases of the next decades. He was soon acknowledged – not least by himself – as the finest orator of his generation. Many senators were very grateful for having Cicero defend them or their clients in court. That did not mean that they would always support him when he sought higher office. Cicero remained the new man and could not boast of the achievements of his family. Yet in the elections for the consulship of 63 BC enough influential voters decided that he was preferable to one of the other leading contenders, Lucius Sergius Catiline. They voted for the new man, and for Caius Antonius. The latter was held in very low esteem, but was considered too lazy to be dangerous – an echo of the alleged reason for giving his brother Marcus Antonius the pirate command in 74 BC.[21]

Catiline tried to win the consulship for the next year and again failed. He was a patrician from an ancient line that had long since drifted away from the centre of public life. In this respect, he was like Sulla – and indeed Julius Caesar – and had the same driving urge to reclaim what he felt was his rightful place at the head of the Republic. Even his enemies had to admit that Catiline had talent, but his reputation was scandalous – again similarities with Sulla and Caesar, and even Mark Antony, are strong. As one of Sulla's supporters he had been especially bloodthirsty during the proscriptions. There were also persistent rumours that he had murdered his own son to please his new wife and allegations of an attempted coup that failed only at the last minute.[22]

Catiline had profited from Sulla's success, but then spent so lavishly that he was soon heavily in debt. He was one of the fast set, mixing with the wild young men and women whose behaviour provided the gossips with plenty of material. Antony must have known him, because Julia's husband Lentulus was a close associate. It is more than likely that many of his friends were drawn to Catiline, who had a reputation for helping to arrange love affairs and being generous with money. He spent to win supporters and tie them to him. Politics was also hugely expensive for anyone in an era when candidates had to out-spend their rivals to advertise themselves and win votes. Catiline's three unsuccessful campaigns for the consulship shattered his remaining credit.[23]

In 63 BC he lost to Cicero, the new man he dubbed a mere 'resident alien' in Rome. The details of what followed are only known from hostile sources. It may well be that Cicero did his best to provoke a crisis, backing Catiline into a corner. Yet he did not imagine or create the rebellion that followed. After brazening things out for a while, Catiline fled from Rome and joined an army being raised by his associates. Eventually they would lead two legions, one carrying an eagle of one of the legions that had fought under Marius.[24]

Mark Antony's stepfather Lentulus was the leader of the men Catiline left behind in Rome, who were later accused of plotting to murder Cicero and other leading men and then start fires to sow confusion in the city. It was far from being a well-organised and disciplined plot. One of the conspirators boasted to his mistress of how he and his friends were going to take over. She promptly took the story to Cicero and continued to keep him informed. Soon afterwards Lentulus made contact with ambassadors sent to Rome by a Gaulish tribe called the Allobroges. They were there to complain of mistreatment by successive governors. Lentulus tried to persuade them to provide cavalry to support Catiline's legions. The Gauls decided to trust to the proper authorities and reported what was happening. Cicero was able to ambush and arrest them, along with one of the conspirators and several incriminating letters. Lentulus had even repeated a prophecy to the Gauls which claimed that three Cornelii would rule Rome. Sulla and Marius' ally Cornelius Cinna were two, and he, Cornelius Lentulus, was destined to be the third.

The Senate having decreed a state of emergency, Lentulus and the other leading conspirators were arrested. A debate then raged as the senators decided what to do. Most favoured immediate execution, but for a while Julius Caesar started to sway their mood in favour of permanent imprisonment. Cato, backed by Cicero and others, managed to convince a majority to enforce the death penalty without formal trial. In honour of his status as praetor, Cicero personally led Lentulus by the hand to the nearby Tullianum, which served as a prison and place of execution. The conspirators were then strangled. Cicero is supposed to have announced simply 'they have lived' – the single word *vixerunt* in Latin.[25]

Antony does not appear to have been seriously involved with the conspiracy. Perhaps he was also still too young to be taken seriously, since he was only twenty, and had not yet taken any formal steps towards a political career. As far as we know he did not take part in any court cases and would not do so in the coming years. Young men tended to prosecute, in part because this was seen as an aggressive action, since if successful it could well end another man's career. Established orators like Cicero usually acted for the defence, since it was considered more honourable to defend a friend or associate even if he was guilty.

Julia was once again a widow. Now in her late thirties, she chose not to remarry. Plutarch reports but discounts a story claiming that Cicero refused to let her have Lentulus' body for proper burial. Her brother-in-law, Caius Antonius, was sent with an army to deal with Catiline. Cicero had helped to secure his colleague's co-operation by a private deal. He had been allocated the province of Macedonia after his year as consul, but he waived his right to this and let Antonius take it instead. The latter believed that the Macedonian frontier offered the prospect of a lucrative war.[26]

Antonius pleaded an attack of gout and was not present at the battle when the rebel army was destroyed and Catiline killed. Instead, command passed to an experienced subordinate. It was common for young aristocrats to accompany relatives on campaign, living with their headquarters and learning the business of leading an army by watching it done. There is no evidence that Antony accompanied his uncle either against Catiline or when he went to Macedonia. Indeed, we know almost nothing about his activities in his early twenties. It was probably to his advantage not to have accompanied his uncle. Antonius was defeated by Thracian tribesmen and when he returned to Rome he was brought to trial in 59 BC on charges of corruption. Cicero loyally defended his consular colleague, but Antonius was condemned and went into exile. With father and stepfather both dead – as we have seen, the latter executed as a rebel – and his uncle now a discredited exile, Antony was running out of relatives able to help his career.[27]

At some point he seems to have married. His bride was called Fadia and was the daughter of a freedman named Quintus Fadius Gallus. There was no political advantage to such a union – and indeed any connection with the family of a former slave was likely to provoke mockery and contempt from the aristocracy. Most likely, Fadius was wealthy, and the marriage helped him to gain respectability while financially assisting Antony. Perhaps the young aristocrat was able to spend some of his wife's money to maintain his flamboyant lifestyle. At best, any aid made only the slightest dent in his crippling debts.[28]

Antony certainly knew many of the leading senators, and especially the younger generation now forcing their way into politics. Although he no doubt knew Julius Caesar, there is no hint of any close connection. Early in his career, Caesar had prosecuted Caius Antonius on charges of corruption and although the latter had not been found guilty there was little love lost between the two men. In 59 BC Antony's friend Curio was a leading critic of Caesar, Pompey and Crassus, enjoying a brief popularity that saw him cheered when he appeared in public. Julia's close family were hostile to Caesar at this stage in his career.[29]

For a while Antony was an enthusiastic supporter of Publius Clodius Pulcher – a man about ten years his senior and already becoming a force in politics. A member of the ancient patrician family of the Claudii, Clodius arranged to have himself adopted by a plebeian in 59 BC. The change of status meant that he could now stand for office as tribune of the plebs, while retaining the prestige and connections of his real ancestry. The tribunate could be used as a powerful platform for an ambitious and well-connected man. It was the post that the Gracchi brothers had used, and it was tribunes who transferred Sulla's command to Marius in 88 BC and gave Pompey his extraordinary commands in 67 and 66 BC. Clodius was easily elected as one of the ten tribunes for 58 BC. He had many supporters amongst the poorer inhabitants of Rome and these proved willing to intimidate and even attack opponents.

The triumvirate assisted Clodius in gaining his plebeian status in this unorthodox way, but it is wrong to think of him as their man. He was soon threatening to attack the laws passed by Caesar during his consulship, before subsequently turning his attentions to Cicero and accusing him of illegally executing the conspirators in 63 BC. The new man was vulnerable and, bitterly disappointed by the lack of support given by other senators and especially Pompey, Cicero fled into voluntary exile. It was Clodius who arranged the annexation of Cyprus to fund the free corn dole he introduced for citizens in Rome.

Clodius was another of the wild-living younger generation, notorious for his womanising. His sisters and brother had a similar reputation. One of the sisters was the 'Lesbia' first adored and then hated by the poet Catullus. Clodius himself had once been discovered disguised as a woman and sneaking into Julius Caesar's house during an exclusively female religious festival. Most people believed he was conducting an affair with Julius Caesar's wife. Caesar refused to testify against Clodius when the latter was charged with sacrilege. Neverthless, he divorced his wife, and when questioned famously said that this was because 'Caesar's wife must be above suspicion'. Clodius was married to Fulvia, herself from a very distinguished family. There were rumours that she and Antony conducted an affair. There may not have been any truth in this, although some years later he would marry her. For whatever reason, Antony broke with Clodius.[30]

At some point, Antony left Italy for Greece and remained there for a considerable time. Ostensibly this was to study rhetoric, and many Romans including Cicero and Caesar had travelled east to do this at a similar age, but both had also already begun their political careers. Antony had not and was probably held back by the burden of his debts as well as his fondness for pleasure. Pressure from creditors may well have been a strong reason for leaving Rome.

[VII]

THE RETURN OF THE KING

Antony had probably already left Rome long before Ptolemy Auletes arrived late in 58 BC. There would anyway have been no reason for the king to seek out the twenty-four-year-old. Instead, he needed to win over enough influential senators to make the Romans commit to restoring him to his throne. He went first to Pompey, both because of their past connection and because of his obvious importance. A Roman senator's prestige was reflected by the level of the people who came as clients to seek his favour. It bolstered Pompey's reputation to have kings coming to him for help and he granted Auletes the hospitality of his own villa in the Alban Hills near Rome.[1]

The city was bigger than his own capital of Alexandria, bigger indeed than any city in the known world, but a good deal less impressive. Alexandria had been planned and was from the beginning built on a monumental scale. Rome developed more gradually over the centuries and was only now beginning to acquire the grand buildings we associate with it. Pompey had already commissioned a massive theatre complex, almost none of which is now visible, but was originally grander than anything else in Rome. Senators lived in old houses near the heart of the city and their prominence was measured by how close they were to the Via Sacra, the route followed by processions on important occasions. Most Romans lived crowded into high-rise blocks (*insulae*), paying a high rent and risking disease and fire. Ptolemy may well have found Rome crude and rather squalid, but he had come because he knew its power.

He had also had a recent taste of the blunt manner of some Romans. En route he stopped at Cyprus and went to seek the advice of Marcus Cato, the man appointed by Clodius to oversee the annexation of the island. The tribune had declared that it was vital to send Rome's most honest man, and Cato had accepted the flattery and the prestigious command. From Clodius' point of view, it also removed a vocal opponent from Rome. Cato performed the task rigorously and without any hint of malpractice and that in itself was rare enough for any Roman senator of his day. He was an ardent follower of Stoicism, a philosophical school that in the form most favoured by the Romans stressed stern duty and self-discipline. He was famous for his simple lifestyle and refusal to compromise – especially since such traditional virtues were what his most famous ancestor, himself a new man, was also renowned for. Yet there was also a touch of eccentricity about Cato. He was a heavy drinker, and sometimes went barefoot and wore just his toga without a tunic underneath, even on official business.

Ptolemy invited Cato to come to him, but was told that if he wanted to talk then he would have to go to the Roman. The timing of the king's visit proved especially unfortunate, for Cato was taking a course of powerful laxatives. This may explain why he remained seated when the king arrived and casually told his royal visitor to sit down. His advice was equally surprising, for he told the king to go back to Alexandria and try to make peace. Otherwise not all the wealth of his kingdom would satisfy the greed of the senators if he looked to Rome for aid. Plutarch claims that Ptolemy was at first convinced and only later dissuaded from following Cato's advice by his own courtiers. This seems unlikely. Cicero had once complained that Cato behaved as if he lived in Plato's ideal Republic rather than the 'cess-pit of Romulus'. Ptolemy knew from experience that Rome was, as another king had claimed half a century before, 'a city up for auction'.[2]

Yet Ptolemy also knew that active Roman assistance would not come at a low price. Once he reached Rome, he borrowed more money from the bankers there and liberally employed this to win the sympathy of prominent men. Berenice IV and her ministers were not idle, and sent a large embassy of leading Alexandrians to speak against the king. Auletes used his borrowed money to block them: some were intimidated and others bribed into changing their opinion. A number – we do not know how many, but it included the embassy's leader – were murdered by hired thugs. The violence caused a brief scandal, and Cicero helped to defend one young senator accused of involvement, but no one was condemned. It was perhaps at this time that Auletes removed himself and went to Ephesus in Asia Minor, where he waited in the security of the famous Temple of Artemis. His agents remained in Rome and continued to spend and plead on his behalf.[3]

Several Romans wanted to be the man tasked with restoring Ptolemy to his throne. That meant there was competition and also that there were plenty of other senators as determined to block them and prevent a rival from winning the prestige and riches which the action would bring. For a while this in-fighting prevented anything from actually happening. Pompey himself wanted to be given the job, no doubt with a new extraordinary command. It is a striking example of the limited power of the triumvirate that he was unable to secure this. Pompey, Crassus and Caesar, who was now in Gaul winning glory in a succession of military adventures, had immense influence, prestige and money, but they could not permanently control public life.

A new complication was added when a Sybilline Oracle – Rome's ancient collection of cryptic prophecies – was 'discovered' and interpreted to mean that Ptolemy should not be restored with the aid of an army. In 57 BC the task was finally given to Publius Lentulus Spinther, consul for that year and due afterwards to go out as governor of Cilicia in Asia Minor. Cicero – now restored from his exile – wrote a series of letters to Lentulus from January 56 BC through to the next year reporting on the debate raging in Rome over the issue. Lentulus was obviously very keen, but in the end decided not to restore Ptolemy, fearing failure if he went without military force and prosecution if he used his army. Either of these outcomes risked wrecking his career.[4]

In the meantime, Berenice IV and her ministers were attempting to consolidate her position. Her co-ruler Cleopatra, whoever she was, died in 57 BC. The oldest of Berenice's two brothers was not yet in his teens and, even if he was in Egypt and under her control, he was too young to be elevated to the throne. Only for very brief periods had a queen ever ruled alone and so she and her ministers looked for a suitable consort. A grandson of Cleopatra Selene (who had married a Seleucid) was located, but then inconveniently died before a betrothal had been arranged. Another candidate from the same dynasty was living in the Roman province of Syria, but its governor refused to let him leave.

Finally, a man with the prestigious name of Seleucus and a very loose claim to royalty was brought to Alexandria and married to the queen. The robust Alexandrian sense of humour quickly nicknamed him 'Salt-fish seller'. Berenice was equally unimpressed and tolerated her new husband's crude manner for only a few days before having him strangled. As a replacement, her ministers now located a certain Archelaus, who claimed to be the illegitimate son of Mithridates of Pontus, but was actually the child of one of his generals. He, too, had been living in the Roman province of Syria, but was able to get away and went to Egypt. The new consort proved acceptable to Berenice.[5]

CAVALRY COMMANDER

In 57 BC Aulus Gabinius became proconsul of the province of Syria – it was he who had prevented one of Berenice's potential husbands from leaving. Gabinius was the man who as tribune had passed the law granting Pompey the command against the pirates in 67 BC. He was still close to Pompey and the triumvirs seem to have backed his successful campaign to be consul in 58 BC. His colleague was Caesar's father-in-law, and they were clearly eager to have well-disposed senior magistrates to guard their recent reforms. In fact, the two consuls bickered, and again this showed the limitations of the triumvirate's power. They could not fully control independently minded and ambitious senators.[6]

Gabinius seems to have passed through Greece en route to his province and recruited the twenty-six-year-old Antony to join his staff. As far as we can tell, this was the first formal public appointment for the latter. Antony had no experience of military life or official responsibility. Nevertheless, he was the son of a senator, the grandson of a consul and an Antonius. He refused to join Gabinius in the junior staff post initially offered to him. Instead, he demanded and got command of some or all of the cavalry in Gabinius' army – the detail is unclear. His rank was probably prefect of horse (*praefectus equitum*) and this could involve command of a single regiment (*ala*) of 400–500 cavalry, or several such units. Publius, the older son of Crassus, was at the same time serving Julius Caesar in a similar capacity.[7]

Before the year was out Antony led his men on campaign in Judaea. During his eastern campaigns, Pompey had intervened in a civil war between brothers of the Hasmonaean royal family, the dynasty that had ruled since the Maccabees had successfully rebelled against the Seleucids. The Roman army had besieged and captured Jerusalem, and Pompey and his officers had gone into the Holy of Holies in the Temple. Although they did not remove any of its treasure, this was still a violation of sacred tradition, which only permitted priests to enter the inner sanctum, and then only as part of a ceremony. The losing brother, Aristobulus, was taken back to Rome by Pompey and held there in comfortable captivity.

Aristobulus' son, Alexander, had escaped and remained in Judaea, and now raised an army of 10,000 infantry and 1,500 cavalry. He rebelled against his uncle, Hyrcanus, and even began to rebuild the fortifications of Jerusalem. Gabinius moved against him and sent Antony and some other officers on ahead. Our sources imply that Antony was in overall command. Although this is possible, we need to be aware that his later fame may have encouraged them to exaggerate his actual importance so early in his career. It is also unclear whether he at first had with him any of the cavalry he was supposed to command. A good deal of the force consisted of Jewish troops loyal to Hyrcanus. There were also some hastily armed Romans – perhaps businessmen active in the area and impressed into service.

At first Alexander withdrew, and a battle was fought near Jerusalem in which he was badly beaten. The bulk of his troops are likely to have been even less experienced than the Roman force, which included elements of the royal army. More than half of Alexander's men were killed or captured and he withdrew northeast to the fortress of Alexandrion in the Jordan Valley. Gabinius now joined his advance force and the rebels were defeated again.

Judea

Antony is said to have killed a number of men in the fighting and displayed conspicuous gallantry throughout the campaign. *Virtus* – which meant far more than virtue or even courage in English – was one of the most important values expected of a Roman aristocrat. Although inexperienced, Antony was physically extremely fit and well practised with his weapons. At no point in his career would anyone ever doubt his physical courage.

Alexandrion surrendered after a siege when Alexander was persuaded to come to terms. Antony may have been left in charge of the force covering the fortress while Gabinius led the main army in a show of force through the countryside. However, Alexander's father Aristobulus managed to escape from Rome in 56 BC and seized Alexandrion. Gabinius sent Antony and two other officers – one of whom was his son – with a force to deal with the fresh rebellion. The most detailed source does not suggest that Antony was in overall command.

Aristobulus abandoned Alexandrion as untenable and retreated across the Jordan towards the fortress of Machaerus. On the way he shed those supporters unable or unequipped to fight, leaving him with 8,000, including about a thousand who had deserted from the royal army. The Romans caught up with the rebels and defeated them, killing or scattering most of the army. Aristobulus and around a thousand men made it to Machaerus and prepared to withstand a siege. The Romans were aggressive and assaulted for two days before he surrendered. Once again the Jewish leader went to Rome as a prisoner.[8]

Gabinius began to look for fresh opportunities for military adventure. Parthia, the powerful kingdom that had emerged in the wreck of the Seleucid Empire, was divided by a civil war between rivals within its royal family. The Roman general scented a chance for glory and plunder, and may already have begun to cross the Euphrates when Ptolemy Auletes made him a better offer. Gabinius was promised 10,000 talents of silver if he used his army to restore the king to power. Antony is said to have been one of the most enthusiastic advocates. As a senior officer he could expect a share of the cash, and that can only have been a very welcome prospect to a man with his great debts.

Sulla's law forbade a provincial governor from leading an army outside of his province without explicit authority. Gabinius ignored this, as well as the official acceptance of the oracle that stated that Ptolemy could not be restored with an army. His legions moved through Judaea and headed south-west to Egypt in 55 BC. With them went a contingent of Jewish troops from Hyrcanus' army, led by Antipater, his senior henchman. The grateful Hasmonaean monarch also issued orders for food and other support to be supplied to the Romans. There was a very large Jewish community in Egypt, particularly in and around Alexandria. The pharaohs, the Persians and the Ptolemies had also made considerable use of Jewish mercenaries. Some of these were tasked with guarding the crossing places at the edge of the Nile Delta at Pelusium. Antipater persuaded them to change sides and let the Romans through.

Plutarch credits Antony with the capture of Pelusium, but it may well be that there was no real fighting and the victory was bloodless. Auletes is supposed to have resented this fact as he had wanted to announce his return by a mass execution of his recalcitrant subjects. Antony is said to have restrained him. Some more serious fighting did occur afterwards, and Berenice IV's husband Archelaus led his men with some determination until he was killed. He did not have much of an army with which to resist the legions. The old system of cleruchies had long decayed and the land was passed on to heirs without enforcement of the obligation to serve. The later Ptolemies had relied heavily on mercenaries, but Berenice and her government lacked the money to hire many of these. Rome's conquest of the eastern Mediterranean had also reduced the number of soldiers for hire, both by recruiting them as allies for the legions and by making the area more peaceful.[9]

After a brief fight, Ptolemy Auletes was restored. One of his first acts was to order the execution of his daughter Berenice IV. No doubt her leading supporters met a similar fate. Antony won the admiration of many Alexandrians because he insisted on giving Archelaus' corpse a proper burial. The two men had known each other when Archelaus had come to Gabinius seeking favour, before he had been approached by Berenice's representatives. Appian, writing in the early second century AD, claims that during this campaign Antony first saw the fourteen-year-old Cleopatra and fell in love with her. This is not intrinsically impossible – she was either with her father and his courtiers, or in Alexandria or another part of Egypt when he returned. She was probably also already striking and charismatic, and there is no reason why Antony may not have found her very attractive. Yet it could easily be just a romantic myth, and even Appian does not suggest that anything actually happened between them.[10]

The Egyptian campaign confirmed Antony's reputation for bravery and dashingly aggressive leadership. On at least one occasion he showed some tactical skill, leading his horsemen to outflank an enemy position that was holding up the main force. Again, though, we should beware of making too much of these early exploits. Plenty of young Romans were brave, dashing and liked by their soldiers. Both in Judaea and Egypt, Gabinius' army was markedly stronger and better equipped than the hastily raised forces opposing them. However stubbornly these fought, they were simply not a match for the Romans. The same was true when Gabinius led the bulk of his army back to his province and suppressed another rising in Judaea, and also in a subsequent campaign against the Nabataean Arabs.[11]

[VIII]

CANDIDATE

In 54 BC a new governor arrived to take over as proconsul of Syria and Gabinius returned to Rome with his newly acquired fortune. Once again Ptolemy had borrowed money from Roman bankers to pay the promised bribe and had paid the bulk, perhaps all, of the promised sum. Gabinius trusted to his money and his connection with Pompey to survive the prosecution that inevitably waited for him at home. His official reports to the Senate as governor had failed to mention his illegal expedition to Egypt, but the truth was already widely known. He had few friends amongst the *publicani* operating in his province – probably because his own extortion restricted their activities – and there were anyway other interested parties who had written to friends in the Senate. Pompey came to see the attacks on Gabinius as a challenge to his own status and strenuously supported him. To general amazement, he was narrowly acquitted of treason for leading an army outside his province. Arraigned on a second charge – and defended by Cicero, who very reluctantly gave in to Pompey's pressure – Gabinius was convicted and went into exile.[1]

Gabinius' successor was no less a person than Marcus Licinius Crassus. His alliance with Pompey and Caesar had come under strain in 56 BC, leading to a renegotiation of the deal. Pompey and Crassus became consuls for the second time in 55 BC. Caesar was granted a five-year extension to his command in Gaul. Pompey had no desire to fight another war, but was given a special command of the combined Spanish provinces, which he was permitted to govern through representatives. He remained just outside Rome to keep an eye on events there. Crassus' ambition was for military glory and the profit of conquest. He had fought for Sulla during the civil war and, later, was the man who defeated the slave army of Spartacus.

This had been a very tough campaign, for the escaped gladiator had smashed a long succession of Roman armies sent against him. Yet for all that, there was little glory in defeating slaves. Crassus had been awarded the lesser honour of an ovation rather than a full triumph for his victory.

Crassus chose Syria as his province and from the very beginning planned to invade Parthia. This war was not authorised by the Senate, but, just like Gabinius, Crassus scented an opportunity. He also knew that he was far less vulnerable to prosecution than his predecessor. His planned war was widely talked about at Rome. One tribune went so far as formally to curse him when he left Rome to go to his province.[2]

Mark Antony did not return to Rome with Gabinius and so avoided becoming the target of any prosecutions following on from the trial of his commander. He may also have been reluctant to go home and face pressure from his many creditors. We do not know whether he considered or was offered a commission to serve under Crassus. New governors brought plenty of their own enthusiastic followers to fill posts in the army and on their staff. Crassus' son Publius had already served with some distinction in Caesar's Gallic campaigns and now acted as one of his father's senior subordinates. There may have been no place for Antony, or no desire on one or both sides for him to serve Crassus.

For whatever reason, Antony did not remain in Syria and take part in the forthcoming invasion. It was just as well. Crassus was over sixty and had not seen active service for the best part of three decades. His leadership proved lethargic and his planning poor. More importantly, the Parthians were far more formidable opponents than the armies of Pontus and Armenia so easily shattered by Sulla, Lucullus and Pompey. Crassus' seven legions were outmanoeuvred by the Parthian cavalry at Carrhae in 53 BC. Publius Crassus was lured away, his detachment wiped out and his severed head thrown into the Roman lines. His father for a while fought stubbornly, but decided that night to retreat. The Parthians pursued the legions relentlessly and Crassus was killed trying to negotiate. The eagle standards of the legions were captured and most of the legionaries surrendered or were killed. Crassus' quaestor managed to rally some and lead them back to Syria, repulsing a Parthian raid that reached as far as the great city of Antioch.[3]

Antony joined Caesar's army instead of Crassus', but we do not know when he arrived in Gaul. Gabinius was in Rome by 19 September 54 BC. It seems unlikely that Antony reached Gaul earlier than that, and he may not have got there until much later in the year. There is no information of how the matter was arranged. Probably he approached Caesar – either directly or through someone known to them both – and asked for a post. Their distant family connection was not in itself enough to guarantee his acceptance, and as we have seen there is no evidence for a prior association.[4]

Antony came from an important family. He had also shown courage and ability in Judaea and Egypt, although we should remember that suitability for the job was rarely the primary concern in Roman appointments. Antony was worth cultivating because of his family and the promise this offered for future distinction. A Roman commander was judged in part by the background of his senior subordinates, and Caesar had struggled to attract many members of leading families. Antony's uncle, the former consul Lucius Julius Caesar, did serve as one of Caesar's legates in 52 BC, and may well have been there earlier than this, but most of his officers came from less distinguished families.[5]

They were drawn in part by the charisma of Caesar, but mainly by his reputation for lavish generosity. Caesar himself had massive debts when he left for his province early in 58 BC. In the next decade he is said to have captured and sold into slavery no fewer than a million prisoners. Shrines throughout Gaul were plundered of their treasure. Caesar became one of the wealthiest men in the world, and his officers also became rich. Many men heavily in debt sought service with him in Gaul to restore their fortunes and this may have been the main motive for Antony. Crassus had a reputation as a miser; Caesar was generous and already successful.[6]

We do not know what rank and duties Mark Antony was given by Caesar. It is often assumed that from the very start he served as one of the legates, the most senior subordinate rank who often commanded a legion or even larger forces. The majority of Caesar's legates were older men, and many had held a magistracy, but there were exceptions to this and so it is possible that Antony had the rank from the time he arrived in Gaul. It is equally possible that he held a more junior post, perhaps as one of the half-dozen tribunes in each legion, or again as a prefect commanding cavalry as in the eastern campaigns.[7]

Caesar left full accounts of his campaigns in Gaul, covering each year's operations in some detail. Antony is not mentioned until the summer of 52 BC. In some ways this is unsurprising, since Caesar was not overgenerous in naming and praising his subordinates. Yet it certainly makes it unlikely that Antony held any important detached command during his first period of service in Gaul. From 58 to 56 BC Caesar had intervened in Gaul beyond the Roman province of Transalpine Gaul (roughly equivalent to modern-day Provence) and extended Roman authority to the Atlantic and North Sea coasts. In 55 BC he bridged the Rhine and led a brief expedition against the German tribes, before crossing the Channel to Britain. He returned to Britain in 54 BC, leading a much stronger force. He did not permanently occupy the island, and his expedition came close to disaster when much of his fleet was wrecked in a storm. This did not matter, for the invasion was a spectacular propaganda success at Rome. He was voted twenty days of public thanksgiving, more than had ever been given to a victorious commander in the past – including Pompey after his eastern victories.[8]

Mark Antony could not have arrived in Gaul early enough to have taken part in the expedition to Britain. In the following winter there was a serious rebellion amongst the tribes of the north-east. A force of fifteen cohorts – equivalent to one and a half legions – was wiped out by a relatively minor tribe. Another legion was besieged in its winter camp. It was commanded by Cicero's younger brother Quintus, who was serving as one of Caesar's legates. Caesar himself led a small column on a risky march to break the siege and end the immediate crisis. The rebellion lost momentum, but was not over. Much of 53 BC was spent in a series of brutal punitive expeditions, with sudden attacks launched on individual tribes before they were ready to resist. Villages and crops were burned, cattle seized and people killed, captured or driven into the wilds.[9]

Antony may well have served in some of these operations. We

cannot be sure, since not all the units of Caesar's army were involved. Some were needed to hold down other parts of Gaul and did not see any actual fighting while performing this deterrent role. Nor can we automatically assume that Antony was given primarily military responsibilities. Caesar required educated and reliable Romans to perform administrative, financial and diplomatic roles. Antony wanted glory, but also needed money, so some opportunities of this sort may have been particularly welcome to him.

At some point in 53 BC Antony finally returned to Rome. It is unlikely to have been later than the beginning of autumn and was probably much earlier than this. He was now thirty, old enough to stand for the quaestorship. This was the most junior magistracy and Sulla had stipulated that election as quaestor automatically meant that the man would also be enrolled as a senator. There were twenty of these magistrates and their duties were primarily financial. Most were sent to the provinces to act as the governor's deputy and to oversee the use and collection of revenue.

Elections and electioneering were carried on according to well-established traditions. A man standing for office dressed in a specially whitened toga – the *toga candidus*, from which we get our word 'candidate' – and so stood out as he walked through the Forum. A candidate took great care to greet citizens as they passed him, especially if they were senators, equestrians or other men whose wealth made their vote important. There were special slaves called *nomenclatores* whose task was to whisper into their master's ear the names of each person they approached. Candidates would be attended by as many and as distinguished supporters as possible. Lucius Julius Caesar is likely to have backed his nephew in this way if he was in Rome. The proconsul Caesar sent letters to make his support for Antony clear and assisted him financially. In addition, officers from the army in Gaul were granted leave to go to Rome and take part in the elections. With all this support, and because he was an Antonius, Mark Antony was one of the favourites to win.[10]

The Roman practice was to hold the consular elections first, ideally at the end of July although there was no set date. Junior posts including the quaestorship were filled by elections held in a different

Popular Assembly at some point after the consuls had been chosen. In 53 BC, however, there were problems. Bribery was widespread, but this in itself was nothing new. More disturbing was the organised violence between supporters of the various candidates. Clodius was standing for the praetorship, promising amongst other things to alter the law so that freedmen's votes would become more significant in the Assemblies. Plenty of the less well-off supported Clodius because they felt that he had their interests at heart – his law as tribune, which introduced a free dole of grain to citizens, was very popular. There was also a hard core of followers who were organised to intimidate any opponent. From Clodius' tribunate in 58 BC, political violence at Rome became more frequent.

Inevitably, other politicians had followed his example. Clodius' most bitter opponent was Titus Annius Milo, who had organised his own gang of hired thugs and gladiators in 58 BC. Now Milo was standing for the consulship. Like many ambitious senators, he was massively in debt and could not afford to lose. Clodius' and Milo's gangs were the largest, but others were formed by some of the other candidates. Intimidation and violence became the norm, and deaths were frequent. Antony was in Rome and soon became involved, even if he probably did not join any of the other groups. His old quarrel with Clodius reignited and on one occasion a sword-armed Mark Antony led a group that chased him into a bookshop. Clodius barricaded himself inside and managed to repel the attack, but Cicero was probably right to claim that only this prevented his murder.[11]

It proved a brief postponement. On 18 January 52 BC, Milo and his wife, accompanied by a band of his gladiators, happened to pass Clodius and some of his supporters at Bovillae, some 10 miles out of Rome along the Appian Way. There was fighting and Clodius was wounded and carried into an inn. A little later some of Milo's men burst in and finished him off. Taken back to Rome by his followers, Clodius' body was carried into the Senate House and cremated, burning the building down in the process. The very heart of Rome's public life was descending into chaos. The consular elections had been delayed again and again, as violence and manipulation of the rules rendered each meeting of the Voting Assembly invalid, and because of this the junior magistrates could not be chosen either.[12]

Finally, the Senate decided to give Pompey emergency powers to raise troops and restore order – it is more than likely that he had manipulated the situation in the hope of this. He was appointed consul without a colleague and without an election, simply to avoid the use of the word 'dictator'. Troops were brought into the city to control the violence and permit elections and trials to occur. Milo was summoned to a court surrounded by guards and the atmosphere was so intimidating that Cicero balked at delivering a speech in his defence. Milo went into exile. Many of Clodius' followers were also condemned, as was another man who like Milo had been a candidate for the consulship. Another of the consular candidates was Metellus Scipio, who was certainly guilty of bribery if not necessarily of violence. However, Pompey's wife had died in the previous year and he now chose to marry Scipio's daughter. After a meeting at Pompey's house, the bribery charges were dropped and not long afterwards he appointed Scipio as his consular colleague.[13]

While all this was going on, Mark Antony was elected as quaestor by the *Comitia Tributa*, a formal meeting of the thirty-five tribes of Roman citizens. For an election, this assembly was normally convened on the Campus Martius – the Field of Mars, where once Rome's militia army had mustered for war. Temporary fences divided the open space into sections and the whole thing was known as the 'sheep-pens' (*saepta*). There were hundreds of thousands of citizens eligible to vote, but votes could only be registered in person and the majority lived too far from Rome to attend. There were four urban tribes and even the poorest members of these could have voted if they chose to do so. As in modern democracies, many seem not to have bothered. It tended to be the wealthy, or those whose work had brought them to Rome, who attended. The tribe and not the individual was what mattered, and the will of each tribe was given equal weight. A lottery determined the order in which the decision of the tribes was announced.

Candidates may have been allowed to make a speech. After that, the presiding magistrate gave the instruction, 'Divide, citizens' – *Discedite, Quirites* in Latin – and each tribe went to its allotted 'sheep-pen'. One by one they would walk over a wooden gangway known as a 'bridge' and drop their written ballot into a basket. One official supervised this, and others were in charge of counting the votes and giving the totals to the presiding magistrate. Once a man received the vote of eighteen of the thirty-five tribes, then he was elected as quaestor. As soon as all twenty posts were filled, then the voting stopped.[14]

Mark Antony was probably one of the first to win office amongst the quaestors of the year. He was now a senator and had taken his first formal step on a public career, following the well-established path. He was probably thirty-one, making him a year older than the minimum age for the office, so had missed winning the quaestorship in 'his year'. This was much less serious at the start of a career than later on.

Yet the traditional process of election should not blind us to the context. There had been months of political violence in which Antony had taken part. Elections were only possible at all because Pompey had been given dictatorial powers to deal with a crisis provoked by internal disorder and not any foreign enemy. Antony had witnessed the power of intimidation and bribery, and seen that only greater force could curb them. He had also watched Pompey manipulate the law and exploit his dominance for his own advantage.

It must have been hard for anyone of Antony's generation to grow up with much respect for the traditional constitution of the Republic. Too much had already happened and then continued to occur before their eyes. Force prevailed, laws counted for little and could not resist it, as leading senators amassed huge debts that could only be recovered if they were successful. Men were ruined, occasionally killed by opponents or succeeded spectacularly. His first taste of public life at Rome is unlikely to have done anything to convince Antony of the strength of the system.

Julius Caesar chose Antony to be his quaestor. Such arrangements were common, and generally considered good, since if there was goodwill between the governor and his deputy then the two were likely to do their job better. Mark Antony went back to Gaul and found himself caught up in a massive rebellion of the tribes, many of whom had been staunchly loyal to Rome. Caesar had intervened in Gaul to protect allied peoples and had used this pretext to extend his operations further and further outside his province. After five years many Gauls realised that they were now effectively occupied by the Romans, who showed no signs of leaving. Many tribes and chieftains did well from the process, for Caesar was generous to loyal allies, making them rich and powerful. Those less favoured saw no prospect of rising to the top while the Romans remained. Some of those who had done well also now decided that they could grow even more powerful if the occupiers left. Tribe after tribe rebelled, uniting under the leadership of Vercingetorix – one of those who seem to have done well from Caesar's favour.[15]

Antony did not leave Rome until after the trial of Milo in April 52 BC and so missed the start of this extremely brutal campaign, which was marked from the very beginning by extreme savagery and ruthlessness on both sides. Caesar was himself caught south of the Alps when the revolt erupted and had to patch together a force to defend Transalpine Gaul, before making a desperate journey to reach his main army. Later in the year, Antony's uncle Lucius Julius Caesar took over the defence of Transalpine Gaul. We do not know when or how the quaestor joined his commander.[16]

Mark Antony is first mentioned by Caesar at the climactic siege of Alesia. As the summer wore on, the Romans had suffered a reverse in a costly and unsuccessful attack on the town of Gergovia. Caesar retreated and was harried by the Gauls. Then he repulsed a heavy attack on his column and seizing back the initiative counter-attacked, chasing Vercingetorix and his army to the hilltop town of Alesia. The legions toiled to construct 11 miles of fortifications surrounding both the town and the Gaulish camp. Vercingetorix had sent to the tribes for aid and these now mustered a massive relief army. As soon as the Romans finished their siege line, Caesar ordered them to build another, even longer one, facing outwards. Both lines were strengthened with forts and in front of them was a network of obstacles and traps.

Caesar did not attempt to attack Alesia, but relied on starvation to defeat his enemy. Vercingetorix expelled the non-combatant population of the town so that food would be consumed only by his warriors. Caesar refused to let the civilians – mostly women, and the very young and very old – pass through his lines. They were left to starve, in full sight of both armies. When the relief force mustered by the tribes arrived, they launched a series of attacks against sections of Caesar's lines, trying to break in. At the same time, Vercingetorix led his men in sally after sally trying to break out. Mark Antony, along with the legate Caius Trebonius, was in command of one of the targets of an especially heavy attack. Caesar tells us that they took men from less threatened sectors as reinforcements and eventually repulsed the enemy.[17]

All of the Gaulish attacks failed. The relief army lost heart and was running out of food, so began to disperse. Vercingetorix was faced with starvation and surrendered. The danger that the Romans would suffer outright defeat and lose Caesar's conquests was over; the fighting was not. Throughout 51 BC there were skirmishes and raids as the last embers of the revolt were stamped out. It was not merely a question of brute force, as Caesar also spent a good deal of time and effort in diplomacy, and was lenient to many of the tribes, especially former allies. Antony took part in some of this fighting, although in one operation in December 52 BC to January 51 BC we are explicitly told that he was left behind with the troops protecting the army's baggage train and headquarters.[18]

Afterwards, Caesar took Antony – and also the *Twelfth* Legion – on a punitive expedition in the north-east against the Belgic Eburones. In many ways these operations had a lot in common with the campaigns in Judaea. Much of the fighting was small scale, opponents weak in numbers and poorly equipped. Aggression and speed of movement were more important for the Romans than careful preparation. When Caesar moved south to deal with the siege of a determined band of rebels at Uxelodunum, he left Antony behind with a force equivalent to one and a half legions to deter the Belgic tribes from rebellion. It was his first independent command in Gaul, and probably the largest of his career so far.[19]

Charismatic leaders were important in keeping resistance going. One of these was Commius, a man who had been made king by Caesar and had proved a loyal ally until the rebellion of 53–52 BC. Antony sent the commander of the cavalry attached to his force to hunt Commius down. In a confused skirmish, this officer was wounded, as was the rebel leader, but the latter escaped. He sent envoys to Antony seeking peace terms, but asking that he never have to come into the presence of a Roman again – earlier in the year Roman envoys had tried to assassinate him during a negotiation. Antony accepted this request and took hostages as a pledge of Commius' future goodwill.[20]

Apart from Alesia, Antony seems not to have participated in any sizeable battles during his time in Gaul. In spite of Shakespeare, he was not with Caesar on 'that day he overcame the Nervii' in 57 BC. Alesia was the only major operation of the war at which he was present. This is worth stating only because of the emphasis in ancient and modern sources on Antony as a soldier. In fact, by this stage of his career, his record was competent, but unexceptional. He was not especially experienced and had usually acted under someone else's command. Soon it was time to return to politics and in 50 BC Antony left Gaul and went to Rome to become a candidate again.

[IX]

'The New Sibling-Loving Gods'

When Gabinius and Antony left Egypt, plenty of Romans stayed behind. Many were soldiers, for the proconsul left a strong force 'with King Ptolemy as a garrison'. Known as the Gabinians, these troops would remain for six years, beginning a Roman military presence that would last almost without break until the seventh century AD. Many were Roman citizens, although some of these soldiers were foreign auxiliaries – we hear later of 500 Gaulish and German cavalry. Overall numbers are unclear, but a strength equivalent to one or even two legions seems quite likely.[1]

Ptolemy Auletes had paid for Roman military force to regain his throne, and only this same force would guarantee that he kept it. Gabinius had no legal authority to invade Egypt, although he would later claim that Archelaus had encouraged piracy in the eastern Mediterranean and so needed to be defeated. Equally, he had no authority to station Roman troops in Egypt to protect Auletes. The king seems from the beginning to have paid and supplied these soldiers – Gabinius also claimed that the only money he had ever accepted from Ptolemy was to pay for the costs of his army. A few years later another proconsul of Syria clearly considered the Gabinians to be still part of the Roman army, and he does not seem to have been alone in this view.[2]

Yet their status was ambiguous. No mention is made of an overall commander, but senior officers seem to have been Roman. Many of the men in Gabinius' army had served in Pompey's eastern campaigns, but presumably their enlistments had not expired by the time the latter returned to Rome. Our sources mention one man who had served as a centurion under Pompey and was later a tribune in Egypt. It is not clear whether he was one of the Gabinians or was recruited independently. Auletes hired as many mercenaries as he could, even enlisting runaway slaves. He may also have sought out experienced Roman officers in need of employment, and men with Italian names appear in the armies of many client kingdoms during this period. These supplemented the Gabinians and in practice all of them acted in every significant respect like a royal army.[3]

Before long the Gabinians were called upon to suppress disorder within the kingdom, which they seem to have done with ease. However, a good deal of their time was spent in garrison in Alexandria. It was a comfortable posting, with the luxuries of one of the greatest cities in the world readily available. Legionary pay was not high in this period – at some point in these years Julius Caesar would double the salary of his legionaries – and Auletes may well have been more generous. Caesar himself later claimed that the Gabinians 'got used to a life and licence in Alexandria and forgot the name and discipline of the Roman people, wed local women, with whom many had children'.[4]

Roman soldiers restored Ptolemy Auletes and kept him in power; other Romans stayed with them to collect the price for this assistance. The king had borrowed vast sums to buy his restoration, since his friends in Rome proved reluctant to assist him purely on the basis of promises. Much of this was owed to a consortium of Roman financiers led by a certain Caius Rabirius Postumus. There were unpaid debts from 59 BC as well as the sum owed to Gabinius, although it is not clear if all of this was paid straight away. Rabirius had gone out to Cilicia with the staff of Lentulus Spinther, in the hope that the latter would restore the king. Disappointed when Lentulus gave up on the idea, the banker joined Gabinius and either accompanied the expedition to Egypt or arrived soon afterwards.

Auletes made Rabirius his senior finance minister (*dioecetes*), so that the Roman would oversee taxation and other royal revenue and take his money directly. The sums involved were staggering, and the king also needed to pay for his own court and continue lavish programmes of spending to secure support. The Ptolemies had from the beginning treated their territory much like a private estate. Scholars may argue over the efficiency of the bureaucracy that governed Egypt, but none doubt that its most important function was generating revenue. Rabirius was now part of this system, and he and his associates dressed accordingly, wearing the Hellenic costume of royal officials rather than the tunic and toga of proper Romans.[5]

With the king's approval, Rabirius enthusiastically set about raising money, involving himself not simply with taxation and the produce of royal land, but royal monopolies and trade tariffs. Egypt was squeezed very tightly at a time when harvests were bad because the inundation of the Nile was low for several years in succession. Probably the irrigation system had been neglected in the years of disruption when the king was driven out. Auletes had also come to power after many decades of serious internal problems and power struggles within the dynasty. Institutions and central authority had decayed, becoming far more corrupt and much less efficient.

It was hard for many of the king's subjects to pay what was demanded of them. Desperation was probably the root cause of the unrest crushed by the Gabinians. The ruthless approach to raising revenue was not in itself enough. For centuries the currency of the Ptolemies had been very stable. Now the silver content of each coin was drastically reduced as the king sought to make his income go further. Having a Roman finance minister helped to deflect the blame away from Auletes himself. Rabirius was intensely unpopular.

The king finally gave in to the demands of the Alexandrians and had the Roman banker imprisoned. Rabirius quickly 'escaped' and fled back to Rome. A good number of merchant ships had already been despatched carrying goods and there were rumours that one had a cargo far more valuable than the mundane contents of the others. Gabinius had already gone into exile and a prosecution was now brought against Rabirius in the hope of seizing the bribe allegedly paid to the proconsul to restore Auletes. Cicero defended the banker, but the trial was probably never completed because of a serious backlog of cases and the political disruptions at Rome. Rabirius survived, although how much he had lost on his dealings with Ptolemy XII Auletes is impossible to know. Julius Caesar took on much of the outstanding debt, in addition to the money still owed to him for his assistance to the king in 59 BC.[6]

Auletes not only survived, but also, with the backing of the

Gabinians, his grip on power was more secure than it had ever been in the past. For all the devaluation of the coinage and the hardships of many of his subjects, he was wealthy and had got away without paying anything like all of his huge debts to the Romans who had assisted him. In his last years his court remained splendid and there was money to spend on grand building projects.

ALEXANDRIA

The remains of much of the Alexandria known to Auletes and Cleopatra now lies under the sea and archaeologists are only beginning to unravel some of its mysteries. In some ways this is appropriate. Alexander the Great chose the site because it was on the coast. The old capitals at Memphis and Thebes had good access to the Nile, but were far from the sea, reflecting the priorities of the pharaohs. Alexander was more interested in securing good communications to his newly won territory. The Ptolemies also wanted their power to be centred on the Mediterranean. In better days their territories had stretched far across the sea. Culturally and ideologically they always looked back to Greece and Macedonia. Economically, they grew rich from trade, as the great surpluses from Egypt's harvest were sold abroad and luxury goods from Arabia, India and beyond were sent further west. Alexandria was a port and, with Lake Mareotis to the south of the city, almost surrounded by water.

It was no coincidence that the greatest monument of the Ptolemies looked out to sea. On an island called Pharos, which lay offshore and sheltered the anchorage, stood the great lighthouse. It was at least 328 feet high and built of white stone in three levels. Commissioned by Ptolemy I Soter and completed under his son, the tower was topped by a colossal statue of Zeus Soter. It was visible a long way out to sea and at night a beacon was kept burning – there is even talk of mirrors to increase the light – ensuring that it still served as a landmark. Not as high as the great pyramids, it was still the tallest structure built by the Greeks or Romans. In the late

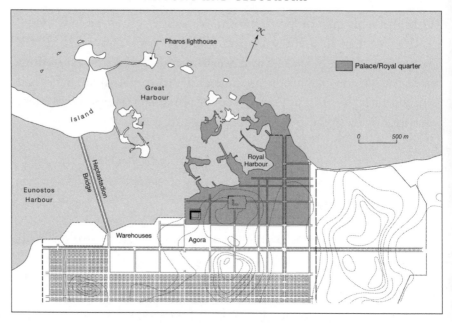

Alexandria

eighth century the highest storey collapsed, but much of the rest survived until the fourteenth century.[7]

There were two great harbours, separated by a mole almost a mile long connecting the shore with Pharos Island. To the east was the main harbour, sections of which were divided into smaller quays. To the west was the second harbour of 'Happy Return' (*Eunostos* in Greek), which had an inner section known as 'the Box' (*Kitotos*), linking with a canal leading eventually to a branch of the Nile. Shipping, warehouses and commerce provided occupations for far more Alexandrians than the royal bureaucracy. There were plenty of very rich families in the city, whose grand houses occupied street after street near the harbour.[8]

A separate quarter, walled off from the houses of the wealthy and probably further subdivided, contained the royal palaces. Quite a few of the Ptolemies had chosen to build their own grand houses, although Strabo's claim that every king constructed a new palace may well be an exaggeration. Other buildings – a theatre is mentioned and was probably dedicated to Dionysus – may have been associated with them to perform a role in ceremonies. Colonnaded courtyards linked the individual palaces and the whole complex was grand in scale and lavish in materials. The Museum complex was also in this area, as was the Sema, the grand tomb containing Alexander's mummified remains and the corpses of the Ptolemies. Originally, Alexander the Great's corpse had been housed in a golden coffin – possibly in the familiar style of an Egyptian sarcophagus, although we cannot be sure. However, Ptolemy XI in his desperate need for funds had melted this down and replaced it with one of glass or crystal.[9]

Alexandria was a consciously Greek city, but its large population was always mixed. It included the biggest Jewish community outside Judaea. There were also many Egyptians, since from the start there were never enough Greek settlers to meet all the demands for labour. Laid out on a grid pattern of streets, the city was divided into five regions named after the first five letters of the alphabet, and the various nationalities seem to have lived separately – the Jews, for example, lived mostly in the region called Delta. On a day-to-day basis there was doubtless much more interaction. In later periods we read of periodic friction between the communities, especially between Jew and Gentile, but this is less clearly attested under the Ptolemies.[10]

Strabo tells us that all the roads in Alexandria were wide enough for 'horse-riding and chariot driving'. There were two main streets at right angles to each other, each far wider and fringed with colonnades. The more famous of the two was the Canopic Street. Altogether, the houses of the wealthy and the royal palaces made up between a quarter and a third of the entire city. There were plenty of other grand buildings, especially temples. A complex system of canals and underwater channels brought the water needed by the city's vast population.

There was work in Alexandria and a good deal of wealth. Successful merchants lived in great houses, as did many landlords whose estates were worked by tenant farmers. For the well-off, life was comfortable, with luxuries and entertainments readily available. It is hard to tell how much or little interest these took in the cultural and intellectual pursuits encouraged by the Museum and Library. For the very poor, life may well have been grim and squalid, as it was for the poor anywhere else in the ancient world. The population of

Alexandria was large and volatile, dependent on a constant supply of food and water from outside. We do not know precisely who or how many of its inhabitants took part in the rioting and protests that at times drove out or killed the kingdom's rulers. Ptolemy Auletes could not rely solely on force in Alexandria, and maintaining an adequate food supply was essential. Other parts of Egypt could suffer from shortages without posing anything like so severe a threat.[11]

Memphis was the second largest city of Egypt and remained the centre for a number of important traditional cults. Unlike Thebes, it had never been involved in a rebellion against the Ptolemies and so had not suffered accordingly. In 76 BC Auletes had been crowned there in a traditional ceremony by the fourteen-year-old priest of the cult of Ptah. These priests were important figures, but their status reflected the dominance of the monarchy. The post of high priest was effectively hereditary, but the actual appointment had to be made by the king. Similarly, the cults and priests were supported by great estates, but did not actually own the land. Instead, the king allocated the revenue from specific properties to them, but the levies passed through the hands of the royal bureaucracy first. In this way, the Ptolemies gained the loyalty of important Egyptians, who in turn helped to keep the wider population content.[12]

For all their patronage of the native cults, Ptolemy XII, like his predecessors, showed far more personal enthusiasm for Hellenic deities. The self-styled 'New Dionysus' had particular reverence for his namesake. Music and dance were ways of worshipping Dionysus, and this as well as taste and pride in his own skill help to explain his staging of musical competitions and his own performances. Luxury, drinking and feasting were central to his version of the cult. The extravagant indulgence of the king and his court mixed religious devotion with symbols of wealth and plenty for the whole kingdom. They were also opportunities for Ptolemy to enjoy himself. One inscription survives in which several Egyptian men claim to have been Auletes' catamites. Each gave himself a suggestive pseudonym and even if they were really erotic dancers rather than actual lovers – the Greek could mean either – then it still gives a flavour of Ptolemy XII's court. Auletes does not appear to have been a very active ruler, except when it came to regaining his throne. He was a survivor, but there is little sign of energy in government, especially after his restoration. The king feasted, performed and indulged himself in pleasure and opulence. Even if this all had an aspect of worship, it was indulgence none the less.[13]

HEIRS

Cleopatra grew from a child into a young woman in these years. We know nothing of her life at this time or how closely she was involved in the daily life and banquets of her father's court. The Greeks and Macedonians as a rule did not grant as much licence to women as to men. Her education may well have continued, but whether her experience of Alexandria in these years had more the flavour of her father's court or of the sober education of the Museum and Library, or indeed more innocent indulgences of the young and rich, is simply impossible to know.

At some point Auletes made a will, one copy of which was sent to Rome. This may have been during the disruptions of 53 and 52 BC, for we are told that it was not forwarded to the Senate's keeping and remained with Pompey. The Romans were asked to guarantee the implementation of the king's wishes 'in the name of all the gods and the treaties which he had made at Rome'. Strikingly he did not leave his kingdom to them, and instead Cleopatra, his oldest remaining daughter, and his oldest son Ptolemy were to become joint rulers. The boy was some seven or eight years her junior and too young to be made sole ruler. He would also need a consort and for the Ptolemies a sister was always a likely choice.[14]

It would not have been safe for Auletes to ignore his oldest surviving child, since this would have invited a challenge to the succession. Nothing is known about the relationship between Cleopatra and her father, and whether or not he sensed promise in her. Perhaps there was genuine affection, especially if she had accompanied him during his exile, but we simply do not know. Similarly, there is no way of knowing if efforts were made to prepare her for the task of ruling. Auletes does seem to have publicly promoted all of his children, who were referred to as 'the new sibling-loving gods' in an inscription from 52 BC. The experience of the past never stopped the Ptolemies from proclaiming family harmony.[15]

By this time, Auletes' health may have been failing. On a frieze from the temple at Dendera, Cleopatra is depicted behind the figure of her father, both making offerings to the Egyptian gods. Some scholars see this as an indication that he had already made her co-ruler with him. If true, then Auletes may have wanted assistance in the task of ruling and perhaps to smooth the succession after his death. On the other hand, Cleopatra was now the most senior female member of the royal family and it may simply be in this capacity that she was shown supporting the king. No source actually claims that she ruled jointly with her father. Some official documents list them both, but these may have come from the early months of her reign and maintained a fiction that her father was still alive – something not uncommon at the beginning of a new reign.[16]

By 51 BC Cleopatra was about eighteen, but it should already be clear that we know very little indeed about her life up until this point or what she was like. Beyond her extensive education and clear intelligence, almost everything else about her character remains conjecture. Declared a goddess and the daughter of a self-declared god, her family had been royal and divine for centuries. The self-confidence of someone born to rule was mixed with the uncertainty and fear of her own family as potentially deadly rivals.

Whether or not she had actually travelled outside Egypt and visited Rome, the young Cleopatra was aware of the overwhelming power of the Roman Republic. She may also have had some under-standing of the unpredictability of the new world power and the dominance of individuals like Pompey. Cleopatra's later career suggest ambition and ruthlessness. It is hard to believe that she did not know from a young age that there would always be people eager to use her to gain power themselves. She was the king's daughter, accepted by him as legitimate, whatever the precise details of her birth. The choices were between being controlled by others or trying to be in control herself. In either case there was a considerable risk of a sudden and violent death.[17]

We can do little more than guess at Cleopatra's character at this stage of her life, but what of her appearance? The question inevitably arises in a way that it simply does not for male figures from the ancient world, or indeed for many women. In part, this is because images are plentiful for most famous names such as Alexander the Great and Caesar. The attitude to Cleopatra is always different, for it is more than simple curiosity. Imagined and reimagined so often over the ages, people have a far more emotional desire to picture the real Cleopatra. Quickly, the question becomes not what she looked like, but whether or not she was beautiful. Even this tends to be almost a simple binary decision, making her either beautiful or ugly – a standard that few people would care to have applied to themselves.[18] The literary sources are of limited help. According to Plutarch,

> in itself her beauty was not absolutely without parallel, not the kind to astonish those who saw her; but her presence exerted an inevitable fascination, and her physical attractions, combined with the persuasive charm of her conversation and the aura she somehow projected around herself in company, did have a certain ability to stimulate others.

Dio wrote more than a century after Plutarch and claimed that Cleopatra 'was a woman of surpassing beauty, and at that time, when she was in the prime of her youth, she was most striking; she also possessed a most charming voice and a knowledge of how to make herself agreeable to every one'.[19]

The passages are less different than tends to be claimed. It is important to note that Plutarch does not say that Cleopatra was not beautiful, simply that she was not the most beautiful woman in the world and that her looks were one part of her considerable attractiveness. Dio does not claim that her beauty surpassed all other women, but that she was very beautiful and also charismatic.

Ideals of beauty change from age to age and culture to culture, and are anyway subject to individual taste. Artistic representations are subject to conventions and vary in their purpose as well as the talents of the artist. The reliefs carved on Egyptian temples were part of a truly ancient tradition and individuals are recognisable only because they are named in the inscription. A young Cleopatra appeared on coins minted in Ascalon. The face on these does not seem especially attractive to modern eyes, but we need to remember that coins were not pin-ups or equivalent to the cover of modern fashion magazines. They were statements of power, and in this case carried a message of the legitimacy of a young queen faced with a serious challenge to her throne and life. The aim was to show power and legitimacy, emphasising that Cleopatra was the rightful heir to the throne of the Ptolemies. The head on coins did not have to be strictly accurate. The Ascalon coins show a prominent, slightly hooked nose and large eyes, both features strongly associated with the Ptolemies.

Later busts of a more mature Cleopatra present even more problems. Identification is almost never secure, and some might easily represent other members of her family, including one of her daughters. Even if they are intended to be Cleopatra herself, they may also have been made long after her death. Most suggest a face that was pleasant, if not exceptionally striking. Many ancient sculptures were originally painted, which would have brought them much more to life. Even so there were limits to the medium and it would be hard to convey vivacity in such a portrait even if this was thought desirable. Both Dio and Plutarch emphasised Cleopatra's voice and charm. Charisma is not readily conveyed in marble or bronze.

Cleopatra clearly had a strong, somewhat hooked nose. Given the tendencies of her family and her lifestyle, she may well have been a little inclined to plumpness, especially in her teenage years. Excessive thinness as an ideal of feminine beauty is a very recent phenomenon, in spite of its fervent promotion by the fashion industry and media. No evidence suggests that she was as obese as some of the other Ptolemies. She was certainly pretty and probably, by most standards, beautiful. A full figure readily becomes voluptuous, and a hooked nose could be hawk-like if we search for more flattering words. She was not necessarily more beautiful than other women, but her real beauty was combined with wit, sophistication, charm and a lively personality. All of this was reinforced by the simple fact that she was a princess and then a queen. Glamour surrounded Cleopatra, magnifying the force of her real beauty and personality. Given our own age's obsession with celebrity, we should have no difficulty in understanding this.

The poet Lucan is the only ancient author to make any reference at all to the queen's complexion. It comes in a scene emphasising the ambition of the queen, the decadent luxury of her court and overpowering ambition of Julius Caesar. He depicts Cleopatra wearing a dress of silk, the material brought originally from China having been rewoven to make it finer and semi-translucent. Such a filmy garment is reminiscent of Ptolemy Physcon. In this case Lucan talks of it revealing much of Cleopatra's 'white breasts' (*candida pectora*). Lucan wrote in Rome some ninety years after the queen's death and it is hard to know whether or not he had seen accurate images of her appearance, let alone her colouring. Much of his poem is highly fanciful. In addition, *candida* normally means white or fair – and in the case of hair can mean blonde – and this begs the question of white or light in comparison to what? Earlier in the same passage he talks of the variety of slaves attending to the guests, contrasting blondes with ruddy complexions (or just possibly red hair) from northern Europe, with dark slaves with curly hair from Africa. This could perhaps imply that Cleopatra was not like either of these in her own appearance, but that is surely pushing the evidence too far. The whole passage is a slender reed on which to rest confident assertions about Cleopatra's appearance.[20]

Apart from this, there is not a shred of evidence about Cleopatra's complexion or the colour of her eyes or hair. This is worth stating bluntly, because so many people keep trying to deduce these or claim to have discovered evidence. At the time of writing two separate TV documentaries have presented reconstructions presenting her as relatively dark-skinned and with brown eyes and black hair. This is all conjecture. As we have seen, there is uncertainty about the identity of Cleopatra's mother and grandmother (or indeed grandmothers if her parents were not siblings).[21]

The Ptolemies were Macedonians, with an admixture of a little Greek and via marriage with the Seleucids a small element of Syrian blood. (There is no evidence to make us question the paternity of any of the line and suggest that they were the product of an illicit liaison between the queen and a man other than her husband. This remains possible, if not very likely, but an uncertain basis for any argument.) The Macedonians were not an homogenous people and seem to have varied considerably in appearance and colouring. Alexander the Great was fair-haired, although it is always difficult to know precisely what this meant. A Roman copy of an earlier mosaic shows him with medium-brown hair. Fair might simply mean not black or very dark brown. On the other hand, several of the early Ptolemies were blond and comparisons of their hair to gold suggest this was more than simply *not* black-haired.

For most of the Ptolemies, including Auletes, there is no mention of the shade of their hair or the colour of their eyes. It is unclear how common blond hair was in the family. (If Cleopatra's mother was a mistress then we know nothing at all about her appearance or ethnic background, although the probability would always be that she was from the Greek or Macedonian aristocracy.) A painting from Herculaneum in the Bay of Naples, which shows a woman wearing the headband of a Hellenistic queen, has sometimes been identified as Cleopatra. She has dark, distinctly red hair. This is not impossible, but there is actually no very strong reason to believe that the image is supposed to be Cleopatra.[22]

Absolutely nothing is certain. Cleopatra may have had black, brown, blonde, or even red hair, and her eyes could have been brown, grey, green or blue. Almost any combination of these is possible. Similarly, she may have been very light skinned or had a darker more Mediterranean complexion. Fairer skin is probably marginally more likely given her ancestry. Greek art traditionally represented women and goddesses as very pale, and a fair skin seems to have been part of the ideal of beauty. Roman propaganda never suggested that Cleopatra was dark-skinned, although this may simply mean that she was not exceptionally dark or simply that the colour of her skin was not important to her critics.

At no point will we need to consider Antony's appearance at similar length and this should remind us that the obsession with Cleopatra's looks is unusual, and not entirely healthy. Not only is there no good evidence, but also there is something disturbing about the desire to base our understanding of her first and foremost on her appearance. Cleopatra was not another Helen of Troy, a mythical figure about whom the most important thing was her beauty. She was no mere passive object of desire, but a very active political player in her own kingdom and beyond.

Cleopatra was born and raised in the real and very dangerous world of the Ptolemaic court in the first century BC. When her father died early in 51 BC, she became a queen. Auletes had planned for his son and daughter to rule jointly. Cleopatra had other ideas.

[x]

TRIBUNE

When Mark Antony returned to Rome in 50 BC his first goal was to enter the priesthood by becoming an augur. This was not from a sudden outbreak of piety, but another step up the political ladder. There were fifteen members of the college of augurs, and along with the pontiffs they were the most prestigious of Rome's priests. They were always from senatorial families and, once elected, the post was held for life. This meant that vacancies were rare and hotly contested when they did occur.

In this case the appointment was prompted by the death of Quintus Hortensius Hortalus, consul in 69 BC and Cicero's rival as the greatest orator of the age. The other members of the college had to choose two nominees. It was common to select men from families who had held the priesthood before, but this was not compulsory. Being selected was a sign of prominence and the ability to call in political favours. Pompey was an augur, and Julius Caesar the senior pontiff or *Pontifex Maximus* – a title now preserved by the pope. The choice between the two candidates was then made by a special assembly consisting of seventeen tribes chosen by lot out of the thirty-five. As in any election, all means from canvassing to outright bribery were pursued to convince the voters. Caesar himself decided to go to Cisalpine Gaul to 'speak in the towns and colonies … and support his bid for the priesthood. For he was happy to use his influence in favour of a man who was very close to him … and especially against the small, but powerful faction, who hoped through the defeat of Mark Antony …' to weaken Caesar's own prestige.[1]

The main priesthoods at Rome were not associated with any particular deities. Augurs had a special role in interpreting messages sent by the gods to show their attitude towards a planned course of action. This might take the form of examining a sacrifice or often simply observing the skies and interpreting the future on the basis of the flights of birds. Cicero was an augur, and although he wrote a book dismissing divination in general, he made an exception in the case of his own college. However, there is absolutely no indication that candidates were judged at all on their knowledge of such things.[2]

Antony was picked as one of the candidates and ran against Lucius Domitius Ahenobarbus, an ancestor of Emperor Nero. The latter was older and much more experienced, having been consul in 54 BC when he had tried and failed to replace Caesar as governor of Gaul. Domitius was also Cato's brother-in-law, which was another reason for him to dislike Caesar and anyone associated with him. Well connected, and from a successful and distinguished family, he could expect to win against his much more junior rival. In the event, Caesar's influence and Caesar's money were lavished through intermediaries to give the victory to Antony. The news of this success reached Cisalpine Gaul before the proconsul had arrived there and begun to canvass. Instead, Caesar toured the communities thanking them for supporting his former quaestor and encouraging them to back Antony in the autumn's election for the tribunate.[3]

There were ten tribunes of the plebs each year and it was a post that a man of Antony's age and experience could reasonably expect to win at this stage in his career. The tribunate was not compulsory and its duties were restricted to Rome itself and never extended to service in the provinces. Yet its powers were considerable. Actively, a tribune could summon the *Concilium Plebis* and propose a bill that the Assembly could then make into a law. The tribunate had been created to protect citizens from the abuse of power by senior magistrates and especially patricians. They possessed the right of veto – literally, 'I forbid' – which allowed them to block any decision or action in the Senate or an assembly. This was not a collective thing and the veto of just one tribune was enough to stop a motion in its tracks.[4]

Caesar's money and backing helped again and Antony was comfortably elected as tribune for 49 BC. Amongst his colleagues were several other men from well-established families. Not all of the candidates Caesar backed were so fortunate. One of his former legates, Servius Sulpicius Galba, tried and failed to win the consulship.[5]

THE ROAD TO THE RUBICON

Caesar was coming to the end of his tenure in Gaul. Since 58 BC he had expanded Roman territory on a grand scale, defeating tribes most Romans considered as traditional enemies. His victories were celebrated by a succession of public thanksgivings and plans were under way to commemorate them by rebuilding on a grand scale the *saepta* voting area on the Campus Martius at Rome. Caesar had been voted his initial command and its five-year extension in bills proposed by tribunes and passed in the Popular Assembly. This was legal, since the People could legislate on anything. In the past, Pompey had benefited in the same way, but it broke the tradition that provinces should be first allocated and then renewed or reassigned by the Senate.

There had been worries about what Pompey would do when he returned to Italy from his eastern campaigns and widespread fear that the successful commander would seize control of the state by force. In the event he had disbanded his army and entered politics as a private citizen in the proper way, which allowed other senators to block him, until in frustration he allied with Crassus and Caesar. Crassus had died in Parthia in 53 BC, unbalancing the alliance. Another very personal connection between Pompey and Caesar had also been removed a year before. In 59 BC Pompey had married Caesar's daughter Julia, his only legitimate child. Caesar's new son-in-law was six years older than he was and yet the marriage proved genuinely happy. Pompey craved adoration, whether from his soldiers, the wider population or a wife, and Julia seems to have been as charming as her father.[6]

Then, in August 54 BC, Julia died in childbirth, and the baby followed her a few days later. Caesar had searched around for another female relation to renew the alliance, but instead Pompey had married into a well-established senatorial family, wedding the daughter of Quintus Caecilius Metellus Pius Scipio Nasica. This man's lengthy name was the product of successive adoptions, which had combined the fortunes of several famous lines. His daughter was simply Cornelia, the feminine form of his name before his own adoption. Scipio himself never gave any evidence of sharing the talent of his famous ancestors, but he was extremely well connected. This encouraged Pompey to marry his daughter and make Scipio his colleague in the consulship of 52 BC. Cornelia was also a remarkable woman and, once again, the marriage to a bride at least thirty years his junior proved extremely happy.[7]

Pompey did not need Caesar as much as he had done in 59 BC. With Crassus gone, there was now no single senator who could match his wealth and importance. In spite of Caesar's new-found glory and great fortune from the conquest of Gaul, Pompey did not yet consider him to be his equal. From at least 52 BC many senators sensed that the two men were becoming much less close. In that year Pompey was made sole consul – dictator in all but name – and his command of the Spanish provinces was renewed. Although he never had any intention of going to the Iberian Peninsula, the provinces gave Pompey control of an army and the immunity from prosecution of a serving magistrate. Once Caesar's command expired in Gaul, then he would have neither of these things. Back in 59 BC he had forced measures through against stubborn opposition. The Roman system allowed acts in the past to be attacked even when they were legal at the time.

Caesar had charisma, which he displayed in his courting of other senators and his frequent seduction of their wives. Anyone who felt that he had seen past this charm tended to loathe him with a hatred that was almost visceral. Cato was one of his bitterest opponents, but there were other men who resented being overshadowed by Caesar's glory and achievements. Several boasted that as soon as Caesar returned home he would be put on trial in a court surrounded by soldiers and condemned.[8]

Simply being brought to trial was a major blow to a senator's prestige, even if he was not condemned. No one had ever thought of prosecuting Crassus, or indeed of charging Pompey with anything.

Caesar refused to risk such an insult to his *auctoritas*. He was equally reluctant to trust for his defence to the friendship of Pompey, both because this would have admitted that the latter was the more important man and because his past record of supporting friends was patchy. Instead, Caesar wanted to go straight from his command into a second consulship in 48 BC, which would give him immunity from prosecution during that year and then the option of taking a province. All ten tribunes of 52 BC were persuaded to pass a law permitting him to stand for election without actually leaving his province and returning to Rome.[9]

The question of how Caesar would return home from Gaul overshadowed public life for more than two years, although this was not to the exclusion of everything else. Individual senators still pursued their own ambitions and agendas, joining in the struggle over this when it suited them. The men who knew themselves as the *boni* (the good) or even the *optimates* (the best) were almost all hostile to Caesar and determined that he should come to Rome as a vulnerable private citizen. They were all from well-established families, who were reluctant to see so much fame, honour and profit from service to the Republic go to someone other than themselves. Many, including Scipio, were heavily in debt and desperately in need of lucrative provincial commands to restore their fortunes. Most had in the past been deeply hostile to Pompey, but now came to believe that they could use him against Caesar.

The dominance of a few old families was well illustrated by consecutive consulships of three men called Claudius Marcellus – two brothers and a cousin. All of them attacked Caesar's position, encouraged by the shift in Pompey's attitude, who had backed the tribunes' law in 52 BC, but over time seemed first ambiguous and then increasingly unsympathetic towards his former son-in-law and ally. One suggestion was to recall Caesar, since after suppressing the rebellion of 52 BC the war in Gaul was clearly over. Pompey did not support this, but wanted the Gallic command to end as soon as the full term expired. There was a divide over precisely when this was and whether the five years granted to him in 55 BC had begun immediately or was in addition to the original five-year term. Pompey was repeatedly questioned over this. In October 51 BC

Cicero's correspondent Caelius Rufus reported the following exchange: "'What if,' someone else said, "he wants to be consul and still retain his army?" To this Pompey responded mildly, "What if my son wants to attack me with a stick?" These words have made people suspect that Pompey is having a row with Caesar.'[10]

Caesar could not legally leave his province without laying down his command, so was unable to talk to Pompey or represent his own interests directly. Instead, he had to work through others, and the profits of conquest were again freely spent to win allies. A massive gift to Lucius Aemilius Lepidus Paullus, one of the consuls in 50 BC, secured his support. He was busy restoring the Basilica Aemilia et Lepida on the edge of the Forum and needed money to pay for the renewal of this monument to his ancestors. In the past he had not been close to Caesar, but had good reason to dislike Pompey, who had executed his father after his unsuccessful coup in 78 BC. It was rumoured that he received 9 million denarii from Caesar.

Another newly purchased ally at first kept the association secret. This was Curio, Antony's friend from youth and now tribune for 50 BC. His open criticism of the triumvirate in 59 BC had been followed by periodic attacks since then, which had often been popular. Everyone expected his tribunate to see more hostility towards them, especially against Caesar. Yet this time there was little enthusiasm outside the self-styled *boni* for attacking Caesar and this would not be the road to popularity.[11]

Curio's father had died some years before, removing one, albeit limited, restraining influence on his son, who marked the event with spectacular funeral games. These included two semi-circular wooden theatres, which were able to rotate and join together forming a single amphitheatre to stage gladiatorial fights. In this period such extremely popular shows could only be staged as part of a funeral. The cost of all this was enormous, adding to the already huge debts that came from Curio's extravagant lifestyle. It was a fragile position. His creditors gambled on his future success, just as they did with other up and coming men, and as with them this gave a desperate edge to his need to reach the very top of public life or face utter ruin.

Caesar is said to have paid Curio 2.5 million denarii by one source, and no less than 15 million by another. The money was vital, but it was not the whole story. Curio had clearly decided that he had other things to gain by allying with Caesar. There was no particular advantage for him in backing Caesar's opponents, since the most ardent of these were as likely to block his own legislation. Curio had married Clodius' widow Fulvia and in other respects was doing his best to cultivate the dead man's former followers. Just like Clodius, Curio was an independent senator with aims of his own and not simply Caesar's puppet. However, Clodius' older brother Appius Claudius Pulcher was tied by marriage to Cato and was now one of Caesar's more enthusiastic critics. Not all members of a family necessarily followed the same line in politics.

Curio did his job well throughout 50 BC, vetoing any senatorial decree that threatened Caesar's right to go straight from his provincial command into the consulship. In April, Caelius described some of this to Cicero:

As for the situation of the Republic, all contention is focused on a single cause, namely the provinces. At the moment Pompey seems to be backing the Senate in demanding that Caesar leave his province by the Ides [13th] of November. Curio is utterly determined to prevent this – he has abandoned all his other projects. ... This is the scene – the whole thing – Pompey, just as if he was not attacking Caesar, but making a fair settlement for him, blames Curio for making trouble. At the same time he is absolutely against Caesar becoming consul before giving up his province and army. He is getting a rough ride from Curio, and his entire third consulship is attacked. You mark my words, if they try to crush Curio with all their might, Caesar will come to the rescue; if instead, as seems most likely, they are too frightened to risk it, then Caesar will stay as long as he wants.[12]

Cicero was at the time a reluctant proconsul of Cilicia and was determined to remain there no longer than the minimum term of a year. Caelius noted earlier in the same letter that he and Curio had helped to prevent an extension of his term. Again, this is an indication that many other issues were fiercely contested as part of, or just alongside, the wider struggle. Cicero had little sympathy for

Curio's support for Caesar, but welcomed his aid in his own case. Pompey remained outside the city, since he, too, could not enter and retain his provincial command. The Senate obligingly met outside the formal boundary (*pomerium*), of Rome.[13]

On 1 December there was a major debate, at which Curio cleverly scored a point against his opponents. The Senate voted by a large majority to recall Caesar from Gaul, while a similar motion to end Pompey's term as proconsul of Spain was defeated by just as big a margin. Both decrees were vetoed by tribunes, and Curio then asked the Senate to divide on the proposal that both men should lay down their commands simultaneously. No fewer than 370 senators backed this and only 22 voted against. If few men actively favoured Caesar, and most were sympathetic to Pompey, the overwhelming majority dreaded the civil war that seemed so very likely if the dispute was not resolved peacefully. The consul Marcellus ignored the outcome and dismissed the meeting, bawling out, 'If that is what you want, be Caesar's slaves!'[14]

By the end of the year Curio had ensured that Caesar remained as proconsul of Gaul, but his direct attacks on Pompey had only fed the tension. All of the issues were carried over into 49 BC. Curio hurried to confer with Caesar and returned early in January with a message from him. By this time Antony had become tribune and taken over the role of defending Caesar's position, aided in this by one of his colleagues, Quintus Cassius Longinus. Both of the consuls were vehemently opposed to Caesar who claimed that one boasted of becoming a second Sulla as the only way of surviving his staggeringly large debts. Men on both sides were desperate and more than a few thought they would benefit should civil war break out. There was also mutual suspicion, not helped by the inability of the main protagonists to meet face to face. On top of that was a deep-rooted confidence that the other side would back down.[15]

Curio brought a letter from Caesar, but Antony and Curio had to insist before this was read out in the Senate. It contained a restatement of his services to the Republic and claimed that he should only have to lay down his command if Pompey did the same. Cicero had now returned from Cilicia and was waiting outside Rome in the hope of being awarded a triumph. To him the letter's tone was 'fierce and threatening'. A motion was passed demanding that Caesar immediately lay down his command, but Antony and Cassius vetoed it. There were still attempts at private negotiation, Caesar writing to many leading senators and offering concessions, for instance that he give up Transalpine Gaul and Illyria, keeping only Cisalpine Gaul and a single legion. This way he would be safe from prosecution, but too weak to risk fighting a civil war. Some of his opponents saw this as weakness, confirming their belief that he would give in if they refused to compromise.[16]

Antony had grown into a big, barrel-chested and thick-necked man. While in Greece he had studied oratory and adopted the flamboyant Asiatic style. He had huge force of personality and threw all his energy into defending Caesar, but he was not a man to whom subtlety came naturally. He was also highly inexperienced politically, having spent little time in Rome since becoming a senator. In later years, Cicero talked of Antony 'vomiting his words in the usual way' when he made a speech. Like Curio, he decided now to attack Pompey's career and especially his third consulship and use of force to restore order. Political exchanges at Rome were often strong, but this was seen as particularly vitriolic and included repeated threats of war. At one public meeting late in December, the tribune elect Antony had been so aggressive that Pompey complained, 'What do you reckon Caesar himself will be like, if he gets to control the Republic, if now his weak and worthless quaestor acts like this!'[17]

On 7 January the Senate passed its ultimate decree, suspending law and calling on 'the consuls, praetors and tribunes, and all the proconsuls near the city to ensure that the Republic comes to no harm'. It was obvious that 'the proconsuls' first and foremost meant Pompey. Attempts by Antony and Quintus Cassius to veto this decree were ignored and one of the consuls told them that he could not ensure their safety if they remained in Rome. There does not seem to have been an actual attack on them, but the two tribunes disguised themselves as slaves and were carried out of the city in a hired cart.[18]

Caesar was at Ravenna, just inside his province of Cisalpine Gaul. With him he had the *Thirteenth* Legion supported by some 300 cavalry. It was a small force, and it was also very unusual for armies

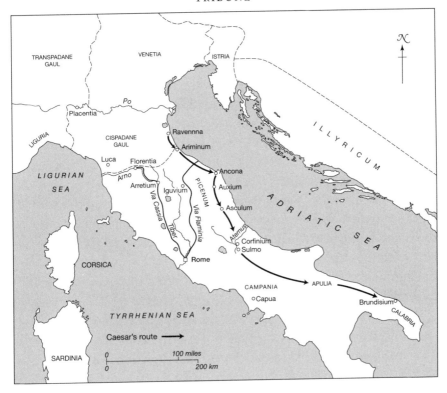

The Italian Campaign 49 BC

to go on campaign in the winter months. Pompey and the hard-line senators opposing Caesar did not think that he could begin the war quickly. They may even have still thought that he would back down, seeing this final proof of their determination.

They were wrong. On the night of the 10/11 January 49 BC, Caesar led his men from Ravenna to Ariminum (modern-day Rimini). When he crossed the River Rubicon – so insignificant a stream that we cannot now be sure of its location – he left his province, where he could legally command troops, and entered Italy, where he could not. He is said to have used a gambler's tag when he did so, the famous 'the die is cast' (*iacta alea est*). Later he would place the blame for the civil war squarely on his enemies, saying that 'They wanted it; even after all my great deeds I, Caius Caesar, would have been condemned, if I had not sought support from my army.' Whatever the rights and wrongs of the conflict, the simple fact was that crossing the Rubicon turned him and all his supporters into rebels.[19]

It is unclear whether Antony, Cassius and Curio joined Caesar at Ariminum or earlier at Ravenna, but the former seems more likely. In either case, the *Thirteenth* was paraded and the proconsul addressed them and explained how he had been forced to act by the bitter and illegal hostility of his enemies, who had lured Pompey away from him. The two tribunes were still dressed as slaves when they were brought before the soldiers to underline the way that his opponents had trampled on the laws. The persons of the tribunes of the people were sacrosanct and yet these representatives of the people had been threatened with violence. All Romans had a deeply emotional attachment to the idea of the tribunate and by the end of the parade the legionaries and their officers were shouting that they were ready to set things right.[20]

Antony was a few days short of his thirty-fourth birthday. Years later Cicero would blame him for starting the civil war. That was a huge exaggeration, for it is hard to see enough trust on either side to have made a peaceful resolution possible. It is fair to say that Antony was an active participant in the actual events that sparked the war. He also showed no reluctance about taking part in an invasion of Italy.[21]

TRIBUNE WITH PROPRAETORIAN POWERS

Caesar did not linger, but pressed on. His opponents were unprepared and had no reliable troops to oppose even the small invading army. Town after town opened its gates to Caesar's men. Antony was sent with a force of five cohorts from the *Thirteenth* to occupy Arretium (modern-day Arezzo). There was no fighting. A little later Curio led another column to Iguvium. The Pompeian commander fled, his soldiers deserted and the townsfolk welcomed the cohorts. From the beginning, Caesar maintained very strict discipline and forbade his soldiers from looting or indiscriminate acts of violence. They were to fight only when actively resisted.[22]

Absolutely no one had anticipated Caesar's strategy. Even men like Cicero who knew Caesar personally and had hoped to avoid the war, expected him to advance like Sulla or Marius, plundering and slaughtering all his opponents. Instead, he paraded his clemency. When he surrounded a large force at Corfinium under the inept leadership of Domitius Ahenobarbus, the town surrendered after a brief siege. Ahenobarbus – Antony's rival for the augurate – and all of the senior officers were allowed to go free, taking their possessions with them. His soldiers nearly all changed sides and joined Caesar, who proclaimed that this was 'a new way of conquest – we grow strong through pity and generosity'.[23]

Early on Pompey had decided that it was impossible to defend Rome. He had very few trained and reliable soldiers. Levies were held, but the raw legions raised in this way would take many months to be trained. Everything had to be improvised and for the moment he and his supporters were weak. Hotheads like Ahenobarbus tried to force him to fight, refusing to obey orders and retire to join him. Attempts at negotiation continued, some involving Antony's cousin, the son and namesake of Lucius Julius Caesar. Both sides repeated their desire for peace and much of this may have been intended to win support from the undecided. The bulk of the Senate, let alone the wider population, felt no strong commitment to either side and tried to remain out of the conflict.[24]

Pompey retreated to Brundisium in the south and began transporting his men by sea across to Greece. There he planned to assemble and train a great army, drawing on the resources of the eastern provinces he himself had organised. Once he was ready, he would return and crush Caesar. As he put it, 'Sulla did it, so why can't I?' Caesar pursued and tried to prevent his escape, but failed to close the harbour. Brundisium fell, but only after Pompey and his forces had escaped.[25]

Caesar had won the first campaign, but he remained a rebel with many strong enemies at large. He lacked the ships needed to follow Pompey, so instead decided to march by land to Spain and defeat the Pompeian legions there. First he needed to make arrangements for the governance of Italy. He returned to Rome, but at first did not enter the city itself. Antony and Cassius as tribunes summoned a meeting of the Senate to a spot outside the *pomerium* on 1 April.

Few attended, and only two of these were former consuls. Never-theless, Caesar took the opportunity to address the meeting and later an Assembly of the Roman people to lay out his case. The Senate decreed that an embassy should be sent to Pompey and his allies in the hope of agreeing a peace. No one was willing to serve on the delegation, however, and so the whole matter was dropped. Needing funds to pay his soldiers, Caesar took money from the Republic's Treasury, in spite of the opposition of another of the tribunes. This was only a few months after proclaiming his willingness to fight on behalf of the rights of the tribunate.[26]

Caesar then left for the campaign in Spain. Antony's brother Caius Antonius was given command of two legions and sent to Illyricum, nearest to the massing enemies in Greece. Curio received the legions that had defected at Corfinium and was sent to Sicily, with orders to proceed to North Africa once this was secured. On his way, the young aristocrat visited Cicero and spoke with his usual freedom, claiming that Caesar's clemency was a sham and that soon he would reveal his true and far more cruel nature, becoming another Sulla.[27]

As well as generals, Caesar needed administrators. Rome was put under the charge of the praetor Marcus Aemilius Lepidus, the younger brother of the consul of 50 BC and a man who would later play a major role in Antony's life. Antony himself was given special propraetorian *imperium* to add to his office of tribune and was tasked with overseeing the rest of Italy. Both men were appointed because they were already properly elected magistrates and also because they came from well-established families. It was still an unprecedented responsibility for a tribune. Antony revelled in the power.[28]

[XI]

QUEEN

Cleopatra was about eighteen when her father died in 51 BC, the oldest of Auletes' four surviving children. Her sister Arsinoe was younger by one or more years and the older of their two brothers was just ten. Their father had intended Ptolemy XIII and Cleopatra to rule jointly. It is normally assumed that they were quickly married in accordance with the family tradition, but no source explicitly tells us this, and it was unusual for a Ptolemaic king to take a wife who was so much older. On the other hand, if Ptolemy XIII had subsequently married then friction would always have been likely between his wife and his sister and co-ruler, so in many respects marriage between the royal siblings encouraged stability. It is also possible that a marriage was planned, but did not actually take place.

We do not know how Auletes died and whether his death was sudden or long anticipated. This means that it is uncertain how far he prepared the way for the succession. There were problems from the beginning. Ptolemy XIII was a minor who could not rule himself and so required some form of regency. There was a long tradition amongst the Ptolemies of giving important courtiers the status of 'friends' or the even greater honour of 'kinsmen', in keeping with Macedonian tradition, which had surrounded Alexander and other kings with 'companions'. A number of important men were associated with the boy and formed a loose faction around him. The dominant figures were his tutor Theodotus of Samos and the eunuch Pothinus. There does not seem to have been any formally appointed regent or regency council, merely a group of prominent men able to influence and effectively control the young prince. All had ambitions of their own and were united only in a desire to increase the importance of Ptolemy XIII and so gain power themselves.[1]

Cleopatra also had her advisers and allies, although we know next to nothing about them. This is because she was older, confident enough to assert herself and unwilling to let anyone else rule through her. From the beginning this created tension. Her favourites doubtless gained prestige and power within the court, but these were inevitably a minority. Other men saw their rivals doing well, as their own influence and importance declined or at best remained the same. If they were unable to ingratiate themselves with the young queen, then the natural alternative was to turn to her brother. Increasing his power would benefit all those who surrounded and supported him.

The teenage queen made her intentions clear very quickly. Ignoring her father's will, Cleopatra made herself sole monarch of his kingdom. Official documents from 51 BC make no mention of Ptolemy XIII. They refer instead to 'Year Thirty, which is also Year One'. The Egyptian system of dating inherited by the Ptolemies was based around the years of rule of each monarch. Year Thirty was the final year of Auletes' reign – tactfully ignoring the period of his exile. Therefore the year marked the end of one era and the start of the new reign of the sole queen. She styled herself the 'father-loving goddess' (*Thea Philopator*), at once stressing her connection with Auletes and ignoring his declaration that his children were 'sibling-loving'.

Her sole rule was also reflected in less official sources. A priest of an association dedicated to the worship of the goddess Isis seems to have prepared a statue to dedicate to Ptolemy XII. When the king died, this man had the inscription altered to celebrate 'Queen Cleopatra Thea Philopator' instead. Time, cost or lack of concern meant that the statue was still of an obviously male figure in the traditional garb of a pharaoh. There is no mention on the inscription of Ptolemy XIII.[2]

On the 22 March 51 BC a grand ceremony was held at Hermonthis in Upper Egypt to enthrone a new Buchis bull, the focus of one of the great animal cults of Egypt. Whenever a Buchis bull died, it was carefully mummified and buried, while the priests searched for a replacement of suitable type, size and colour. The Buchis bull was supposed to change colour during the course of each day. The animal cults of Egypt often attracted the scorn of Greek and Roman observers, but that did nothing to prevent their popularity, which extended beyond the indigenous population to many settlers from outside. Most famous was the Apis bull whose shrine was at Memphis, but there were others. The Buchis bull was believed to be in some way the physical manifestation of Montu, a god of war, and was also sacred to other deities. Hermonthis lay on the opposite bank of the Nile to the Upper Kingdom's capital city of Thebes and had immense prestige.

An inscription from Hermonthis, recording the burial of this Buchis bull more than twenty years later, stated that:

> He reached Thebes, the place of installation, which came into existence aforetime, beside his father, Nun the old. He was installed by the king himself in the year 1, Phamenoth 19 [22 March 51 BC]. The Queen, the Lady of the Two Lands, the Goddess Philopator, rowed him in the boat of Amen, together with all the barges of the king, all the inhabitants of Thebes and Hermonthis and priests being with him. He reached Hermonthis, his dwelling place . . .[3]

Such inscriptions were formulaic, so that we need to be cautious about reading too much into the details. 'He was installed by the king himself' was a traditional formula and did not usually mean that the king was in fact present. We do not know if it anyway refers to Auletes, or less probably Ptolemy XIII, or is simply used vaguely to mean Cleopatra herself, in this traditional religious role of the pharaoh.

Many historians chose to take the description of her participation literally. If this is correct, then it would be striking that the new queen was willing to travel to the south of her realm so early in her reign, removing her from Alexandria and the court for a period of a least a few weeks. Ptolemy Auletes was generous to the temple cults, and this can be seen as an extension of his patronage, taken a stage further by a young queen able to speak the Egyptian language. Upper Egypt does seem to have been consistently loyal to both father and daughter, which could suggest that this attention was rewarded. Cleopatra certainly continued to build temples and fund the cults. Another inscription records that she gave money to pay for the ceremonial feasts accompanying the instalment of a new Apis bull. However, in this case the sum involved was no more than 421 silver coins, making the gift generous, but not on an especially grand scale.[4]

It is certainly possible that the eighteen-year-old Cleopatra actually did go down the Nile and play a role in the rituals of the Buchis bull. She does seem to have enjoyed theatre, perhaps felt a genuine religious commitment to the cult and may also have wanted to show herself as queen in a very public role. The 'rowing' would never have to be more than symbolic. Extending this to a deep commitment to traditional Egyptian religion and culture remains a very large step even beyond this, as does the claim that 'she was indeed queen of Egypt' in contrast to earlier Ptolemies. We do have to remember that her participation may have been entirely symbolic, consisting of financial support and official words of approval issued from distant Alexandria. It was obviously in the interests of the priests of the cult to portray royal involvement as direct and true, in an ideal rather than literal sense. Once again we simply do not know, making this a flimsy piece of evidence on which to base sweeping statements about Cleopatra's policies and attitudes.[5]

EXILE

There was no tradition of a Ptolemaic queen ruling alone for any length of time. Cleopatra was intelligent, capable and ambitious, but she was also young and inexperienced. Perhaps she believed that she could be the exception to this, but her position was always precarious and it was difficult to keep enough of the court and wider aristocracy satisfied. The Roman attitude was almost as vital, but remained unclear. Although news of Auletes' death had reached Rome by the summer of 51 BC, the Senate took no action to recognise the new queen or to enforce the terms of her father's will. There were plenty of other matters occupying the senators' minds and a general indifference to Egypt's affairs. It had after all taken Auletes more than a decade and concerted lobbying and bribery to gain the formal acceptance of the Roman Republic.[6]

Crassus' unprovoked and disastrous invasion of Parthia was followed by a series of heavy Parthian raids into the Roman provinces. In 50 BC, the Roman proconsul governing Syria was Marcus Calpurnius Bibulus, son-in-law of Cato. Bibulus had the misfortune to be Julius Caesar's contemporary, and in a succession of magistracies was overshadowed by his far more charismatic and able colleague. In 59 BC the two men were consuls and after vain attempts to block Caesar's legislation, Bibulus had retired to his house. He produced a stream of scurrilous attacks on his colleague, whilst all the time proclaiming that public business was invalid because of bad omens. People joked that the year was the consulship of Julius and Caesar rather than Caesar and Bibulus.[7]

Like Cicero, Bibulus had only reluctantly gone out to govern a province, but once there he seems to have tried to do the job to the best of his limited ability. With only the remnants of Crassus' army at his disposal, he sent two of his sons to Alexandria to summon the Gabinian troops. This does suggest that these were still seen as part of the Roman army, although it is just possible that he simply saw them as Roman citizens and so obliged to serve the cause of the Republic. Whatever Bibulus' view, the Gabinians and their officers did not recognise his authority. Not only did they refuse to answer to leave Egypt, but they also promptly murdered the proconsul's sons.

Cleopatra had the ringleaders arrested and sent in chains to Bibulus for punishment. As one source puts it, 'No greater favour could have been offered to a mourner. But when offered it, he made grief yield to moderation and had the slaughterers of his flesh and blood returned to Cleopatra immediately unharmed, saying that the power to punish them should be the Senate's, not his.'[8]

The young queen had demonstrated her loyalty to Rome and asserted some degree of control over the Gabinians, who formed such a major part of the royal army. It is not known what happened to the prisoners once they were returned to her by Bibulus. Cleopatra had been able to arrest these men, but had not been able to get the Gabinians to go to Syria, assuming that she wanted this. The queen's willingness to hand these officers over for execution can scarcely have endeared her to their colleagues.

Much of Auletes' unpopularity in 58 BC came from his fawning attitude to Roman power. Many Alexandrians, and in particular many of the well-off and influential, seem to have resented this. It is more than likely that Cleopatra's actions following the murder of Bibulus' sons caused a similar reaction, but we should be careful not to push this too far. It was not a simple question of pro- and anti-Roman factions at court. Instead, any perceived weakness or mistake made by the queen was bound to be exploited by the faction surrounding her brother. Discontent amongst army officers weakened Cleopatra and aided men like Pothinus and Theodotus.

At some point in 50 BC the queen's sole rule ended and she was forced to acknowledge her brother as co-ruler. For a while there seems to have been co-operation between the two, at least officially. There are relatively few formal documents from this period, but Ptolemy XIII more often than not is named first. This may simply be because a king would normally be considered the dominant partner, but perhaps reflects the real balance of power. On 27 October a decree was issued in the name of the king and queen forbidding any excess from the harvest being stored locally and commanding that all of this was to be transported to Alexandria. The death penalty was to be imposed on anyone violating this decree and 'whoever wishes shall inform ... about contraventions of this order, on the understanding that he shall receive a third part of the property of the person found guilty, or, if he be a slave, shall be freed and in addition receive the sixth part'. Harsh penalties for violating royal decrees were not unusual.[9]

In this case, the harvests seem to be have been bad for several years in succession as the annual inundations were low. At the same time the royal bureaucracy pressed hard to levy taxation on what was produced. Other documents from this period hint at widespread hardship and shortages. In some cases the peasants took the traditional route of protest by fleeing from the lands they were supposed to work.

Alexandria was large and had a volatile population. Food shortages there were likely to cause rioting, which could quickly destabilise any regime. Therefore the royal decree may simply have been intended to make sure that however bad the situation was, the inhabitants of the great city were adequately fed. Yet there may be more to it than this. Some scholars have suggested that Cleopatra had already left the city and gone to Upper Egypt to rally support against her brother. If so, then the law was designed to deny her the food supplies she would need to feed any army she raised.[10]

More probably, the relations between brother and sister had not yet broken down into actual conflict. The measure could just as easily have been intended to keep all resources under the close supervision of Ptolemy's supporters and so deter Cleopatra from resorting to open resistance. It is more than possible that for a year or so there was the same sort of uneasy truce that had at times operated between Ptolemy Physcon and his two queens.

By the end of 50 BC the official dating system spoke of 'Year One, which is also Year Three', and the former clearly referred to the reign of Ptolemy XIII. Cleopatra may still have been in Alexandria when Pompey sent his elder son Cnaeus Pompey to the royal court in 49 BC. Having evacuated Italy, Pompey and his allies were busy organising the great army that was intended to smash Caesar, either in Macedonia or by returning to Italy itself. Therefore envoys were sent to gather men and resources from all the provinces and allied kingdoms of the eastern Mediterranean. Pompey's past connection with Auletes may well have encouraged him to send his son to the Ptolemaic court, although it is more than likely that he also visited other regions. Cnaeus got at least some of what he requested. Five hundred Gallic and German cavalry drawn from amongst the Gabinians were despatched to join Pompey's army, which included many contingents of allied troops to support the legions. In addition, he received sixty oared warships, apparently fully equipped and crewed. Egypt also sent wheat to feed the Pompeian forces.[11]

Plutarch claims that Cleopatra – now about twenty – seduced Cnaeus Pompey, but none of our other sources mentions this and it is highly unlikely that Octavian and his propagandists would not have thrown such a charge at the queen. She may or may not have met the Roman envoy, but he clearly was left in no doubt that Ptolemy XIII's advisers were in charge of the kingdom. The senators who were with Pompey's army considered themselves the legitimate governing council of the Republic even though they were far from Rome. When Cnaeus Pompey returned they met and formally recognised the rule of the young Ptolemy XIII. Absolutely no mention was made of his sister. There is also no hint that Ptolemy's aid to the Romans made him in any way unpopular with his subjects, highlighting the fact that it is wrong to see this as a simple struggle between pro- and anti-Roman factions.[12]

At some point in late 49 or early 48 BC, Cleopatra left Alexandria and went to raise an army. Arsinoe went with her. A much later source claims that they went first to Upper Egypt, seeking support in the Thebaid. Perhaps not enough men rallied to the queen's cause or her brother's control of the food supply was simply too tight. For whatever reason, Cleopatra and her sister fled to Syria. In just a few years she had gone from queen to exile.[13]

Her father was only the most recent of the Ptolemies to be driven from their kingdom, only to regain power at a later date. Cleopatra was not resigned to her fate, but determined to build up her strength until she could either defeat, or at least negotiate with, her brother and his advisers. She received an enthusiastic welcome from the city of Ascalon on the coast of Palestine. Originally one of the five main Philistine cities from the Old Testament period, it was now a bustling port. Alliance with the Ptolemies had allowed the city to break away from the kingdom of Judaea and become independent. In gratitude they had on several occasions minted coins bearing the Ptolemies' eagle symbol. Now a series was produced carrying Cleopatra's head. These are the images emphasising family traits such as the large eyes and prominent hooked nose to prove the legitimacy of her claim to power.[14]

Why Ascalon's leaders chose to support Cleopatra against her brother is unclear. Assistance may also have come from other quarters, and she may have hired or been given troops by the Nabataean kingdom, the capital of which was at the famous city of Petra. By the summer of 48 BC Cleopatra had an army and was ready to return.

Ptolemy XIII and his ministers knew that his sisters were coming back. The royal army was mustered under the command of a general named Achillas, who now joined Pothinus and Theodotus as part of the inner circle controlling the young king. Julius Caesar says that:

> Achillas ... had twenty thousand armed troops. These consisted of the old soldiers of Gabinius. . . . To these he had added recruits drawn from the ruffians and bandits of Syria and the province of Cilicia and the neighbouring regions. Meanwhile many condemned criminals and exiles had joined them; also our runaway slaves were sure of a welcome in Alexandria if they enlisted in the army. If any one of them was apprehended by his owner, he would be saved by the common support of the other soldiers.[15]

It was a strong force, better trained and more experienced than the army Cleopatra had managed to assemble. It was always important in a civil war to show supreme confidence, since caution would readily be interpreted as weakness and so might make people wonder whether to change sides. Ptolemy XIII was still in his early teens, but was dressed in splendid armour and the royal cloak to lead his soldiers in person. The faction surrounding him were unlikely to have wanted to let the boy out of their sight and close control; they are also unlikely to have trusted each other.[16]

Achillas did not wait at Pelusium to meet the invaders, but marched the army another 30 miles or so to the east to wait at Mount Casius. It was a strong position and the forward move was another expression of confidence. Cleopatra's army arrived and took up a position facing them. For days the two armies stared at each other. Such stand-offs were common in ancient warfare; battle usually required the consent of both sides. If an army remained in a strong position, then its opponents were rarely willing to attack it at such a disadvantage. Probably Ptolemy's army was much stronger than that of his sister. Her invasion of Egypt had bogged down before it had really begun.

Then Pompey the Great arrived in Egypt for the first time in his long career.

[XII]

CIVIL WAR

Pompey ought to have won the civil war, for he had far greater resources at his disposal and appeared to have much wider political support. He had lost Italy, but that was principally a blow to prestige and did not seriously reduce his capacity to fight. By the summer of 49 BC Caesar had outmanoeuvred the Pompeian armies in Spain and forced them to surrender. The leaders were permitted to go and duly returned to Pompey. The junior officers and soldiers switched sides or were demobilised. The legions in Spain had been the most experienced under Pompey's command, but they were trapped in a strategic backwater and the campaign decided nothing. If Caesar had been beaten, then the civil war would have been over, for the rebel could not afford to lose even once. To Pompey the defeat was of only minor significance and, more importantly, the campaign had given him time to prepare for the real confrontation. Organisation had always been Pompey's forte and the fifty-eight-year-old seemed rejuvenated as he gathered and trained his army in Greece.[1]

There was also encouraging news from other theatres, as Caesar's subordinates failed to match his successes. Caius Antonius led one and a half legions into Illyricum, but was overwhelmed and captured. Curio at first did well against weak opposition and had enjoyed a bloodless victory in Sicily – a minor reverse for Pompey's cause. The Pompeian commander of the island was Cato, but he had no significant forces and decided not to waste citizens' lives in a futile defence, so left and went to Greece. Curio then took two of his four legions over to North Africa. Lack of transport ships severely restricted the Caesareans, just as it had prevented Caesar from following Pompey across the Adriatic, and the invasion was a gamble. At first the risk paid off and his legions of recently captured Pompeians proved remarkably loyal, with only a handful of desertions. One enemy army was routed at the cost of only a single fatality. Curio had very little military experience, but was bold and charismatic. He was also fighting against an opponent with hastily raised soldiers and inexperienced officers. In the early campaigns of the civil war, both sides contained a high proportion of unskilled amateurs.

Then things started to go wrong. King Juba of Numidia was a staunch ally of Pompey – not least because while on an embassy to Rome he had been insulted by both Caesar and Curio. Acting on false intelligence, Curio force-marched his men in the hope of ambushing the king's vanguard. He won a minor victory, but then realised that the entire Numidian army was closing on his position. Impulsively, Curio chose to fight. He was killed and only a handful of his men escaped. There was panic and chaos when these survivors reached the troops left back at the Caesarean base camp on the coast, a horde of fugitives swamping the boats trying to take them off. The historian Asinius Pollio was one of the few who managed to get away by ship to Sicily. Juba executed all those who surrendered, in spite of the protests of his Roman allies.[2]

By the end of 49 BC one of Antony's brothers was a captive of the enemy, and the severed head of his old friend Curio had been triumphantly presented to King Juba. His cousin, the younger Lucius Julius Caesar, was with the Pompeian forces in Africa and would lose his life during the course of the war. The boy's father remained a Caesarean. The Roman aristocracy was close knit and everyone had some connections in the opposing camp.

The split in the senatorial class was not even and its more distinguished members – including nearly half of the former consuls – actively supported Pompey. This gave him a deep political strength and an impression of legitimacy, which Caesar could not match. In spite of his victories in Italy and Spain, Caesar was a rebel and the Pompeians could still make a better claim to be defending the Republic. Only a handful of ex-consuls actively supported Caesar and these included three discredited men recalled from exile. One was Gabinius, and another was Antony's uncle, Caius Antonius, although the nephew was later accused of having done little to encourage Caesar to recall him. Cicero was contemptuous of the

Caesareans, dubbing the ones he saw accompanying their commander in March 49 BC as a 'rabble'.[3]

Like Antony and Curio, quite a few Caesareans came from noble
families, but they were generally young, had reputations for wild
living and radical politics, both of which had drained away their
inheritances. The older men who followed Caesar were the failures
and the desperate, descendants of the men who had backed Marius
and paid the price, survivors of Catiline's rebellion or those who
had fallen foul of the courts. Caesar had a well-proven record for
generosity, saying that he would reward even bandits if they served
him well. Some had simply taken a pragmatic judgement of who
was likely to win the conflict. Cicero's correspondent Caelius
believed that Pompey had the better cause, but Caesar the better
army, and so became a Caesarean.[4]

The Pompeians had little to offer men like Antony. Not only did
Caesar promise lavish reward once victory was won, but also there
was the chance of important commands and responsibilities in the
meantime. There were plenty of Pompeians who had been consul
or praetor, and who had governed provinces and led armies. Such
men expected to receive tasks in keeping with their status. Had he
been a Pompeian, there were no imaginable circumstances where
the thirty-four-year-old Antony would have been given such an
important task as the supervision of Italy.

Caesar had far fewer distinguished men to call upon. Antony was
an elected magistrate, and was also an Antonius, both of which made
him more qualified for this task than most of the other Caesareans.
It is also clear that Caesar had confidence in his ability to do the job,
although interesting that for the moment he did not choose to
employ him in a more overtly military role. As we have seen,
Antony's military experience was still relatively modest and it is
quite possible that he had been as much or more an administrator as
a soldier during his years in Gaul. Caesar did take his fellow tribune
Cassius Longinus with him on the Spanish campaign, and left him
behind as provincial governor. Cassius had both a brother and a
cousin fighting for Pompey, but the appointment was to prove a bad
one for other reasons.

Antony did a better job as tribune with propraetorian power in

Italy. The peace was kept, with no upsurge of Pompeian resistance. In the meantime, progress was made in preparing the army and fleet for crossing to Macedonia. How much either of these things was a direct result of Antony's personal involvement is impossible to know, as we have very little information about these months. Plutarch claims that he was energetic in organising and training the troops, and popular with the soldiers for his generosity. In contrast, he was supposed to have shown little energy when it came to receiving petitions from civilians. He does seem to have travelled widely, visiting many of the towns of Italy. People noticed Antony, and this was not always a good thing for the Caesarean cause, because he paraded his power. Cicero claimed that:

> A tribune of the people was driven in a British chariot, preceded by lictors crowned in laurel [the symbol of victory], and in the middle a mime actress carried in an open litter; respectable men from the towns were obliged to greet her, and address her as Volumnia, rather than her stage name. Following behind were his shameful companions – a whole band of pimps – and at the back his mother, attending her wicked son's mistress just as if she was a daughter-in-law.[5]

This description comes from a speech made years later, but although the orator may have exaggerated a little, there is evidence from the time that he was not inventing the whole story. In May of 49 BC he mentioned in a letter that Antony carried his mistress 'about with him in an open litter just like a second wife, and had seven other litters with male and female friends'.[6]

At some point in the last few years Antony had married for the second time. We do not know what happened to his first wife, but he may have divorced her because of her undistinguished family. Instead, he married his first cousin, the daughter of Caius Antonius. This connection made it seem all the more strange that he did little to encourage Caesar to recall Antonius, but the marriage seems not to have been a happy one. A year later he would divorce Antonia amidst rumours that she had taken a lover. Gossip claimed that Antony had affairs with the wives of several other men, but Roman society did not grant the same licence to a wife as it did to a husband.[7]

Antony himself reserved his passion for his mistress in a relationship that lasted several years. She was a freed slave, and the name Volumnia was the feminine form of her old master's name. Professionally she was known as Cytheris. Taking a mistress was common for Roman aristocrats and there existed a distinct class of courtesans, some of whom became famous. These women were usually foreign, and often freed slaves, but were educated and witty, stylish and in many cases able to sing, dance and play musical instruments. Quite a few, like Cytheris, had first won fame on the stage in the mimes – stories told through dance and music in which women took part, unlike drama where female parts were generally performed by male actors.[8]

Such a mistress could not be taken for granted. Suitors competed to win her favour, offering gifts and ultimately providing a house or apartment for the lover to live in. Both parties knew that the affair would not be permanent, and a mistress could end the relationship if she found a more appealing protector. Able to flatter and flirt in a way that would have been socially unacceptable for a wife, expensive mistresses offered exciting and glamorous company in affairs that were spicy, but without long-term commitment. Cytheris had already had an affair with Servilia's son Brutus, a man whose philosophical leanings and sober nature seem so opposite to Antony's character. Considerable licence was allowed to senators' sons during their adolescence – a period that the Romans felt lasted into the late thirties. Yet they were expected to show at least some discretion, and this was something Antony seems never to have mastered or even thought necessary. A story circulated that he had a chariot pulled by a team of lions rather than horses. Whether or not such an absurdly impractical and dangerous experiment was actually made, it gives an idea of what people were willing to believe about him.[9]

He paraded his power in a way that was both blatant and vulgar, giving the impression of enjoying himself in luxurious debauchery instead of labouring diligently. For Cicero, this confirmed his worst fears that Caesar would eventually throw off the façade of clemency and preside over a bloodbath. The orator believed the war to be unnecessary and had tried to encourage a negotiated settlement. He had been shocked by the militancy of many leading senators, then dismayed by the evacuation first of Rome and then of Italy itself. Yet he was still drawn to Pompey and more comfortable siding with him and his allies than Caesar and his 'rabble'. For a while he stayed in Italy, avoiding taking part in the meetings of the Senate at Rome or committing himself in any way to Caesar. His protégé Caelius Rufus and several friends who were with Caesar repeatedly encouraged him to take this step, or at the very least maintain his neutrality. Another voice came from his son-in-law Dolabella, but Cicero despised the man. The marriage to his daughter had been arranged by his wife while he was away in Cilicia and without his approval.[10]

Antony kept an eye on Cicero, for it was obvious that the famous orator was tempted to leave the country and join the Pompeians. In early May, Cicero mentioned that he had repeatedly written to the tribune, assuring him that he planned nothing rash, but expressing a desire to go abroad, perhaps to Malta, and avoid all involvement in the war. Antony had replied:

Had I not such strong affection for you – far greater than you think – then I would not have been disturbed by the rumour which has spread about you, particularly as I believed it to be untrue. However, because I am so very fond of you, I cannot pretend to myself that the report, even if false, does not greatly worry me. That you are about to go abroad I cannot believe, given your love for Dolabella and your [daughter] Tullia, the finest of women, and because you are so highly esteemed by all of us. . . . But I felt it unbecoming in a friend not to be concerned even by loose talk, particularly as our disagreement made things more difficult for me, the whole thing caused more by my jealousy [Antony uses the Greek word] rather than any wrong deed of yours; for I wish to assure you that nobody is more dear to me than you, apart from Caesar, and I am sure Caesar counts Marcus Cicero amongst his foremost friends. And so, my dear Cicero, I implore you not to make a mistake . . . and not to flee from one [Caesar], who, even if he cannot love you – for that is now impossible – will always want you to be safe and held in the highest honour.[11]

Again, Cicero assured Antony of his resolution to remain neutral and asked permission to leave Italy and go somewhere peaceful. Antony was unhelpful:

> Your plan is quite correct. For anyone who wants to remain neutral should not leave his homeland, while the man who leaves is seen to take one side or the other. However, it is not my place to determine whether anyone has the legal right to leave. The task Caesar has given me is not to permit anybody to leave Italy. It really does not matter what I think of your plan, since I am not permitted to allow you to go. I think you ought to write to Caesar and ask his permission. I have no doubt that you will be successful, especially as you assure us of our friendship.[12]

Some of this may have been a smokescreen, for Cicero had secretly arranged some time before for a ship to be ready to transport him. When he finally slipped away, it was to go directly to Pompey.

MACEDONIA

Caesar came back from the Spanish campaign in the autumn of 49 BC. En route he had to deal with a mutiny amongst the *Ninth* Legion encamped in northern Italy. The soldiers complained that they had not yet received the rewards he had promised them, but the real cause was said to be the tight discipline that prevented them from plundering. Boredom during a lull in the fighting fostered the discontent. Caesar arrested the ringleaders and executed a proportion of them, restoring order very quickly.[13]

There was no consul to preside over the consular elections for 48 BC. Caesar suggested that the praetor Lepidus be allowed to perform this task, but the college of augurs refused to accept this. Presumably Antony had voted in favour, and Pompey and Cicero were both in Macedonia, but there must have been enough other members of the priesthood to block this idea. Instead, Caesar had Lepidus declare him dictator and held the elections himself. It was common for a dictator to be appointed to oversee voting when a consul was unavailable, but never before had one been named by a praetor. The legality was questionable, but there was no other obvious solution. The senators with Pompey did not presume to hold elections of their own and instead simply extended the command of all elected magistrates on their side.[14]

Caesar was elected to a second consulship, with Publius Servilius Vatia Isauricus as his colleague and, that task done, then resigned the dictatorship. After eleven days he left Rome and went to the army mustering at Brundisium, eager to press on with the war. Antony and his other subordinates had gathered a considerable number of transport ships, but there were still nowhere near enough to carry the entire army and only a dozen warships to escort them. Cutting baggage to the bare minimum, Caesar managed to cram 15,000 legionaries and 500 cavalry into the available ships. On 4 January 48 BC he set sail, reaching Epirus and disembarking without meeting the enemy.

Antony does not seem to have been elected to any magistracy for this year, but continued to wield *imperium* either as an extension of his extraordinary tribunate or now as one of Caesar's legates. He did not go with the expedition to Greece, but was one of those left behind with instructions to bring more soldiers as soon as possible. This proved longer than expected. Caesar had sneaked across because the Pompeians had not expected him to risk the voyage and begin a campaign in winter. Now they were waiting, with a fleet of some 500 warships under the overall command of Bibulus.[15]

For a while it was impossible to break the blockade and Bibulus showed himself an especially ruthless opponent, burning captured ships with their crews still on board. Some of this was deliberate atrocity intended to terrify the enemy. There was also the long years of jealousy and loathing for Caesar himself, and perhaps the bitterness of a father whose sons had been murdered. Oared warships carried a very large crew of rowers in proportion to their size and there was little space for food and fresh water. This meant that a navy was heavily dependent on land bases. Caesar tried to break the blockade by seizing the ports and coastline suitable for landing. It was a tough campaign and at some point the exhausted Bibulus fell ill and died.[16]

The blockade continued unabated, preventing news as well as supplies and men from reaching Caesar. As the weeks dragged on, he is said to have decided that the only way to get things moving was to return to Italy himself. Sneaking out of camp, he secretly set sail in a small boat accompanied by a handful of slaves. In spite of his immense self-confidence – as the storm grew worse he assured the captain of the vessel that everything would be fine because he carried 'Caesar and Caesar's good fortune' – the weather proved too bad and they had to turn back. Another story claims that he then sent messengers to give orders summoning the rest of the army. The order was to be given first to Gabinius, and if he did not instantly obey, they were to give it next to Antony, and finally to a third officer if Antony failed to act.[17]

The last story is probably an invention, for there is no good evidence that the loyalty of his subordinates was ever in question. It is possible that Caesar became nervous, although as usual his *Commentaries* present a picture of perfect assurance in his ultimate success. In fact, Antony does seem to have worked hard to get across the Adriatic, because the Pompeian squadrons not only patrolled the sea, but also raided Brundisium itself and tried to close the port altogether. On one occasion Antony set up an ambush, luring the enemy ships close into the harbour and then overwhelming them with a swarm of small rowing boats packed with soldiers. After this success, and finding it difficult to land on shore and fetch water without falling prey to Caesarean cavalry patrols, the Pompeian squadron withdrew.[18]

Antony finally broke the blockade and led some 10,000 legionaries and 800 cavalry to land at Lissus in the north of Greece on 10 April. It was the largest independent command of his career so far and he handled it competently, but it was short-lived. Caesar managed to hear of his arrival and the two halves of the Caesarean army were united before Pompey could intervene. They were still heavily outnumbered by the Pompeians, especially in cavalry, but had the advantage that most of their legionaries were veterans confident of victory. Caesar offered battle and, when Pompey declined to risk an engagement, he decided to strike at the Pompeians' main supply depot at Dyrrachium on the coast. His opponent swiftly realised what was happening, and managed to get there first.

A surprise attack having failed, Caesar turned instead to blockade, trying to hem the Pompeians in against the sea by building a line of fortifications on the high ground. Pompey responded by ordering his men to construct their own fortified line, aiming to build it quicker and so prevent the enemy from completely encircling them. Caesar's men toiled just as they had done at Alesia. Antony was now in command of the *Ninth* Legion, the same veteran formation that had mutinied the previous year. The tough old soldiers – the formation had been raised before Caesar arrived in Gaul in 58 BC and had seen constant service since then, being described as 'veterans of exceptional courage' – once again laboured and fought hard.[19]

There was a series of small-scale engagements to control key ground on which to build the fortifications. Early on the *Ninth* seized a hilltop position and began to fortify it, but were soon under a hail of missiles from enemy skirmishers and artillery. As casualties mounted Caesar ordered a withdrawal, but when the legionaries pulled back they were hard-pressed by the enemy. Troops were brought up to cover the retreat. Then Caesar decided that he did not want the enemy to think they had chased his men away. Antony was ordered to charge back up the hill, which he did, the *Ninth* routing their pursuers and inflicting heavy losses. After this, they were able to retreat unmolested.[20]

Pompey had a large force of cavalry, and in the confined plain outside Dyrrachium there were limited supplies of forage and so the horses began to suffer. Yet overall his men had more food than Caesar's soldiers, who were making do with minimal rations. Some gathered a local root called charax and baked it into a substitute for bread. Pompey had far more men, and since he was on the inside, these had a shorter distance of fortified line to build. It was a race Caesar's men could not win and it soon became clear that they would not be able to complete the encirclement. Even so, they repulsed a succession of Pompeian assaults on sectors of the line. Three cohorts of the *Ninth* managed to hold one fort for an entire day, although in the process almost every man was wounded. Caesar claims that 30,000 enemy arrows were collected from within the fort and the shield of one centurion was struck by no fewer than 120 missiles. This man lost an eye during the fighting, but remained on his feet and kept fighting. Antony led up the reserves, which finally drove the attackers away.[21]

Yet the pressure continued and, after a lull when Pompey's men strengthened their line, he launched another assault that finally punched a hole in a vulnerable section of Caesar's line. Caesar countered with an attack of his own on what seemed to be an isolated enemy camp containing a single legion. The *Ninth* was part of a force of thirty-three cohorts sent to overwhelm this position, but after initial success the attackers got lost and the attack bogged down. Failure turned to panic when the enemy rushed reinforcements to the spot and drove the Caesareans back. Casualties were heavy – 960 soldiers and thirty-two tribunes and centurions. The Pompeians also captured thirty-two standards as well as some prisoners, who were subsequently executed.[22]

It was a serious setback and forced Caesar to acknowledge that he had failed in his objective. There was little point remaining where he was and allowing the soldiers to suffer with no prospect of success. Under cover of darkness he sent away his baggage train and his wounded under the guard of a single legion. The main part of the army followed later, leaving only a rearguard, which managed to convince the enemy that nothing was amiss. After a while these, too, followed on. At last Pompey realised what was happening and sent his cavalry in pursuit. Caesar's horsemen were outnumbered and their mounts probably in as poor a condition as those of the enemy cavalry. However, they were closely supported by a strong force of legionaries and able to drive off the pursuers.[23]

Caesar's men now marched through country untouched by the recent campaign and found it much easier to gather supplies. The town of Gomphi refused to let them in, so he stormed the place and allowed his men to sack it in a drunken orgy of looting and destruction that was credited with restoring both their morale and health. It was also a dreadful warning that persuaded other communities in the path of the army to be more welcoming.[24]

Pompey followed. Dyrrachium had been a clear victory and

vindicated his strategy of avoiding battle and slowly wearing down the enemy army. Caesar had left the coast to march inland and was now cut off from Italy and any reinforcement or supply convoy. Pompey had twice as many legionaries, and many more cavalry and allied soldiers. Some of the senior senators in his camp urged him to ignore Caesar and return to Italy, but he was reluctant to leave the campaign unfinished and permit his enemy to escape. Therefore the main question was whether to continue to avoid battle and harass the Caesarean army, whittling it away until it withered from lack of food or was forced to surrender. This would take time, but seems to have been Pompey's own choice. The other option was to rely on his advantage in numbers and crush the enemy in battle.

That was the view of most of the senior senators and some whispered that Pompey only wanted to prolong the campaign because he revelled in exercising supreme command. Confident of success and eager to enjoy its spoils, they put steady pressure on the commander to risk a battle. This was the great disadvantage that came with the political benefits of having so many distinguished men in one camp. Cato was sent off on detached duty largely because Pompey became tired of his acidic comments. Cicero was equally unpopular, for he found himself almost as disgusted by the leading Pompeians as he had been by Caesar's followers. Unlike his opponent, Pompey did not have a completely free hand. His character was also different, for he craved popularity. For whatever reason, he chose to give battle. Caesar readily accepted the offer.[25]

On 9 August 48 BC, near the small town of Pharsalus, Pompey formed his 45,000 legionaries into three lines of cohorts, each one ten ranks deep. His right flank rested on the River Enipeus, but the left was on an open plain and it was here that he massed most of his 7,000 cavalry, placing them under the command of Labienus, Caesar's old legate from Gaul. Caesar matched the frontage of the enemy infantry, forming his 22,000 legionaries in three lines of cohorts, each of which was in a shallower formation. Mark Antony was given command of the left flank, resting on the river. On the very left of the formation his *Ninth* Legion was so depleted in numbers that it was merged with the *Eighth* Legion to form a more viable unit. Caesar had about 1,000 horsemen to face the massed enemy cavalry.

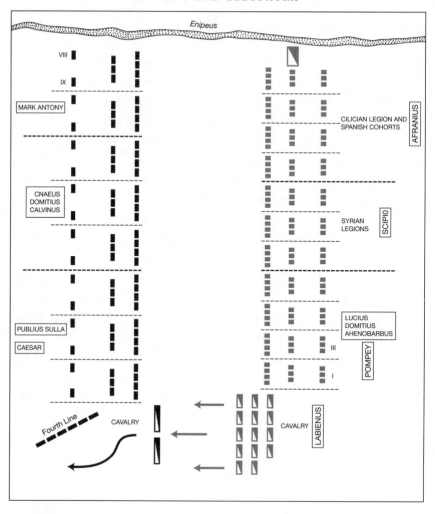

The Battle of Pharsalus, first phase

Caesar took six cohorts from the third line of cohorts and stationed them behind his mounted troops. In the dust thrown up by so many marching feet and hoofs, and with the cavalry screening their front, the Pompeians do not seem to have noticed this deployment.

Pompey relied solely on the great cavalry attack to sweep Caesar's horsemen away and then roll up the right flank of his army. It was not a subtle plan, but it could well have worked. Instead, his inexperienced cavalry had merged into one great unmanoeuvrable mass by the time they drove back the Caesarean horse. Suddenly the

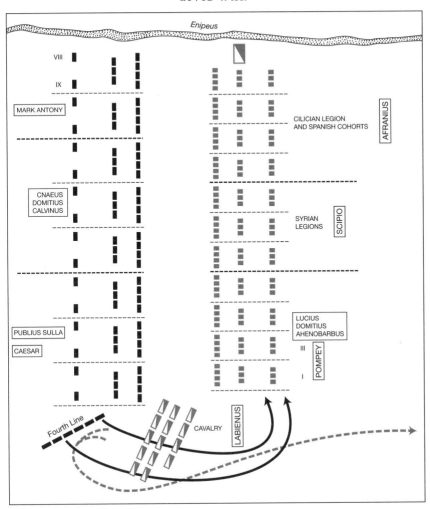

The Battle of Pharsalus, second phase

cohorts of the fourth line advanced through the clouds of dust and stampeded the Pompeian cavalry into a panicked flight. In the centre the Pompeian infantry had not charged to meet the Caesarean legionaries. They were slowly driven back, and when the fourth line swung round against the flank left exposed by the rout of the cavalry, the entire army began to dissolve.

We know little about what Antony did during the battle, but it is safe to say that he performed well, and Plutarch claims that his valour was conspicuous throughout the campaign. His role was not one that required any great tactical decision making, for all the key moves were made on the right flank under Caesar's direct supervision. Nevertheless, the flanks were considered places of honour and it was a mark of trust that Caesar gave him this major responsibility. It marked him out as one of Caesar's senior subordinates. Later, there was criticism that he was overly bloodthirsty during the pursuit, killing men Caesar had wanted to capture, but this may simply be propaganda. Ahenobarbus was one of the most conspicuous Pompeians to be killed and Cicero later blamed Antony for his execution, but the majority surrendered or escaped.[26]

Pompey was one of the first to flee the battle. When his grand cavalry attack failed, he does not seem to have had an alternative plan. He had been reluctant to fight in the first place, and now despaired. He made his way to the coast, gathered his family and a small force and set sail. For a while he was uncertain of where to go, but determined to rebuild his strength and continue the struggle. Soon he thought of Egypt, remembering his past support for Auletes and his family, the presence of the Gabinians as the basis for a new army and the country's wealth and resources.[27]

When Pompey the Great came to Egypt it was not as conqueror, but a fugitive.

[XIII]

CAESAR

Pompey's small flotilla of ships reached the coast near Mount Casius on 28 September 48 BC, just a day short of his fifty-ninth birthday. Ptolemy XIII's army was waiting for him, the boy king splendidly attired as a commander, but the faction that controlled him had already decided how to welcome the visitor. Pompey's friendship no longer seemed so attractive in spite of his long connection with Auletes. He was coming to Egypt in the hope of rebuilding his power, which meant that he must take from the kingdom and had little to give in return. He would want money, grain and men, and some of the king's advisers feared that the Gabinians might well be willing to join him. Ptolemy XIII's government risked being stripped of the very resources that guaranteed its power. Even then, Pompey was more than likely to be defeated again and his conqueror would scarcely be well disposed towards them. Instead, there was an opportunity to win Caesar's favour.

A small boat put out carrying a welcoming party consisting of the army commander Achillas and two Roman officers from amongst the Gabinians – one of them the tribune Lucius Septimius, who had served under Pompey back in the 60s. It was a small delegation in an unimpressive craft and scarcely a mark of honour, but they claimed that the conditions made it impossible to employ a more dignified vessel or to permit Pompey to bring his own ship to the shore. Instead, they invited him to climb down and join them, so that they could take him to be properly greeted by the king.

Pompey agreed. He and his companions may well have been suspicious, but it would have destroyed what little prestige he had left to seem frightened by the representatives of a mere client king. His wife Cornelia and most of his staff watched as Pompey climbed down into the boat and was rowed ashore. On the way, he spotted something familiar about Septimius and, addressing him as 'comrade', asked whether they knew each other.

The tribune's response was to stab his old commander in the back. Achillas joined in the attack, as presumably did the centurion. It was a brutal, clumsy murder and afterwards Pompey's head was hacked off and taken to the king. Another senator was taken prisoner and later executed. Ptolemy's warships then launched an attack on the Roman flotilla and several ships were destroyed before the rest managed to escape. (Thirteen centuries later, Dante would consign the boy alongside Cain and Judas to the circle of hell reserved for traitors.)[1]

Caesar arrived in Alexandria a few days later. Ptolemy's court must have been aware that he was on his way, because Theodotus was waiting for him and triumphantly produced Pompey's head and his signet ring. These did not prompt the hoped for reaction. Pompey had been Caesar's enemy, but before that he had been his ally and son-in-law; he was also a Roman senator of immense prestige and fame who had been cut down on the whim of a foreign king and his sinister advisers. It is arguable whether or not Caesar could have extended his vaunted 'clemency' to his most powerful adversary, and in any case unlikely that Pompey could have brought himself to accept it.

Caesar refused to look at the severed head and wept when he saw the familiar ring. His horror and disgust may or may not have been feigned. Cynics said that it was very convenient for him, since his enemy was now dead and yet someone else would take the blame for the crime. His emotions were probably mixed, with relief that his opponent could not renew the struggle mingled with a sadness at the loss of a rival and a former friend. With Crassus and Pompey now both dead, there was really no other Roman left with whom it was worth competing.[2]

If the boy king's advisers were disappointed at Caesar's reaction, they were dismayed at what he did next. For the Romans disembarked and then marched in a column to take up residence in part of the complex of royal palaces. Caesar was consul and he proceeded in full pomp, with twelve lictors carrying the fasces walking ahead of him. It was a blatant display of Roman confidence and authority, suggesting the arrival not of an ally, but of an occupier. The Alexandrians had a fierce sense of their own independence. Some of the royal soldiers left to garrison the city immediately protested and crowds soon gathered to jeer the Romans. Over the next few days, several legionaries wandering on their own were attacked and killed by mobs.

Caesar was not at the head of a large army and had only two legions with him. One, the *Sixth*, was a veteran formation, but after years of heavy campaigning it now mustered fewer than 1,000 soldiers. The *Twenty-Seventh* had about 2,200 men, which meant that it was below half its theoretical strength. Its legionaries were far less experienced and the formation had originally been raised by the Pompeians, but had been renumbered when it was captured and the men swore a new oath to Caesar. To support these Caesar had 800 cavalry, who may well have been the bodyguard unit of Germans he usually kept with him. Horses are far more difficult to transport than soldiers and there is a fair chance that most or all of these men were transported without their mounts.[3]

It is tempting to criticise Caesar for tactlessness in parading through the city and antagonising the Alexandrians, especially since he had so few soldiers and could not hope to dominate a population numbering hundreds of thousands. Some would see this as habitual Roman disdain for the feelings of other nations and unthinking arrogance reinforced by his own recent victories. It was more likely calculation. Caesar had no particular reason to expect hostility when he came to Egypt, but knew he had only a small force actually with him. The murder of Pompey was intended to please him, but could also be seen as a threat. Had he slipped quietly through the streets of Alexandria the impression would have been one of fear. This is unlikely to have made the population less hostile, for they had a long tradition of resenting Roman influence, and it could easily have made them more aggressive.

There were several reasons for him to stop in Egypt. Although eager to pursue Pompey, he had already paused in several communities, raising money, dealing with local problems and also placating and pardoning those who had supported the Pompeians. He needed the eastern provinces to accept his supremacy and to be stable, for confusion would more easily provide opportunities for his remaining enemies to continue the civil war. Above all else, Caesar needed funds. The Republic had been massively disrupted by two years of conflict and he needed to find the money to ensure that everything kept running. One major expense was paying his army, which had swollen massively in size as Pompeian soldiers surrendered. It would have been unwise to demobilise these men, and even more dangerous if they were not regularly paid and provided for. The Ptolemaic kingdom was wealthy, offering grain to feed soldiers and revenue to pay them — the same things that had attracted Pompey. Caesar needed to be sure that these resources were kept under his own control and did not fall to recalcitrant Pompeians.

Caesar decided to stay, and soon the decision was reinforced when a change in the weather made it impossible for his ships to leave. Soon after landing he had sent orders for more legions to join him, but this would inevitably take time. At some point, Ptolemy XIII himself and much of his court including Pothinus also arrived in Alexandria. Achillas and the main army of 22,000 men remained to the east for the moment, watching Cleopatra's forces.[4]

The Roman consul informed the king and his court that he and his sister must disband their forces 'and settle their dispute through law rather than weapons with himself as judge'. There was also private business. Caesar declared that the heirs of Auletes still owed him 17.5 million denarii according to the agreement of 59 BC and also the loans to Rabirius Postumus, which he himself had underwritten. He demanded 10 million of this to be paid to him immediately to support his army.[5]

Pothinus was by now the king's *dioecetes* — the same post held by Rabirius Postumus until he had fled from Egypt — and so the finances were his direct responsibility. Caesar's very presence was unwelcome, his interference in a civil war that seemed virtually won was appalling and his demands more than could readily be met. It may also have been politically dangerous for the regime that controlled the king to be seen to give in to Roman pressure. Pothinus suggested to Caesar that he ought to leave Egypt for he must have more pressing business elsewhere. For a while — perhaps for weeks — there was an uneasy truce. Caesar occupied part of the royal palaces and brought the king and his courtiers under his control to show the people that the violence was provoked by 'a few private individuals and gang-sters' and not by the boy himself. Pothinus met Caesar's demands to feed his legionaries, but gave them the poorest grain he could find. Feasts in the palaces were served on old tableware in direct contrast to the normal opulence of the Ptolemaic court. It was a double message, telling Caesar that his demands could not quickly be met and suggesting to the locals that the Romans were bleeding the kingdom dry.[6]

THE LOVERS

At some point, Cleopatra arrived. Caesar barely mentions her in his own brief account of his time in Alexandria and the fuller narrative written by one of his officers adds very little information about her. Neither suggest she played any important role in events and do not even hint at intimacy between the Roman consul and the Hellenistic queen, but this is in keeping with the generally impersonal style of Caesar's *Commentaries*. Plutarch and Dio both say that the two had been in contact for some time by messenger, although they differ over who initiated this.[7]

If Caesar was to arbitrate in the dispute between brother and sister, then it was natural that he should want to speak to both of them. Even if he chose to back Ptolemy XIII, he would need to deal with Cleopatra or risk the civil war between them continuing and thus leaving Egypt unstable and a source of potential trouble in the future. There was actually little to recommend such a full endorsement of the boy king and the men who controlled him. These had so far failed to deliver properly the supplies and money he wanted, and the attitude of Pothinus was scarcely that of a loyal and suitably subservient ally. Wherever he had gone, Caesar issued judgements as he saw fit, usually emphasising his clemency, but always making clear that this was something he could give or withhold. Backing Ptolemy XIII could easily have seemed to be giving in to coercion. It would also have aligned him very closely with Pompey's murderers. At the very least, he needed to make sure that Ptolemy and his court worked hard to win his approval.

Until Caesar's arrival, Cleopatra's bid to regain power had stalled and looked likely to end in failure. She clearly lacked the military power to defeat her brother's army and there is no trace at this stage of major political defections to her cause. Caesar had relatively few soldiers with him, but he represented the power of the Roman Republic in an especially real sense, since he was victorious in Rome's civil war. His public disgust at Pompey's murder, his refusal fully to endorse her brother's regime and, most of all, his willingness to talk to her all suggested that he might be persuaded to favour her. In a way now traditional for the Ptolemies, Cleopatra quite naturally wanted to harness Roman power to support her own ambition.

The twenty-one-year-old exiled queen left her army. It is not heard of again, suggesting that the soldiers dispersed. Perhaps the money to pay them had run out or, since she did not have enough strength to win, Cleopatra decided it would be better to appear as the pitiful exile preferring to rely on Roman justice rather than force. Caesar may have formally summoned her to Alexandria, and is certainly likely to have known that she was coming. That did not mean that he could ensure her safe arrival. The Romans controlled only a small part of the city. Outside that area were many soldiers from the king's army. Pothinus, Theodotus and indeed the young Ptolemy himself are unlikely to have welcomed his older sister. Given the past willingness of the Ptolemies to slaughter their own family, the more or less discreet murder of a sister was not only possible, but likely.

There is no good reason to disbelieve the stories that Cleopatra sailed secretly into the harbour at Alexandria, using stealth or bribery to avoid her brother's guards. Only Plutarch tells the famous story that she was then taken across the harbour in a small boat and into the palace by a single faithful courtier, Apollodorus of Sicily. They waited until night fell, so as not to be seen, and the young queen was concealed in a bag used for carrying laundry – not the oriental carpet so beloved of film-makers. Apollodorus carried the bag into the palace where Caesar was staying and brought her to his room. Once there, he could undo the tie fastening at the top of the bag, so that the material dropped down as the queen stood up, revealing herself almost like a dancer popping out of a cake.

Some reject the story as a romantic invention, pointing out that Caesar would scarcely have permitted a stranger carrying a mysterious burden to come into his room. Yet their earlier correspondence makes it likely that he knew that either the queen herself or a message was on its way and so demolishes this objection. Apollodorus' arrival would not then have been so unexpected. Others would modify the story, suggesting that instead of hiding in a bag, the young queen wore a long hooded cloak, throwing this back to show herself when brought into Caesar's presence. This is possible, but there is no direct evidence for it. The appearance of a story in just a single source does not automatically mean that it is an invention, especially since the accounts describing Caesar and Cleopatra in Alexandria are quite brief. It was in the best interest of the king and his advisers to prevent his sister from reaching Caesar and beyond the latter's power to guarantee her safety until she was actually with him. That she came without any ceremony and with at least a degree of stealth makes perfect sense.[8]

Cleopatra was staking everything on winning Caesar's favour. It was a desperate gamble, but her invasion had been blocked and this was her last resort. It was also a courageous move, for there was a real risk that she could fall into her brother's hands and, even if she did not, there was no assurance that her pleas would be successful. Perhaps Dio was right and she had recognised Caesar's 'disposition, which was very susceptible, to such an extent that he had his intrigues with ever so many women – with all, doubtless, who came his way' and so 'trusted in her beauty for all her claims to the throne'. Both Plutarch and Dio see her as deliberately planning the encounter, doing everything to attract the Roman consul. In this context, suddenly revealing herself from an opened sack was dramatic and flirtatious. Dio claimed that she had carefully dressed and made herself up to appear at once attractive, regal and distressed. It was a performance, but just because it was calculated does not mean that it was not also exciting for both of them.[9]

She was twenty-one, had already been driven from her realm and was now hoping to return. The affair with Cnaeus Pompey is unlikely to be more than gossip, and the marriage to her brother may not have happened and could certainly not have been consummated. While many of the Ptolemies took mistresses and other lovers, the same licence was not granted to their wives and daughters. It is more than likely that Cleopatra was a virgin when she met Caesar, and that he and Mark Antony were the only two lovers she ever took. It was no coincidence that each was the most powerful man in the world at the time. Inexperienced perhaps, Cleopatra was clever and self-confident in her own beauty and charm. It really does not matter which of these was the more powerful, they combined to make her extremely attractive. She hoped to win Caesar's backing and probably felt that seducing him was the best way.

Caesar was fifty-two, more than a decade into his third marriage and with a long series of extramarital affairs behind him. He was a serial seducer of other senators' wives – as we have seen, Pompey, Crassus and Gabinius were amongst the many he had cuckolded – and was supposed to have slept with plenty of chieftains' daughters and wives during the years in Gaul. Behind his womanising was more than a simple desire to have sex with lots of attractive women. His longest affair was with Servilia, a woman as ambitious, intelligent, witty, well educated and attractive as he was himself. Caesar liked excitement, perhaps even an element of danger. Cleopatra was a lot like him in so many ways, and like Servilia was much more his equal. She was also a queen and there is an added appeal to the idea of royalty, especially in a member of a dynasty who could claim a connection to Alexander the Great.[10]

In spite of the big age difference, Caesar was still considered a handsome man, even if his hairline was rapidly receding. He was a dandy, very fussy about his appearance and a man who set the fashions at Rome, and was lean and fit after long years spent on campaign. His charm was very difficult for anyone to resist. He was experienced, utterly self-confident and now controlled the most powerful state in the world. There was a lot to attract the young Cleopatra.[11]

The tendency then and now is to see this encounter as the seduction of the Roman by the eastern queen. Sometimes this is painted in damning moral terms, with Cleopatra as little more than a whore. More recently, fashions have changed and, instead, historians emphasise an empowered woman taking control of her own life. Each of these views contains an element of truth, but neither is fair either to the queen herself or the situation. Cleopatra certainly used her charm and her body to get what she wanted. She really had nothing else left.

Yet for all that the twenty-one-year-old hoped to seduce, it was Caesar who was far more experienced and was used to taking what he wanted. Cleopatra was young, physically very attractive, lively and charming. He would have wanted to bed her even if she had not been so desperate to gain his support. Politically – and people like Caesar and Cleopatra would never entirely forget politics – she would be a useful asset, showing her brother and his advisers that he had other options than supporting their regime. Both Caesar and Cleopatra wanted something from the other, and were willing to seduce and manipulate to get this. He was no doubt fully aware of this and, given her intelligence, there is a fair chance that so was she. Physical attraction was no doubt there and very probably on both sides, for in spite of his age Caesar's success with women shows that his charm was very real. Passion seems certain and genuine love most likely developed. The politics added extra spice and gave the whole affair an excitement that was probably exhilarating to both of them.

Cleopatra arrived in the evening and spent the night in Caesar's bed. There is no record that she knew Latin and they presumably spoke Greek to each other, for Caesar was fluent in the language. The next morning Ptolemy XIII and his advisers discovered that his exiled sister had returned to Alexandria. It must quickly have sunk in that she was offering the Roman consul something that they could not match, still less surpass.

The boy king rushed out of the palace, tore off his royal diadem and shrieked of betrayal to the crowd that rapidly gathered. Caesar had him brought back inside, which only turned the crowd into an angry mob, but the people calmed for a while when the Roman made a speech to them. Soon afterwards he announced that Auletes' will would be fully enforced. Ptolemy XIII and Cleopatra would rule Egypt jointly. In addition, their younger brother Ptolemy XIV and their sister Arsinoe were to rule Cyprus. The latter was clearly in the palace by this time, although there is no evidence for when and how she arrived. Ptolemy XIV may also have been with the court, but none of our sources says anything about him at this time and he was still only eleven or ten years old.[12]

This was a major concession, returning to the family territory annexed by Rome a decade earlier. It is possible that Caesar was readier to do this because the province had been set up by Cato, serving on the special commission created for him by Clodius. Alternatively, his concern may have been more practical. Cyprus had been an extra burden to the governor of Cilicia, was difficult for him to supervise and there had been cases of severe misbehaviour and extortion by Roman businessmen operating there. Throughout his career Caesar showed concern for protecting provincials from mistreatment, or he may simply have thought this was an effective way of keeping the island stable and secure.[13]

THE ALEXANDRIAN WAR

At a stroke Ptolemy XIII was expected to accept as co-ruler the sister who had tried to exclude him from power altogether. Pothinus and the other inner circle of advisers stood to lose even more. To strengthen his own hand he sent messengers to Achillas and summoned the royal army to Alexandria. It was a provocative move, and Caesar arranged for two senior courtiers, who had in the past gone on Auletes' behalf to Rome, to go to the army. Achillas was in no mood for talking and had the men attacked. One was killed and the other badly wounded, but carried away by his attendants.[14]

Caesar did not have enough men to risk battle outside the city and could not respond to this provocation. When Achillas arrived in the city he launched an assault almost immediately. Caesar's men were able to hold their own after heavy fighting, largely because the restricted space made it difficult for the enemy to take advantage of their numbers. In the harbour were some seventy Ptolemaic warships. These included the squadron of fifty that had been sent to support the Pompeians. For much of the time these had been led with great success by Cnaeus Pompey himself, but when news of the defeat at Pharsalus had arrived they had abandoned him to return home. Now, Achillas was eager to seize them and then use them to prevent Caesar from retreating or getting reinforcements by sea.

The Romans struck first. After heavy fighting, Caesar's men were able to secure control of the warships long enough to burn them. In the confusion the fire spread to the buildings near the harbour. Several were destroyed, including a warehouse used for storing scrolls from the Library. Achillas quickly threw a cordon round the areas occupied by the Romans. He raised a militia from the Alexandrians and seems to have found plenty of willing volunteers. The buildings in this part of Alexandria were large and strongly built of stone. Both sides built stone ramparts across the streets to block enemy attacks and also fortified the houses themselves, knocking down interior walls with battering rams where necessary. Achillas left the bulk of the labouring and guard duty to the militia, keeping his own soldiers in reserve for major assaults and to meet any Roman counter-attack. For the moment Caesar's men held their own, but the pressure steadily mounted.[15]

Throughout the early stage of the fighting, Cleopatra, Ptolemy, Arsinoe, Pothinus, Theodotus and other courtiers all lived together with Caesar in the beleaguered palace. Caesar supervised the fighting by day and in the evenings returned to dine. At night he had the twenty-one-year-old queen as lively companion and lover. In spite of this prospect, for the first time in his life he took to staying up late, drinking and feasting with his friends and companions, although it was claimed that this was through fear of assassins. His barber overheard Pothinus plotting murder, and this and other reports were enough for Caesar to order the eunuch's execution. That did not mean, however, that Caesar had no more enemies within the palace.[16]

Caesar and Cleopatra were lovers, but in spite of this he maintained his decision that she should rule jointly with her brother. Perhaps this was simply politic, but since he was already besieged and the royal army and most of the city were hostile there was no obvious reason for such caution. It is an indication that although he was fighting a war against supporters of Ptolemy, he was not so besotted with his new mistress that he was happy to give her everything. In any case, Cleopatra no doubt was confident that she could dominate her younger sibling. We do not know how she spent her days, whether she watched as her lover went out to fight. Many of the combats during these days would have been readily visible from the higher buildings.

Arsinoe had been offered joint rule of Cyprus, but clearly decided that there was an opportunity for far higher things. She slipped away from the palace accompanied by her tutor, the eunuch Ganymede, and perhaps other advisers, and joined Achillas. There was some friction as the general resented taking orders from a teenage girl and her teacher. This problem was solved in the traditional way for the Ptolemies when Achillas was murdered. Ganymede took his place and Arsinoe was proclaimed queen. No mention seems to have been made of a consort, but perhaps it was simply assumed that she would rule with her brother, Ptolemy XIII.[17]

The eunuch tutor probably had no military experience, but in the event prosecuted the siege well. Seawater was diverted to run into the cisterns used by the Romans, rendering their water supply undrinkable. Caesar set his men to digging new wells, and fortunately they were able to find them. He had now been reinforced by the *Thirty-Seventh* Legion, another former Pompeian formation, which managed to sail into the harbour, bringing supplies of food, as well as military equipment including artillery.

Ganymede decided that he must cut Caesar off from the sea. Considerable ingenuity was exercised in assembling a fleet. Patrol boats from the Nile were brought to the city and old, half-forgotten warships resting in various royal dockyards were found and repaired. Beams were taken from the roofs of major buildings including gymnasia and reshaped into oars. Yet it was easier to gather ships than it was to train the crews that would operate them to the peak of efficiency. In a series of battles fought in and around the great harbour, Caesar's outnumbered vessels – many of them manned by Rhodians and other Greek allies – more than held their own.[18]

Caesar decided that controlling Pharos Island was the key to holding the harbour and keeping access open to further reinforcements. His men had seized a small foothold on the island early in the siege. Now he launched an attack, landing ten cohorts of legionaries and capturing a larger area. On the next day a follow-up attack to secure the long bridge began well. Then a group of sailors were panicked and the confusion and fear spread to the legionaries, who fled back to the boats from which they had landed. Caesar was already on board one vessel when a stream of fugitives swarmed over the side. He dived into the sea and swam to the safety of another boat. Some sources say that he left his reddish-purple general's cloak behind and that this was carried off as a trophy by the enemy. Suetonius denies this, but most accounts agreed that the middle-aged commander showed remarkable nonchalance, swimming with his left hand above the water to protect some important documents.[19]

Whether or not Cleopatra watched this encounter – and at such a distance she could anyway have seen little detail – she must have known fear over the fate of her lover. If Caesar died, then the Romans would be defeated and she was unlikely to survive. The siege continued into the first weeks of 47 BC. At this point a deputation of leading Alexandrians came to Caesar and begged him to send Ptolemy to them, since they were weary of the tyranny of Arsinoe and her tutor. Perhaps they were genuinely unpopular, although it is equally likely that the men involved were simply out of favour with the new queen and hoped for better from her brother. The struggle for power amongst the royal family and the elite who hoped to manipulate them never slackened for a moment during the fighting with the Romans. There was never any question of uniting against the foreign occupier.

Caesar let the boy go, even though the lad pleaded not to be sent from his presence. Once free, and his sister removed or at least made subordinate, Ptolemy readily urged his army on to fight against the Romans. Ganymede disappears from our sources and may have perished in the power struggle. Some of Caesar's officers are supposed to have mocked his naivety in being fooled by a child. The author of the *Alexandrian War* instead believed that he had cynically let Ptolemy go to divide the enemy command.[20]

Things were turning in Caesar's favour, and soon he heard of the approach of a relief army, which had marched overland and stormed

Pelusium. This force may not have included a single Roman and was led by Mithridates of Pergamum – the child of one of Mithridates of Pontus' generals and, rumour said, the bastard son of the king himself. Once again, Antipater led a Jewish contingent on behalf of Hyrcanus II the High Priest. Ptolemy 'led' the bulk of his army away from Alexandria to meet them. Caesar followed. In the street fighting in the capital, the Gabinians and the rest of the royal soldiers had performed well. In such situations the burden of command falls mainly on junior leaders. In the more open country of the Delta, they were quickly outmanoeuvred and out-fought. The successive changes of high command were unlikely to have helped.

Caesar won a rapid victory. The royal army was destroyed and the young Ptolemy XIII drowned in the Nile as he fled. Arsinoe was taken prisoner; Pothinus and Achillas were already dead. Theodotus, the remaining man held most responsible for the murder of Pompey, somehow managed to escape to Syria.[21]

Cleopatra had gambled and won. She had gone to Caesar, becoming his ally and his lover. Now he confirmed her as queen, but a marriage was arranged to Ptolemy XIV because it was against tradition for a woman to rule alone. He was young, and she would make sure that no faction of manipulative courtiers would coalesce around him. The king and queen were given Cyprus as well as Egypt, restoring something of the glory of the kingdom in past years.

Caesar spent longer than he needed in Egypt after the war was won. For a time, perhaps even for months, he and Cleopatra took a long cruise down the Nile. The Ptolemies were famous for their vast pleasure boats, but enough other vessels crammed with soldiers accompanied them to turn this into a grand procession. It was a statement of the power and legitimacy of the queen – and to a lesser extent her brother.[22]

Yet Caesar did not have to go in person to make such a statement. He would leave behind three legions to ensure that his nominee remained in power and she did not become too independent. There was a political dimension to the cruise, but it would be a mistake to see that as its sole, even main purpose. Caesar had been almost constantly on campaign for more than a decade. Weary, facing a world in which he must single-handedly sort out the problems of the Republic, which no longer contained rivals worth competing against, the appeal of a pleasure cruise is obvious. In Alexandria he had seen the tomb and corpse of Alexander. Now he could view the antiquities of ancient Egypt, which intrigued Greeks and Romans alike. All the while he had the company of his clever, exciting and beautiful young lover, helping him to forget his age and his cares. In hindsight, the months Caesar spent in Egypt were a serious mistake, allowing the surviving Pompeians time to recover and renew the civil war. Yet in the circumstances it is hard to blame him.

Cleopatra was pregnant by the time her lover left, called away to deal with a new war in Asia Minor.

[XIV]

MASTER OF HORSE

Antony had done well at Pharsalus, but in its aftermath Caesar once again preferred to employ him in an essentially political rather than a military role and he was sent back to Italy. Definite news of Pompey's defeat took some time to reach Rome. Caesar seems to have been reluctant to boast of triumphing over such an illustrious Roman or perhaps wanted to delay the news until Pompey himself was taken or killed. Reports came slowly and were mingled with plenty of rumour, so that the Senate's initial response was cautious. Antony landed in Brundisium in the autumn of 48 BC, bringing with him a substantial part of the army from Macedonia. By this time the scale of Caesar's victory was evident and the senators were desperate to show their loyalty by voting him honours.

Caesar was given a range of powers, including the right to declare war and peace, and to deal as he chose with captured Pompeians. He was also named dictator for the second time. This was not a short-term expedient, allowing him to hold elections, but a means of making legal the supremacy that he already in fact possessed. The traditional six-month limit to the dictatorship was extended to a year. Sulla had had no time limit to his dictatorship so this was marginally more moderate.[1]

The decision to become dictator was presumably made by Caesar himself and then tactfully suggested to a willing Senate. Equally, he must have selected Antony to be his subordinate or Master of Horse (*Magister Equitum*). Strangely, this proved more controversial than the dictatorship itself. Some of his fellow augurs questioned whether it was legitimate for anyone to be Master of Horse for longer than six months. At thirty-five, Antony was also young for such a senior position, especially since he had so far only been quaestor and tribune. The objections were brushed aside.[2]

In the absence of the dictator, his Master of Horse was effectively the most powerful man in the Republic. There was a lot for Antony to do. The legions returning to Italy needed to be kept occupied and content to prevent any repeat of the mutiny of the previous year. There were also all the normal tasks of government to keep going. When a dictator was appointed, the *imperium* of other magistrates lapsed. Elections for the most senior magistrates for 47 BC had in any case been postponed until Caesar returned, and only those such as tribunes, who were selected by the *Concilium Plebis*, campaigned and were elected.

Antony now had even greater power and responsibilities than in the previous year and, once again, showed little restraint in enjoying them. Cicero later claimed that Cytheris rushed to greet him at Brundisium when he landed. This does seem to have been much more than a casual affair and Antony was happy to be seen in public with his mistress. He also continued his friendships with other actors and performers, spending a good deal of time in their company. Back in Rome, he attended the wedding celebrations of the actor Hippias and the next day appeared in his official capacity considerably the worse for wear. Presiding over a meeting of the People's Assembly, he was obviously badly hung over. Suddenly nausea overtook him and he vomited into the cloak held out by one of his companions – or into his own lap in Cicero's probably exaggerated version. Antony does not appear to have cared. Years later when attacked over his heavy drinking, he replied with a pamphlet called *On his Drinking* which boasted of his prowess. Rather than bow to convention he preferred to shock.[3]

There was a similar spirit in his choice of company. Loyalty to friends regardless of their social status may often be admirable, and Antony genuinely seems to have enjoyed the lively companionship of actors, dancers and musicians. Probably, much like today, the theatrical culture was one in which flattery was as warmly given as received. Yet no one could ever really forget that he was who he was, and none of his companions could forget that he merely deigned to spend time with them. Antony was utterly convinced of his high birth and how this and his own merit meant that he deserved to be one of the most important men in the Republic. He did not need the approval of other senators to confirm this, and no doubt enjoyed their dismay and disgust. Whatever they thought of him, he remained an Antonius. At the moment, he also effectively had supreme power and even the most disapproving of them must come to him to ask for any favour.

Antony summoned and presided over meetings of the Senate. This and other public business he tended to conduct with a sword at his hip. A Roman magistrate inside the city was supposed to be overtly civilian. Antony ignored the convention and was also frequently escorted by soldiers. Others had done the same during the civil wars, as had Pompey in his sole consulship of 52 BC, but it was not the way the Republic was supposed to be seen to function. Antony was blatantly a conqueror and keen to enjoy the fruits of victory.[4]

Cicero complained that many of Pompey's supporters before Pharsalus had already been dividing up the spoils they planned to take from the Caesareans and anyone who had been neutral. Now Antony led the Caesareans in a similar race to profit from victory, although they did remain bound by Caesar's refusal to treat neutrals as his enemies and his willingness to pardon those who surrendered. It did not matter too much, because there were plenty of wealthy, eminent and dead Pompeians whose assets could be seized. Antony confiscated a grand house to live in, as well as other spoils, and tended to make decisions favouring himself and his friends, including some of the actors and others considered disreputable.

The victory in Macedonia had also created other problems. Some Pompeians had surrendered directly to Caesar. He was said to have been especially pleased to welcome Servilia's son Brutus, but the latter's brother-in-law Cassius was also pardoned in this way. Cicero and some others had travelled back to Italy, assuming that Caesar would swiftly return and they could ask him in person for clemency. Instead, the newly named dictator had chased after Pompey and then become embroiled in the Alexandrian War.

Cicero's status was unclear, especially since he had not yet formally laid down his *imperium* as proconsul of Cilicia, so was still accompanied by his lictors. Antony had been ordered by Caesar not to let former enemies come back to Italy without his specific approval. The Master of Horse therefore informed Cicero that he must leave and wait in the provinces somewhere or risk punishment. The latter responded by saying that he had been encouraged to return by his son-in-law Dolabella, a staunch Caesarean who had assured him of Caesar's goodwill. Antony passed a decree exempting Cicero and one other by name from the ban on returning to Italy. The orator was less than pleased to be singled out so publicly. His nervousness only increased as the months wore on and Caesar did not return from Egypt, while news came that the Pompeians were raising strong forces in North Africa.[5]

Antony was neither subtle nor tactful in the way he wielded power and this did nothing to make Caesar's new regime popular. There were also very many problems to deal with and, even if he had not spent so much energy in feasting and pleasure, it is quite possible that he would not have been able to cope. As it was, discontent was allowed to fester and only needed a spark − or the appearance of an ambitious leader − to turn into violent disorder. Festivals were given, mostly in Caesar's name and generally at his expense, but this did nothing to resolve the deeper unrest.[6]

DEBT, PROPERTY AND LAND

Antony was one of many on both sides who went into the civil war massively in debt. It was not just a problem restricted to the aristocracy. Life was expensive, especially in Rome itself where most people lived in rented accommodation. In the past, leaders such as Catiline had rallied many to their cause with the cry of 'new tablets' (*novae tabulae*), promising to abolish all existing debts. Plenty of debtors had hoped for the same from Caesar, but in 49 BC he proved moderate. Debts were to be paid, but property valued at pre-war prices to make this easier.

Caelius Rufus had joined the 'worse cause' with the 'better army', but after his return from Caesar's Spanish campaign had steadily come to regret his decision. Elected praetor for 48 BC, he felt that he had been wrongfully denied the prestigious position of urban praetor in spite of earlier promises and his own opinion of his worth. In his last surviving letter to Cicero he claimed to be sickened by the other followers of Caesar and spoke of their unpopularity amongst the wider population. Hoping to exploit the discontent, he proclaimed a sweeping relief of debt. Servilius, Caesar's consular colleague for 48 BC, acted swiftly and the Senate passed its ultimate decree, just as they had done in 49 BC against Caesar and at other times of crisis. Caelius was stripped of office and fled from the city. He tried to join Milo, whom Caesar had refused to recall from exile, but who had in fact returned and was raising rebellion in Pompey's name. Milo was killed in some of the initial fighting. Caelius tried to bribe some of Caesar's auxiliary soldiers to defect, but was arrested and executed.[7]

This brief rebellion had occurred before Antony left for Macedonia, but he was already busily preparing at Brundisium. As far as we can tell he was not involved in its suppression in any active way. Yet in 47 BC he would be at the heart of a new crisis sparked by the same issues. Coincidentally, the leader was again an associate of Cicero's, this time his wild son-in-law Dolabella, who had returned early from the Macedonian campaign on the grounds of illness. Once back in Rome, he copied Clodius and had himself adopted by a plebeian so that he could stand for election as tribune for 47 BC. He was successful, but soon began to quarrel with one of his colleagues, Lucius Trebellius, and the two men's supporters grew increasingly violent.

Dolabella announced that he would abolish existing debt. Since he had borrowed on a scale far greater than his capacity ever to repay, cynics suggested that the move was mainly for his own benefit. Even so, there were plenty of other people who welcomed it. Dolabella was willing to intimidate the rest, and there were soon fatalities in the clashes between his men and the followers of Trebellius. Antony was away from Rome dealing with unrest amongst the legions and his ban on individuals carrying weapons in public inside the city was ignored. In an unprecedented move, he had named his uncle, Lucius Julius Caesar, as urban praetor, but the now ageing former consul proved ineffectual. When the Senate once again passed the *senatus consultum ultimum*, he was unable to marshal enough force to deal with the problem and, apart from the tribunes, there were no other magistrates to assist him in seeing that the Republic came to no harm. Dolabella and his gang occupied the Forum to make sure that the People's Assembly would pass his debt relief bill.

Antony may initially have been close to Dolabella, and the two men must certainly have known each other well. The latter was popular and at first it seemed wise to support him. However, other important Caesareans advised him to resist the tribune and a personal hatred developed when Antony became convinced that his wife Antonia was having an affair with Dolabella. The Master of Horse brought a strong force of soldiers to the city and stormed the Forum. There may have been little bloodshed, although a few executions occurred. Dolabella survived, but was forced to abandon his programme.[8]

The whole episode had echoes of Clodius and Milo, and all the other violent disputes that had disrupted public life for so many years. Antony had restored order by force, just as Pompey had done in his sole consulship in 52 BC. Nevertheless, the way that he had done this made the Master of Horse unpopular. It also gave people little confidence in the stability of Caesar's regime. Twice in as many years the Senate had had to pass the same ultimate decree that it had used against Caesar himself, initiating the civil war in the first place. The propertied classes feared that radical measures to abolish existing debts were still likely. If Caesar failed to return from Egypt and the east, then no one could be sure just how his followers would behave. That was assuming that the recovering Pompeians were not able to turn the tide in the civil war and return vengefully to Italy.

The problems amongst Caesar's army only added to the sense of nervous uncertainty. Armies that are busy tend to remain under control. Mutinies usually occur in periods of rest and idleness, when resentment over real or perceived grievances has time to grow. The disorder amongst the *Ninth* Legion in 49 BC had come during a lull in campaigning. After Pharsalus, most of Caesar's veterans had been shipped back to Italy. Once there, they were left in Campania with little to do apart from wait for new orders, and it was more than a year before Caesar returned. The same discontent that had provoked the earlier mutiny again came to the fore. Men remembered Caesar's promises to give them discharges as well as money and land to allow them to support themselves and a family. They had so far received nothing and yet the war seemed to be over.

This time the trouble was centred around the *Tenth* Legion, a unit which Caesar had specially favoured from the time of his arrival in Gaul. In battle, this legion was normally deployed in the place of highest honour on the right flank of the line and often Caesar himself chose to stay with it. Yet many of its men were long overdue for demobilisation, felt that the war was already won and wanted to settle down and enjoy the rewards deserved by their long and faithful service. Many of the tribunes and centurions were sympathetic, for their own promised bounties were very generous indeed. Sticking together, the *Tenth* and other legions refused to accept orders from some of the more senior Caesareans sent by Antony to calm them. The need to suppress the violence caused by Dolabella and restore order at Rome had prevented the Master of Horse from confronting the mutineers in person.

Caesar finally landed in Italy in September 47 BC and hurried to Rome. Along the way, he met Cicero, and reassured the nervous orator of his goodwill. At Rome he appointed magistrates for the remainder of the year, giving the consulship to two of his loyal supporters. Caesar acted quickly, replacing the confusion of the last year with definite action and continuing his generally moderate approach to major problems, including the burden of debt. When the dictator was actually present, his regime seemed a good deal more stable and less repressive than when government was left to his subordinates.

The mutiny took a little longer to resolve. Caesar sent Sallust – the future historian – to the legions, but he was attacked and barely escaped with his life. The legions then marched on Rome to demand that their grievances were met. Caesar rode into their camp himself. He unnerved the mutineers by his calm, and then broke their spirit by addressing them not as 'comrades' (*commilitones*) in his normal way, but as 'citizens' (*Quirites*) – not soldiers at all, but mere civilians. In Gaul he had once shamed the army into advancing, by telling them that he would go on alone with just the *Tenth* Legion if the others refused to follow. Now he singled out the *Tenth* in a different way, saying that he would accept all the others apart from them back into his service. In the end, the veterans of the *Tenth* were begging him to decimate them – executing one soldier in ten – just so long as he would take them back into his service. Caesar graciously granted the request, did not execute anyone and would soon lead the *Tenth* to Africa where it would again fight with great distinction.[9]

Antony did not accompany Caesar when he set off to fight the Pompeians in Africa, nor was he given any formal role to perform in his absence. In contrast, Dolabella did go with the army, although it is possible that this was to ensure that he got up to no more mischief. Caesar had decided not to extend his dictatorship, and instead became consul for the third time for 46 BC. The Senate had granted him the right to ignore the usual restriction and hold consecutive consulships. As a colleague he took Lepidus, the man who as praetor had looked after Rome in 49 BC.[10]

By December Caesar was in Sicily, waiting to embark with his army for the crossing to Africa. Before he left Rome he began the public auction of the property of dead Pompeians. Antony was one of the most enthusiastic bidders, so that he was still sharing in the spoils of victory even if for the moment he held no office. Amongst his purchases were Pompey's grand house in the newly fashionable region known as the *Carinae* (literally, 'keels'), which led off from the Via Sacra, and several of his country estates. Dolabella also purchased a good deal of property during these auctions.[11]

Both men were greatly surprised when Caesar insisted that they must actually pay the high sums they had bid, since they had clearly expected either to pay less or nothing at all. Antony paid grudgingly, and we do not know enough about his personal fortunes to say whether he was now able to do this from his own funds or again needed to borrow, but the latter seems likely. Antony continued to live well beyond his means, trusting to future success to stave off creditors. Pompey's house and country villas became the scenes of wild feasts and celebrations, as the great man's wine cellars were consumed or given away to friends by their new owner. Cicero no doubt exaggerated when he attacked Antony for his excesses, but it is doubtful that he had to invent very much.[12]

Another person to benefit from the auctions was Caesar's mistress Servilia, who purchased several estates at a knock-down price. Gossips claimed that around this time she had arranged for Caesar to sleep with her daughter, who after the Roman fashion was simply called Tertia, or 'third'. Cicero joked that there was a 'third' off the price. Her husband was Cassius, who at the moment was relieved simply to have been pardoned by Caesar, although it is possible that this encouraged his later resentment of the dictator.[13]

Antony divorced his wife Antonia around this time and publicly alleged that she had betrayed him with Dolabella. He still had Cytheris as his mistress and remained happy to be seen in public with her. Marriage for a senator was normally a political act, where any emotional attachment either came later or was coincidental. In the case of Antony's third marriage there may have been more to it than this, for he seems quickly to have taken a new wife as well and, at least on his side, the passion was genuine. This was Fulvia, the widow of Clodius and Curio, and the match made sense politically. She was also clearly a formidable character and accounted one of the great beauties of her day. Perhaps Antony had been infatuated with her for years and the rumours that this had caused his split with Clodius were genuine.[14]

Caesar may have wanted to give the impression that Antony was out of favour as a way of distancing himself from the excesses that had occurred while his Master of Horse was in charge. Perhaps he also wanted to let Antony know that his approval could not be taken for granted. However, it is also worth noting that there were other loyal supporters to reward, and it is possible that even as a private citizen Antony continued to work informally on Caesar's behalf. Since he held no office, we hear little about Antony's activities in 46 BC. Caesar defeated the Pompeians at Thapsus in April, and was back in Italy by June, and Rome by July. However, Cnaeus Pompey, along with Labienus and other die-hard Pompeians, had raised another army in Spain, and by November Caesar had set out for war once again.[15]

Dolabella went with Caesar to Spain and was wounded during

the fighting that led to the victory at Munda. Antony remained behind, but in 45 BC he journeyed through Gaul to greet Caesar on his victorious return. If there had been a breach between the two men, then it was now healed, for Caesar treated Antony with great honour, letting him ride in the same carriage. More was to come. Caesar would once again be consul in 44 BC and this time he chose Antony as his colleague, even though at thirty-nine the latter was still several years below the legal age for the office.

Antony was excited by his return to favour and rushed back to Rome, where he celebrated in a tavern. When it was dark, he came to his own house – once Pompey's – in an exuberant mood. He came in disguise, posing as one of his own slaves with a message for Fulvia from her husband, and was promptly ushered in to her presence. She was worried, fearing that he wrote because something bad had happened – a natural fear, made all the more powerful since she had already been widowed twice. Cicero claims it was actually a passionate letter in which he promised at long last to be devoted only to her and to give up Cytheris, but there is no way of knowing whether there was any basis for this. As Fulvia started to read, the 'slave' suddenly took her in his arms and kissed her.[16]

[XV]

NOT KING, BUT CAESAR

Cleopatra's first child was a boy. We do not know when he was born, although some time late in 47 BC seems most likely. Inevitably, the baby was given the name Ptolemy, and in later years this was extended to 'Ptolemy called Caesar'. From quite early on the Alexandrians nicknamed him Caesarion ('Little Caesar').

Caesar never formally acknowledged the baby as his son – there would have been little point. Cleopatra was not a Roman citizen and the child was illegitimate, so by Roman law he could have no official status or inherit any of Caesar's property. On the other hand, Caesar does not seem to have done anything to prevent the informal use of his name. After his assassination there would be debate over whether or not he was actually the boy's father. Antony claimed that Caesar had said in front of witnesses that the child was his and some people claimed a strong physical resemblance. Others were equally vehement in denying his paternity and both sides had a vested interest in proving their case. One of Cicero's letters written just months after Caesar's death makes it clear that wider opinion saw the child as his.[1]

In the course of three long marriages, Caesar had fathered just one child – his daughter Julia, born back in the early 70s BC. He does seem to have been eager for more children, especially a son to continue the family line, but was disappointed. On top of this, his numerous affairs produced no certain illegitimate children, although a century later at least one Gaulish aristocrat boasted that he was the product of an illicit liaison between his great-grandmother and the proconsul Caesar.[2]

This has led some scholars to question whether Caesar was capable of having children by the time he met Cleopatra. Such things are inherently hard to prove and not entirely predictable, even in this day and age. Apart from this there could easily be other explanations for the failure to produce more than one child – even assuming there were not other pregnancies that ended in miscarriage or a stillborn baby, which went unrecorded in our sources. The second marriage ended in divorce and may well have been unhappy. Caesar and Calpurnia were married for fourteen years, but after the first few months he left for Gaul and they were apart for a decade, and afterwards only reunited during his brief visits to Rome. Quite simply the couple had little opportunity to conceive.

As far as we can tell, Caesar did believe himself to be the boy's father and was most probably right to do so. Absolute certainty would require the sort of intimate knowledge that is rare enough for the recent past, let alone the ancient world. Apart from those who denied the boy's paternity, none of our other sources hints that Cleopatra took another lover at this time. Once again, it is worth stressing that there is no good evidence for any men in her life apart from Caesar and later Antony.[3]

Caesar first saw the boy when his mother brought him to Rome late in the summer of 46 BC. Suetonius tells us that he had summoned the queen to the city, but it is unlikely to have been primarily from a desire to see his son. Nor was the main reason romantic. Cleopatra also brought her brother and husband, Ptolemy XIV, with her. The whole royal party was accommodated in a villa in Trastevere owned by Caesar and technically outside the boundary of the city. This was well within the traditions of Roman hospitality. Ptolemy Auletes had stayed in one of Pompey's villas during his visit to Rome.[4]

Arsinoe was also in Rome at this time, but as a prisoner. Between 21 September and 2 October, Caesar celebrated four triumphs in succession – one more than Pompey in his entire career. The second of these was over Egypt and the Nile, and amongst the floats carrying paintings of the campaign and trophies of victory was a statue of the Nile as a river god and a flame-belching model of the Pharos lighthouse. Amongst the prisoners was Cleopatra's younger sister. At the end of his Gallic triumph, the chieftain Vercingetorix, held captive since his surrender at Alesia eight years before, was ritually strangled. The death of the enemy leader confirmed Rome's total victory in a conflict.

Dio tells us that the Roman crowd was overwhelmed with sympathy for the teenage Arsinoe. It is most unlikely that Caesar had ever considered having her executed. Women had been included amongst the famous prisoners in earlier triumphs, but had never been executed as part of the ceremony. Arsinoe was kept as a prisoner – as was the four-year-old son of King Juba, who had been part of the triumphal procession for the victory in Africa. She was soon sent to live as an exile in the Temple of Artemis at Ephesus. Cleopatra's attitude towards her sister at this stage is not recorded, but later events suggest that it was scarcely warm. During the triumph, Caesar's soldiers enjoyed the traditional entertainment of singing ribald songs about their commander. Some of the verses joked about his affair with Cleopatra. We do not know whether she ever heard about this.[5]

Caesar did not live in the villa with the royal party, but that is not to say that the affair was over. He doubtless spent time with the queen whenever he could, as before enjoying her wit, intelligence and companionship, as well as making love. Yet he was exceptionally busy and as usual drove himself hard, drawing up new plans and legislation, and responding to petitions, as he strove to deal with the great backlog of public business. There was little time for pleasure. Caesar was also no more faithful to his mistresses than he was to his wives. During the months in Africa he had bedded another queen, this time Eunoe, the wife of King Bocchus of Mauretania.[6]

Cleopatra's rule was based on Rome's approval. The royal army had overwhelmingly supported her brother. Many died or were dispersed during the Alexandrian War and those who survived were of questionable reliability, so that the legions left behind by Caesar were the main insurance for her rule. Their commander Rufio was a man Caesar trusted, but interestingly he was the son of a freedman. The appointment may purely have been made on merit, but it is also likely that Caesar wished to avoid having a more senior subordinate stationed in Egypt, given the Alexandrians' reaction to his own symbols of office. The troops were there, but some illusion was preserved that they were controlled by the monarch and not the other way around. Another reason for appointing Rufio to command the garrison may have been that he was not prominent enough to be dangerous.[7]

In 46 BC the Roman Senate formally recognised Cleopatra and Ptolemy XIV as rulers and friends of the Roman people. Caesar had arranged for Auletes to be granted the same status in 59 BC for precisely the same reasons. According to Suetonius, he also lavished presents on the queen, but the most important gain she made was this confirmation of her rule. It was not too long ago that prominent Romans, including Caesar, had talked of annexing Egypt as a province. Cyprus had actually been taken, and although Caesar had given this back to her, there was no absolute assurance that he would not change his mind.[8]

He and the queen had been lovers in Egypt, at a time when both were threatened by forces loyal to her brother. It would have been only natural if she were worried that his support would not necessarily continue more than a year later. If she had heard the stories about Caesar's other affairs, then Cleopatra's concern would naturally have grown. Perhaps she felt that Caesarion would help to confirm the bond between them, although if she understood Roman law and society to any extent then this would have been less reassuring. In the event, she must have been more than satisfied with the visit to Rome. On a personal level it was clear that strong affection – perhaps genuine love – remained. This could well have been deeply important to the twenty-three-year-old queen. Yet in the end the most essential thing was the political endorsement and assurance that her rule would continue with the full backing of Rome.

In return, Caesar gained a stable Egypt, unlikely to rebel or to let its resources fall into the hands of a Roman rival. No doubt Caesar also enjoyed having the queen near him again. The months spent with her after the Alexandrian War represented the only real rest he had had for well over a decade. In addition, Cleopatra brought with her specialist assistance for some of his projects. Rome's lunar-based calendar of 355 days relied on adding an extra month on alternate years, but the system had been neglected and abused for a long time and was now hopelessly out of tune with the natural seasons. Caesar replaced it with the Julian calendar – the month of his birth was renamed July in his honour. Apart from a minor readjustment, this is the calendar of 365 and a quarter days that we still use today. Much of the work on this project was carried out for him by Sosigenes, an astronomer from the Museum at Alexandria. Inspiration, and perhaps actual assistance, came from Alexandria for another project, namely the creation of grand public libraries, one containing Latin and the other Greek literature, in Rome.[9]

Caesar left in November for the Spanish campaign. Cleopatra and the royal party may already have begun the journey home before this. If not, then they left soon afterwards, for there was no reason for them to stay in Rome in the absence of the dictator. There is no evidence for the frequent assumption that she remained in the city for eighteen months and it seems highly unlikely that she would have been willing to be absent for so long from her own realm. Perhaps the party visited Cyprus on their way back, but this is pure conjecture.

THE IDES OF MARCH

Caesar returned from Spain late in the summer of 45 BC, but did not enter Rome itself until October, when he celebrated a fifth triumph. In the past these ceremonies had at least nominally been over foreign enemies – for instance, the African triumph was over King Juba rather than his Pompeian allies. This time it was blatantly a celebration of the defeat of other Romans. Even so the crowds turned out to cheer. The Senate had decreed no less than fifty days of public thanksgiving, something never before openly given for a victory in a civil war.[10]

More and more honours were voted to Caesar. He was made dictator for ten years in 46 BC, and for life in 45, and allowed to be consul simultaneously for ten consecutive years. On top of formal powers there were monuments and statues, creating a status that seemed more than human and came close to divinity. Caesar is supposed to have refused some of the most sycophantic awards, but still accepted many others. Most were well within the traditions of honouring successful generals and statesmen, but in combination these were on a massively greater scale. There were also generous rewards to his followers. Two of his legates were granted triumphs for the Spanish campaign, and there was no precedent for anyone apart from the army commander receiving such an honour. In addition, Caesar resigned his sole consulship for 45 BC and had two of his followers elected as replacement or suffect consuls for the remaining months of the year. One of these men died on 31 December and Caesar held a fresh election to elect another replacement for the remaining hours of the day. Cicero joked that this man was so vigilant that he did not even sleep during his term of office. Privately, he and others were outraged at such cavalier treatment of the senior magistracy.[11]

Caesar had little patience with formality and tradition, in part because of his temperament and the habit of commanding an army and issuing orders, but also because there was so much to do in very little time. There was an enormous programme of land settlement to provide for his discharged veterans and the unemployed and impoverished citizens living in Rome itself. Caesar was determined to carry this out without the confiscation and upheaval of Sulla's colonisation programme. Few people objected to what Caesar was doing, and most of his reforms were seen to be sensible and for the good of the Republic. Yet they did resent the way he rushed everything through. Cicero found himself being thanked by cities in the provinces whose petitions had been granted in Senate meetings at which he had supposedly been present, but which as far as he could tell had never occurred.[12]

Caesar once said that the 'Republic is nothing, merely a name without body or shape', and his behaviour in these months did show a lack of concern about appearances and convention. He possessed supreme, personal and permanent power. So far he had studiously avoided the name and symbols of Rome's ancient kings, but he had accepted the right to dress in the manner supposedly adopted by the kings of nearby and long-vanished Alba Longa, from whom he claimed descent. On 26 January 44 BC, he celebrated the festival of the Latin games, much of the ceremony being performed on the Alban Hills outside the city. As he processed back, the crowd hailed him as 'king'. Rex was a family name as well as a title, so he simply responded by saying that he was, 'Not king, but Caesar.'[13]

Yet incidents continued that made many people unsure – especially if they were senators who resented his power. On 15 February came the Lupercalia festival in which his fellow consul Mark Antony played a key role. On that day he acted as the leader of the priests of Lupercal, who according to the ancient rite raced through the heart of the city clad only in a leather loincloth, and flicking a goatskin whip at anyone they passed. This was considered lucky, especially for women, increasing the chances of pregnancy and making a safe and easy birth more likely. Caesar was sitting on a raised platform in the special ornate chair awarded to him by the Senate and at the end of the ceremony Antony ran up to him. The almost naked consul was holding a royal diadem, which he offered to the dictator. Caesar refused, prompting cheers from the watching crowd. Antony offered the crown again and the cheering increased when the dictator once again refused to accept kingship. Afterwards, he had the diadem placed in the Temple of Jupiter on the Capitoline Hill, because the god was Rome's only king.

It was a strange episode, and while almost everyone agrees that it was deliberately staged, there is less consensus over its purpose and inspiration. Most are reluctant to believe that Antony acted on his own initiative and suspect that Caesar knew at least in broad outline what was going to happen. Even at the time, no one seems to have been sure whether the whole thing was intended to reassure people that he did not want to be king or, as cynics would see it, was testing the water to see whether or not public opinion would approve. If it was intended to convince public opinion that Caesar had no ambition to be king, then it certainly failed.[14]

The year had started well for Antony and his family. His brother Caius was praetor, having survived his captivity during the civil war, and his other brother, Lucius, was tribune. The Antonii were doing well with the promise of more to come. Antony and Caius could both expect to go out to govern provinces after their magistracies. It is possible that the dictator had already allocated the important province of Macedonia to his fellow consul. Caesar himself also planned to leave Rome and expected to be away for three years. He would go first to fight the Dacians on the Danube, before going east to lead a grand invasion of Parthia and finally get revenge for the defeat of Crassus.[15]

Caesar planned to lay down his consulship before he left, allowing a suffect consul to replace him. He had already nominated the consuls and half the praetors for the next two years. Caesar's choice for suffect consul was Dolabella, showing his renewed faith in him. It was probably also no coincidence that this would mean that two of his most distinguished supporters would hold office after he left. However, to set against this, the consuls for the next year were loyal Caesareans, but by no means distinguished in family or personality. Although the dictator nominated the consular candidates he still went through the formality of letting the people vote for his choices. When the Popular Assembly filed into the *saepta* to sanction Dolabella's election, Antony used his powers as augur to see a bad omen in the heavens and halt the proceedings. Caesar could not fully control Antony, who was an important man in his own right, and was determined to continue his vendetta against his adversary from 47 BC.[16]

Rivalries still continued between Roman senators, but the normal rhythm of public life was suspended. Cicero despaired of a Republic where the courts barely met and the Senate fawned on a dictator who privately made virtually every key decision with his advisers. Many could understand such a suspension of normality if it was temporary. Servilia's son Brutus had met Caesar on his way back from Spain in 45 BC and had then hoped that 'he was going over to the good men'. Cicero did not believe this, and Brutus soon changed his mind.[17]

It did not matter that Caesar ruled well, or that he spared and promoted his opponents – both Brutus and Cassius were praetors for 44 BC and could realistically expect the consulship in a few years' time. The most fundamental principle of the Republic was that no one individual should hold permanent supreme power. Caesar now blatantly possessed this and showed no sign at all of resigning – in fact, he called Sulla a 'political illiterate' for retiring from the dictatorship. His title did not really matter. Many Romans, especially amongst the propertied classes, loathed the name of king, but Caesar had monarchic powers whatever his title and they hated this even more.[18]

Marcus Junius Brutus – technically, after his adoption by his uncle he was named Quintus Caepio Brutus, but his earlier name is more usually used – was the son of the formidable Servilia and had long been recognised as one of the up and coming men of the new generation of senators. His father had been executed by Pompey in 78 BC as one of the supporters of Lepidus – the father of Caesar's consular colleague in 46 BC. Brutus refused even to speak to Pompey until he joined him at the start of the civil war. He was much closer to Caesar and was to have married his daughter Julia until the betrothal was severed and the girl married to Pompey instead. Brutus was a year or two older than Antony. His character was sober and overtly respectable, although it is claimed that he also had an affair with Cytheris before she became Antony's mistress. Caesar said that 'Whatever Brutus wants, he wants badly', and an incident during Cicero's term as governor of Cilicia confirms this. Having loaned money to the city of Salamis on Cyprus at 48 per cent interest – four times the legal rate of 12 per cent – he badgered a succession of governors to give his agent troops and let him extract the payment by force.[19]

Brutus idolised his mother's half-brother Cato, pursuing a similar dedication to stern philosophy. Cato not only refused to surrender and accept Caesar's mercy after the defeat of the Pompeians in Africa, but also took his own life in a spectacularly gruesome manner. He tried and failed to stab himself to death with a sword, and his son brought a surgeon and had his wounds treated and bound up. Left alone to sleep, Cato ripped the stitches apart and pulled out his entrails with his own hands.[20]

In contrast, Brutus surrendered after Pharsalus, was welcomed by Caesar and subsequently given office. Guilt fuelled his adulation of his uncle. He wrote a book praising Cato and persuaded Cicero to do the same. Caesar made no attempt to restrain them, but did reply with his own *AntiCato*, which took the form of a vicious attack on his character in the most scurrilous tradition of Roman invective. Brutus also divorced his wife and married Cato's daughter – and his cousin – Porcia, the widow of Bibulus. Nagged by the years of gossip about Caesar and his mother, and driven by the stern example of his uncle and the family boast that an ancestor had forced out the last of Rome's kings almost five hundred years before, Brutus began to 'want badly' to remove the dictator.[21]

He had three sisters, married respectively to Cassius, Lepidus and Servilius Isauricus, Caesar's colleague in the consulship in 48 BC. This reinforced his mother's closeness to Caesar and suggested that his future was bright. Cassius was also doing well, although he was said to have been bitter because Brutus was preferred to him for the office of urban praetor in 44 BC. He had been Crassus' quaestor in the invasion of Parthia and had led the survivors of the disaster back to Syria and then repulsed an enemy raid that reached Antioch. Cassius had made a good deal of his own leadership at this time of crisis.[22]

Brutus and Cassius were the leaders of a conspiracy of some sixty senators. These included other former Pompeians, but also some disillusioned Caesareans: Caius Trebonius had been suffect consul in 45 BC, and Decimus Brutus – Marcus Brutus' cousin – was promised the consulship for 42 BC. Both had served Caesar loyally and well in Gaul and the civil war and had been rewarded accordingly. Their motives were mixed, but all of the conspirators had a deep sense that it was wrong for the Republic to be dominated by one man. Most genuinely believed they were acting for the good of Rome. They would not have been Roman senators had they not also been aware that the men who killed the tyrant could expect to be amongst the leaders of the Republic in the immediate future.

Trebonius had cautiously sounded Antony out in the summer of 45 BC when the latter was going to meet Caesar, hoping that he might join the conspiracy. Antony refused, but said nothing to the dictator. Perhaps he misunderstood or felt that it was just an old friend complaining and letting off steam, uttering threats that were never fully serious. Brutus was adamant that no one apart from Caesar should be killed and forced those who wished to murder Antony as well to give in. If only the dictator died, then perhaps everyone would realise that this was necessary for the Republic and no new conflict would result.[23]

The conspirators knew that they had limited time before Caesar left the city to begin his campaign. He was readily accessible, for early in the year he had dismissed the bodyguard of Spanish soldiers that had protected him since his return from the Munda campaign. Caesar either did not take the reports of plots seriously or no longer cared very much, and most probably felt that showing supreme self-confidence at all times was the best way of preserving his regime.[24]

After his death rumours would circulate of various things he had planned to do, as the dispute between his supporters and killers escalated into a new civil war. One of the more bizarre was the claim that he wanted to be allowed to marry as many women as he liked for the purpose of producing children. Cleopatra, Caesarion and presumably Ptolemy XIV had come to Rome for a second visit some time late in 45 or early in 44 BC. Caesar had drawn up a new will after returning from Spain, which made no mention of Caesarion, which does not suggest that he was planning such a break with Roman law and tradition. Perhaps he wanted to spend time with his lover, but once again the main reason was doubtless political. For the planned Parthian expedition, grain from Egypt would be a major source of supplies for the Roman army – just as Auletes had helped to support Pompey during his eastern campaigns.[25]

The presence of the queen, once again installed in Caesar's villa across the river, may have made the dictator seem even more like a Hellenistic king. It was an extra provocation, but a minor one and, even if she had not been in Rome, the conspirators would surely have acted in the same way. Suggestions that Cleopatra was a major influence on Caesar's thinking and policies make little sense, and even in the propaganda war after his death were a minor thread. Appian tells us that he had a statue of her placed next to the one of the goddess Venus in the Temple of Venus Genetrix and that it was still there a century and a half later. This building was the centrepiece of the new Forum Julium and Caesar had vowed to build it before the Battle of Pharsalus if his ancestor the goddess brought him victory. The Forum was not actually complete in 44 BC and Dio tells us that Augustus brought at least one statue of the queen back to Rome thirteen years later, so it may be that Appian was confused. On the other hand, the statue may have been one of the goddess, or of Isis, who was often equated with her, and simply been modelled on Cleopatra, rather than formally an image of her.[26]

While in Rome, Cleopatra seems to have copied her father's example and cultivated important Romans with gifts. Cicero went to visit her, but never received the books he was promised and bitterly resented having to pay court to a foreign queen. Perhaps senators also felt that they could gain Caesar's favour through her, although how far this was true is impossible to say.[27]

On 15 March – the Ides in the Roman system – Caesar attended a meeting of the Senate in one of the temples forming part of Pompey's huge theatre complex. Antony had gone to his house to accompany him, as had Decimus Brutus. After some reluctance, caused by some unfavourable sacrifices and the nervousness of his wife Calpurnia, Decimus persuaded Caesar to go to the session. The conspirators were waiting, having gathered early in the day, using Cassius' son's coming of age as a pretext. They were supported by a group of gladiators owned by Decimus Brutus and stationed near by, but were determined to do the deed themselves. They greeted Caesar as he got out of his litter. Trebonius drew Antony aside for a private word, delaying him outside the temple, while the others went in. They did not want the burly consul to be in his proper place sitting beside Caesar, rightly judging that his instinctive reaction would be to fight.

Antony must have heard the noise. Perhaps Trebonius then told him what had happened. The other conspirators had clustered around Caesar to petition him. Then they struck, producing knives and all trying to reach and stab at him. Caesar was wounded twenty-three times, although it was thought later that only one wound would have been mortal. In the confusion, some of the conspirators accidentally struck each other and Brutus was wounded in the thigh. The dictator seemed surprised, then angry and stabbed back with his sharp stylus pen. When he fell, it was to collapse beneath a statue of Pompey.

The watching senators were stunned, then terrified. They fled, streaming out of the temple to reach the sanctuary of their homes because no one knew what would happen next. Antony fled with them.[28]

XVI

CONSUL

Antony spent much of the Ides of March barricaded inside his house. He had thrown off his consular robes and disguised himself as a slave when he fled – the latter an ironic repeat of his flight from Rome at the beginning of 49 BC. In the past, Roman politicians who resorted to violence had never stopped with the death of just one man and there was no reason to expect anything else now. Apart from the conspirators, as yet no one else knew of Brutus' insistence that only Caesar be killed. Like Caesar's own clemency to his defeated opponents, this attitude was surprising. Antony was Caesar's fellow consul and political ally and knew himself to be an obvious target. Lepidus, Caesar's *Magister Equitum*, similarly took refuge in his own house, as did the vast majority of the Senate, anticipating a bloodbath. Some may have feared death at the hands of the conspirators and their supporters, others at the hands of Caesar's vengeful supporters. All were nervous that mobs of looters would take advantage of the chaos.[1]

The news of the murder would have taken longer to cross the River Tiber and reach Cleopatra. No doubt she was stunned, probably grief-stricken and certainly nervous, but she was in no real danger unless Rome descended into total anarchy. Politically she was irrelevant, and she may already have known enough about Roman public life to realise this and that the conspirators would have no reason to think her worth the trouble of killing. Whatever new regime emerged following the death of the dictator, it would be formed by Romans. The queen could not play a part in this process and could only hope for an accommodation with the leaders who emerged. She had lost her political protector and her lover. It was impossible to know how Rufio and his legions would react to the news of Caesar's death and whether she would be able to cling on to power without her Roman backer. Cleopatra did not flee from Rome as soon as she heard of the assassination, fearing for her own life or that of her child. She remained there for several weeks, watching events.[2]

An already depleted Senate had suffered a further cull of its leading members during the civil war. Caesar had enrolled hundreds of new senators, but few of these men had much prestige or political influence. His enlarged Senate of some nine hundred members was very light at the top. When Caesar lay dead, Brutus had called out Cicero's name, for he was one of the very few distinguished former consuls who might now lead a restored Republic. The sixty-two-year-old orator had not been aware of the conspiracy and ran away in the general panic.

The conspirators had wound themselves up to stab the dictator to death in a flurry of wild blows. They do not seem to have prepared well for what would happen next, and were taken by surprise by the stampede that left them alone in the temple. They raised a freedman's cap on a pole as a sign that citizens had gained their freedom once more, just as a slave put on this headgear on the day his master granted him liberty. (The French Revolutionaries would one day adopt the same symbol.) Then, joined by Decimus Brutus' troop of gladiators, they climbed up on the Capitoline Hill, Rome's ancient citadel, and waited to see what would happen next. Three of Caesar's litter-bearers returned and carried his body home.[3]

Caesar's supporters did not appear seeking vengeance, nor did citizens of all ranks rush to cheer the men who had heroically killed the dictator and restored liberty. Rome was stunned, and only slowly and tentatively did it begin to stir again. A trickle of senators made their way up to the Capitoline to congratulate the conspirators. Cicero was one, and he was warm in his praise, but neither he nor any of the others stayed very long. Dolabella was another visitor, and either then or in the next days he assumed the garb and status of a consul. Warm in his praise for the assassins, he saw no reason not to take the office allocated to him by the dictator. Brutus and Cassius addressed the thin crowds now milling about in the Forum. There was no great enthusiasm for their justification of the murder and even the money they distributed failed to produce an outburst of support. Appian noted the irony of men who expected their fellow citizens to embrace liberty at the same time as they bribed them.[4]

Later in the day, Antony must have realised that no attack was imminent. Like any Roman senator, he sought council from family, friends and political associates. He met with Lepidus and other prominent Caesareans such as Aulus Hirtius, the man nominated as one of the consuls for 43 BC. Given her strong character, and no doubt a reluctance to mourn a third husband, it is likely that Fulvia played a very active part in encouraging Antony. Lepidus commanded the only legion in Italy. At least some of his troops were near Rome and on the 16th he brought them into the city. Technically, now that the dictator was dead, the power of his *Magister Equitum* ought to have lapsed, but the soldiers responded to Lepidus' orders and that was all that really mattered for the moment. Antony and Hirtius restrained him from using the troops to launch an immediate attack on the conspirators, and the former went to Caesar's father-in-law, Calpurnius Piso, and with his support obtained the dictator's will from the Temple of Vesta.

In the meantime, Brutus made a speech to a crowd that had gathered on the slope of the Capitoline, but once again failed to fire their enthusiasm. Most people had not seen Caesar as a tyrant and could see no advantage to themselves from his death. There were large numbers of discharged veterans in Rome, waiting to be allotted farms, and these now feared that a Senate led by the conspirators would end the dictator's colonisation programme. Brutus vainly tried to reassure them that they would receive their land. There was growing hostility towards the conspirators and the house of a senator who had publicly supported them was menaced by a mob.

On 17 March, Mark Antony as consul summoned a meeting of the Senate. It was convened in the Temple of Tellus, not far from his house and away from the Capitoline. Lepidus' soldiers, supported by veterans, stood on guard outside. Most senators, including Cicero, attended, and whatever their attitudes to Caesar, the universal hope was for stability and peace. The conspirators remained where they were, still guarded by their gladiators and depressed by their failure to recruit citizens as supporters.

The fundamental question was whether the murder had been justified. If Caesar was a tyrant then it was, and everything he had done was illegal. The problem with this was that he had done so much. Many senators owed office and privilege to the dictator. Brutus and Cassius were praetors, and Decimus Brutus was named as proconsul of Cisalpine Gaul for the following year and consul in 42. If Caesar's acts were declared invalid then they had no right to these offices and nor were Antony or Dolabella consuls, nor any other provincial governor or magistrate entitled to hold power. Caesar's decisions spread far beyond the Senate, to the colonists and the many provincial communities granted status or rights by his decisions. Individuals had a lot to lose, but as importantly there was the risk of plunging all of government into chaos. It would take time to hold new elections and their outcome would be uncertain. Many of Caesar's appointees were below the legal age to hold a particular office – Dolabella by more than a decade. Even when this was not the case, launching an electoral campaign would have been expensive and its outcome uncertain. Yet if Caesar was not a tyrant, then the conspirators were murderers and deserved to be punished. A good number of senators sympathised with Brutus, Cassius and the others. More were simply afraid that condemning them would provoke the bloodbath and perhaps civil war, which they had feared on the Ides itself.

Antony advocated a compromise. Cicero was willing to support him and the vote was actually taken on the proposal made by the orator. The conspirators were not to be prosecuted or held respons-ible in any way. At the same time, all of Caesar's acts were confirmed, and on the following day he was granted the right to be given a public funeral and his will was formally recognised. It was illogical, but for the moment it was enough to keep the peace. Cicero later claimed that it was the best that could be hoped for once it was clear that the conspirators were not to be formally vindicated and Caesar condemned, but at the time he may have been more optimistic. That evening Antony and Lepidus sent their sons as hostages up to the Capitoline and entertained Brutus and Cassius to dinner with every sign of goodwill. Cassius' and Lepidus' wives were sisters, both daughters of Brutus' mother Servilia.[5]

TRUTH AND RECONCILIATION

In describing the months that followed it is especially important to avoid any sense of inevitability or view things as a simple conflict between the conspirators and the Caesareans. The latter were not a coherent party or even faction with common policies, but a loose collection of people who had chosen for various reasons to support him. Caesar's position in the state had been personal, his powers awarded to him individually. He was dictator for life and controlled an enormous army of soldiers who had taken an oath of loyalty to him – as had the Senate not long before the Ides. There was no heir waiting to assume his powers and lead his army, nor even any indication that either Caesar or anyone else assumed that there should be.

Antony was Caesar's fellow consul and a distinguished supporter, but he lacked Caesar's wealth, reputation and *auctoritas*, and the network of clients who were tied to him by past favours. The dictator's status and importance were the product of years of effort, as well as civil war, and could not readily be taken over by anyone else. What the legions would do was hard to predict. Many were composed of soldiers originally recruited by the Pompeians. On the whole, these men had responded well to Caesar's rewards and promises and had proved loyal to him. That did not mean that they would automatically obey someone else, simply because they had also served Caesar. In 44 BC Antony commanded no troops, although he had been allocated a province containing legions for the next year. Brutus and Cassius could similarly expect provincial commands after their year as praetors, but at the moment none of the con-spirators commanded any soldiers. Decimus Brutus was due to govern Cisalpine Gaul, which had an army well placed to intervene in Italy, but he had not yet left Rome to take up his post. Lepidus had just the one legion and that was not really enough to dominate Rome for very long. If political rivalries became violent and civil war broke out, none of the key players could be confident of victory.[6]

Caesar was dead, and if no one could expect to replace him as the overwhelmingly dominant man in the Republic, then there were still new opportunities. Antony was consul, but he was also an Antonius, something he would stress repeatedly in the coming months. He expected to be one of the leading men in the state and win office and honours accordingly. He also still needed money, for although he had done well from the civil war, he had not yet acquired the wealth to finance either his lifestyle or his career. Barely forty, he could expect to be active in public life for decades. He wanted further honours, and perhaps eventually the sort of dominance Caesar had shown to be possible. He had much to be grateful to the dictator for and had liked Caesar as a man, but a Roman aristocrat with his background was never fully anyone else's man. His own success, and the success of his family, came first. Avenging Caesar's murder would not in itself make Antony's own position stronger or more secure, at least for the moment.[7]

Similarly, the conspirators wanted acceptance and not conflict. Success and security for them would come only if senators and the majority of all other classes approved of their action. They, too, were mainly young men by the standards of Roman politics. Brutus and Cassius were in their late thirties and few of the others were much older. One of the reasons they wanted their 'free' Republic was so that they could advance further in public life, unrestricted by a dictator. Dolabella was younger still, probably no more than thirty, and although one of Caesar's supporters, it can have seemed no bad thing to the conspirators that Antony's new consular colleague was a man he detested. Bitter personal rivalries were a very traditionally Roman way of restricting the power of individuals. Apart from that, the restoration of liberty could not very well have begun with attacks on the consuls. Brutus in particular hoped that the willingness of Antony to meet was an indication that he too saw that the Republic could not function as it should while there was a permanent dictator. This did not mean that he and the others did not watch Antony as warily as he watched them. All of them were looking to advance their own position in the new Republic.

Cassius is said to have argued against permitting Caesar a public funeral and allowing Antony to conduct it, but allowed himself to be overruled by Brutus. This proved to be a mistake, although it is possible that refusing the dictator this honour would have produced even greater resentment. The simple truth was that Caesar had been popular with many citizens. On 20 March the funeral was held in the Forum itself, witnessed by a large and volatile crowd. Details of the dictator's will had already been released and it was known that he had left his extensive gardens in the city to become a public park. Valued in itself, it was a reminder of Caesar's generosity to many and what little support there had been for the conspirators ebbed even lower. Shakespeare's version of the speech Mark Antony made on this occasion is justly famous and gives a good flavour of the power of an orator to move the Roman crowd. However, our sources are divided over what he actually said. Caesar's body was displayed, dressed in his regalia and laid on an ivory bier. The bloodstains on his official cloak were clearly visible.

Antony seems to have begun by listing some of the many honours voted to Caesar by the Senate, leading up to the oath to support and protect him that all senators – including the conspirators – had taken. The irony was as heavy as the Shakespearean repetition of Brutus as an 'honourable man'. From this he moved on to speak of some of Caesar's great deeds and gradually became more emotional. He pulled the cloak off the corpse and held it up to show the tears made by the assassins' knives. Someone shouted out a famous line from an old tragedy – 'to think that I saved those men so that they could destroy me!' The terms of the will were read out. There was dismay that Decimus Brutus was mentioned as one of the lesser heirs, showing once again how fond Caesar had been of the men who killed him. Apart from the gift of the gardens, each citizen living in Rome was to receive a gift of 300 sesterces. A wax effigy of the body had been made and was now raised into the air on a crane of the type used in the theatre or games. It was slowly rotated, displaying all twenty-three wounds, which were graphically marked on the model.

Emotion spilled over at the sight. Helvius Cinna, a loyal supporter of Caesar and a respected poet, was mistaken for another man named Cinna who had supported the conspirators and was beaten to death.

Angry mobs went to the conspirators' houses – as prominent senators, many will have lived on the slopes of the Palatine edging the Forum – but they found none of them and after a while came back to cluster around the corpse. The cremation was to have occurred outside the city in the Campus Martius, but now the crowd hastily heaped up a pyre on the spot, dragging anything wooden from the Forum and its shops. Like Clodius, Caesar was burned in the heart of Rome. Veteran soldiers threw their decorations onto the burning pyre and women threw their jewellery. Amongst the crowd were many non-citizens from all over the empire. For nights to come some of Rome's Jewish community went to the spot, publicly mourning the man who had been generous to their people.[8]

Antony had helped the wider population's simmering resentment to boil over into rage. The conspirators feared for their lives – they never appeared in public, never once felt safe enough to attend a meeting of the Senate. Over the next month all of them slipped away from the city. Antony had the Senate grant Brutus and Cassius special dispensation to leave, because normally as serving praetors they were expected to remain in Rome. Decimus Brutus and Trebonius soon set out for the provinces allocated to them by Caesar. From now on, the conspirators could only hope to influence politics through friends and family who remained in Rome. The self-proclaimed 'Liberators' had been forced to leave Rome, making it much harder for them to challenge Antony's current dominance.[9]

Hatred of the conspirators did not mean a wave of popular enthusiasm for Antony's leadership. Soon after the funeral, an altar was set up on the spot where Caesar had been cremated. There was no official sanction for this, and the main leader was a man called Amatius, who claimed to be Marius' grandson and so Caesar's relation. Dolabella dispersed the crowd and removed the altar. Amatius and his followers set it up again and this time it was Antony who took action and had the man executed. The deep affection for Caesar and anger against his murderers was sometimes useful, but both consuls wanted to keep it under control.[10]

On the 17th the Senate had agreed to ratify all of Caesar's acts, including those that had been announced, but not yet implemented. It was obvious that the allocation of land to veterans had to continue if the large numbers of the latter were to be kept in order. Brutus and Cassius had tried to win these men over by getting them granted the right to sell their new farms if they wanted, something that Caesar had forbidden since he wanted the men to settle permanently. Antony had taken possession of Caesar's papers from his widow Calpurnia and presented to the Senate a steady stream of the dictator's decisions to be put into force.[11]

Soon, he was announcing things that had not been mentioned in Caesar's lifetime and Cicero and others believed were his own inventions. The dictator had granted Latin status to much of the population of Sicily and now Antony had them made full Roman citizens. King Deiotarus of Galatia had supported Pompey in the civil war and had his kingdom substantially reduced in size by Caesar. Now the lost power and territory was restored. There were rumours of a bribe and Cicero claimed that Fulvia had done much to arrange the business. It was felt a bad thing for a Roman senator to be influenced too much by his wife, so this may be no more than routine denigration of Antony. Yet many aristocratic women were influential behind the scenes of public life so there is nothing inherently implausible about it.[12]

To Cicero it seemed that although the tyrant was dead, tyranny continued, as one man issued a stream of arbitrary decisions. This was a little unfair. Antony wrote him an ostensibly courteous letter in April, asking his permission to recall from exile one of the orator's old enemies, an associate of Clodius. Cicero accepted as politely as he could, believing that Antony would have gone ahead anyway. There was certainly a poorly veiled threat in the consul's letter: 'Though I know your fortune, Cicero, is above any danger, yet I think you would rather enjoy old age with peace and honour rather than anxiety.'[13]

Antony was determined to get his way, but he was also very busy and this no doubt fed his impatience. There was a great deal of business to be done, for Caesar had had so little time and the government of the Republic had not functioned well for many years. Especially in the provinces, there were communities and individuals pressing for recognition, appealing for favours or seeking arbitration in disputes. While it may have been preferable to Cicero that the Republic function more traditionally, this would have meant these delegations waiting patiently until the Senate had time to consider their cases. The delays would have been long, without any certainty that the matters would be decided at all, let alone in a way satisfactory to those involved. Most provincials had readily taken to dealing with a single supreme individual, in preference to the slow and tortuous securing of favours through the Senate.

As consul, Antony therefore busied himself addressing a long series of different issues. It was simply quicker to assert that each decision had actually been made by Caesar, since this ensured approval. There is no doubt that he was also exploiting the situation to strengthen his own position. Favours granted to Romans and provincials brought him bribes, but also placed the individuals and communities in his debt for the future. There was a new land bill, extending the colonisation programme. Former centurions – Cicero maliciously claims also veteran rankers from the *V Alaudae* Legion raised from Gauls – were to be included in the juries for major trials, which represented a substantial growth in their importance. The centurions were the single most influential group within each legion and well worth cultivating. Caesar had portrayed them in an heroic manner in his *War Commentaries* for the same reason.[14]

Antony effectively wielded immense patronage and used this as any Roman would to gain more clients. He became richer and more influential. His consulship would only last until the end of the year. At the moment he had more power than anyone else, and he needed to do enough with this to improve his position when the office lapsed. Potential rivals and enemies were for the moment weak, but there was no guarantee that they would stay that way. Antony needed wealth, connections and prestige to both compete in the future and make himself safe from attack. There was no assurance that Brutus' reluctance to kill anyone other than Caesar would last forever.

Antony won over Lepidus by ensuring that he became *Pontifex Maximus* in place of Caesar. He also betrothed his daughter to Lepidus' son to reinforce the alliance, although the children were too young for the wedding to take place. Antony had accepted Dolabella's assumption of the consulship because it was both better than any alternative and a well-known decision of Caesar. He helped him to secure the province of Syria for a five-year proconsulship. Syria was wealthy and contained a substantial army as part of the preparations for Caesar's Parthian War. Dolabella had the prospect of leading this expedition and successful eastern wars were always lucrative. For a man whose debts were still vast – he had been unwilling and unable to repay the dowry when he divorced Cicero's daughter – this was very attractive.[15]

The spring of 44 BC was a time for new alliances and arrangements, as individuals strove to build up their own power and connections. They acted through a mixture of ambition and fear, so familiar to Roman politicians of the last generation or so. The renewal of civil war and violence was a real possibility, perhaps almost inevitable. Antony and everyone else hoped to make themselves safe and strong enough to profit from the opportunities to come. Caesar's murder had radically shifted the balance of power within the Roman state and the readjustment to the new reality took time.

CAESAR'S SON

Cleopatra may well have waited in Rome to receive formal recognition of her power, and perhaps confirmation of her status as a friend of the Roman people. Cicero mentions that she had left Rome in a letter dated 16 April 44 BC. Later, there would be false rumours that she had perished on the journey home, and some have interpreted a later letter written by Cicero to mean that she was pregnant, presumably with another child of Caesar. This seems unlikely, since it is not mentioned in any other source and a more natural reading would make this a reference to Caesarion. Nervous about her hold on power in Alexandria, it was sensible for the queen to return as soon as she had made some effort to secure approval from Rome.[16]

Soon after Cleopatra decided to return to her own kingdom, an eighteen-year-old youth arrived in Rome. His name was Caius Octavius and he was the son of Caesar's niece Atia. His father had died some years before, but had held the praetorship and been expected to rise further. Atia had then married Lucius Marcius

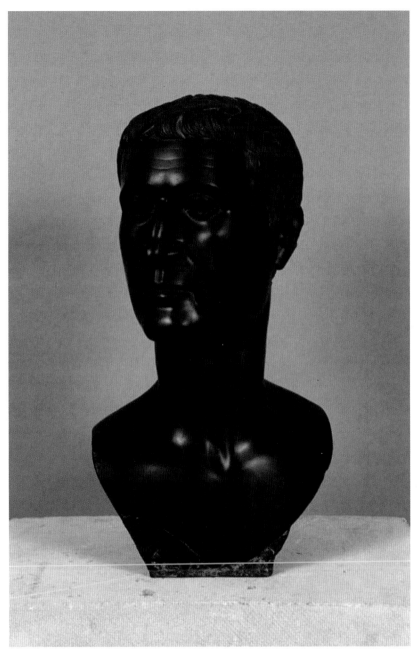

Bust of Mark Antony. Generally accepted as a portrait of Mark Antony, this bust shows similar, if more subtle features than his coin portraits. The latter portray a thicker-set, rather bull-necked individual. Antony was proud of his muscular appearance and physical strength, which he felt evoked his ancestor Hercules. (NTPL/Paul Mulcahy)

The Egyptian Cleopatra. On the south wall of the Temple to Hathor at Dendera Cleopatra and her son Caesarion are depicted in the style of the pharaohs of distant antiquity. Although still no more than a child when the carvings were made, Caesarion stands on the right, as tall as his mother. (Rowan)

The Greek Cleopatra. This bust now in Berlin is widely accepted as a portrait of Cleopatra and presents a far more Greek image of the queen. Her hair is fastened back into a bun and she wears the diadem of Hellenistic monarchs. (Photo Scala)

Coin portrait of the young Cleopatra *(below).* This silver coin was minted by the city of Ascalon in 50–49 BC, and depicts the young Cleopatra. The strong, rather hooked nose of the Ptolemies is emphasised. (British Museum)

Idealized beauty. This bust from Italy is identified as Cleopatra largely on the basis of the royal diadem, which may originally have included the uraeus symbol of the Ptolemaic kings. It has softer features than other portraits. (Corbis)

Image of Power. This later coin portrait of Cleopatra strongly emphasises the large eyes and beak-like nose familiar from coins of the Ptolemies. Coins were statements of power and legitimacy far more than faithful portraits. (Hunterian Museum, Glasgow)

The fair-haired Alexander *(above)*. Alexander the Great is describ[e]d as fair-haired, like many of Cleopatra's family. In this mosaic, a Roman copy of a Greek original found in Pompeii and constructe[d] more than three centuries after his death, the king of Macedon is depicted with medium brown hair. (Bridgeman Art Library)

The father. Cleopatra's father Ptolemy XII styled himself the 'New Dionysus', but was less respectfully dubbed 'the bastard' or the 'oboe-player'. This portrait hints at the family tendency to be plump, or even obese. (Jastrow)

The royal hand. This papyrus records the granting of favours to one of Antony's commanders by Cleopatra. The single word beneath the main text – the Greek for 'let it be so' – is in a different hand, and may have been written by Cleopatra herself. (Reuters/ Corbis)

Caesar *(far left)*. Probably the only portrait of Caesar made during his lifetime, this bust from Tusculum gives us some idea of the man who became Cleopatra's first lover. (W&N Archive)

Pompey *(left)*. Pompey the Great had been Caesar's son-in-law and ally, but became his most powerful opponent and the dispute between the two men led to the Civil War. (W&N Archive)

House of the Griffins. Underneath the Palace of the Emperor Domitian on the Palatine Hill in Rome are the remains of houses from the first century BC, still with the original decorations on their walls. The so called 'House of the Griffins' gives us a taste of the decor of an aristocratic house in Antony's day. (Author's collection)

The physical heart of the Republic. Taken from the slopes of the Palatine Hill, this view of the Forum Romanum shows the third century AD Senate House of curia in the centre, and the rostra to the extreme left. The structures were different in Antony's day, but stood in the same general are This was the heart of Rome's public life. (Author's collection)

Funeral of a dictator – temple of a god. Just to the left centre of this view of the Forum Romanum is the Temple of the Divine Julius, with its modern semi-circular metal roof. To the rig is the Temple of the Vestals. Antony presided over Caesar's funeral in the Forum. (Author's collectio

Agrippa. Marcus Vipsanius
Agrippa was a contemporary
and close friend of Octavian. His
family was obscure, but he proved
himself a capable administrator,
gifted general, and admiral of
genius. Octavian trusted him
with considerable responsibilities,
and he was content to rise as the
assistant of his friend. (Bridgeman
Art Library)

Cicero. Marcus Tullius Cicero was the greatest orator of
his age. As consul in 63 BC, he executed Antony's stepfather Lepidus. In 44–43 BC Cicero would lead the
opposition to Antony himself, delivering the Philippics, a
series of speeches, savaging his character and deeds. As a
reprisal Antony had his severed head and hand nailed to
the rostra. (Bridgeman Art Library)

The victor. Octavian joined Antony in the triumvirate, but just over a decade later the allies fell out. Octavian won, created the imperial system and took the name Augustus. He had some forty years in which to justify his own actions and damn Antony's reputation. This statue shows the finished product, the 'father of his country' who had restored the state to glory. (Bridgeman Art Library)

Seapower. This sculpture from Praeneste shows a stylised image of a Roman warship. The size of the marines is exaggerated in proportion to the vessel, but note the tower on deck, intended to allow men to throw or shoot missiles down onto enemy ships. (Photo Scala)

Controlling Italy. The modern-day harbour on the site of ancient Puteoli, with Cape Misenum just off to the left in the background. This was one of the busiest ports of Roman Italy, and it was in this bay that Antony and Octavian negotiated with Sextus Pompey. (Author's collection)

Octavia. Accounted a great beauty, Octavian's older sister Octavia was in her early thirties and already a widow when she was married to Antony to cement the alliance. She bore him two daughters, and from this line came no fewer than three of Rome's emperors. (AKG Images/Nimatallah)

The triumvir. This coin depicting Antony the triumvir was minted in 43 BC and suggests the raw physical strength of the man. (W&N Archive)

Livia. Octavian married Livia while she was pregnant, making her former husband divorce her and then give the bride away. Although well connected, his haste suggests a real passion for this attractive and fiercely intelligent woman. (Author's collection)

Barbarian bodyguards. This statue of a Gaulish warrior gives a good idea of the aristocratic fighters encountered by Caesar's army in Gaul. In later years Antony gave Cleopatra a bodyguard consisting of several hundred of these warriors. (The Art Archive/Gianni Degli Orti)

Roman ruler of the east *(left)*. The older Antony appears even more bull-necked on this later series of coins. His titles are recorded as augur, imperator (or triumphant general) three times, twice consul, and triumvir to restore the state. On the reverse of the same coin *(below left)*, Antony's son Antyllus is shown. For all the honours given to Cleopatra and her children, this coin series promoted his Roman son and heir. (British Museum)

Deadly opponents *(below)*. This terracotta statuette of a Parthian horse archer emphasises the very different fighting style of Rome's eastern neighbour. The great strength of the Parthian army lay in its cavalry. A few were heavily armoured cataphracts, but the majority were unarmoured bowmen, relying on speed to avoid enemy missiles. (Bridgeman Art Library)

Actium today. This aerial view of the Bay of Actium today helps to show why it was difficult for Antony's fleet to break out. Antony's main camp lay on the far side of the estuary. His smaller camp, and Octavian's position were just out of shot on the nearer side. (Harry Gouvas collection)

Actium fresco. This wall painting shows a naval battle and is often identified as the battle of Actium. It gives some idea of the confusion as oared warships tried to manoeuvre into favourable positions to attack the enemy, like an enormous dogfight. (The Art Archive/Gianni Dagli Orti)

Harmony of the new regime. In later years, when Octavian had become the Emperor Augustus, he paraded his family as ideals of harmony and traditional Roman virtue. Included amongst them were Octavia and the two daughters she had borne to Antony. The younger Antonia is in the centre, holding the hand of her young son Germanicus. The older Antonia is to the right, with her head covered. Antony's son by Fulvia, Iullus Antonius, fell victim to a scandal involving the emperor's daughter Julia, which saw her exiled and him executed, and is not depicted. (Author's collection)

Pride, loyalty and pay. In preparation for the Actian War, Antony minted a series of coins to pay his army. On the front these showed a warship, symbolising the substantial fleet funded in part by Cleopatra. On the reverse these coins depicted a legionary eagle, flanked by two of the signa standards carried by the sixty centuries in a legion. (Author's collection)

Antonia Minor. Antony and Octavia's youngest daughter was married to the younger son of Livia, the child with whom she was pregnant when married to Augustus. (Author's collection)

Spoils of war. Amongst the spoils Octavian brought back from Egypt were two obelisks. This one now stands in the Piazza di Montecitorio. (Author's collection)

The dramatic
finale. Romance
surrounded every
aspect of Antony
Cleopatra's affair
but most of all th
deaths, as reflecte
these two ninete
century painting
Ernest Hillemach
'The dying Anto
being raised up
by Cleopatra' (to
depicts a very ea
Cleopatra and
her maids raising
up a surprisingly
tidy Antony usin
ropes. Note the
hieroglyphics
decorating the w
of the mausoleur
(The Art Archive
Gianni Degli Or
In the second
picture, the
orientalism is ma
especially erotic.
Jean Andre Rixe
'Death of Cleop
shows the queen
naked, instead of
clothed in her ro
robes. She and th
maids are utterly
Egyptian, so muc
so that Charmio
depicted in profi
much like the
stereotypical wal
paintings behind
(AKG Images/E
Lessing)

Philippus, who was consul in 56 BC. Octavius was Caesar's closest male relative and at the age of just twelve the boy had given the oration at his daughter Julia's funeral in 54 BC. The dictator had taken an interest in the boy, enrolling him in the college of pontiffs in 47 BC, and he had joined the campaign against Pompey in Spain, although illness had prevented him playing a very active role. At the start of 44 BC he was in Apollonia on the Adriatic, waiting to take part in Caesar's Parthian War.[17]

The first report of Caesar's death brought with it news that he had made Octavius his principal heir and also adopted him as his son, which meant that he was to inherit his name. The Romans took adoption very seriously, and it was a common means for childless men to perpetuate the family name and ambitions. There is no indication that he knew of the provisions of the will before this and they were certainly not common knowledge in the dictator's lifetime.

It is important to remember how young and inexperienced Octavius was in 44 BC, for only then can we hope to understand the amazement at his immediate acceptance of the legacy and his determination to take not only Caesar's name, but also his political dominance. His stepfather Philippus advised him to decline the legacy, and for some time refused to address him as Caesar. Antony was even less welcoming when the youth arrived in Rome in April and came to see him. He would not hand over Caesar's papers or private funds, which he was employing to great effect. Later in the year he would dub Octavius a boy 'who owes everything to a name', but at this stage Antony was reluctant even to acknowledge that name in any formal way.[18]

Some of Caesar's former supporters were more enthusiastic, impressed by the 'boy's' immense self-confidence. A group of wealthy men, including Rabirius Postumus, provided him with the funds to go to some of the colonies set up for Caesar's veterans and begin recruiting soldiers. Borrowing from these men, and selling some of his own property, he also began to pay citizens the gift Caesar had promised in his will. Generous bounties, combined with the appeal of Caesar's heir and anger that the conspirators had gone unpunished, soon produced hundreds of volunteers from amongst the veterans. Caius Julius Caesar Octavianus – scholars conventionally call him Octavian to avoid confusion – started to become a political force. For the moment his power was still minor, but his swift rise was remarkable and unsettling.[19]

Brutus was still in Italy, but did not risk returning to Rome. As praetor he was responsible for the games that formed part of the festival of Apollo, the Ludi Apollinares. Afraid to go, he had agents arrange the spectacles and spent a lot of his own money and effort in the hope that this would win him more support. Octavian personally presided over the Ludi Victoriae Caesaris, voted to commemorate the Battle of Pharsalus, again paying for this with borrowed money. A comet appeared during the celebrations, and normally such things were seen as a bad omen. Octavian, however, persuaded people that it was a sign of Caesar's ascent into heaven to become a god. Now the youth, who turned nineteen in August, was not simply Caesar, but the son of the divine Julius. A statue of Caesar with a star on his head was placed in the temple he had built to Venus Genetrix. An altar was again set up in the Forum, and in time would be the site of a temple to the new cult.[20]

Brutus and Cassius finally left Italy. At Antony's bidding the Senate had allocated them unimportant provinces without troops, but they ignored these tasks. Brutus went to Athens, ostensibly to study. Decimus Brutus was in Cisalpine Gaul and controlled the closest army to Italy itself. Antony had been allocated the province of Macedonia, which contained six well-trained and numerically strong legions, most of which were destined for Caesar's projected campaigns. At the start of June he carried a bill through the Popular Asssembly that granted him for five years both Cisalpine Gaul and the extensive province of 'long-haired Gaul' conquered by Caesar. Decimus Brutus' command was to be terminated and Caius Antonius would be sent to Macedonia as its governor. Antony would take over Decimus Brutus' legions and also bring most of the troops from Macedonia across to his new province, although one of these six legions was given to Dolabella. Such a move was unorthodox, but the Roman people could vote for anything and so it was not technically illegal. This did not mean that Decimus Brutus was willing to accept his replacement.[21]

Antony had already recruited his own force drawn from Caesar's veterans and employed them as a bodyguard in Rome itself. As consul he had *imperium*, but the small private army raised by Octavian was illegal in every way, comparable to the legions Pompey had once enrolled from his family estates. In Spain, his surviving son Sextus Pompey still led the Pompeian forces that had survived the defeat in 45 BC. Attempts by Cicero and others to have him rehabilitated after the Ides of March had failed. Soon, Brutus and Cassius would also assume command of armies without any authority to do so. All of the key players had decided that only the control of legions gave them any real security. Civil war was brewing and threatened once more to plunge the whole Mediterranean world including Egypt into conflict and chaos. For monarchs like Cleopatra, there were severe risks of backing the wrong side or simply that the wealth of their kingdom would draw Roman leaders desperate for funds to support their armies. Caesar had given the Republic brief stability. For a few months after his death there had been uneasy peace. Now even this was breaking down.[22]

XVII

'ONE OF THREE'

To curb the rise of Octavian, Antony had made some public offers of compromise with Brutus and Cassius, but this alienated many of his supporters who were staunch Caesareans and loathed the assassins. It was a difficult, probably impossible balancing act. In August Calpurnius Piso criticised Antony in the Senate. Cicero, who had planned to go abroad, was sufficiently encouraged to return to Rome, but failed to attend a meeting on 1 September, pleading fatigue from his journey. In his absence Antony attacked him and then proposed fresh honours for Caesar. The next day Antony was not in the Senate, but Cicero did go and delivered a speech that would later form the basis for his *First Philippic*. The original *Philippics* had been delivered by the famous Athenian orator Demosthenes, warning his fellow citizens of the danger posed by King Philip II of Macedon, the father of Alexander the Great. Cicero's first speech was fairly moderate, but still represented a concerted attack on Antony's position and actions.

The consul responded angrily, although it was not until 19 September that he lambasted the orator in a speech. Antony blamed him as the real instigator of the Ides of March, criticising him for his 'ingratitude' to a man who had treated him generously in 48 BC and, in true Roman fashion, freely damning his character and politics. Cicero retired to the country and wrote his *Second Philippic*. This was never delivered as a speech, but took the form of a pamphlet, and copies were sent out to a few associates, although opinion is divided on how widely it was circulated. The text replied in kind, liberally slinging invective at Antony's whole life and career.[1]

About this time, Antony had a statue of Caesar erected on the Rostra in the Forum, which referred to him as 'father and benefactor'. Such a statement made it harder to agree any com-promise with the conspirators. Then he accused Octavian of sending an assassin to murder him. Cicero was deeply suspicious of the 'young Caesar', but was cheered by this news and slowly began to wonder if the boy might be useful. It was probably no more than a rumour. Octavian had little to gain by killing Antony and could not yet risk an open confrontation. A few weeks later, his hand became stronger.[2]

Three legions of the Macedonian army arrived at Brundisium, and a fourth was soon to follow. By the vote of the people, these soldiers were placed under Antony's command and their officers had obeyed the summons to come to Italy. They were well trained, and it is reasonable to think that they were strong in numbers and perhaps even close to their full strength. Antony had no prior connection with these units, which had been training in Macedonia since they were formed in 48 BC. Their officers had all been appointed by Caesar and both they and the men were loyal to his memory. They did not know Antony and he did not know them. When he went to meet them in October 44 BC there were angry complaints that he had done nothing to avenge Caesar's murder.

Antony promised the soldiers a special bounty of 100 denarii apiece, less than half of a legionary's annual pay of 225 denarii. Octavian's agents had already visited the camps and promised the men 500 denarii, and ten times as much on the eventual discharge, and so the legions were unimpressed, jeering the consul. It is always worth remembering that officers received far larger sums, so that the centurions and tribunes stood to become very wealthy indeed. Caesar had broken the spirit of the mutinous *Tenth* Legion with supreme self-confidence and a single word, backed by limited pun-ishment. They were his 'comrades', men he had led to victory after victory for twelve years, with whom he had shared hardships and on whom he had lavished rewards, decorations and praise. The bond between soldier and commander was deep and not to be shattered by one disagreement.

Antony and these legions were strangers to each other. On top of that he had no great victories of his own to show and there were no stories of his rewards to his own soldiers. He lacked Caesar's experience and his gifts, as well as his charisma, and when the soldiers jeered, he lost his temper and tried to bully them into submission. Demanding the names of malcontents from the officers, he ordered executions, although he may have stopped short of a full decimation. Cicero claimed that the victims of this purge included centurions as well as ordinary soldiers, and he seems unlikely to have invented such a detail. It is a lot less likely that the men were killed in front of Antony and his wife, so that their blood spattered onto Fulvia, who was egging her husband on. She may well have been with Antony and possibly urged him to take strong action, but the rest will have come readily to Cicero's imagination and such invective was rarely expected to restrict itself to the actual truth.

The punishment made the troops angry and resentful, and that was a mistake when Octavian's agents were still promising far more attractive service under Caesar's son. The discontent and Antony's wrath had fallen mainly on the *Fourth* Legion and the *Martia* Legion, whose number has not been preserved and seems to have preferred being known as the war god Mars' own. As these troops marched north from Brundisium both of these units deserted Antony and marched under discipline to join Octavian. They brought with them some supplies, including a number of war elephants.[3]

The young Caesar had already gathered some 3,000 volunteers from amongst the veterans and had led these to Rome earlier in November. Few of them had proper weapons and equipment, and they showed a reluctance to back him against Antony. They were also disappointed that he was taking no immediate action to punish the conspirators. Caesar's heir had yet to prove himself and his strength and connections were still modest, so he left Rome and began recruiting again. When the fully equipped and trained *Fourth* and *Martia* legions joined him, he at last had the basis for a proper army. Alongside them he formed new versions of Caesar's old *Seventh* and *Eighth*, as well as a praetorian cohort of picked troops to act as bodyguard and an elite reserve. The young Caesar now had more than 'just a name'. He had an army.[4]

One legion remained faithful to Antony and another soon arrived at Brundisium and joined him. These were the *Second* and *Thirty-Fifth*. Their loyalty was helped at the end of November when he gave them a bounty of 500 denarii, matching Octavian's promise. He also had a substantial force of auxiliaries, including light infantry and Moorish light horsemen. At some point, he re-formed Caesar's old *V Alaudae*, the 'Larks', originally recruited from Gauls and then given citizenship. There was little to be gained by fighting Octavian at the moment, nor was there any pretext. Instead, Antony decided to march to Cisalpine Gaul and occupy the province allotted to him by the Popular Assembly. Before he went, he made those senators who gathered to see him take an oath of loyalty to him. His soldiers did the same and could probably be relied on more readily to keep it. Given time, Antony had the knack of getting troops, and especially officers, to like him. He now had a force of perhaps 10,000–15,000 men. It would be his first campaign as overall commander.[5]

CONSUL OR PUBLIC ENEMY?

Decimus Brutus refused to give up Cisalpine Gaul. Earlier in the year he had led the provincial garrison on an expedition against the Alpine tribes. He won some small victories, sharing the rigours of a campaign with his men and rewarding them with plunder to 'make them firm for the defence of our concerns'. He told Cicero that he thought he had 'succeeded; for they have practical experience of my liberality and spirit'. There were two legions already in Cisalpine Gaul and soon after his arrival Decimus Brutus began raising another two. Antony also continued to recruit, forming three new legions by the beginning of 43 BC. These new units were inexperienced and needed intensive training before they would become effective. All seem to have been quite small in size, far below their theoretical strength. The normal practice was to establish a cadre, appointing officers and setting up the structure for the entire legion, and then allocate recruits as these became available. This made practical sense, but there was also a propaganda element. An army of four or six legions sounded impressive, even if in reality most of these units were mere shadows of their normal size.[6]

Decimus was determined to retain the province and the army, although it is probable that his command was supposed to expire at

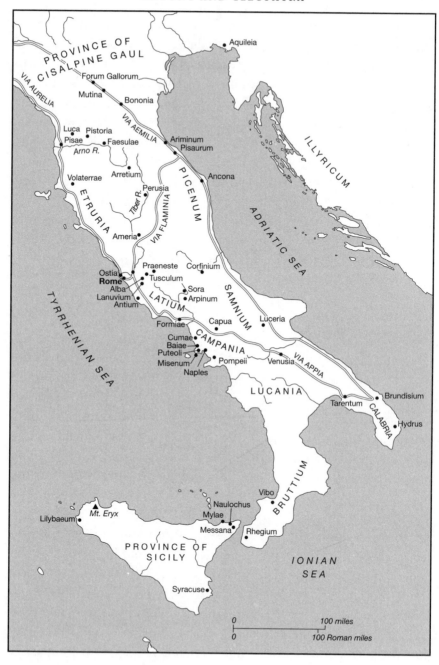

Italy

the end of 44 BC. He was unwilling to face Antony in the open and perhaps still hoped that fighting could be avoided. Slaughtering his baggage oxen and smoking the meat to bolster his store of food, he took his army into the town of Mutina and prepared to defend it. Antony established a blockade, but does not seem to have attempted a direct assault. He, too, was reluctant to begin an open war, and anyway it was winter, with poor weather and difficult conditions for foraging. Brutus' men were doubtless happier to be billeted in a town rather than camping in siege lines outside.[7]

From late in 44 BC Cicero lobbied hard to have the Senate name Antony as a public enemy and formally declare hostilities against him. Most senators were reluctant to take this step, and Fulvia and Antony's mother Julia were very visible expressing their dismay that a consul of Rome should be condemned in his absence and without trial. Some senators had connections to Antony, although his two uncles, Caius Antonius and Lucius Julius Caesar, were never more than lukewarm in their support and at times hostile. Many had no particular sympathy for Decimus Brutus or the other conspirators; almost all feared the return of civil war and felt that any compromise would be preferable. To Cicero's disgust, the Senate sent a delegation of three former consuls – Caesar's father-in-law Calpurnius Piso, Octavian's stepfather Philippus and Sergius Sulpicius Rufus – to negotiate with Antony.

The fear of civil war was the most powerful emotion, made worse because it remained so uncertain what the sides would be and who was likely to win. Lepidus was now proconsul of Transalpine Gaul and Nearer Spain, and Asinius Pollio governed Further Spain. Both were Caesareans, but that did not mean they would automatically ally themselves with Antony, and the latter was in any case busy enough trying to contain the resurgent Sextus Pompey. On 1 January 43 BC, the new consuls Hirtius and Pansa took office. They were also Caesareans, although they had not been especially close to Antony in recent months.[8]

Antony's brother Caius had gone out to Macedonia, but the legion left there had been subverted by Brutus. Caius was placed under arrest and Brutus took his place as governor and was soon recruiting more soldiers. More violent confrontations had already erupted in the eastern provinces. On his way to Syria, Dolabella had visited Asia, the province allocated by Caesar to Trebonius. Feigning friendship, Dolabella had taken the proconsul by surprise and had him killed. Cicero claimed that Trebonius was tortured first and there were grisly stories of his severed head being thrown about like a ball until the face was unrecognisable. While Dolabella enthusiastically plundered Asia, Cassius went to Syria and brought the army there under his control. He and Brutus now led armies and governed provinces without any authority to do so. At Rome, Cicero struggled and eventually succeeded in getting this recognition for them.[9]

Sulpicius died on the way back from meeting Antony. The other two delegates returned in February and reported that the latter was willing to give up Cisalpine Gaul, as long as he kept the other Gaul and retained command of his six legions for five years. Antony was insistent that before this period lapsed, Brutus and Cassius must have given up their own commands, tacitly accepting that they held them. He also demanded formal recognition of all his acts as consul and, in due course, discharge bonuses for his soldiers equal to those promised by Octavian.[10]

Since the beginning of the year, the consuls had led the Senate in making preparations for war. Both gathered armies and Octavian was awarded propraetorian *imperium*, although he was still a private citizen. A man with his own fiercely loyal army simply could not be ignored. Decimus Brutus was also confirmed in his command. The Senate rejected Antony's terms, but only after a fierce debate. Lucius Caesar blocked the move to name Antony as a public enemy. The *senatus consultum ultimum* was passed, but rather than a formal declaration of war, the crisis was termed a *tumultus* – something closer in sense to a state of emergency. In many ways the situation was similar to the build-up to war in 49 BC. Both sides were reluctant to commit themselves irrevocably and still hoped that the other would make concessions. There was another attempt to form a delegation to go to Antony, but this came to nothing. Lepidus sent letters urging compromise. Yet while all this went on, Decimus Brutus' army was steadily consuming its stocks of food and would starve or surrender if not relieved within a few months.[11]

By the start of spring, Hirtius, Pansa and Octavian were ready to move – two former Caesareans and Caesar's son marching against Antony to save one of the dictator's murderers. Cicero had decided that the dangers of recognising Octavian were outweighed by his usefulness. He provided three of the seven legions marching to relieve Mutina, the only experienced troops in an army that otherwise was formed of levies. For the moment he placed the *Fourth* and the *Martia* under Hirtius' command, but the soldiers remained loyal to him. Brutus and Cassius both felt that Cicero and the Senate were unwise to trust the young Caesar, but as was so often the case they did not suggest any practical alternative. Three veteran legions could not be ignored and had a fighting power far greater than their numbers. Cicero felt the nineteen-year-old could be used, saying, 'we must praise the young man, decorate him, and discard him' (*laudanum aduluscentem, ornandum, tollendum*).[12]

Hirtius approached Mutina first, but on his own did not have the strength to attack Antony, and this remained true even when he was joined by Octavian. To let Decimus Brutus know that relief was on the way, they tried lighting beacons, but in the end the news was carried by a man who sneaked through the lines and then swam a river. The same method was used to reply and in the coming days Decimus also employed carrier pigeons with some success. In April, Pansa led the four newly raised legions to join them.[13]

Antony had word of his coming and saw an opportunity to destroy these inexperienced troops before the enemy forces combined. It was similar to the bold attacks he had led in Judaea and Egypt, if on a much larger scale. He decided to take the *Second* and *Thirty-Fifth* legions, along with two elite praetorian cohorts (one his own and the other raised by one of his supporters), and some of his enrolled veterans, as well as supporting cavalry and light troops. Yet unlike Judaea and Egypt, this time his opponents were a lot more capable. Hirtius and Octavian moved first, sending the *Martia* and their own praetorian cohorts to rendezvous with Pansa's column. On 14 April the combined force advanced towards the town of Forum Gallorum, moving along the Via Aemilia, which at this point ran on a causeway through patchy marshland. Patrols spotted some of Antony's cavalry and then noticed the gleam of helmets and equipment amongst the long reeds.

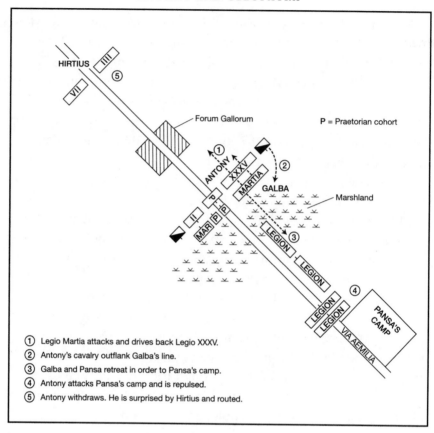

The Battle of Forum Gallorum

Remembering the executions of the previous summer, the men of the *Martia* boiled over with rage and attacked immediately, supported by the two praetorian cohorts. As yet they had only spotted Antony's cavalry and skirmishers, for the *Second* and *Thirty-Fifth* were concealed in Forum Gallorum itself. It was a confused, unplanned engagement and the broken terrain produced several separate combats. Pansa sent two of the raw legions up in support, but the battle was already well advanced before these arrived.

The commander of the *Martia* was another of Caesar's former officers named Servius Sulpicius Galba, and he later reported that they had formed the ten cohorts of the *Martia* and the two of praetorians in a single line – an unusually shallow formation for a Roman army. On the right, he led eight cohorts of the *Martia* and drove back the *Thirty-Fifth* no less than half a mile. This left his flank exposed and Antony's cavalry led by the Moors began to envelop the line. In the confusion of this fluid combat, the general found himself riding amongst Antony's soldiers. Antony himself was some distance behind him, for a Roman commander was expected to direct and encourage from just behind the fighting line. Galba was spotted as he fled back to his own troops. Chased by the Antonians, he had to sling his shield behind him to stop himself being killed by his own side when the recruits coming up in support mistook him for a bold enemy leader.

The veteran soldiers of the Macedonian legions fought each other with a grim and, according to Appian silent, savagery. Octavian's praetorians were ground down as they stubbornly held the Via Aemilia itself. On the left side of the road, there were only two cohorts of the *Martia* and Hirtius' praetorians. Before long Antony's cavalry was threatening their flank. They were forced to retreat and soon the whole line was giving ground. Pansa was wounded by a missile, but the resistance of the experienced troops permitted the whole army to withdraw to its camp without suffering catastrophic losses. Antony pressed them and tried to make the victory decisive by storming the camp. His men were now weary and the enemy still numerous and determined enough to repulse them.

Antony led his men back to their camp some miles away. They were cheered by their success, but physically tired, emotionally drained and hungry after hours of waiting, marching and fighting. Caesar would probably have camped on the spot and brought supplies to them. Antony saw no danger and as the column marched carelessly along, Hirtius led the *Fourth* and the *Seventh* in a surprise attack. The Antonian soldiers fled, surrendered or were killed. The eagle standards of the *Second* and *Thirty-Fifth* were captured, along with half of their other standards, and the two effectively ceased to exist as units. The survivors spent the night in the houses of Forum Gallorum.[14]

The blockade of Mutina was still intact, but Octavian and Hirtius moved the combined army closer. A week later they tried to break through the siege lines. A battle developed and Antony was defeated, making him abandon the siege and retreat. When news reached

Rome, the Senate was finally persuaded to declare him a public enemy. Yet control of events was slipping away from Cicero and the others eager to prosecute the war against Antony. Hirtius had been killed as he led his men into the Antonian camp. Pansa succumbed to his wounds soon afterwards. Octavian was left in command of the entire army and this was clearly very convenient for him. There need not have been anything suspicious about the consuls' deaths and neither is it certain that he would not have found them sympathetic to him if they had lived. Neither had shown much enthusiasm for the conspirators.

Octavian asked the Senate for a triumph. Cicero tried and failed to get him the lesser honour of an ovation. Caesar's triumph after the Munda campaign in 45 BC had shocked people for blatantly commemorating a victory in a civil war. Less than two years later it seemed much easier to discuss such things. On the whole, the Senate was relieved to see Antony defeated, but was not inclined to be generous. Rewards to the soldiers of the *Fourth* and *Martia* were reduced and Octavian was not included in the commission tasked with providing land for the soldiers on discharge. It was a sign that moves were now under way to 'discard' the young Caesar.[15]

ALLIANCE AND PROSCRIPTION LISTS

Antony had been outmanoeuvred and out-fought during the campaign. Once again, it is worth emphasising that this was his first campaign in sole command and his military experience of large-scale operations was limited to Italy in 49 BC and Macedonia in 48 BC. The civil wars were fought by improvised armies containing many inexperienced amateurs. Yet he was at his best during the retreat, sharing the same poor rations as his men, even drinking stagnant water and eating wild fruit and roots scavenged during the march into the Alps. There was encouragement when he was joined by Publius Ventidius Bassus with three legions recruited from the colonies set up for Caesar's veterans. Ventidius had himself served Caesar in Gaul and the civil war, which probably made it easier for him to re-enlist these old soldiers.

Octavian's veterans were bitterly opposed to serving under Decimus Brutus, whom the Senate now appointed to overall command of the forces in Cisalpine Gaul. The young Caesar himself was scarcely any more enthusiastic. The victors were divided amongst themselves and this prevented any concerted pursuit, helping Antony to escape into Transalpine Gaul, where Lepidus controlled a powerful army that included many experienced soldiers and officers. The former *Magister Equitum* had proclaimed his loyalty to the Republic on numerous occasions, but Cicero and many others found it difficult to trust him. It did not help the situation that around this time Cassius received formal recognition of his command, while even Sextus Pompey was finally appointed to a naval command instead of being simply a rebel. Caesar's enemies seemed to be growing strong and little incentive was being offered to former Caesareans to support the Senate. The veterans were frustrated by the failure to punish his assassins. For Lepidus, as for the other leaders at this time, power and security depended ultimately on control of his army. His men struggled to see Antony as the real enemy and his best troops were re-enrolled veterans, for Lepidus had re-formed several of Caesar's legions including the *Tenth*.

The two armies camped near each other. Antony made no hostile moves, and no doubt encouraged his men to fraternise with those of Lepidus. Plutarch tells us that he had not shaved since the defeat at Mutina – a mark of mourning Caesar himself had employed until he avenged the massacre of fifteen cohorts at the hands of rebels in 54–53 BC – and that he wore a black cloak. Within days, the army defected to Antony en masse. Lepidus claimed to have been forced to follow his men, but it seems more likely that he preferred to join Antony as he had little to gain from fighting him. One of Lepidus' legates committed suicide, but everyone else seems to have been happy at the change. In Spain, Pollio protested his loyalty for a little longer, but also eventually aligned himself with Antony. Joined by all the governors of the western provinces, Antony and his allies controlled something like eighteen or nineteen legions. Many were small in size, and not all could be safely deployed in the civil war, but the quality of the troops was high. Within months of his defeat, Antony had grown far stronger militarily.[16]

Decimus Brutus was in no position to confront them. Some of his troops defected and he fled, only to be captured and held prisoner by a Gallic chieftain. Octavian had command of his own and most of the legions of Hirtius and Pansa – with new recruits, some eight legions. He sent some of his centurions to Rome, demanding that he be elected to the now vacant consulship. There was a rumour that Cicero would be his colleague. The orator had vainly tried to persuade Brutus to bring his army from Macedonia to Italy and provide forces to face Antony and his allies. The Senate refused to consider a man who was still weeks short of his twentieth birthday. In response, Octavian marched his army south from Cisalpine Gaul, this crossing of the Rubicon no more than incidental.

Pansa had left one legion behind to protect Rome. Three more were summoned from the province of Africa. All of them defected to Octavian when he camped outside the city. Reluctantly – Cicero most reluctantly of all – the senators went out to greet him and agree to his terms. He was elected suffect consul on 19 August 43 BC, with Quintus Pedius as colleague. The latter was also a relative of Caesar and had been named as a secondary heir in the will. Octavian's adoption was also officially confirmed. Both Antony and Dolabella had finally been condemned as public enemies in the previous months. Now this was repealed and, instead, the surviving conspirators as well as Sextus Pompey were outlawed. There were rewards for the soldiers, each of whom received immediately 2,500 denarii from state funds – half of what they had been promised on discharge.[17]

Octavian took his army north again. He was not marching to war, but the military basis of power was blatant when he met with Lepidus and Antony for three days on an island near Bononia. Finally, all of Caesar's associates joined in alliance against the conspirators and anyone else who opposed them. They agreed to form a 'board of three to restore the state', the *tresviri rei publicae constituendae*. Unlike the informal alliance between Pompey, Crassus and Caesar, this was formally established in law when they reached Rome and their powers voted to them for five years. Antony and Lepidus retained the provinces already under their control, and Octavian was given Africa, Sicily and Sardinia. Between them the triumvirate soon led more than forty legions, although many of these formations were small in size and some consisted mainly of untested recruits.[18]

The law creating the triumvirate, the *Lex Titia* after the tribune who proposed it, was passed by the *Concilium Plebis* on 27 November 43 BC. It granted the three men power to make law without consulting either Senate or people, and made them the supreme judicial authorities. Elections were controlled as they had been under Caesar's dictatorship. Antony and his two colleagues publicly rejected Caesar's policy of clemency, since his mercy had spared the men who subsequently murdered him. More urgently, their army was now vast and the soldiers had been promised generous rewards. The triumvirs needed money to pay and the quickest way to get this was to take it from the wealthy. Instead of Caesar, they chose to copy Sulla and began a new set of proscriptions. Enemies were to be killed and so, too, were many men whose chief crimes were to be rich and not to have sufficient ties to the triumvirate.

A connection to just one of them was not always sufficient. Octavian is said to have wanted to spare Cicero, but Antony was determined that he should die and had his way. In return he sacrificed his uncle, Lucius Julius Caesar. Lepidus allowed – some claimed that he inspired – the addition to the lists of his brother Lucius Aemilius Lepidus Paullus, the man whose loyalty Caesar had bought during his consulship in 50 BC. It is not clear how many people died in these purges. Appian claims that as many as 300 senators and 2,000 equestrians were killed, but these might equally be the overall number of names on the proscription lists. Lucius Caesar went to his sister Julia and Antony's mother protected him. Plutarch claims that she confronted the men who came to kill him, blocking the doorway and said repeatedly, 'You shall not kill Lucius Caesar without first killing me, the mother of your commander!' They gave up and Antony later granted his uncle a pardon after his mother had accosted him in the Forum. Lepidus' brother escaped to Miletus and lived on in exile.[19]

They were not the only survivors. Many of the proscribed were hidden or managed to escape abroad and take refuge with Sextus Pompey or one of the conspirators. Yet many did die, and there were even more stories of savagery and betrayal. Cicero calmly faced his executioners on 7 December. His brother and nephew had already been killed, but his son was in Greece and joined Brutus' army.

The proscription lists consisted solely of men. Their children did not suffer, unless they had sons already come to manhood. No women were included or deliberately harmed, and their own property was untouched. They did run risks if they protected proscribed husbands or children, although there is no record of any actually being killed. Women were credited with both saving and condemning. Julia was able to save her brother; Fulvia was said to have cajoled Antony into adding names to the list. The sources are hostile to her, but a woman who had lost two husbands might well have scores to settle. For all the savagery of the civil war and proscriptions, a measure of restraint remained. Julia certainly spent time in Rome when her son was declared as a public enemy, and Fulvia may also have been there. Servilia, her daughters and Brutus' wife were similarly able to live in the city and lobby on behalf of the conspirators when Antony was dominant, and later when the triumvirs arrived and Brutus and Cassius were now enemies of the state. Struggles with a rival politician did not require the death or exile of his family and only adult male relations were at all likely to be attacked. Despite the brutality of the civil war, some conventions were still respected. All sides purported to be fighting for the Republic against its enemies; ideology played no major part, and it was only men who could hold power, so only men who were both acceptable to fight and worth killing.

The overwhelming majority of all classes had hoped to avoid a renewal of civil war after the Ides of March. The conspirators were too young and not yet of sufficient status and influence to take control of the Republic. Brutus wanted to emphasise that they had acted reluctantly to remove a tyrant and restore the Republic and the rule of proper law. Yet even if he and his colleagues had wanted to take charge of the state, it is unlikely that they could have done so. Dislike of the dictatorship, and sometimes of Caesar personally, did not automatically transfer into enthusiastic support for Brutus, Cassius and the others. Most senators had no appetite for going to war to protect the conspirators or to destroy Antony. Cicero tried to rally support for this cause and never really succeeded, but in many ways the conspirators were a liability, permanently resented by Caesar's veterans and many of his more senior associates. The orator may have made things worse, forcing a crisis and demonising Antony, provoking a war that he failed to win. Civil war might have broken out anyway. Fear and the difficulty of trusting political rivals contributed as much to this conflict as they had to the struggle between Caesar and Pompey. Once again, policy played little or no part, and the essence of the struggle was personal rivalry.

On the 15 March 44 BC, Antony was consul, but had no troops under his command. By the end of 43 BC, he shared supreme power far greater than the consulship and was joint leader of the most powerful army in existence. None of this would have come if he had simply completed his term as consul and then become proconsul of an enlarged Gallic province. Antony had taken advantage of the opportunities offered as order broke down and the Republic lurched towards civil war, and he had survived the dangers that accompanied them. There is no reason to suggest that he followed a planned path. Like any Roman aristocrat, he was determined to rise to the top of public life, to gain as much power, influence, wealth and glory as he could. It should also be emphasised that he was legally elected consul and allocated a province and command of an army. The conspirators had a far weaker constitutional position.

This was even more true of Octavian, who had been similarly opportunistic. His rise was even more spectacular than Antony's and could not have happened so quickly had he not been 'praised' and 'decorated'. Neither he nor Antony had much reason to respect the traditions of a Republic that they had never seen working properly. What both men planned for the future, other than a general desire to excel, is unlikely to have been very clearly developed even in their own minds. There was still a war to be fought and vengeance to be exacted for the death of Caesar.

XVIII

GODDESS

In May 44 BC Cicero passed on a rumour that Cleopatra and 'that Caesar of hers' had died on the way back to Egypt, which he hoped was true. A month later he would write baldly, 'I hate the queen' (*Reginam odio* in the pithy Latin) and also complained about the behaviour of a courtier of hers called Ammonius. This had not prevented him from visiting the queen during Caesar's lifetime and accepting the offer of gifts 'that had to do with learning and not derogatory to my dignity'. That these presents had never materialised did much to feed his dislike and he railed at the 'arrogance of the queen herself'. Cleopatra left agents behind in Rome to look after her interests and the outburst seems to have been prompted by a question of whether or not he would assist them. Rome was always full of men lobbying on behalf of rulers and communities and trying to persuade senators to support them.[1]

This short paragraph in a long letter dealing with many other things is the fullest mention of Cleopatra in all of Cicero's correspondence or other writings. It rather misses the point to expound on the orator's difficult relationships with women, as if explanation needs to be found as to why he did not like her. Far more significant is the fact that he mentions Cleopatra only briefly and on just a handful of occasions in 44 BC, and never again after that. If the queen had played any role in the developing power struggle at Rome, she would have figured far more prominently, even if the comments were hostile. For the moment, neither she nor Caesarion mattered enough to attract much concern, or even hatred, from leading Romans.[2]

Perhaps the journey back to Alexandria was eventful. Sea travel often proved dangerous in the ancient world and the threat of disease was ever present. If there were perils en route, then Cleopatra and her son survived them. So did her brother and consort, Ptolemy XIV, assuming that he had been with them in Rome, which seems most likely. Yet by the end of August 44 BC the teenage boy was dead. The Jewish historian Josephus, writing a century later, says that Cleopatra had him poisoned. His attitude to the queen was generally hostile, but in spite of this there is little reason to doubt the story. Most of the Ptolemies who met violent deaths did so at the behest of their own family. Still, it is just possible that the youth died of natural causes.[3]

If so, then the death was very convenient for Cleopatra. Serious rivals for the throne could only come from within the family, most of all from siblings. Caesar had confirmed brother and sister as joint rulers, perhaps because he understood that the sole rule of a queen was unlikely to be accepted and perhaps also to honour the spirit of Auletes' will. With her Roman lover and protector alive, Cleopatra could be confident of controlling her consort. Now that Caesar was dead and Ptolemy XIV was growing to maturity – he was fifteen or sixteen – this was far less certain. There was a very real threat that influential courtiers and Alexandrian aristocrats would coalesce around the king and see increasing his power as the path to wealth and influence for themselves. Cleopatra had narrowly survived and prevailed in the struggle with Ptolemy XIII and can have had no wish to repeat the experience.

There would be nothing particularly unusual for the Ptolemies – or indeed any of the other Hellenistic dynasties and in later centuries Rome's emperors – about the use of assassination in dynastic politics. His removal left Cleopatra and Arsinoe as the only surviving children of Auletes. The younger sister remained in comfortable captivity in the Temple of Artemis at Ephesus. She was a threat, and had already once proclaimed herself queen back in 48 BC, but for the moment a distant one, and anyway beyond Cleopatra's reach. Arsinoe would need powerful backing to attempt a return to the kingdom and such support could only come from a Roman. This made it all the more important for Cleopatra's agents to continue courting influential men at Rome, just as her father had done throughout his life. There were no doubt others there willing to speak and bribe on behalf of

Arsinoe as well. In 44 BC Antony appears to have announced that the younger sister should be released and made ruler of Cyprus, although it is unclear whether anything had been done to implement this before his acts were abolished.[4]

Cleopatra knew that only Roman support could secure her own rule, and that nothing could guarantee this, especially as the Republic began to descend into civil war. Antony dominated, then seemed to fall, before emerging once again to control the Republic with the other triumvirs. Their power was based upon their military strength and the only thing that would supplant them would be superior force. This made the legions left in Egypt by Caesar a valuable asset to any ambitious Roman leader. At some point a fourth unit had joined the three stationed there in 47 BC, and Aulus Allienus had taken over command from Rufio, who disappears from our sources. Probably this was part of the preparations for the projected Parthian campaign. In the past these troops had bolstered Cleopatra's rule. Now their very presence was a danger, risking direct involvement in Rome's civil war.[5]

When Dolabella sent a messenger to Alexandria asking the queen to send the legions to him, it may almost have been a relief and she readily obeyed. This was probably early in 43 BC. Dolabella had taken a long time before going to his province of Syria, and the delay allowed Cassius to get there first and rally support. Fighting had already broken out following a mutiny of some of the legions stationed in the province, which two of Caesar's governors had struggled to suppress. Both sides now buried their differences and joined Cassius. Allienus had not heard of this when he led his army into the province. Taken unawares, and faced with eight legions to his own four, he surrendered and his troops defected to Cassius. There seems to have been very little enthusiasm for serving under Dolabella, as well as a desire to be on the strongest side, even if it was led by one of the conspirators. When he finally arrived, Dolabella was besieged in Laodicia, but could not hold out and committed suicide before the garrison surrendered in the summer of 43 BC.[6]

Cleopatra had obeyed the instructions of a consul of the Republic and quite probably had been glad to assist a man fighting against one of Caesar's murderers. Yet the latter had won and was unlikely to be well disposed towards her. The legions gone, she had only a small force of mercenaries left under her control. This might be sufficient to control minor internal unrest, but would be pathetically inadequate to meet any invasion by a Roman army.[7]

Fortunately, Cassius was busy, as he and Brutus prepared for the inevitable confrontation with the triumvirs, and had no time to go to Egypt. Instead, he demanded support in the form of money, grain and warships. Cleopatra stalled, pleading a succession of bad harvests that made it impossible for her to give him what he wanted immediately. Soon, she would have heard of the emergence of Antony, Octavian and Lepidus at Rome, of the declaration of Brutus and Cassius as public enemies, and the triumvirate's pledge to avenge Caesar. All of this must have been welcome and convinced her that it was better to resist Cassius and support the triumvirs. This made sense if she expected them to win, since she would want the victors to confirm her in power. The pragmatic politics of survival probably combined with natural hatred of the men who had murdered her lover. For the moment, she could not openly declare her allegiance and continued to promise to aid Cassius, just not at that time.

The conspirator soon grew suspicious and directly sent instructions to Serapion, Cleopatra's governor of Cyprus – and just possibly the same man used as an ambassador by Caesar in the Alexandrian War. This official readily obeyed, independently of the queen. Cassius controlled Ephesus and he seems to have decided to make use of Arsinoe, perhaps giving her back nominal rule of Cyprus itself. This was a threat to Cleopatra and might force her to agree to his demands. If not, then in due course she could be replaced by her more pliant sister.

Cleopatra prepared a squadron of warships just as Cassius had requested. However, in 42 BC she led them in person, not to help the conspirators, but to join up with the triumvirs, who had at last launched their offensive. It was a bold move, unusual for a female monarch, although in some ways less surprising from the woman who had in 48 BC raised an army and invaded Egypt to seize back her throne from her brother. Yet courage and confidence do not in themselves bring fortune or success. Her earlier invasion of Egypt had bogged down into stalemate. This time the weather took a hand and many of the warships were wrecked in a storm. Cleopatra herself fell ill. Perhaps it was seasickness, but since she had travelled by sea before, most likely it was something more serious.

The battered remnants of the expedition eventually trailed back to Alexandria. Undaunted, Cleopatra ordered the construction of new warships to replace the losses. In the event, the war was decided before she could take part. The contribution of Egypt was a tiny, almost insignificant part of the struggle between the huge armies led by the conspirators and triumvirs. Yet the cost to Cleopatra was considerable at a time of economic hardship and once again the silver content of her coins was reduced. Standing aside would not have endeared her to whoever won, and Arsinoe was there as a viable alternative to be imposed by Roman force. Cleopatra needed to gamble on doing enough to win the favour of the victors, without provoking their opponents so badly that she did not survive the war.[8]

Surviving, and still more profiting from the struggles within the Roman Republic was a delicate balancing act, made harder as alliances changed. At different times both Antony and Cassius were willing to take power from Cleopatra and give it to Arsinoe. It was not until the end of 43 BC that the civil war became more firmly a conflict between Caesar's supporters and the conspirators.

ISIS AND HORUS

As well as coping with the unpredictable threats and opportunities offered by Rome's internal conflict, Cleopatra had the ever-present task of maintaining her rule in her own kingdom. After the death of Ptolemy XIV, she did not attempt to reign as sole monarch, but straight away took Caesarion as co-ruler. Still an infant, the boy was completely under his mother's control, a situation likely to last at least until he became an adult and married. For the moment, the kingdom had both a king and a queen, and there was no danger of separate and rival factions emerging around mother and son. Caesarion was sole heir, offering the prospect of long-term stability for the regime. Cleopatra had no husband, and as far as we can tell took no lovers, so that there would not be any other children and potential rivals. The aristocracy in Alexandria and the members of the royal court had little alternative but to accept the current regime, at least for the moment.[9]

The long years of disruption during Auletes' reign and the disputes between Cleopatra and her siblings had badly damaged the administration and infrastructure of the kingdom. Royal projects, such as maintaining the irrigation systems, had been neglected. When the inundations were poor each year from 43 to 41 BC, this neglect made the situation worse. Cleopatra was being no more than truthful when she told Cassius that the harvests were bad. As usual, the royal administration attempted to manage the situation, employing the food stores from past levies and the current taxation. Hunger could readily prompt unrest. Like most administrations in the ancient world, Cleopatra's government were especially careful to placate the wealthier classes and the populations of the main cities. Volatile Alexandria was not to go short of food, although Josephus claims that the Jewish community there did suffer. Significantly, royal officials were also warned not to extract too high a levy from the tenants of the great landowners.[10]

As far as possible, Cleopatra tried to keep all of the different communities living in her kingdom content to accept her rule. An inscription survives from this period confirming the right to asylum of fugitives taking refuge in a synagogue at Leontopolis, a town with a sizeable Jewish settlement. The text is in Greek, apart from the last line, which is in Latin and says, 'The queen and king have given the order.' Even after the legions had left, a good proportion of the mercenaries serving as soldiers and policemen were probably Romans, lured by comfortable conditions and generous pay, just as Gabinius' men had been in the past.[11]

There is some suggestion that regional officials were given considerable freedom in these years, probably continuing the policy of Auletes. Inscriptions celebrate the achievements of Callimachus, a *strategos* in the Thebiad, and make only the briefest mention of the king and queen. Cleopatra's government may also have introduced a new style of decree, the decision given royal approval by a simple 'let it be so' (*ginestho* in Greek). These were sent to senior officials, whose task it then was to copy them and send them round to all the relevant officials.[12]

Money was short, but just like her father Cleopatra continued to be generous to the temple cults of the kingdom, cultivating the most important part of the native population. She completed work on the great temple of the goddess Hathor and her son Ihy at Dendera. Its southern, rear wall was covered in reliefs depicting Cleopatra and Caesarion in traditional regalia making an offering to the two deities of the temple and other important gods. 'Ptolemy Caesar' stands tall and in front of his mother, holding out a gift of incense, while she shakes the *sistrum*, the sacred rattle used in the rites of the goddess Isis. Artistically at least, traditions are maintained, the pharaoh and his female counterpart fulfil their roles as the representatives of the gods on earth, the direct link with heaven, ensuring that order prevails over chaos and Maat is preserved.

Temple building gave work to the construction force, honour and status to the cult involved and its priesthood, and provided grand monuments celebrating the regime. Soon after Cleopatra returned from Rome, work seems to have begun on a grand 'birth-temple' for Caesarion at Hermonthis. Such structures had a tradition stretching back into the distant past. This one was considerably larger than was normal, and was also unusual in that it does not seem to have been closely associated with an existing temple. Sadly, the structure no longer survives, having been demolished and replaced with a sugar processing plant in the middle of the nineteenth century, but fortunately a few photographs and more extensive drawings were made before this occurred.

One relief showed multiple scenes of childbirth, and some or all may represent Cleopatra herself. She is described in hieroglyphs as 'The female Horus, the great one, the mistress of perfection, brilliant in counsel, the mistress of the Two Lands, Cleopatra, the goddess who loves her father'. Elsewhere, she is also named 'the image of her father', although on this section the cartouche was left blank and not filled in with her name. Being known as the female Horus was a clear indication of rule – for kings were the representatives of

Horus on earth – and yet Cleopatra never receives all the titles of a pharaoh.[13]

At face value, tradition seems very much alive in the temple cults supported by Cleopatra. If anything, there seems to have been more revivals of very ancient practices, imagery and titles during her reign. It is also possible to see echoes of the ancient cults in the queen's own life. Just as her father had been the 'New Dionysus', Cleopatra styled herself the 'New Isis'; just as Dionysus had grown from a god of wine into a much more powerful and all-encompassing great god of victory and prosperity, so too the Egyptian goddess Isis had changed into an international cult. There was a temple to her at Athens in the fourth century BC and during Cleopatra's lifetime there were determined, but unsuccessful attempts made to suppress her cult in Rome itself.

We know much more about Isis as a goddess worshipped by Greeks and other foreigners than in her Egyptian form. Plutarch, whose biography of Antony is such an important source for Cleopatra's life as well as his own, elsewhere provided the longest account of the Isis story. Sister and wife of Osiris, they were children of the Sky goddess. Osiris and Isis ruled Egypt as king and queen, teaching the people how to grow crops and prosper, to follow laws and worship the gods. However, their jealous brother Seth murdered Osiris. After considerable adventures, Isis found her husband's body in a distant land, but as she brought him back to Egypt, Seth stole it away, chopped the corpse into pieces and flung them to the winds. Helped by Anubis, the jackal-headed god of the dead, Isis found all the fragments – apart from the penis, which had fallen into the Nile and been consumed by fish. She sewed the pieces together, fabricated a new penis and breathed life back into her husband's body. They made love and in due course she gave birth to their son Horus. Osiris then left the land of the living to rule the world of the dead. Isis protected the boy until he grew old enough and was able to overthrow his wicked uncle. Mother and son then ruled Egypt.[14]

It is hard to know how far Egyptians would have recognised Plutarch's version of the story or, indeed, even be sure that most Greek worshippers of Isis believed the same myth. Few ancient religions had clearly developed and universally accepted theology or even traditions. Cults varied from region to region, and the same deity was often perceived and presented in very different ways although given the same name. Greek settlers in Egypt had equated the local divinities with familiar gods and goddesses, worshipping them in their own way, while the native population persisted in their traditional beliefs. In Egypt and elsewhere, for the Greeks Isis expanded to take on attributes of Athena, Demeter and Aphrodite – wisdom, fertility, law, as mother and as wife, as source of rebirth and resurrection with the promise of an afterlife. Finding Osiris a little too alien, the Ptolemies devised a new consort for her, in the god Serapis. Egyptians never seem to have adopted the new god, but his worship was common amongst the Greeks in Egypt and spread abroad through association with the popular Isis. The Isis cult seemed exotic to Greeks and Romans alike, with its shaven-headed priests, *sistrum* rattles, dramatic rituals and deeply emotional experiences. It had the appeal of ancient and faraway wisdom, even if it may well have borne little resemblance to the traditional cult of Egypt.

We cannot say whether Cleopatra chose to associate herself with Isis because it made practical sense to become the personification of such a powerful and popular deity or for more personal, emotional reasons. Perhaps it was a mixture of the two. To be born a Ptolemy set someone apart from the rest of humanity, for they were divine and successors to Alexander the Great. If she did genuinely feel herself to be Isis, it would surely have been in some variant of the Greek perception of the goddess. The traditional imagery at Dendera, Hermonthis and other shrines was conventional, changing little over the centuries. It did not mean an active participation in the cults by the monarch – something especially unlikely for the infant Caesarion. Temples were not churches regularly attended by great congregations, but sacred houses for the gods, entered only by the priests as part of the perpetual cycle of rites. If some very old formulae and images were revived under Cleopatra, the initiative is most likely to have come from the priestly cults, given money and royal favour and permitted to oversee the rituals as they saw fit.

The Isis story of a murdered husband and the infant son who needed protection until he matured and could face the killer had a parallel in Cleopatra's own life. As she was Isis, Caesar could be the

GODDESS

dead Osiris or Serapis, and Caesarion would be Horus. Yet apart from the name Ptolemy Caesar, there is no allusion to Cleopatra's murdered lover in any of the monuments and iconography aimed at an Egyptian audience. These were far more concerned with stressing her own and her son's legitimacy as rulers and their roles as divine representatives on earth. Horus, the good ruler of Egypt, is shown over the head of Caesarion in the form of a bird on the Dendera relief. The blessing of the gods who protect Egypt and ensure prosperity was the important thing. There is no place for a dead father or the need to avenge his death.

Perhaps there was a hint of this in the monument called the Caesareum, which Cleopatra devoted to Caesar in Alexandria, although it is not clear when work began on this, and it may well have been later in her reign. It is all too easy to forget that the monuments in the overtly Hellenic city have almost all been lost and focus only on the great and very Egyptian temples that survive. In Greek, Caesarion was titled 'the father-loving and mother-loving god' (*Theos Philopator Philometor*) and 'Ptolemy called Caesar'. After the death of Ptolemy XIV, Cleopatra herself had dispensed with the title of 'sibling-loving', perhaps aware of the irony, but remained the 'father-loving goddess' (*Thea Philopator*).

Caesar was honoured, but there was never any attempt to present him either to Greeks or Egyptians as Cleopatra's husband or consort, still less as king or pharaoh. He was a distinguished father to Caesarion, but the boy was first and foremost a Ptolemy, and it was through and with his mother that he rightfully ruled. Even if Cleopatra had a strong desire to avenge her lover's death, she lacked the capacity to achieve this. She could aid the triumvirs, and it is striking that she attempted to do so in person, but it was beyond her capacity to do more than assist one side in Rome's civil war. At this stage there is absolutely no trace of friction between Octavian, Caesar's adopted son, and the real, if illegitimate, son Caesarion. The latter had no status at Rome. On top of that he was still a small boy, ruling nominally in Egypt only through his mother's need for a consort. The Romans took adoption very seriously, viewing the bond as effectively as close as a blood relationship. While it might be mildly embarrassing to have a foreign, bastard son of the dictator as a visible reminder of the human Caesar's indiscretions, there was nothing to make Caesarion more of a concern to Octavian. In no meaningful way could he be a rival and assuming that anyone could have considered this at so early a stage is misguided.[15]

Cleopatra had regained her throne through Caesar's intervention. Her priority after his death was to survive and remain in power. This she did, disposing of her brother, fending off her sister and keeping control of Egypt, if not of Cyprus, against ambitious officials and any other rival. At the same time she managed to avoid having her kingdom seized or plundered by a Roman leader eager to exploit its resources and tried to help those she hoped or guessed would win. She managed to avoid direct collaboration with any of Caesar's murderers, although had this become unavoidable it is doubtful that she would have refused this at the cost of losing her kingdom for the sake of personal hatred. Cleopatra was a pragmatic politician and she managed to survive a difficult few years. She was queen and her son was king. Together they promised long-term stability, which in itself helped to deter any challenges to their rule. Cleopatra had done all that she could to achieve this and done it well. Yet in the truly long term, everything depended, as it always did, on Rome and its leaders.

[XIX]

VENGEANCE

On 1 January 42 BC Lepidus began a second consulship with Lucius Munatius Plancus as colleague. Being consul was prestigious, but he shared far greater power with Antony and Octavian as triumvirs. Together they made all important decisions, and neither magistrates nor the Popular Assemblies could contest them. The formalised murder of the proscription lists continued, a blatant warning of the cost of opposing the triumvirate.

Cicero's killers took his head directly to Antony, who was said to have been at dinner when they arrived. In a story echoing the ones told about Marius and Marcus Antonius, he is supposed to have gleefully held the severed head in his hands. According to Dio, Fulvia was even more exultant, grabbing the grisly trophy and mocking the orator. She took pins from her hair – like every aristocratic Roman woman she affected a fashionably elaborate hairstyle – and jabbed them into the orator's tongue.[1]

The story may be an invention, although it should be remembered that Cicero had been one of the bitterest opponents of her first husband, publicly accusing him of revolution and incest and later praising the man who ordered his murder. More recently, his *Philippics* had lambasted Antony, savaging his character and edging the Senate steadily towards declaring him a public enemy. Fulvia had lived in Rome during those months and had found herself under attack in the courts, as Antony's enemies and plenty of opportunists sensed a chance to take her property. There were debts she and her husband had taken out and purchases they had made, which she now struggled to pay. Cicero's long-time correspondent Atticus had helped the beleaguered Fulvia, appearing in court with her and loaning her funds to prevent bankruptcy.[2]

There is no evidence that Cicero had taken a personal role in the attacks on Fulvia, but more than anyone else he had shaped the climate in which they occurred. Antony and his wife had plenty of reasons to loathe the orator. Whether or not they actually toyed with his severed head over dinner, they certainly did carry out a very public form of revenge. Antony had ordered the officer in charge of the soldiers sent to kill Cicero to cut off the orator's right hand as well as his head. Both head and the hand were then nailed to the Rostra at the heart of the Forum. The head that had uttered and the hand that had written the *Philippics* paid the price and served as an appalling warning of the cost of opposing Antony and the other triumvirs.[3]

Atticus went into hiding when the triumvirate occupied Rome, for as well as assisting Fulvia he had aided the families of Brutus and Cassius and been closely associated with Cicero and other opponents of the triumvirs. However, when Antony learned 'where Atticus was, he wrote to him in his own hand, telling him not to be afraid but to come to him at once; that he had erased his name ... from the list of the proscribed'. A friend who was hiding with him was also pardoned as a further gesture of goodwill. Antony sent a detachment of soldiers to escort the two fugitives, since it was night and it would take time for the news of their reprieve to circulate. Until then, they were at risk from anyone hoping to claim the bounty on their heads.[4]

On another occasion, Antony is supposed to have pardoned a certain Coponius, who was probably a former praetor. His wife had gone to the triumvir, sacrificing her honour for her husband's life. Antony slept with her and in payment removed her husband's name from the proscription lists. Dio claims that Antony and Fulvia were willing to accept money to remove a man's name from the list, but that he always substituted another name to fill the gap. Otherwise there are no stories of Fulvia seeking pardon for anyone, and she was accused of getting one man proscribed so that she could buy up property he owned next to some of her own. Octavian was forced to pardon another man when the latter's wife concealed him in a chest and had this brought into the triumvir's presence at a performance in the theatre. The crowd was so obviously in favour of a pardon that the young Caesar was compelled to issue one.[5]

The massacre inaugurated by the proscriptions was a stain on the record of all three triumvirs. At the time, Octavian may have been hated more than the others, since such viciousness was even less becoming in a youth. Apart from that, it was felt that at his age he really ought not to have made too many political enemies. In later years, when he was the Emperor Augustus, there was a concerted effort to disassociate himself from the bloodstained triumvir and blame the cruelty on his two colleagues. This no doubt heightened the attention given in our sources to Fulvia as the angry harridan urging Antony on to ever greater savagery.

We need to be cautious about accepting all the stories told of these years, since many no doubt grew in the telling, and the roles of Antony, Fulvia and Lepidus were all emphasised to cover the guilt of Octavian. Yet the truth was savage enough and clearly scarred the Romans' collective memory. Large numbers of books were written recounting tales of the proscribed and how they were saved or betrayed. These have not survived, but the traces in Appian and other later sources give a good idea of their flavour, focusing on the courage of some of the men who died and the loyalty and treachery of those who protected or betrayed them. Sextus Pompey was widely praised because he not only gave refuge to the proscribed, but also sent ships out looking for them along the coast of Italy.[6]

The proscriptions were meant to intimidate and succeeded in this – the exemplary punishment of Cicero made clear that no one was safe, no matter how distinguished. The triumvirs were hated, but also feared, and no voices spoke out against them in the Senate. They had also hoped to raise money and in this respect they were somewhat less successful. People were afraid to bid at the auctions of the property of the proscribed, worried that a display of wealth could be dangerous and lead to their own names being added to the lists. As importantly, some of the men who had profited from Sulla's proscriptions had been publicly shamed in subsequent decades and in some cases forced to give up their purchases. Some of the confiscated property went as bounty to the killers and informants, and the revenue raised by the rest proved disappointing.[7]

Desperate for money, most of all to pay an army that now

numbered more than forty legions, the triumvirate looked for other sources of revenue. One of the most unorthodox announcements was that 1,400 of the most prominent women in Rome would have their property publicly assessed and pay a levy based upon this. Women had never before been called upon to pay tax to the Republic, although during the worst crisis of the Punic Wars they had voluntarily donated their jewellery to the state.

The decree was deeply unpopular with the women affected. In a properly Roman way, they went first to the female relatives of the triumvirs, asking for them to bring their influence to bear. Fulvia is supposed to have turned them away. Once again, this may be mere propaganda, although it is worth remembering that she may have wondered why such solidarity had not been shown to her when she was being dragged through the courts and war waged against her husband. Led by the daughter of Hortensius – the man whom Cicero had supplanted as the greatest orator of the day – the women gathered in the Forum and appealed both to the crowd and the triumvirs. The former were sympathetic and, sensing this, the latter made no attempt to have their lictors and other attendants clear the demonstrators away by force.[8]

It is striking that only women risked open opposition to the triumvirate in Rome itself. This was a testament to the fear inspired by the proscriptions, but also the confidence that their violence would only be directed against men. One woman who had hidden her husband asked to be executed with him when he was arrested. The killers refused and so she starved herself to death. The triumvirate were not willing to be seen to attack women, but even so the protest was only partially successful. The number of women to be taxed was reduced to four hundred. Around this time similar levies were announced on the property of male citizens.[9]

WARLORDS

The triumvirate was established and maintained by military force, whatever veneer of legality was created around it. Public opposition from aristocratic women in Rome itself was spectacular, but no more than a minor nuisance. The only people capable of putting serious pressure on the triumvirs were their own soldiers. They needed to raise funds for many reasons, but the greatest was always to provide for their legionaries. The best of the triumviral legions consisted of Caesar's veterans. These were loyal to the dictator's memory and eager to avenge his murder, but were far less firmly committed to any of the current leaders. In 44 BC Octavian had outbid Antony for the loyalty of the *Fourth* and *Martia* Legions. As each of the competing leaders sought to outdo their rivals by promising ever more lavish rewards, the expectations of the troops grew. Aware of their own power, they had to be persuaded to serve. Standard pay was now dwarfed by the frequent gifts of substantial sums of money, backed by the promise of farmland at the end of their service. With more legions under arms than at any time in the past, the sums of money involved were colossal. The triumvirs occupied the centre of the Republic at Rome itself, but their control of the wider empire was more limited.

Sextus Pompey's power was steadily growing, especially at sea, and he was able to threaten parts of Spain, North Africa, Sicily and the other major islands in the western Mediterranean. All of the provinces and allied states in the east were denied to them by Brutus and Cassius. Cleopatra managed to avoid supplying the conspirators with much active aid, but was lucky to escape retribution. Other leaders and communities who protested that, although loyal to Rome, they had received no instructions from the Senate to obey Brutus or Cassius, were brutally punished. Cassius invaded Rhodes, defeating its fleet and plundering the city itself. When some communities in Judaea refused to give him the money he demanded, he had their populations sold into slavery. Brutus stormed the city of Xanthus in Lycia (modern-day Turkey) and sacked it, although to some extent his victory was marred by the suicide and burning of their own property by some of the population. The liberty proclaimed by the assassins brought little comfort to the allies and subjects of Rome. Cassius also managed to avenge Pompey, when he arrested and executed Ptolemy XIII's former tutor, Theodotus, who had persuaded the king's council to murder the fleeing Roman back in 48 BC.[10]

Brutus and Cassius needed funds to provide for their own armies, which had grown to more than twenty legions. Many of these formations had once taken an oath of loyalty to Caesar, although some of the soldiers had before that served Pompey until his defeat at Pharsalus. Only a few of the units had actively campaigned under Caesar's command, and most had been raised and trained for his planned Parthian War. The bond to Caesar's memory was there, but it was less strong than in the legions formed from his veterans. They had rallied to the conspirators for various reasons, ranging from dislike of men like Dolabella and Caius Antonius, to some admiration for Brutus or Cassius, or perhaps simply a sense that momentum was on their side. They would remain loyal only if treated well and both commanders began to reward their troops every bit as lavishly as the triumvirs, and for this reason squeezed provincials and allies for revenue.

Cassius had been Crassus' quaestor when he invaded Parthia in 54 BC. A year later, when most of the army was killed or captured at Carrhae, Cassius led the survivors back to Syria, and then staunchly defended the province, winning a few small victories against Parthian raiders. He still had something of a reputation in the east, and this no doubt helped him to recruit and win allies in the area, but ultimately both he and Brutus were successful because they controlled the strongest armies in the region. After his quaestorship, Cassius seems to have had no other military experience until 49–48 BC. Participation in the Macedonian campaign seems to have been the sum total of Brutus' service with the army.

Neither man was an experienced commander. Their recent campaigns had been fought against other Romans or were one-sided conflicts against allied communities. Cassius rather dramatically celebrated his defeat of Rhodes by minting coins depicting the goddess of victory. Brutus' coins bore the cap of liberty and the assassin's dagger on the reverse, but he aped Caesar by having his own head shown on the face. Perhaps it was felt that his reputation and name needed to be emphasised to inspire support. Yet in some ways one of the most striking features of these years is how far the conspirators' behaviour mirrored that of the triumvirs, although they did not stoop to the level of proscription. Caius Antonius was killed as a reprisal for the execution of Decimus Brutus, but otherwise they put to death few Roman citizens, although they did not show similar restraint with provincials and allies. Brutus perhaps showed some reluctance, but his seizure of power in Macedonia was clearly premeditated and once he had resolved to use violence he was determined to do so effectively. Had the conspirators won the war, it is a little hard to see how they could have restored the traditional Republic they revered.[11]

Both sides had a cause. Sextus Pompey's power was growing, but the triumvirs knew that Brutus and Cassius were the more serious threat in the immediate future. They were older, politically more significant with more sympathisers in the Senate and had murdered Caesar. Brutus and Cassius claimed to be fighting to restore the Republic, which had now unlawfully been seized by three dictators instead of one. Political slogans were backed on both sides by immediate and promised rewards. For the triumvirs, Caesar's veterans were enthusiastic to punish his assassins – not that this made them any less demanding of payment. For Octavian – 'who owed everything to a name' and his connection with the great Caesar – the need to gain vengeance was personal and imperative, an aspect of *pietas*, the respect and duty owed to parents. Sextus Pompey similarly placed his dead and unavenged father and brother at the centre of his public image. He took his father's name of Magnus and also called himself Pius. Such slogans meant a lot to many Romans and piety, whether of fathers and sons or slaves and masters, whether honoured or disgraced, figured heavily in the tales of the proscriptions. Octavian was accused of parading his own piety to his adopted father while scorning it in others, killing sons and fathers alike in the proscriptions and demanding that neither protect the other.[12]

The loyalty of the legions could be inspired by a cause, as long as this was backed by the soldiers' trust that they would be rewarded. This faith was not in a side, but a personal bond, almost a contract, with their commander. Soldiers followed a general and they might leave him to serve another if they felt it was in their own interest. When Antony, Octavian or Lepidus offered rewards to their legionaries it was in their own name. The same was true of Brutus and

Cassius. Brutus, not the Senate or the Republic, gave generous bounties to his legionaries and he personally guaranteed all future rewards. The soldiers were reluctant to trust that a commander allied to their own general would fulfil his promises. This meant that each side in the coming conflict consisted of more than one army. Octavian's and Antony's legions were distinct groups, as were those of Brutus and Cassius. This would have a major impact on the course of the war.[13]

Once again, the decisive campaign would be fought in Macedonia, just like the contest between Caesar and Pompey. Then, Caesar had fielded eight legions to Pompey's eleven. In 42 BC Brutus and Cassius probably had seventeen legions, while Antony and Octavian brought no fewer than nineteen to the main battles. Both sides had several other units in supporting roles. If these were at full strength then the triumvirs ought to have had 95,000 legionaries to the conspirators' 85,000. Appian says that the conspirators' legions were under strength, but claims that Octavian's – and perhaps by extension Antony's – legions were full. Both sides are also credited with substantial numbers of cavalry, and this time the conspirators had the advantage, fielding 20,000 horsemen to the triumvirs' 13,000.[14]

These are staggering figures. The Philippi campaign may have involved exceptionally large armies, although as an aside Dio actually claims that it was not the largest-scale encounter of Rome's civil wars. It would be striking if Brutus and Cassius had been able to muster double the number of infantry and almost treble the total of cavalry gathered by Pompey in 49–48 BC. Neither Alexander the Great nor Hannibal had ever led so many horsemen. Logistically, feeding so many soldiers, mounts and baggage animals would have been a mammoth task, especially since the campaign was protracted and lasted well into the autumn months. Commanding such large forces – especially for relatively inexperienced generals and senior officers – would have been almost as difficult. Early in the next century, the future emperor Tiberius would find it too difficult to control an army of ten legions and so divided them into several smaller forces.[15]

As noted already, it added greatly to a commander's prestige if he led a large number of legions. Having lots of units also created plenty of posts as officers, providing opportunities to reward followers. When ordinary soldiers received the equivalent of a decade or more of pay as a single bounty, a centurion stood to receive some five times as much, and a tribune double that total. Grants of land would also be on a similar scale. Many aristocratic young Romans who had been studying in Athens, including Cicero's and Cato's sons, as well as the poet Horace, were drawn to Brutus' prestige and needed to be rewarded with suitable commissions.[16]

It is probable that the legions on both sides were well below strength. At Pharsalus, Pompey's units had been at about 80 per cent strength and Caesar's less than half the proper size for a legion, and yet both functioned effectively. Octavian's and Antony's legions may have been larger than the enemy formations as Appian claims, but an average size of 5,000 is very unlikely. Even if the total forces for both sides were halved, that would still mean that some 90,000–100,000 legionaries – the bulk of them Roman citizens, although the conspirators are known to have recruited some provincials as well – fought at Philippi, supported by substantial numbers of cavalry. This would still make it a significantly larger encounter than any of the battles in the civil war of 49–45 BC, and the armies far bigger than was typical for Roman field forces. None of the commanders, including Antony, had any experience of leading such substantial numbers, and very many of the officers and soldiers they led were inexperienced. This too would shape the campaign.

PHILIPPI

In 42 BC the triumvirs decided to leave Lepidus to watch over Italy, while Antony and Octavian went east to deal with the conspirators. It may have been for this reason that he was given the consulship. He loaned several of his legions to each of his colleagues and in the course of the campaign these would be integrated into their own armies, coming to see their new leaders as the source of rewards. Antony was the dominant figure in the triumvirate and Octavian could not be denied the opportunity to avenge his father and win glory, so Lepidus was the logical choice to leave behind.[17]

Like Caesar in 49 BC, the triumvirate faced an enemy who was much stronger at sea. Brutus and Cassius resolved upon essentially the same strategy adopted by Pompey, waiting to meet their opponents in the east. This gave them the chance to harass and intercept the enemy at sea. In late summer the triumvirs sent an advance force of some eight legions to Greece. These crossed without misadventure, but the conspirators' fleet made it difficult for any convoy carrying supplies or reinforcements to reach them. Antony was effectively blockaded at Brundisium for several weeks. Octavian had begun building up a force of warships to deal with Sextus Pompey and it was only when these had sailed round southern Italy that the blockade was broken. Antony and Octavian with their main armies were able to cross to Macedonia.[18]

The Via Egnatia, built by the Romans in the second century BC, crossed the top of the Greek Peninsula from the Adriatic to the Aegean coast and was the natural path for an army to follow. The advance guard had pushed almost to the Aegean and occupied the most commonly used pass through the mountains. Brutus and Cassius ferried their combined army over the Dardanelles and, with the assistance of a local Thracian chieftain, found another pass that allowed them to outflank the position. The triumvirate's advance guard withdrew to Amphipolis on the coast. Brutus and Cassius followed them as far as Philippi. Then their advance stopped and they took up a strong position outside the town, blocking the line of the Via Egnatia.[19]

Antony arrived at Apollonia some time in September 42 BC. Octavian's army was lagging behind, for he had fallen seriously ill. In spite of this, Antony took his own legions and the advance guard forward and camped in front of Philippi. It was a gesture of confidence, which unnerved the conspirators. Although they had a temporary advantage in numbers, they do not appear to have made any effort to provoke a battle and Octavian was able to join Antony ten days later. The conspirators planned to wear the enemy down. Brutus and Cassius camped separately, but constructed a ditch and wall joining the two camps. They were well supplied, with ready communications to the coast and plentiful sources of water from the local springs. Brutus was in the north and Cassius in the south. Antony and Octavian constructed a single camp down on the plain and had to dig for wells, although these soon provided an adequate water supply. It was harder to draw enough food and fodder from the surrounding countryside. The Philippi campaign would more closely resemble Dyrrachium than Pharsalus or any of the other pitched battles of Caesar's civil war.[20]

Antony and Octavian repeatedly formed their armies up in front of their camp. Brutus and Cassius did the same – and were indeed encouraged when the enemy held a lustration, a ceremony that ritually purified the army behind their own rampart, seeing this as a sign of caution. However, they were unwilling to advance any great distance in front of their own fortifications. This meant that their armies kept the advantage of the slightly higher ground, while the wall and towers behind could support them with missiles and offered a ready haven for retreating troops if things went badly. Antony and Octavian were unwilling to attack in these conditions, for that would risk failure and certainly involve heavy casualties. They continued to deploy and challenge the enemy, but apart from some skirmishing there was no serious fighting. Octavian's army formed on the left of the line, facing Brutus, while Antony's legions were on the right, opposite Cassius' men.

Unable to provoke a battle, Antony decided to threaten the enemy flank, building a new line of fortifications reaching past Cassius' camp and then at right angles to the conspirator's position. If completed this would allow the triumvirs to cut the enemy's lines of communication, forcing them either to withdraw or risk a battle. Work began in secret, with men detached from each unit while their colleagues formed line of battle as usual facing towards the enemy. The deception was helped because the work started in an area of marshland, where the tall reeds obscured what was happening. For ten days the fortified causeway progressed and it was only then that it became visible as soldiers openly garrisoned the new line. Yet it was far from complete and Cassius' response to the threat was to set his own men working on a line extending south from his camp. His intention was to cut across Antony's fortifications, preventing

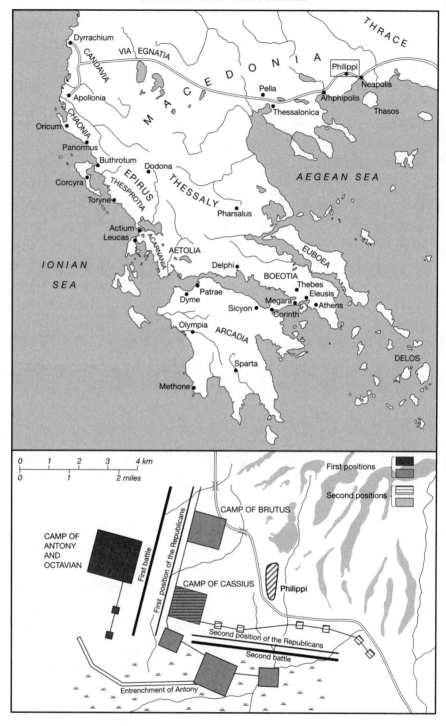

Top: Greece and Macedonia
Below: The Battles of Philippi

their extension and isolating any of the redoubts left behind his own line.

On 3 October Antony realised what was happening. It was about noon and the rival armies had deployed for battle as usual. It is possible that Brutus and Cassius had already decided to launch a demonstration or perhaps even a major attack to cover the construction work. Octavian was still seriously ill and was not with his army. He does not seem to have appointed anyone else to supreme authority, but even if he had done so, it would have been hard for that individual to inspire the same enthusiasm and obedience from his men, given the very personal bonds of loyalty and reward in these years.

Antony took the troops on the extreme right of his line and led them diagonally uphill, evading Cassius' main line and striking at the new wall. Soon afterwards the main armies on both sides engaged and heavy fighting developed. In the meantime, Antony and his men stormed through the new line of fortification, which was not yet complete, and brushed aside a counter-attack by another part of the enemy work party. He then turned and assaulted Cassius' camp itself. This was strongly fortified, but contained few defenders, since the bulk of the legions were either in the main line or had been working on the new wall. Antony, keeping the momentum of his attack going by personal example, broke into the camp. When news of this spread to the main fighting line, Cassius' legions collapsed into rout. Roman troops were often made nervous by the fear of losing their possessions and that was no doubt a particular concern to legionaries so generously paid by their commanders.[21]

While this was going on, what was effectively a separate action was being fought to the north, where Brutus had launched an attack. His legions advanced in some confusion, several units moving off before they received the orders. It all suggests an inexperienced general with equally inexperienced staff officers trying to control an unusually large and not very well-disciplined army. (All of this would still be true even if, as suggested, the numbers involved were substantially less than is usually believed.)

In the event, it worked well, for Octavian's men lacked the clear authority of a commander altogether and were not ready. It may have made things worse that for so many days they had deployed in battle order and yet nothing had happened. Brutus' line was longer than that formed by Octavian's troops, who were quickly outflanked. Octavian's line collapsed, with three legions being badly cut up – one of them the *Fourth*. Brutus' men swept on and broke into the triumvirs' camp, which they proceeded to loot. Octavian was not there – he later claimed that his physician had had a dream warning him to leave the camp. Critics said that he spent three days hiding in a marsh, completely out of touch with his army.[22]

Each side had overwhelmed the enemy on one flank. Brutus does not seem to have made any real effort to keep in communication with Cassius and did not know of his defeat until too late. He is said to have noticed that the general's tent had been struck in his ally's camp. Antony had led the attack on the wall and camp in person, energising the men he was with, but as a result losing touch with the wider picture. It would probably have been difficult for him to regain control over Octavian's leaderless men anyway. Both sides simply withdrew to their own positions. Casualties may have been heavier amongst the triumvirs' men, but the conspirators suffered a very serious blow when Cassius lost heart. Unaware of Brutus' success, he mistook a party of friendly cavalry for the enemy – he was short-sighted and took their greeting to one of his officers as a cry of triumph – and ordered a slave to kill him. By coincidence, it was his birthday.[23]

For nearly three weeks the armies went back to watching each other warily. Brutus quickly issued a generous bounty to Cassius' soldiers, hoping to keep their loyalty. They remained in their separate camp and there were signs that the two armies struggled to co-operate. A hillock near the camp that had been permanently picketed by Cassius was abandoned on Brutus' orders – perhaps simply as a mistake – and was quickly occupied and fortified by Octavian's men. Unable to provoke another battle, the triumvirs reverted to Antony's plan of getting around the enemy flank, building on this gain.[24]

On 23 October Brutus felt forced to offer battle again, from fear of this threat to his supply lines and also suspicions about the loyalty of the soldiers. The second battle was fought at a right angle to the first battle and he no longer had such an advantage of position. Ironically, the triumvirs had just learnt that a convoy carrying two of their legions, one of them the *Martia*, had been caught by enemy ships and destroyed. A deserter brought the news to Brutus, who refused to believe it, and the sources suggest his mood was fatalistic by this stage. The battle was hard fought, but the triumvirs' men made steady progress, Appian says they drove Brutus' legionaries back step by step, like men pushing heavy machinery. There is no evidence for any great tactical subtlety and it was simply a slogging match. In the end Brutus' men broke and fled. He kept elements of four legions together during the retreat, but soon lost heart and, with assistance, committed suicide.[25]

The triumvirs had won an overwhelming victory. Brutus and Cassius were both dead, as was Cato's son and many other prominent aristocrats. Others surrendered and only a few continued the struggle, most drifting to join Sextus Pompey. The prisoners at Philippi are said to have hailed Antony, but jeered crudely at Octavian. The latter was certainly held to have been more vicious in executing a number of captives. A number of the prisoners who were pardoned chose to join Antony and would follow him loyally. He also won credit for treating Brutus' corpse with honour, even wrapping it in his own general's cloak according to one account. The body was decapitated and then cremated, and Antony had the ashes sent to Brutus' mother Servilia. The head was sent separately to Rome – the sources are divided over whether Octavian or Antony ordered this – but was lost at sea.[26]

Philippi was the greatest victory of Antony's career. At the time and since, no one has seriously doubted that he played a far greater role than his younger colleague in winning the two battles and in the campaign as a whole. It was Antony who threatened to outflank the enemy line, precipitating the first battle, and then led his men into the enemy camp. His personal courage could not be doubted, unlike Octavian. Yet it had been a campaign fought by large and clumsy armies, containing many inexperienced soldiers, led by equally inexperienced generals and senior officers. Antony had seen far more military service than Brutus and Cassius as well as Octavian, but he had never in the past commanded such a large force. He had been bold, just as he had in Judaea and Egypt, and when he joined Caesar in Macedonia in 48 BC. He had been equally aggressive at Forum Gallorum and had suffered a bad defeat after his initial success. This time he had succeeded, but this might not have been the case if he had been unlucky or faced more able opponents.

Amongst the spoils of the victory at Philippi, Antony added a fine, and unusually tall, bay horse to his stable. It had originally been owned by a man named Seius, but the latter had been executed on Antony's orders, either in 44 BC or when he had been Caesar's deputy in Italy. Dolabella purchased the horse and later took it with him to the east. When he was defeated and took his own life, the bay passed to the victorious Cassius. Now he, too, was dead and Antony became the possessor of a fine, if rather unlucky animal.[27]

[xx]

Dionysus and Aphrodite

Victory at Philippi brought new problems for the triumvirate. Tens of thousands of their soldiers were due for discharge. These men had been promised farms and most expected these to be on good land in Italy. The property confiscated from the proscribed and the dead supporters of Brutus and Cassius provided only a small part of what was needed. It was already obvious that territory would have to be seized from individuals and communities to be given to the soldiers. The task of overseeing this process was given to Octavian. His health was still poor – indeed he was so ill on the journey back to Italy that it was widely assumed he would die – and this was one good reason why he should return home. Redistribution of land on such a vast scale was bound to be a difficult job and likely to be an extremely unpopular one. No one would welcome having their land confiscated, while the veterans would balk at any provision that seemed less than generous.[1]

Antony was surely glad to see this controversial task taken on by his colleague and content to remain in the east. Several commanders who could be expected to be loyal to him were in Italy and the western provinces. The most important was Quintus Fufius Calenus, who as governor of Caesar's conquests in Gaul controlled eleven legions. Lepidus was already being marginalised, under suspicion of colluding with Sextus Pompey. The third triumvir was left in control of only the province of Africa, a region that was anyway not fully secure. Antony and Octavian divided the remaining provinces and armies between them.[2]

For the moment there was plenty for Antony to do. The provinces and allied states of the eastern Mediterranean had been caught up in Rome's internal struggles for much of the last decade. Levies of men, money, food and other resources had been imposed by a succession of leaders, most recently the conspirators. Leaders and communities had suffered, many had lost power, some had been deposed and a few killed. A small number had been lucky enough to avoid the worst depredations and had even grown in power. Virtually all had recently given aid to the conspirators.

It was important to reorganise the entire region, to restore order and stability. Antony and the other triumvirs also needed money to pay their armies, which would still be very large even after the veterans had been demobilised. Many of the soldiers captured at Philippi were immediately enrolled in the triumviral legions. It was better than letting them go and running the risk that they would happily enlist with other leaders eager to fight their way to power. The eleven legions organised after Philippi contained many prisoners as well as men whose discharge was not yet due. There was also the question of the long-delayed Parthian War. A campaign on that scale required years of preparation, but Antony was probably already planning to undertake it. Philippi had bolstered his military repu-tation, but true glory could only be won against a powerful foreign enemy and one whose humiliation of Rome had not been avenged. The eagles of Crassus' legions remained trophies of the Parthian king.[3]

Antony was the obvious candidate from amongst the triumvirate for the task of reorganising the east. He was older than Octavian, who was just twenty-one, and his reputation was much greater. He was also in robust health, unlike his younger colleague. In addition, neither of his colleagues had spent anywhere near as much time in the Hellenistic east. Antony spent the winter of 42–41 BC in Athens, a city he knew well from his time studying there in the 50s BC. He happily adopted Greek styles of dress, attended lectures and dramatic performances, and actively relished the physical exercise and display of the gymnasia. Plenty of Romans, including serving governors and army commanders, had in the past thrown themselves into Hellenic culture in this way. Brutus had spent several months at Athens in 44 BC, posing as nothing more than a visitor, keen to share in the traditions of the city. He was popular as a result, and so was Antony. The Athenians and other Greeks could not ignore or ever hope to challenge the reality of Roman rule. When leading Romans displayed a love of Greek culture, to some extent acknowledging its superiority, then it made it easier for them to accept this hard fact.[4]

From early on, delegations came to Antony, asking for favours, arbitration in disputes and redress from penalties imposed on them by the conspirators or other grievances. In the spring of 41 BC he crossed into Asia Minor and travelled through the province, dealing with petitioners and raising revenue. He also feasted and celebrated, enjoying power and wealth as he had always done. Plutarch says that musicians, dancers and actors from the provinces rushed to join his household. When Antony processed into Ephesus, he was preceded by dancers dressed as Bacchantes, the wild female devotees of the cult of the wine god Dionysus/Bacchus, as well as boys and men garbed as satyrs. The crowd there and elsewhere readily hailed him as the god. This was Hellenic culture as well, if a different side of it to the educated tastes of aristocrats in Classical Athens.[5]

Other Romans had also been hailed as gods in the eastern provinces, most recently Pompey and Caesar. The Rhodians had hailed Cassius as 'Lord and King', to which he had bluntly replied that he was neither, but a killer of both. Such sentiments did not prevent him from plundering the captured city. Antony had no need to use force, but made very heavy demands on the provincials. All told, he demanded something like nine years' worth of normal levies, but wanted them paid in just two years. Some of this he spent in spectacular gifts to his disreputable followers. A cook who had prepared a feast for him was rewarded with a house taken from an aristocrat. When Antony announced that he required a second levy from the province before the end of the year, an orator named Hybreas managed to dissuade him by asking whether the Roman general could also arrange for a second harvest. Hyrbreas continued by pointing out that since Antony had already collected 200,000 talents from them, he must realise that they had no more to give – and if Antony had not received the money, then he ought to be talking to his officials rather than the poor provincials.[6]

Antony liked blunt speech, especially when it was leavened with humour. It was widely believed that he was often manipulated by others who pretended to be plain speaking. There were other ways of influencing Antony. He liked women, and it was believed that many eastern rulers felt it easier to let their wives persuade the Roman. There were two claimants for the throne of Cappadocia, and the mother of one of them, Glaphyra, caught his eye. She had been the mistress of Archelaus, the dynast of Comana, until he was called away to marry Berenice IV. Although illegitimate, her son was his child and so possessed royal blood. For a while at least Glaphyra was believed to have become Antony's mistress. A snatch of verse written by Octavian claimed that 'Antony screws Glaphyra, so Fulvia as revenge wants to nail me'. For the moment she was not persuasive enough, and the rule of Cappadocia went to the other claimant.[7]

When there was no special persuasion involved, Antony generally favoured communities that had suffered for opposing Brutus and Cassius and punished their enthusiastic supporters. The inhabitants of the Jewish towns enslaved by Cassius were freed and their property restored. Rhodes gained some territory and was exempted from taxation for the moment, as was Lycia, where Brutus had stormed Xanthus and extorted money from other cities.

The tyrant of Tyre seems to have been deposed, both for his enthusiasm for Cassius and using this as a pretext to seize Jewish territory. When Antony wrote to the city he addressed his letter to 'the magistrates, council and people' and stressed that his recently defeated 'adversaries' had not been granted commands by the 'Senate, but they seized them by force'. Tyre was ordered to return to the rule of Hyrcanus any territory taken from Judaea. In a letter to Hyrcanus, Antony spoke of the tyranny of Brutus and Cassius as an offence against the gods, and how he wanted 'to let our allies also participate in the peace given us by God; and so, owing to our victory, the body of Asia is now recovering, as it were, from a serious illness'.[8]

The triumvirate needed money, and no doubt some communities found Antony's rule just as oppressive and demanding as that of Brutus and Cassius. Perhaps some felt that they were worse off and there was little sign of recovering. However, we do know of leaders who had aided the conspirators and yet were confirmed in power.

Antipater, the second in command and military commander of Hyrcanus, had by this time been murdered, and power passed to his sons Herod and Phaesel. The former had proved especially willing to meet Cassius' demands for money. In spite of this Antony confirmed them in power, no doubt feeling that they would keep the generally pro-Roman Hyrcanus secure.[9]

Antony continued his progress through the provinces. Hostile sources characterise this whole period as one of indulgence, loose control that allowed unscrupulous followers to abuse their position, arbitrary decisions and squeezing the provincials for money. Yet, where his decisions are known in any detail, they seem reasonable, and certainly well within the character of Roman provincial administration in this period. The triumvirs desperately needed revenue, but this need would not go away and it was important for them to restore long-term stability to the empire. Antony and his colleagues had to create a situation where the provinces and allies would supply them with a substantial and steady income year after year.

TARSUS

In 41 BC Antony summoned Cleopatra to come to him at the city of Tarsus in Cilicia – later home of St Paul, who dubbed it 'no mean city'. We do not know whether she had already sent envoys to him on his journeys, but this is quite possible. Like all the other rulers of the region, she needed to be sure that her power was confirmed and the triumvirs would adhere to the recognition they had given to her joint rule with Caesarion. Her kingdom was the greatest single source of grain and money in the eastern Mediterranean, so it was obviously a prime concern for Antony to ensure that he could draw on these resources, both for the moment and for the eventual war against Parthia.[10]

Questions had been raised over her conduct during the struggle with the conspirators. Serapion in Cyprus had actively aided them, and the queen herself had promised much to Cassius, even if she had not delivered anything, while her attempt to join the triumvirs with a fleet had failed. It is worth remembering that an alternative to Cleopatra existed. Antony had paid a long visit to Ephesus. During that time he may well have confirmed the rights of the great Temple of Artemis there. It is inconceivable that he had not had some contact with Arsinoe, or at least her representatives. Antony had backed her claim in 44 BC and there was no assurance that he would not now decide that replacing Cleopatra with her younger sister might allow him to exploit Egypt's and Cyprus' resources more effectively.[11]

Antony sent Quintus Dellius to Alexandria to summon the queen. Dellius had already defected from Dolabella to Cassius, and then Cassius to Antony, and in later years wrote a racy history of the period, which has not survived, but may well have influenced Plutarch's account. He claimed to have realised at once that Antony could be swept away by a woman like Cleopatra. Guessing that this would happen and that she would win his favour, he decided that it would be advantageous for him to assist the queen. Dellius encouraged her to dazzle Antony, assuring her that he could readily be persuaded to do what she wanted.[12]

Cleopatra did not hurry her journey to Tarsus. A succession of letters arrived demanding that she hasten, but she ignored them all, determined to appear at a moment of her own choosing and in the most spectacular style. Unlike her meeting with Caesar, there was no need to sneak into his presence. Drawing on her family's long tradition of building luxurious pleasure craft, she transferred into a specially prepared ship for the final stage of her journey up the River Cydnus into Tarsus. Its sails were of rich purple, the prow of gold and rowers plied silver-tipped oars to the music of flutes, oboes and lyres. Her father would no doubt have been proud of such a performance. Everything about the craft was lavish and incense in generous quantities was burned so that the fine smells wafted onto the banks of the river.

Cleopatra 'herself reclined beneath a gold-embroidered canopy, adorned like a painting of Aphrodite, flanked by slave-boys, each made to resemble Eros, who cooled her with fans. Likewise her most beautiful female slaves, dressed as Nereids and Graces, were stationed at the rudders and ropes.'[13]

Aphrodite was one of the many goddesses whose character had

been subsumed into the Hellenised cult of Isis, and Cleopatra was the New Isis. However, it is probably a mistake to see her as rigidly bound by this association. Plutarch's description does not suggest an especially Egyptian – even an idealised Greek vision of Egyptian – flavour to this performance. It was about spectacle, and most of all about glamour and wealth. Some see it as solely designed with Antony's tastes in mind. One historian dubbed it 'a vulgar bait to catch a vulgar man'.[14]

It soon had the impact Cleopatra had intended. Plutarch tells us that a crowd quickly gathered to watch the progress of the royal barge along the river. Antony was supposedly receiving petitions in front of a large gathering in Tarsus itself. Then rumour started to spread that the goddess Aphrodite was on her way, and people began slipping away to see the wondrous spectacle. In the end, Antony and his household were left on their own and so trailed along behind. The cry went up that Aphrodite had come to feast with Dionysus for the good of all Asia. It did not matter if for some this meant Aphrodite/Isis and Dionysus/Osiris, while for others different aspects of the deities were important. There was genuine enthusiasm for the display, well within the traditions of the Hellenistic monarchies and drawing on even older roots.

Antony sent an invitation for Cleopatra to join him at dinner. She declined and instead suggested that he join her. The banquet that followed was brightly illuminated by carefully arranged clusters of lamps. The luxury, opulence and spectacle of the Ptolemaic court were displayed to full effect. On the following night Antony entertained the queen to another banquet, but in spite of their best efforts his household could not match the royal display. The triumvir, and master of the eastern Mediterranean, responded with deprecating humour.[15]

Cleopatra was clever and witty, and is said to have lowered the tone of her humour to suit Antony's tastes. Now around twenty-eight – 'at an age when the beauty of a woman is at its most dazzling and her intellectual powers are at a height' according to Plutarch – she was confident and sophisticated, her charisma probably even more powerful than when she had met Caesar. It is unsurprising that Antony found her both attractive and challenging. She needed to win over the man who could confirm or depose her, so it is reasonable to believe that she deliberately set out to seduce him and that from early on he wanted her as a lover. As with her first encounter with Caesar, both the queen and the triumvir were no doubt aware that desire and political advantage mingled, that each hoped to seduce the other and gain from the encounter. It was exciting. Cleopatra had only ever given herself to one other lover and he had been the most powerful man in the Roman world. For Antony, it was a measure of his own importance that the queen might be available to him. He was in his early forties, closer in age than her first lover had been. He was vigorous, roughly handsome, experienced and very confident. His power made him an acceptable as well as expedient lover.[16]

The physical and emotional attractions were strong for both of them. Cleopatra had also displayed the abundance of her realm. Even after years of bad harvests, Egypt could still somehow fund this opulence and it was a clear promise that the queen could mobilise this wealth to Antony's service. She had another advantage in Caesarion, although it is unclear whether or not she had brought the boy with her to Tarsus. Tradition and experience showed that it was difficult, probably impossible, for a Ptolemaic queen to rule as sole monarch. Joint rule with Caesarion gave her regime the promise of stability.

We know nothing about Arsinoe's appearance and whether or not she could equal her older sister in charm and glamour. She was a potential rival to Cleopatra, but was probably more useful to both Cassius and now Antony as a lever to control the queen. Cleopatra was already established and had maintained control of her kingdom remarkably well since Caesar's death. She had an heir and co-ruler who would be fully under her control for at least another decade. Arsinoe could not match this, and it would have been a major risk dethroning Cleopatra and installing the younger, unmarried and childless sister. Annexing Egypt and reclaiming Cyprus as Roman provinces held little appeal, for the burden of administering them directly would have been heavy when all of the east needed reorgan-isation after the upheavals of the civil wars. It was far better to let the already established monarch arrange to supply what the triumvirate needed.

Soon after her arrival in Tarsus, Cleopatra and Antony became lovers. Within a year she would bear him twins, a son and a daughter. The queen was confirmed in power, with Caesarion as king and co-monarch. On Antony's command, Arsinoe was taken from the sanctuary of Artemis, whose rights he had recently confirmed, and executed. There is no evidence to connect her with an unusual octagonal-shaped tomb at Ephesus. There is indeed no particular reason to associate this structure with the Ptolemies or any other royal family. Another victim of Cleopatra's success was a young man who claimed to be her dead brother, Ptolemy XIII. This lesser threat to her was executed at the Phoenician town of Aradus.[17]

ALEXANDRIA

Antony spent the winter of 41–40 BC with Cleopatra in her capital. Alexandria was an important city, so that the choice could be justified on practical grounds, but it is clear that the key factor in its selection was that it would allow him to spend months with his lover. No doubt work continued and deputations from kings and cities wound their way to Egypt, seeking audience with the triumvir. As in Athens the previous winter, Antony donned various items of Greek dress. There were philosophical lectures, drama and dance, as well as the life of the gymnasia and other sports. Antony and Cleopatra went on hunting expeditions, no doubt on a grand scale. Horses and hunting were obsessions of Greek, and most especially Macedonian, aristocrats. It is quite possible that Cleopatra was an accomplished rider – we certainly read of one of her female ancestors helping to command an army from horseback.[18]

Another pursuit was fishing. Eager to guarantee the success of his efforts, Antony had slaves swim underwater and attach fish to the hooks on the end of his line. Plutarch tells us that Cleopatra easily saw through the deception and on the next day sent one of her own people down, who fixed a salted fish from the Black Sea to the hook instead. Antony hauled in the long-dead trophy to general laughter. His lover suggested that he give up, since as a great victor he should fish for cities, countries and whole continents.[19]

Cleopatra flattered Antony and watched in admiration as he exercised or was just a lively companion as he drank or gambled with dice – a particular passion for many Romans, including Octavian. Eating and drinking were particular concerns, in keeping with the traditions of the Ptolemaic court. Together with their intimates, both Roman and Alexandrian, the couple formed a club they named 'The Inimitable Livers'. A few years later one of the courtiers involved in these entertainments set up an inscription dubbing himself 'The Parasite', calling Antony a god as well as 'Inimitable at sex'.[20]

Everything was on an extravagant scale. Plutarch's grandfather used to repeat a story told by a friend who had been studying medicine in Alexandria at the time and had become friendly with one of the royal cooks. Amazed by the sheer quantity of food being cooked one evening, he was surprised to be told that the company was very small. Multiples of everything were prepared to be ready at different times, so that Antony could be served almost instantly whenever he demanded the next course. Presumably the staff were happy to dispose of the unused food. In recent years, Egypt had suffered from poor harvests and outbreaks of famine. Yet the much paraded opulence of the Ptolemaic court never faltered.[21]

The extravagance was deliberate and emphasised, not simply in the food, but also in the decorations of the palaces and even the tableware. In the first feast at Tarsus, Cleopatra had used golden and jewelled tableware and covered the room in rich tapestries. All of this was given away to the guests, the richest luxuries going to Antony. On the next night everything was even more lavish and expensive, and once again it was given away. Cleopatra provided Ethiopian slaves bearing torches to escort them and their goods home. On another occasion, she let clouds of rose petals flutter down onto the gathering. Luxury and excess were celebrated, and it is certain that the displays at her own court in Alexandria were on an even grander scale. It may have been around this time that Antony acquired a set of golden chamber pots.[22]

Sometimes the group would wander the streets of Alexandria at night, with Antony and Cleopatra – and presumably also their followers – dressed in the simple clothes of slaves. Antony would behave rowdily, mocking passers-by and even looking into houses, while his lover is supposed to have watched. The disguises were unconvincing, but a lot of Alexandrians were happy to play along, replying to mockery with abuse of their own. A few were even willing to let Antony pick a fight with them and more than once he is supposed to have returned with bruises from these adventures. There was a long tradition of such displays by aristocrats and many Alexandrians were happy to indulge their queen and her Roman guests. They said that Antony only ever revealed the serious face of a tragic actor to his own countrymen, but with them showed the mask of a comic actor.[23]

Over the winter months the Alexandrians indulged them and they seem to have been popular. Antony continued to work, even if his pleasures were more conspicuous and received more attention in our sources. He enjoyed the affair with Cleopatra, as he had enjoyed other affairs earlier in his life. This one was made special because she was a queen in a lavish court. The flavour of these months was very Hellenic and that appealed to him as well. Yet in the spring of 40 BC Antony left to deal with a pressing crisis in Italy. Soon there would be more problems as the Parthians invaded Syria and raided deep into the Roman provinces.

Antony and Cleopatra would not see each other again for three and a half years. Love may well have been genuine on one or both sides, but at this stage there was no overwhelming urge for them to remain always together. The rule of Cleopatra and Caesarion had been confirmed and Antony assured that he could call upon the resources of their kingdom. Their political ambitions were, for the moment, satisfied.

[XXI]

CRISIS

Much to everyone's surprise, Octavian had recovered from his illness late in 42 BC. Back in Italy, he threw himself into the grand colonisation programme needed to satisfy the veteran soldiers due for discharge. At the very least there were tens of thousands of these men, even if most legions in these years were greatly under strength. Land was confiscated from an initial list of eighteen towns, but this was not enough, and almost forty communities suffered to a greater or lesser extent. Most senators had enough influence to protect their own property in these regions and so perhaps did the wealthiest local inhabitants. The burden fell more on those of middling income, without powerful friends. By a strange coincidence, three of the greatest poets of the age, Virgil, Horace and Propertius, all saw their family's land confiscated and given to retired soldiers. It was clearly a traumatic episode for many Italians. The behaviour of the veterans and the commissioners assigning them land rarely helped, and there were accusations that they were taking more than they had been allocated and generally intimidating their new neighbours. On the other hand, the veterans resented the slow pace of the process and were ready to resist any attempt to give them less than they had been promised.[1]

Antony's surviving brother Lucius was consul in 41 BC, with Publius Servilius Vatia Isauricus, the man who had been Caesar's colleague in 48 BC, holding the post for a second time. There was resentment amongst the many dispossessed and wider discontent because the power of Sextus Pompey had grown. He overran Sicily and dominated the sea lanes, preventing much of the supply of grain from reaching Italy. Rome relied on imported food – Sicily was a major supplier – and the triumvirate was blamed for the shortages.

Octavian was in charge of the colonisation and he was also there in Italy. The resentment focused on him, for Antony was away in the east and Lepidus was already acknowledged as the least of the three.

Lucius Antonius sensed an opportunity to gain from this festering discontent. He was a Roman senator, determined to rise to the very top, winning glory, reputation, power and wealth. It is a mistake to see him simply as Antony's agent. His brother may have indicated general support, but did not order his actions in this year – indeed, the slow pace of communications would have made this impractical. Fulvia was initially reluctant, but eventually encouraged her brother-in-law, sending her children to Lucius for him to show to Antony's veterans and raise support. Yet it was difficult for the soldiers to sympathise with those dispossessed by the colonisation process. Clearly, Fulvia felt that she was acting for Antony's good by turning against Octavian. The latter's verse suggests that she was jealous of Glaphyra and others claim that she hoped also to win her husband back from Cleopatra. As so often in these years, strong personal emotion mingled with political ambition.

The result was a confusing period of unrest and civil war, in which allegiances were often unclear. Lucius seized Rome, but could not hold it. He raised an army and ended up being blockaded by Octavian in the town of Perusia (modern-day Perugia). Lead sling bullets survive from the siege, some simply proclaiming allegiance to one of the leaders, but others with slogans jibing at Lucius' baldness or targeting Fulvia's sexual organs. Asinius Pollio, Plancus and Ventidius Bassus were all in Italy with their legions and were seen as Antony's men, commanding legions loyal to him. However, the three generals could not agree on what to do and bickered with each other. They postured and demonstrated, but stopped short of practical aid. Clearly, they had no instructions and this, combined with their own sense of what was good for their personal ambitions, stopped them from intervening. Without help, Lucius surrendered early in 40 BC.[2]

The consul was spared, and so were his soldiers, but there may have been some executions and Perusia was plundered and burned. Lucius was soon despatched to govern Spain. Fulvia fled from Italy, in search of her husband. Antony's mother Julia also decided to leave Rome, but chose a circuitous route to reach her son. She went first to Sextus Pompey, who welcomed her and then sent her with an escort to Antony, with an offer of alliance against Octavian. It seemed that Perusia was only the first campaign of a new civil war, pitting one triumvir against another.

Octavian was also trying to conciliate Sextus. He had divorced Fulvia's daughter, claiming that the marriage had never been consummated. If true, then it suggests that he had been cautious about the alliance from the start, although it may simply have been that she was exceptionally young, even by the standards of Roman brides. Instead, he married Scribonia, sister of Sextus' father-in-law and one of his leading supporters. Pompey's son does not seem to have viewed the young Caesar any more warmly as a result.[3]

A NEW DEAL

None of our sources accuses Antony of provoking the conflict (which is known as the Perusine War). At most they claim that he failed to restrain Fulvia and Lucius. Some of this was clearly intended to emphasise his inability to control his own wife. Realistically, he was too far away to play a direct role in the rapidly changing situation in Italy. It is also worth saying that Antony rarely deliberately initiated a confrontation at any stage in his life. He was ambitious, seeking power and then revelling in it. After the Ides of March he reacted to the assassination and gradually turned opinion against the conspirators, but even then did not himself provoke an open conflict with them. Throughout he seems to have been content to let them continue in public life, as long as this did not conflict with his acquisition of power, patronage and wealth. Similarly, in the following months, as Cicero and others increased the pressure upon him, Antony responded angrily, but was not fully prepared for war when it came. In part, this was because he underestimated his opponents, both the senators and the young Caesar, but it also seems to reflect his nature. There is little trace of long-term strategy at any stage in his life, beyond a general desire to rise to the top. Lucius played a strong part, but on balance it does seem that the sources are right to see Fulvia as the main force behind the opposition to Octavian.

Antony had not wanted a confrontation with Octavian, although no doubt he would happily have profited from the new situation if his wife and brother had won. This did not mean that he could pretend the conflict had not happened. Antony left Alexandria and went to Syria, but in spite of a Parthian invasion, he hurried from there to Athens, where he met Julia and Fulvia. He thanked Sextus Pompey's envoys for bringing his mother, but sent their master a cautious reply. If war did break out with Octavian, then he would treat Sextus as an ally. If it did not, then the agreement to form the triumvirate held and so all he could do was encourage his colleagues to negotiate with Sextus.[4]

He seems to have received Fulvia coldly, which made it easier to absolve himself of responsibility for the Perusine War. She may already have been ill and was said to be heartbroken. Fulvia died later in the year, after Antony had left Athens. Lucius Antonius also succumbed to illness soon after taking up his post as proconsul in Spain. There is no hint of foul play in either case. In many ways more damaging for Antony was the death of Calenus, the governor of Gaul, in the summer of 40 BC. Octavian went in person and took over the province without a struggle, taking command of its eleven legions. The balance of power was shifting, making the outcome of the impending civil war very hard to predict.[5]

Antony returned to Italy. He did not go alone, but led a fleet of 200 warships. There were few if any transport ships and he had only a small army. En route he was joined by more ships and soldiers led by Cnaeus Domitius Ahenobarbus, the most important Republican leader to continue the struggle after Philippi. Asinius Pollio had already arranged the reconciliation, so that Antony was calm as the other fleet approached and duly saluted him as general. The added strength was welcome and Ahenobarbus had the prestige of a distinguished family, but the new allies proved a liability when the combined fleet arrived at Brundisium. In the past, Ahenobarbus had often attacked the port. The garrison refused to admit this known enemy and treated Antony in the same way.[6]

The triumvir responded angrily, landing near by and besieging the city. A new civil war seemed to be beginning. Octavian gathered his forces and marched south, setting up his own blockade around Antony's forces. There was some skirmishing. Antony took 500 cavalry on a raid, which caught three times that number of enemy horsemen by surprise and overwhelmed them. Octavian raised levies from amongst the veteran colonies, but when the men heard that they were to fight Antony, most of them turned around and went home. It was not so much a sign of enthusiasm for – or even fear of – Antony, but a feeling that there was simply no good reason to fight a civil war. This mood was general amongst Caesar's old officers and soldiers on both sides. They fraternised and soon felt confident enough to make their feelings known to their commanders.

Their armies did not want a war, and it is unlikely that Antony and Octavian were themselves enthusiastic, for neither had much to gain. There was still too much to be done for one of them to feel confident that he could control the empire at present. If Antony destroyed Octavian, then there was no assurance that Sextus Pompey, or whoever emerged as the dominant leader in the west, would be any less of a threat in the future. Neither side was properly prepared for war, which made the outcome even less certain. Fighting would have been a dangerous gamble for both Antony and Octavian, and it was only the fear that the other one was determined to fight that made the prospect at all acceptable to either of them. In the past, mutual suspicion and fear had fostered more than one civil war. This time, the reluctance of the rival armies forced their leaders to hold back. Serious fighting did not occur and that made it easier for Antony and Octavian to negotiate.

The talks were conducted by Asinius Pollio for Antony and a young equestrian named Caius Maecenas for Octavian, with the senior officer Lucius Cocceius Nerva, who had the confidence of the troops, as a neutral. No one was there to represent Lepidus, reflecting the continuing decline in his importance. Maecenas was one of Octavian's earliest supporters and closest friends, and over the years proved himself a wily political operator, as well as later a patron of poets like Virgil and Horace. By September 40 BC, these three had put together what is known as the Treaty of Brundisium. Antony and Octavian split the empire between them, leaving

Lepidus with only Africa. Octavian kept Gaul, so that he now effectively controlled all of the western provinces, while Antony held the east. The boundary between the two was set at Scodra in Illyria. Antony seems to have been formally charged with the war against Parthia, while Octavian was to regain Sicily and the other islands occupied by Sextus Pompey, unless the latter proved willing to negotiate a peace. This was the only concession to Sextus and he clearly felt cheated. Ahenobarbus did better, receiving a pardon. He had been condemned along with Caesar's assassins, although it seems that he was not actually part of the conspiracy. A few others were pardoned, and Antony and Octavian each executed one of their more prominent followers. Antony killed a somewhat shadowy agent of his named Manius, because he had encouraged Lucius and Fulvia to rebel. He is also said to have told Octavian that one of his generals had offered to defect to him. The man was summoned on a pretext and then killed, the triumvirs getting the Senate to pass its ultimate decree to give a veneer of legality to the death.[7]

Concordia (concord) was proclaimed and soon being celebrated throughout Italy. Whatever their attitude to the triumvirate, the fear of fresh civil war was deeply felt and the relief genuine. As so often, a marriage alliance confirmed a political bargain. Fulvia had died – Antony is said to have felt guilty about his coolness towards her in Athens, but in all respects this was remarkably convenient. Octavian's older sister Octavia had recently been widowed, when her husband Marcellus, the consul of 50 BC, died. She was about thirty. Roman law stipulated that ten months should pass between the death of one husband and the taking of another, since this would make clear the paternity of any child. Antony and Octavian had the Senate pass a special decree exempting Octavia from this and the wedding was celebrated almost immediately.

Antony and Octavian had coins minted showing the face of the other. Antony also issued a series with Octavia on the reverse, making her the first Roman woman to appear on coinage. Another of Octavian's coins showed clasped hands as a further sign of the new concord. The poet Virgil wrote of a new golden age, to be ushered in by the birth of a boy – clearly a hoped for child of Antony and Octavia. In the event, she actually bore him the first of two daughters, but by that time the mood had already become less optimistic.[8]

Antony and Octavian each celebrated an ovation when they went to Rome late in the year. It was a lesser ceremony than a triumph, but still impressive, although it was not quite clear what victories were being commemorated. Much like the honours to Caesar, it marked the triumvirs out as greater than normal magistrates. The crowds may well have cheered the processions. Yet the population was far less enthusiastic when more extraordinary taxes were announced. To make matters worse, Sextus Pompey refused to be ignored and was effectively blockading the major sea lanes to Italy. Food was short and prices high. People did not blame Sextus but the triumvirs for not coming to terms with him. Octavian was threatened by a mob when he appeared in the Forum with very few bodyguards. Missiles were thrown and he was injured.

Antony brought a small force of soldiers along the Via Sacra to help his colleague. Perceived as more favourable to a peace with Sextus, no stones were thrown, but a determined crowd blocked the path. When he tried to force his way through, they began to lob missiles at him. Antony retreated, gathered more soldiers and then attacked the Forum from two directions. He and his men cut their way to Octavian and his party and managed to bring them out. Corpses were dumped in the river to conceal the number of deaths. In the end the crowd dispersed, but it was clear that their resentment was only held in check by the naked force of the triumvirs.[9]

It was now clear that they needed to deal with Sextus and since they did not have the naval power to defeat him, negotiation was the only option. Approaches were made through relatives, including Sextus' mother. There were preliminary talks in the spring of 39 BC off the resort city of Baiae and for the first time Pompey's son met Caesar's son and his ally Antony. The rival sides stood on specially prepared platforms sunk into the beach within comfortable earshot, but offering security from sudden attack. It was not enough to overcome mutual suspicion and the talks broke down. Finally, off Misenum in the late summer a second meeting was held and an agreement reached.

Sextus Pompey was in his late twenties and had never been

enrolled in the Senate, even before he had been outlawed in 43 BC along with the conspirators and other enemies of the triumvirate. Now he was named as governor of Sicily, Sardinia and Corsica – all of which he anyway controlled – and also the Peloponnese in Greece, which he did not. Sextus joined Antony in the college of augurs, and was nominated for a consulship in 33 BC. (He would still have been too young for the office, but such breaches of the old laws no longer caused much comment.) In return, he agreed to end his naval blockade. Much to his credit, Sextus also insisted on restoring rights to the proscribed and other exiles, allowing them to return and take back at least a quarter of their property. Only the few surviving conspirators were excluded from this pardon. The proscriptions were to be ended. Runaway slaves who had served in his fleet were granted their freedom.

The Peace of Misenum for a while brought to a halt the civil wars that had split the Roman Republic since 44 BC – indeed, virtually since Caesar crossed the Rubicon in January 49 BC. There was genuine celebration when the news spread, especially when trade began to flow more normally and the food shortages in Rome and elsewhere came to an end. The immediate celebrations involving the leaders on each side seem to have begun rather nervously and it was rumoured that most of those attending the great banquet to mark the event carried concealed daggers. When Antony and Octavian both dined on board Sextus' flagship, one of his admirals is supposed to have suggested cutting the cable and disposing of them, seizing power in one fell swoop. The response became famous, for Sextus said that he could not break faith in this way and wished that the man had simply acted without seeking his permission. From the beginning, the truce was uneasy.[10]

ATHENS

Having spent almost a year in Italy, Antony set out again for the east, taking Octavia with him. It was perhaps a sign of affection, for although the marriage was one of political convenience, at least at the beginning it seems to have been reasonably happy. Antony readily responded to affection, and his new wife was both attractive and intelligent. It was widely believed that he had fallen in love with her, yet there was probably more to it than this. Roman provincial governors did not take their wives out to their provinces. Even during civil wars, this was extremely unusual and Pompey the Great's wife Cornelia was a rare exception. There was no threat to Octavia if she remained in Italy – as Fulvia had done in 44 BC, and Brutus' and Cassius' wives throughout the civil war. She was indeed the clearest symbol of the renewed alliance between her brother and husband. The most likely reason for her accompanying Antony was that all concerned felt it was a good idea to keep this symbol with him as reminder of the new, closer bond with Octavian.

The couple spent the winter together in Athens. Octavia was well educated, but Roman women got few opportunities to travel abroad and this was probably her first visit to the famous city. Their daughter, Antonia the elder, was born before they arrived and Antony made a show of laying aside many of his formal duties for the quiet life of a private citizen. His attendants were reduced to a minimum, and once again he dressed in Greek fashion and attended lectures and exercised in the gymnasium. With his wife he dined in the local manner and took part in the cycle of religious festivals, which involved sacrifices and other rituals as well as sumptuous feasting. One Stoic philosopher dedicated a book to Octavia. Antony accepted the civic office of *gymnasiarch*, dressing up in the white shoes and robe and carrying the staff of office. It was an annual post tasked with overseeing the lives and education of the ephebes, the youths training in the gymnasium.

The Athenians played along with the charade, just as the Alexandrians had pretended not to recognise the Roman general and their own queen when they dressed as slaves. Yet the Panathenaic festival games were named Antonian in his honour. At the same time they proclaimed Antony as the 'New God Dionysus', and he and Octavia as the 'Beneficent Gods'. There seems to have been some form of sacred alliance or marriage between the New Dionysus and the city's own goddess, Athena. Antony accepted this as an honour, but also insisted on a substantial sum of money from the city as dowry for his new bride.[11]

In spite of this and other levies, Antony was once again popular with a Greek audience, especially the Athenians. The Romans taxed them anyway, and at least he showed respect to their culture. The honours were not unprecedented – Caesar had also allowed himself to become *gymnasiarch* – and were part of a wider promotion of his status. Appian claims that he received few delegations over the winter months, although he accepted and responded to letters. Although the triumvirs often presented their actions as con-stitutional, and referred their decisions to the Senate for approval, the provincial and allied communities were fully aware that real power lay with Octavian and Antony. Cities approached them dir-ectly for favours. The city of Aphrodisias set up a series of long inscriptions on the wall of its theatre recording decisions made by the triumvirs and stated baldly that:

> Whatever rewards, honours, and privileges Caius Caesar or Mark Antony, triumvirs to restore the state, have given or shall give, have allotted or shall allot, have conceded or shall concede by their own decree to the people of Plarasa or Aphrodisias, all these should be deemed as having come justly and regularly.[12]

It was clear that the Senate would not challenge any decision of the triumvirs. Aphrodisias was in Asia Minor, and thus clearly within the provinces allocated to Antony, and it is interesting that they felt free to approach Octavian independently, and that he was willing and able to make decisions in response. Other communities appear to have acted in the same way. There is much less evidence for civic life in the western provinces – in part, because this was less developed in many areas – but it seems more than likely that some of these went to Antony rather than Octavian for favours and rulings. On the other hand, perhaps there were simply more problems needing attention in the east, for the recent Parthian invasion had spread disorder over a wide area.

At the end of the winter, Antony resumed the full pomp and ceremony of his rank as triumvir, donned the uniform of a Roman magistrate and general, and made it clear that he was available to receive petitioners.

[XXII]

INVASION

Cleopatra gave birth to twins in 40 BC. The boy was named Alexander and the girl Cleopatra. A few years later they would be dubbed 'the Sun' and 'the Moon' – Alexander Helios and Cleopatra Selene. It seems to have been at this point that Antony openly acknowledged them as his children, but no doubt he was informed of their birth soon after it occurred. Whether or not he and Cleopatra had formal contact in these years, they certainly took care to keep informed about the other's activities. Personal feelings aside, this was simply sound politics.[1]

Antony already had at least three children. His first marriage to the freedman's daughter Fadia seems to have produced offspring, but these may have died young – the fate of so many infants in the ancient world. Antony's daughter Antonia is generally held to be the child of his second wife and first cousin, Antonia, and not of Fadia. Fulvia gave him two sons, Marcus Antonius, also known as Antyllus, and Iullus Antonius. In 39 BC Octavia bore him the first of two daughters, both of course called Antonia, and known as Major and Minor to distinguish them in modern studies. Unlike Caesar, who had lost his only recognised child when Julia died, for Antony there was less of a novelty when his royal lover bore him twins.[2]

There were anyway far more worrying concerns for both Antony and Cleopatra. Early in 40 BC, a Parthian invasion swept through Syria. It was led by Pacorus, son of King Orodes II and favoured heir to the throne. With him was Quintus Labienus, son of the man who had been Caesar's ablest legate in Gaul, but who had defected – or perhaps returned to an older allegiance – to Pompey at the start of the civil war. The elder Labienus had died at Munda. His son –

another of the young men who so dominated public life and the civil wars after Caesar's death – sided with Brutus and Cassius and was sent by them to seek help from Orodes II. In 49 BC Pompey had made a similar request and few Roman leaders showed any reluctance in seeking foreign allies to win a civil war. Yet this was still politically sensitive and the attempt to win over the Allobroges by Lepidus and the other conspirators had utterly discredited them in 63 BC. In any event, the Parthian king proved cautious and gave no active support to either Pompey or the conspirators. Labienus was still with him when Philippi was lost and Brutus and Cassius took their own lives.[3]

What happened next was unprecedented. The figure of the exiled prince or aristocrat serving as a mercenary with a foreign monarch was a common enough one in the ancient world, especially amongst the Greek cities. Both of the fifth century BC Persian invasions of Greece included such exiles, providing information in the hope of being restored to power through foreign aid. However, Roman senators did not behave this way. There were no Roman aristocrats with Pyrrhus or Hannibal when they led their armies into Italy. Even when the competition between ambitious Roman senators became violent, no one imagined they could be restored to power by a foreign army. Subordinate allies were acceptable, but not the prospect of accompanying an invading enemy.

Labienus was amongst the proscribed and could expect to be executed if he was caught. Presumably he concluded that the Republic no longer existed and any means were acceptable to defeat the tyranny of the triumvirs. He still saw himself as a Roman general and would issue coins with the proper symbols of office. He also styled himself Parthicus, but this seemed ironic since such titles were only taken by men who defeated a foreign enemy and he served alongside the Parthians. Our sources portray him as persuading Orodes II to attack the Roman provinces. More probably he provided useful intelligence of the vulnerability of their defences and offered the hope of persuading some of the soldiers to defect, for in truth the Parthian king is unlikely to have needed much encouragement.[4]

When Crassus launched his unprovoked attack on Parthia, Orodes

II had been king for barely four years and only recently defeated a rival for the throne. Attempts to placate the Roman commander failed, but then came the sudden, overwhelming defeat of the invaders at Carrhae. Orodes and his main army were not there and the victory was won by a member of one of the great Parthian aristocratic houses. This man celebrated his success too blatantly and was soon executed by the king. Even so, the Parthians quickly recovered all the territory lost to Crassus, attacking deep into Syria in the following years.

The Roman Republic was an aggressive neighbour. The decades of internal conflict also made it highly unpredictable. Parthia was itself an empire created by aggressive warfare. Roman and Parthian armies had defeated most of their enemies in the near east with almost disdainful ease. Now, Carrhae seemed to show that the legions were also no match for the armoured cataphracts and fast-moving horse archers that were the great strength of the Parthian army. For much of the next decade, Orodes had other problems to deal with and restricted himself to minor interventions in Rome's civil wars. Caesar's plans for a grand expedition to Parthia were no secret, and Dolabella and Antony in turn talked of fulfilling this ambition. Before Antony went to winter in Alexandria at the end of 41 BC, he sent a cavalry raid to plunder the city of Palmyra, which lay beyond the borders of Syria. The Parthians saw this as clear confirmation of future aggressive intent.[5]

By 41 BC Orodes II was free from other threats and had the benefit of the detailed information provided by Labienus. Defeating Rome would also greatly strengthen the position of his chosen heir, Pacorus, and ideally prevent any challenges from Orodes' other sons or relatives when the throne passed to him. The main target of the war was Syria, once the heartland of the Seleucid Empire that the Parthians themselves had supplanted. Culturally and geographically, it seemed a natural addition to Orodes' realm.

Roman resistance was feeble. Most of the garrisons in the area were survivors from Brutus' and Cassius' armies. Some defected to Labienus. Antony's commander on the spot managed to put together a small field army, but was quickly defeated and killed. The city of Tyre resisted a siege – hence Antony was able to land there on his way to Greece in the aftermath of the Perusine War – but almost all of the rest of Syria was swiftly conquered. Pacorus gave limited support to further attacks. Labienus moved into Asia Minor, but seems to have led only the Roman troops he had been able to raise and was not accompanied by any Parthians. Even so, this was enough to overrun a large area. Some communities resisted. The outspoken orator Hybreas who had persuaded Antony to reduce taxation, now convinced his home city to turn on the garrison Labienus had installed. These were defeated, but the Roman general soon attacked again. Hybreas had by this time fled, but one of his estates was devastated. Another city seems to have been saved by freak weather conditions and set up an inscription praising the god Zeus for his intervention.[6]

Throughout the region, numerous kings, tyrants and other leaders had been driven away from their communities in the last few years, often because they had backed the wrong side in a Roman civil war. Many of these men fled to Orodes or his allies, and were now installed as sympathetic local rulers. Pacorus sent a small Parthian force into Judaea to back Antigonus in his bid to seize power from his uncle, Hyrcanus. The former promised his allies payment in the form of money and also five hundred women, many of them of royal or aristocratic family and so useful as hostages as well as a harem. Antigonus was the son of Aristobulus, whom Antony had helped to defeat in 56 BC, and there was clearly substantial support for the challenger. Hyrcanus and Herod's brother Phaesel were captured. Antigonus mutilated his uncle, apparently biting his ears. A man who was not physically whole could not be high priest and so this immediately brought his rule to an end. Phaesel died in captivity, perhaps through suicide.[7]

Herod escaped, taking with him his extended family and many of the women from the royal court promised as a prize to the Parthians. Installing these in the fortress of Masada, overlooking the Dead Sea, he went to seek aid from the king of the Nabataean Arabs. Rebuffed, he turned instead to Egypt. At Pelusium, Herod and his party were detained by Cleopatra's garrison, until she sent permission for them to be escorted to Alexandria. The queen received them with friendship and offered Herod employment as a general in her own army. One account claims this was for an expedition she was planning, but gives no further details of this. It may simply have been that she wanted a capable commander for her mercenaries, not least as defence against the Parthians should they decide to advance against her. For the moment Cleopatra had no legions to protect her realm. There was no incentive for her to join the Parthians, who if anything were successors to the Seleucids and so unlikely to favour her interests.[8]

The offer was not accepted. Herod in his later propaganda may simply have wanted to stress that he was immune to the famous seductress, but there were more important reasons for him to decline. Antigonus was already seeking recognition of his rule from Rome and it was not impossible that he would be successful. Herod wanted to go in person and lobby the triumvirs and anyone who could influence them. He left Alexandria. Cleopatra made no effort to hinder him and presumably found another, less famous, commander for her forces.

SUBORDINATES OF GENIUS

Antony's priority was to deal with the situation in Italy and it was some time before he did anything about the Parthians. Even after the renewal of the alliance at Brundisium, he clearly felt it necessary to stay in Italy. Instead, he sent Publius Ventidius Bassus with an army to take command in Asia and if possible recover the provinces there as well as Syria. Other commanders, including Asinius Pollio, went to Macedonia to fight wars against the tribes on its frontiers. At the same time Octavian sent subordinates of his own to deal with problems in Gaul.[9]

Ventidius Bassus' career was a remarkable one for a Roman general. As a child in Picenum he had been caught up in the Social War, the last great rebellion of Rome's Italian allies. His father may well have died in the conflict, but the young boy and his mother marched amongst the prisoners in the triumph held by Pompey's father, Pompeius Strabo, to commemorate his victory over the rebels. Ventidius restored his fortune by breeding mules, selling many to the Roman army, and seems to have established himself as a contractor skilled in providing transport for the legions. Julius Caesar enlisted him and he served in ever more senior posts in the campaigns in Gaul and the Civil War. Caesar made him a senator and nominated him for the praetorship, and then for bringing several legions to join Antony after Mutina he was rewarded with a brief consulship at the end of 43 BC. During the Perusine War, he was one of the commanders who failed to help Lucius Antonius in any meaningful way.

With a proven track record in logistics, Ventidius soon also demonstrated a considerable flair for tactics. Labienus was driven from Asia with very little fighting. He had too few men to face Ventidius without Parthian support, which did not appear for some time, probably not until he had actually retreated from Asia into Syria. In the Taurus Mountains, probably to the south of the pass known as the Cilician Gates, Ventidius lured the combined enemy army into attacking him on ground of his own choosing. The Parthians were overconfident, convinced of their superiority after Carrhae and the easy victories of the last year. Their uphill attack was a disaster, repulsed with heavy losses. Labienus escaped and went into hiding, but was arrested and killed by one of Antony's governors some time later.

Pacorus and the strongest part of his forces had not been at the battle. It was late in the year and they may well have withdrawn to winter nearer the Euphrates. In the spring of 38 BC the prince led a new invasion of Syria. Ventidius' army was still dispersed in its own winter quarters, but a well-crafted deception plan managed to convince the enemy to advance by a slower route and gave him time to concentrate. At Mount Gindarus, the Roman general used much the same tactics as the year before. He took up a strong position, keeping some of his troops concealed, and lured the enemy into attacking him by sending forward a weak force with orders to pull back as soon as it was heavily engaged. The Parthians still despised their Roman enemies and the ambitious Pacorus was eager to prove his own worth by leading the charge to victory. He took the bait and was routed by the sudden Roman counter-attack. Pacorus was killed and the Romans paraded his severed head around the provinces and allied communities. This was proof of Roman strength and perhaps also revenge for Crassus, who had been decapitated by the Parthians.[10]

While Ventidius was winning glory, Antony's attention remained focused on Italy. The peace with Sextus Pompey proved short-lived and in 38 BC war erupted once again. Propaganda dismissed him as a pirate, the leader of runaway slaves, and – after his eventual defeat – played down the real threat he had posed. It was true that he was always strongest at sea, able to raid the Italian coastline, but not to establish a permanent presence. Octavian may well have provoked the struggle, confident of rapid success. Instead, his fleets were twice smashed by the Pompeians and suffered further losses in storms. At one point, the son of the Divine Julius was a fugitive with just a handful of attendants. Throughout his entire career, he never came closer to defeat and death. Desperate, Octavian asked Antony to come to Brundisium for a conference, but was not there when the latter arrived. Impatient, his colleague waited for only a few days before sailing back to Greece.[11]

By this time news had reached Athens of the victory at Gindarus. Ventidius had followed up his success by advancing against the kingdom of Commagene, which had supported the enemy. He began to besiege the capital Samosata, amidst rumours that he had accepted a bribe from the king. Plenty of the recently installed rulers of the kingdoms and cities in the area were lavishly giving gifts to Ventidius and his officers in an effort to buy recognition from the Romans and remain in power. Antony arrived in person before the end of the summer to complete the siege. However, it proved more difficult than he had expected and, with the campaigning season almost at an end, he allowed the king to make peace on very generous terms. In November 38 BC Ventidius was back in Rome and rode in triumph along the Via Sacra where he had once shuffled as a prisoner. He was the first commander to win a triumph over the Parthians and it was the great culmination of his career. The 'muleteer', as he was mockingly dubbed, was at least in his late fifties and getting old for an active command. He may also have been ill, for he died not long afterwards and was granted the further honour of a state funeral.[12]

In 37 BC Octavian again asked Antony to meet him at Brundisium. He came, accompanied by a fleet of 300 warships, and the town was too nervous to admit them into the harbour. Antony went to Tarentum, and the conference occurred there instead. Lepidus was notably excluded. It took much of the summer to negotiate a new deal, aided it was said by the pregnant Octavia, who conciliated her brother and husband. In the end, Antony backed Octavian in the war against Sextus, who was stripped of his post as augur and the promised consulship. The five-year term of the triumvirate had expired at the end of 38 BC, without anyone taking particular note. Now, to restore the constitutional veneer of their rule, they gave themselves a further five years of power. They were still triumvirs – as presumably was Lepidus in spite of his marginal role. As so often, marriage alliances were to confirm political unity. Antony's son by Fulvia, Antonius Antyllus, was betrothed to Octavian's daughter Julia. Since the boy was not yet ten and the girl an infant of two years, the marriage itself was to occur at some point in the future.[13]

In practical terms, Antony promised to supply 120 ships to reinforce Octavian's fleet for the struggle with Sextus. In return, Octavian was to send him a thousand veteran praetorian guardsmen, presented as a special gift to Octavia. There was also to be a strong force of legionaries. Appian gives the figure of 20,000, quite possibly a round figure for four legions. However, Plutarch says that the promise was to provide just two legions. The ships and crews were promptly delivered. There was no sign of the promised troops, but since both the eastern expedition and the main effort against Sextus were scheduled for the following year this did not at first seem to matter.[14]

It was much to Octavian's advantage that his ablest subordinate would be present to direct the coming campaign. Marcus Vipsanius Agrippa was a contemporary and close friend of Caesar's adopted son. Of obscure family, which limited his personal ambition, he was content to serve his more famous associate. From the beginning he assisted Octavian, serving in the early campaigns, at Philippi and in the Perusine War. As time passed, and he gained practical experience, he proved to be a highly gifted commander. In 38 BC he was away in Gaul quelling a rebellion of the tribes in the south-west and in his absence the campaign against Sextus Pompey went badly. Voted a triumph on his return to Rome, he declined to celebrate it since this would have highlighted the failure of his friend. Now, Agrippa carefully prepared and trained a new, stronger fleet, for the coming struggle.[15]

The eastern provinces were still disturbed in the aftermath of the Parthian occupation. Herod had succeeded spectacularly well when he went to Rome in 40 BC. Not only did both Antony and Octavian welcome him, but they also had the Senate recognise him as king. This gave an air of tradition to the proceedings, but since Antony and Octavian walked on either side of the newly named monarch, escorting him from the meeting, it was obvious where real power lay. In spite of this approval – as much a sign of favour to both triumvirs' connections with his father Antipater – it took rather longer for him actually to regain control of Judaea, Galilee and Idumaea. Ventidius Bassus sent an officer with troops to support him, but these proved ineffective, amidst more rumours of bribery. Later, Roman assistance proved more effective and at one point he was even given command of two legions – an exceptional favour for an allied leader. Jerusalem was captured after a siege lasting several months. Antigonus was subsequently flogged and beheaded on Antony's direct orders. Herod was king, but from the beginning was far from popular.[16]

Antony spent the winter of 37–36 BC in Antioch, but responded angrily to Jewish deputations complaining about their new monarch. He ordered one group to be forcibly ejected from his presence and several were killed by his guards. Antony had plenty to do reorganising the provinces and preparing for the attack on Parthia, which now seemed very vulnerable. Orodes II was devastated by the news of Pacorus' death and perhaps unable to check the growing power of factions within the court. In 37 BC he abdicated in favour of another son, Phraates IV, who inaugurated his reign by massacring most of his brothers – there were about thirty of these – as well as his son and Orodes himself.[17]

Civil war loomed in Parthia, and suggested that Antony could exploit this internal weakness to win a great triumph. So far his military career had largely consisted of fighting other Romans. He had never commanded an army against a foreign enemy. Pompey the Great had started in the same way, but his position and authority as Rome's greatest commander had been confirmed only after the victories over the pirates and Mithridates. If Antony could defeat the Parthians – and Ventidius had shown that they were far from unbeatable – then he could fulfil the plan of Caesar, perhaps even place himself alongside Alexander the Great as the conqueror of the east.

It was a tempting prospect, but before it could be fulfilled lay a winter of work to prepare the way. This did not mean that Antony did not feast and celebrate. Octavia was not with him, having returned to Italy after beginning the journey east in the aftermath of the new agreement at Tarentum. This may well have been because her pregnancy was advanced and perhaps proving difficult. She would give him a second daughter, Antonia Minor, in January 36 BC. Her brother Octavian had already divorced the mother of his only child, since Scribonia was no longer useful as a connection with Sextus Pompey. Instead, he had married Livia Drusilla, member of one branch of the great patrician clan of the Claudii and married to a husband from another branch. This man, Tiberius Claudius Nero, had fought against Octavian at the time of the Perusine War, and he, his pregnant wife and their young son, the future Emperor Tiberius, had all been hunted fugitives. Soon afterwards he was pardoned, a divorce was arranged and he played the part of the bride's father in the ceremony marrying her to Octavian. When her son was born not long afterwards, he was sent back to Tiberius to be raised in his household.[18]

Octavian would remain married to Livia until his death half a century later, and although they would fail to have children, the marriage proved very successful in every other respect. In her youth she was considered beautiful, and throughout her life she proved herself fiercely intelligent – the Emperor Caligula dubbed her Ulysses in a frock (*Ulixem stolatum*) after Homer's wily hero. Later Roman historians would depict her as a political manipulator, and in the twentieth century Robert Graves would reinforce this image in his novel *I, Claudius*. The haste of the marriage suggests genuine passion on the part of Octavian. There were also longer-term political advantages in an alliance with such a distinguished group of families.[19]

It was not just Antony who feasted and play-acted the role of a god. At the height of the struggle with Sextus Pompey, when Italy was again blockaded and food prices high, Octavian, his new bride and their friends took part in a feast that became infamous. There were twelve guests and each took the part of one of the twelve Olympian deities. Octavian dressed as Apollo. They ate and drank in spectacular luxury. It is worth remembering that Octavian and many of his closest companions were still only in their twenties and yet they saw themselves as masters of the Republic. If this makes revelling in power and wealth less surprising, it does not make it any less tactless. Octavian continued to be widely hated. At least Antony's excesses were conducted far away and not in the very heart of a Rome threatened with starvation.[20]

Antony did not choose to spend the winter alone. He summoned Cleopatra. There was politics to be done, and Egypt would be an important supplier of grain to feed his soldiers and money to pay them. Many other leaders also came in person or sent representatives to Antioch. Perhaps Cleopatra took the twins to see their father. It certainly seems to have been now that he openly acknowledged them and they were named Sun and Moon. Such recognition had no status in Roman law and Antony made no effort to do more than this admission of paternity. Yet his welcome to the queen was warm and more than purely diplomatic. Once again they became lovers. Before the end of the winter Cleopatra was pregnant for the third time.

[XXIII]

'LOVER OF HER FATHERLAND'

Antony needed Cleopatra. Plutarch claims that the need was primarily physical and emotional, as his old passion for her had built up until he could no longer control it. An exciting and vivacious royal mistress may well have seemed a far more appealing companion for the winter months than a heavily pregnant wife. In the event, Antony would never again see Octavia, and in the remaining years of his life he was to spend more time with Cleopatra than away from her. There is no reason to believe that this is what he expected – or necessarily wanted – to happen, at least at this stage. He had certainly not repudiated his wife in any way. Cleopatra remained a mistress, if an illustrious one, and Antony had never worried about discretion when it came to lovers. Feasting with the Ptolemaic queen differed only in scale from processing around Italy with Cytheris.[1]

The Roman triumvir found the Ptolemaic queen very attractive and it is hard to believe that he did not love her, but Antony loved readily and not exclusively. It continued to be widely believed that he was susceptible to good looks and that this would influence his decisions. Herod had married Mariamne, the daughter of Hyrcanus, the mutilated and deposed king. The marriage alliance gave him some connection with Judaea's royal dynasty, but relations were not easy with his mother-in-law Alexandra. The faction around the former queen arranged for portraits of Mariamne and her younger brother Aristobulus to be sent to Antony. They were encouraged in this by Dellius, the same man who had first summoned Cleopatra to meet Antony at Tarsus.

Aristobulus was sixteen, tall for his age and handsome, while his sister's beauty was famous. Antony was suitably impressed. Herod managed to prevent the boy from going in person to meet the triumvir, fearing that he would readily be granted whatever he requested. There were even said to be fears that Antony would take the youth as a lover. Herod's family was obscure, and worse than that he was an Idumaean, from an area forcibly converted to Judaism under the Maccabees and never accepted as fully Jewish. Judaea had been plagued by violent power struggles within the royal family for more than a generation. There was little reason to suggest that the new king would be any more secure on the throne.[2]

Antony needed the eastern Mediterranean to be stable. It was important that the local rulers and communities be loyal and secure against any counter-attack once he began his Parthian expedition. The kingdoms needed to be stable enough not to require strong garrisons and committed enough to supply him with all that he needed in terms of troops, resources and money. The Romans often preferred to employ client kings instead of directly governing. Antony reduced the eastern provinces to three – Asia, Bithynia and a smaller version of Syria – and greatly strengthened the power of a handful of kings. Most, like Herod, were from outside the existing dynasties, so that they owed their position to Antony. It was now that Antony appointed Glaphyra's son to rule Cappadocia, replacing the man he had installed in 41 BC.[3]

Boundaries were redrawn, kingdoms expanded at the cost of their neighbours or former Roman provinces and monarchs made or deposed. Pompey had tended to favour cities, but now Antony relied more on kings. Yet overall there was little difference between the aims and methods of the two Roman leaders, or indeed of Caesar's measures to secure the east after Pharsalus. Each Roman leader wanted his settlement to function, but would also have understood that they were placing monarchs and leaders in each community firmly in their debt.

Cleopatra and her realm were an important part of the jigsaw that made up the territories under Antony's control. Thus, as well as love, sex and feasting, there were sound political reasons for bringing her to Antioch late in 37 BC. There is no hint of her delaying her arrival as she had at Tarsus, for Cleopatra was fully aware of the importance of the decisions being made by her former lover. It no doubt added to the enthusiasm with which she renewed the affair and she was further encouraged when he proved very generous. Cyprus may have been confiscated after the support given to Cassius by her governor Serapion. Either now, or at some earlier stage, it was returned to her control. Cleopatra was also given Crete, as well as part of Cyrenaica to the west of Egypt, some of Cilicia and Syria, all previously directly governed as Roman provinces. Her realm now embraced virtually all of the Syrian coastal strip, including Phoenicia, Ituraea inland and part of the Decapolis (the 'Ten Towns' of the Gospels) near the Sea of Galilee, and sections of the Arab kingdom of Nabataea. Tyre remained an independent city, but Herod only retained Gaza as a Mediterranean port.

Antony was generous to his mistress and Plutarch claims that opinion at Rome was shocked. Perhaps this was true, but if so this did not have any tangible results. The grants to the queen were in keeping with his general reorganisation. She was loyal to Rome, and to Antony personally, and there was every reason to believe that she would enthusiastically and effectively exploit the resources of these territories on his behalf. Cilicia was especially rich in timber, something that Egypt itself lacked in any significant quantities. It was thus especially useful for the queen, helping building projects, and was clearly also intended to permit the construction of ships. Some would no doubt be warships to strengthen Antony's fleet. As important were the transport vessels that would carry grain from Egypt to the Syrian coast from where it could be taken to his legions.[4]

Cleopatra now ruled most of the territory controlled by the Ptolemies at the very height of their power in the third century BC. Yet Antony had not given in to her every desire. Herod's kingdom of Judaea lay surrounded on three sides by her lands, but remained distinct. The region had been disputed by the Ptolemies and Seleucids over the centuries and would have made her expanded kingdom more coherent geographically. Cleopatra wanted Judaea, but was never able to cajole Antony into granting it to her. This did not deter her from trying – she kept a close interest in the affairs of the kingdom and remained very friendly with Alexandra. Herod was Antony's own appointee – one of the only decisions affecting the area made jointly with Octavian. He held on to his newly won throne, although he lost most of the coastline of the kingdom. Also given to the queen was a region near Jericho, rich in date palms and groves of the balsam bush. The latter was the famous 'balm of Gilead', which provided highly prized incense used in rituals and was also believed to have medicinal qualities. The Nabataean kingdom gave up its territory close to the Dead Sea, which provided a rich supply of bitumen – again important for shipbuilding amongst other things.

Herod and the Nabataean king leased these regions back from Cleopatra, paying her a substantial annual rent from their profits. At some point Herod took on the responsibility for the other monarch's payments. His main aim may have been political, improving relations with his neighbour, but it was also a reflection of the profitability of the trade in bitumen, so that he could expect to make money on the deal. Profit to Rome was inevitably indirect. Cleopatra had gained valuable new sources of income and, in turn, Antony could expect to be able to draw upon her wealth to support his own enterprises. Elsewhere, the communities that found themselves part of the Ptolemaic kingdom on the whole continued to run their own affairs, just as they had done if previously part of the Roman province, autonomous or included within another kingdom. There is some sign that aspects of the Roman provincial administration continued to function in Cyrenaica under Cleopatra's rule, except that tax revenue and other income now went to her.[5]

The queen had done well out of the deal at Tarsus. She was not unique in this, as several monarchs had found their power bolstered by Antony's reorganisation of the east. Yet, even when set within the context of the wider restructuring of the eastern Mediterranean, his royal mistress was probably the greatest beneficiary. A stronger Ptolemaic kingdom seemed useful to Antony. Unlike her father, Cleopatra had not contracted huge debts to prominent Romans, but there was never any doubt that the resources of her kingdom were at Antony's disposal. What she had been given could as readily be taken away.

Cleopatra's success at Antioch has tended to blind historians to the precariousness of her position. She still relied on Roman support to remain in power and there was no imaginable situation in the future where this dependence would end. Continued Roman backing was less certain, although for the moment Antony's good-will and generosity were secure. Yet his needs and inclinations might change in the future, nor was it certain how long he would remain in the east and whether his power would endure or decline. Cleopatra had to keep on proving her loyalty and effectiveness as an ally and personally hold on to Antony's affection. It may well be that the love was also genuine on her side, but even if it was not, she simply could not afford to lose his interest.

No Ptolemy was safe on the throne for long. Cleopatra's siblings were dead, but by 37 BC Caesarion was ten. As he advanced into his teenage years, the boy would be less and less easy to control. There might come a time when he was no longer content as nominal co-ruler with his mother. Given the characters of his father and mother, it would be surprising if he was not ambitious. Even if he was not, and Cleopatra felt able to dominate him, then there were bound to be courtiers and Alexandrian aristocrats who felt that their own power could be increased by promoting the status of the young prince. At some point, Caesarion would marry, adding an extra element to court politics. His bride – even if Cleopatra Selene was chosen – might prove equally independent. An adult king seen to be dominated by his mother was unlikely to be popular. In the even longer term, Alexander Helios would automatically be seen as a potential alternative ruler.

A woman could not rule on her own for long. The birth of Caesarion had in due course allowed Cleopatra to dispose of her brother and rule with a consort who fulfilled the necessary titular role of king and pharaoh, but who could be fully controlled. Yet in the longer term he and the other children were potential rivals as much as assets. Family history made it doubtful that Cleopatra's children would prove uniquely able to live in harmony. They might become threats to her or to each other. The only assurance against this was for her to retain the close support of Rome, and the only guarantee of this was to hold fast to the affection of the Roman with greatest power in the region. Neither Cleopatra nor any of her children could hope to challenge Rome and win. Her first Roman protector had been killed and she needed to make the most of her second. Gaining territory brought her prestige and, as importantly, wealth with which to reward loyal followers. There was even the possibility that she could prevent an eventual power struggle amongst her children if her territory was large enough to divide into several realms. It was a method the family had used in the past, admittedly with mixed success.

Antony needed Cleopatra and her kingdom politically, and revelled in her love and company. Her need for him – or someone like him, with his power – was even stronger and more pressing, since losing his support would remove the ultimate surety of her power. If normal politics were free to resume in Alexandria, then once again exile and death became real possibilities.

THE NEW EMPIRE

The year 37–36 BC was for Cleopatra's regime 'the Year Sixteen, which is also the Year One'. It was sixteen years since she had succeeded to her father's throne in 51 BC – remembering again that the ancient system of counting had no zero and so began with one. The period of her exile and the sole rule of Ptolemy XIII before Caesar returned her to power was tactfully forgotten. Nor were the years of joint rule with Caesarion referenced in the new system of dating.

There are other signs of the importance of this year for royal propaganda, as Cleopatra began to style herself 'the younger goddess' (*Neotera Thea*), and 'lover of her homeland/fatherland' (*Philopatris*) as well as the familiar 'father-loving'. Caesarion's titles did not change, and he remained the 'father-loving and mother-loving god'. Cleopatra herself was honoured in her new territories and sometimes also by neighbouring communities. Caesarion received little or no attention outside Egypt.[6]

The connection with the grants of territory ceded to her by Antony is obvious. Cleopatra 'the goddess' (*Thea*) was evoked, the Ptolemaic princess who in the second century BC married three Seleucid kings in succession and was mother of three more – one of whom she murdered. (She was the daughter of Cleopatra II and so sister of Cleopatra VII's great-grandmother.) Syria, Ituraea and some of the other territories had more recently been ruled by the Seleucids than the Ptolemies. Cleopatra clearly felt it was worthwhile promoting the memory of her namesake by becoming the 'younger goddess'.

What was meant by her 'homeland' is less obvious. For some, it has been proof of her deep attachment to Egypt itself. Yet there does not seem to be any particular reason why she would have chosen to express this at this particular point in her reign. Far more plausible is the suggestion that Cleopatra was now associating herself with the memory of Alexander the Great. Thus the homeland was specifically Macedonia, but more generally the wider area of his conquests and the Successor kingdoms. The appeal was to her newly gained territories, reminding them of older, indeed pre-Roman, unity. It is hard to say whether the audience was receptive. Equally, the word was vague and may well have been interpreted in different ways by people in the various regions now ruled by the queen. Perhaps there were some in Egypt, even some who considered themselves more Egyptian than Greek, who saw this as a sign of genuine affection in their monarch.

Cleopatra strove to keep Egypt stable and productive. For practical reasons she favoured the more important, and potentially dangerous, sections of the population. Alexandria was given precedence over the countryside and the southern regions, while the aristocrats of the great city were favoured even more. She continued her policy of temple building and support for the cults maintaining the country's traditional religion and as a result retained the loyalty of the important Egyptian priestly classes. There is no real evidence that she did anything to improve the lot of the poorer Egyptians, but then there was no particular reason to expect this. They were important as a labour force, working the fields and producing the annual harvest that provided the great bulk of the crown's income. The 40s BC had suffered from disruption of the irrigation systems and government in general, as well as a series of poor inundations. Although things may have begun to improve, and as far as we can tell the cycle of flooding had returned to its more normal levels, the yield was unlikely to have been as high as in earlier periods of stability. A fair proportion of the profits also went to aristocrats in Alexandria and elsewhere, to ensure their loyalty.[7]

There were some other sources of royal revenue. The trade from the Red Sea ports to Arabia, and beyond that to India and Sri Lanka, was promoted by the queen and proved very lucrative. The principal advantage of the new territory was as fresh sources of income. Resources like timber were practically useful, both for shipbuilding and construction in general. Cleopatra also ordered balsam shrubs to be brought from Jericho to be replanted in Egypt to provide a more immediate supply. She was not the first Ptolemy to introduce a new crop to Egypt, as in the early period there had been an unsuccessful attempt to cultivate a type of cabbage from Rhodes. On the whole, the Ptolemies were not great innovators in methods of production.[8]

Developing groves of balsam shrubs would not yield a quick result and the greatest gain was in the immediate rent. Cleopatra had become substantially wealthier and much of this wealth came directly in cash through taxation. Money was important to reward supporters, both within her kingdom and important Romans, and also to maintain the splendour of her court. That in itself helped to keep Antony's favour, but far more important was the ability to supply her Roman protector with wealth and resources at the time and in the quantities he needed. For all her wider profile in the new territories, and the propaganda of past Hellenistic monarchs, there was never any attempt to conceal that she ruled by Roman consent. Several series of bronze coins were struck by Syrian cities within her new realm bearing the queen on the face and Antony on the reverse. Antioch began to issue silver coinage with Antony's head and the titles 'imperator for the third time and triumvir' translated into Greek, with a very Roman-looking Cleopatra on the other side.[9]

This is well illustrated by her continued involvement in Judaean affairs. Cleopatra and Alexandra corresponded, although much of the communication had to be done in secret and we are told Herod's mother-in-law used a minstrel as courier. Amongst her languages, Cleopatra was fluent in both Hebrew and the Aramaic used for much everyday communication in Judaea. At one point, Alexandra attempted to smuggle herself and her son out of Jerusalem to seek refuge in Egypt, an idea allegedly suggested by Cleopatra. The plan was to conceal them in coffins, but Herod's informers had kept him abreast of the plot and they were watched and then caught in the act.

As an Idumaean from outside the priestly families, Herod himself could not be both king and high priest, as Hyrcanus and his predecessors had done. The temple cult required the appointment of a high priest, and although his wife's brother Aristobulus was the obvious candidate, he could prove a dangerous rival. Herod chose someone else, prompting Alexandra to appeal for assistance to Cleopatra. The latter backed her and in turn appealed to Antony. His support left Herod with no choice, so he dismissed the present incumbent and elevated Aristobulus to the post. A little later he arranged for the 'accidental' drowning of the youth. Alexandra was kept virtually as a prisoner.[10]

Cleopatra could intervene in Judaean affairs because she was able to influence Antony. Only the triumvir could order Herod to take any action, and Antony was unlikely to remove a monarch who proved a loyal and effective client. He would not give Cleopatra Judaea, nor let her independently interfere outside in the kingdom's affairs. She had influence rather than power. On the journey back from Antioch she stopped in Judaea and was entertained by Herod. There was business to conduct over the lease of the land near Jericho. Josephus, no doubt drawing on Herod's own memoirs, claims that Cleopatra did everything she could to seduce the king. He not only resisted, but also considered having her murdered. The claims seem unlikely, and no doubt Herod merely wished once again to stress his ability to resist the famous seductress. On the other hand, Cleopatra may well have alternately flirted and threatened, keeping Herod off balance in the negotiations. It would be no bad thing for her if her neighbour was nervous, making him more likely to give in to her requests.[11]

The size of her territory should not conceal the essential weakness of her position. Land, wealth and influence were all dependent on Roman, and specifically Antony's, favour. Cleopatra remained a client monarch, if one on a grand scale, and she should not be considered in any way ruler of an autonomous or allied kingdom. The new territories were gifts, not conquests. Cleopatra had no significant military resources and could not have taken any of these lands. Nor would she be able to hold them without Roman backing. The royal army was tiny and barely adequate for internal control of Egypt itself. It was over a generation since the system of cleruchies had lost any real connection with military service and become simply a type of land ownership. The only royal troops were mercenaries and there were fewer of these in the world as Roman control increased. At some point Antony gave his lover a bodyguard of 400 Gallic and German horsemen, drawn from warrior societies famed for their loyalty.[12]

Cleopatra could never fight Rome with even the remotest chance of winning. The same was true of Herod and all the other eastern client kings and communities. They were simply a useful way for the Romans to control the eastern Mediterranean and would survive as long as no more attractive alternative presented itself to the Romans. From the beginning, Egypt and to some extent all the Ptolemaic possessions had been run as royal property, with the primary aim of extracting a steady revenue for the monarch. This was still true, only now the system was also employed to feed much of this profit on to Antony. Neither he – nor before him Caesar – had any role to play in the official titles and propaganda employed in Egypt itself. There it was the queen and her son who served as pharaohs and ensured balance in the world. In that context, it did not matter at all that they were in no way genuinely independent.[13]

The power of the Ptolemies had relied ultimately on Roman support for at least a century before Cleopatra became queen. In her lifetime, Roman power throughout the entire eastern Mediterranean had grown even stronger and was clearly not about to disappear. She was highly successful within this context, but it would always be as a dependant of Rome. For the moment, Rome meant Antony. Simply being his lover may possibly have kept her in power. Yet it was being so useful and reliable, just as much as her personal charm, that brought her new lands to rule on his behalf. Cleopatra had survived, and that in itself was no mean feat in these disturbed times. That she was a woman, and ruled effectively if not nominally as the sole power in her kingdom, made this even more of an achievement.

[XXIV]

'INDIA AND ASIA TREMBLE':
THE GRAND EXPEDITION

After the winter at Antioch, Mark Antony finally began the long talked about war to punish the Parthians and avenge Crassus. Some in Italy may have felt that Ventidius' victories and the killing of Pacorus had already satisfied Roman honour, and it is possible that Octavian encouraged this view. Yet it was far from universal and the Parthians still had the legionary eagles and other standards taken at Carrhae as trophies of Rome's humiliation. Ventidius' victories had been defensive, driving the invaders from Roman and allied territory. Antony was now ready to humble the Parthian king in his own homeland.[1]

By Roman standards, there were good reasons for an attack on Parthia, not least to restore the façade of the legions' invincibility and to deter future invasions of Syria. Antony also had strong personal reasons for fighting this war. He was forty-seven, had been consul once and had shared effectively dictatorial powers with his triumviral colleagues since 43 BC. It was a highly unorthodox career – if not quite so spectacularly so as that of the twenty-seven-year-old Octavian – and only made possible by the disturbed times. As we have seen, for all his success Antony had never commanded in a war against a foreign opponent and, indeed, had only limited experience of such conflicts at a junior level from his service with Gabinius and Caesar.

The highest glory for a Roman aristocrat was to defeat a foreign enemy and, ideally, an especially dangerous or exotic one. This was deeply embedded within their psyche and reflected in a political system that gave both military and civil power to the senior executive officers of the Republic. Winning a foreign war brought clean glory, and equally clean plunder, without the stigma of killing or plundering fellow citizens. A foreign victory could make a man's fortune as well as his reputation. It was something neither Antony nor Octavian had so far done. It might help to overshadow the brutal path they had taken to controlling the state.[2]

PREPARATIONS

Antony's preparations were on a grand scale. Late in 37 BC, or very early in 36 BC, one of his generals, Publius Canidius Crassus, mounted a show of force in the kingdom of Armenia and then operated against the tribes to the north, defeating the Iberi and Albani. Armenia had been defeated by Pompey, but, although a Roman ally, had close cultural connections with Parthia. From the beginning Antony may well have planned to use it as a base for his invasion. It was said that Caesar had intended to do the same thing, avoiding the open plains of Mesopotamia where Crassus' army had been destroyed, instead striking into the more broken country of Media Atropene (roughly modern-day Azerbaijan). This was felt to be far less favourable to the cavalry, which formed the heart of any Parthian army. The Iberians and Albanians were unlikely to have presented any threat to the planned expedition. Operations against them were a useful way of winning glory and giving at least some of the legions the confidence and experience of recent victory.[3]

Other lessons had also been learned from Crassus' defeat. Ventidius had demonstrated the effectiveness of infantrymen armed with bows, slings and javelins, and Antony ensured that he had large numbers of these to support his legionaries. In a missile exchange, the horse archers would no longer have things all their own way. There would also be a very strong contingent of cavalry accompanying the army. Antony is said to have had 10,000 auxiliary horsemen, mostly from Spain and Gaul. More mounted troops were provided by the eastern kingdoms. King Artavasdes of Armenia brought 6,000 horsemen – a mixture of heavy cataphracts and light horse archers much like the Parthians themselves – as well as 7,000 infantrymen. Altogether, Plutarch claims there were 30,000 allied troops, but does not say how many of these were cavalry. With the

Gauls, Spaniards and the core of 60,000 legionaries, he suggests a total of 100,000 men for Antony's army. In a rhetorical flourish, he claims that throughout central Asia and even in India beyond, people trembled at the rumours of so huge a force.[4]

As usual, it is a little hard to know how to treat these numbers. Plutarch does not say how many legions took part in the operation, although later he mentions that two were detached and refers to the presence of the *Third* Legion. The latter is the only named unit mentioned in our sources, but it seems likely that other legions associated with Antony, for instance *V Alaudae*, also took part. Velleius Paterculus says that Antony had thirteen legions altogether, but does not give a figure for their strength. Other sources claim that there were fifteen, sixteen, or seventeen legions. For no very convincing reason, most modern scholars opt for an army of sixteen legions. Appian says that that was the number Caesar had intended to employ on his own Parthian expedition, supported by 10,000 cavalry. Crassus' army had been half the size, with eight legions.[5]

It is extremely unlikely that any of the legions mustered their full theoretical strength. Many veterans had been discharged after Philippi from units that were unlikely to have had their full complement in the first place. Recruits had been drawn from the survivors of the conspirators' men, but there had also been casualties in the campaigns fought since then. Antony seems to have had trouble recruiting from Italy and the troops promised by Octavian in 37 BC had not appeared. He had recruited some legionaries from the provinces, since we hear of such inexperienced troops supporting Herod in Judaea. Many of these may not have been citizens.[6]

Antony's army was certainly large, although 2,000–3,000 is once again probably a good estimate for the average strength of his legions, and it is unlikely that the overall force was as big as Plutarch suggests, at least in terms of combatants. On the whole they were the pick of his troops, for other forces remained in Macedonia and probably also as garrisons within the eastern provinces. The army contained some experienced units and individuals, as well as more recent recruits. It was well balanced in terms of the different troop types and generally well equipped. One disadvantage was that the different contingents had limited experience of working together as a single army, but this was probably inevitable in such a large operation.

Moving the food and other equipment needed by the men and mounts was a formidable task and accompanying them was a very large number of pack and draught animals, attended by slaves and other camp followers. These were more mouths to feed and, in the end, the capacity to supply his force was more likely to limit its size than availability of troops. Equipment carried in the baggage train included large numbers of ballistas and other siege equipment, notably a battering ram 80 feet in length, presumably carried in sections. This was no mere raid, but an invasion by an army capable of capturing strongly fortified positions.[7]

Neither Antony nor any of his officers had experience of leading and controlling such a large army. Perhaps there had been more men in the combined armies at Philippi, but there his own and Octavian's forces had remained clearly distinct. It had also proved a relatively simple campaign, with the main manoeuvres limited to a small area around Philippi itself. Almost all of Antony's military experience had been gained in Italy or one of the more settled provinces, where the roads were generally good and geographical and topographical information fairly easy to obtain. Even Gaul was quite well known to Caesar's army by the time Antony had joined it. Now the context would be different, advancing into a region never before explored by a Roman army. Far more reliance would have to be placed on local guides. If the size of his army was something new, so was the sheer scale of the theatre of operations and the distances involved.[8]

Roman commanders were bold by instinct and training, and Antony was no exception. In his early exploits under Gabinius, Antony had been a dashing cavalry leader, good at seizing opportunities and, on a small scale, gaining surprise by sheer speed of movement or outflanking the enemy. He relied on similar methods in the larger operations of the civil wars, and boldness had succeeded at Philippi. Then – and indeed in almost every campaign throughout his career – operations had been completed within a single year. Later, Antony would be criticised for delaying the invasion so that he could spend longer with

Cleopatra at Antioch, then rushing away at its end to return to her arms. This was unfair, and he must have been aware that Caesar had expected his Parthian War to last for several years. Yet his own experience was of quick campaigns and perhaps he struggled to plan for anything longer.[9]

This time the enemy was likely to prove more dangerous than the hesitant, almost supine performance of Brutus and Cassius in 41 BC. Parthian armies were extremely good when well led. In 40–38 BC the army had been overconfident, lured into fighting at a disadvantage by Ventidius Bassus. It could not be assumed that it would make the same mistake again and with such a strong mounted arm it was highly mobile. In defence of their homeland, the Parthians could also be expected to be numerous, most probably significantly outnumbering Antony's cavalry if not his entire army. So many horses created major supply problems, especially if operations extended beyond the spring and summer. However, within his own and allied territory, the Parthian king was better placed to ensure adequate supplies of food and fodder, which could be protected behind the walls of his cities.[10]

The war would present Antony with new problems and the challenge of a mobile and effective enemy. Yet his army was large and reasonably well prepared. If he lacked experience at this level, then in some ways this had also been true of Caesar when he took command in Gaul. Antony was still in his forties, the prime of life for a Roman general, and he had wider authority than even Pompey had wielded during his eastern command. There were plenty of reasons to forecast a grand success, which would hugely enhance his status and power.

Phraates IV had been king for barely a year and after his bloody accession still faced rivals from amongst the aristocracy. A nobleman named Monaeses fled to Antony and was promptly rewarded with the revenue from three cities in the provinces. The Parthian aristocrat assured the Roman that the new king was loathed and that many others would defect to his side if he attacked. Antony was encouraged, even when Monaeses decided to return to his homeland early in 36 BC and be reconciled with his king. It seemed clear evidence of an unstable and vulnerable kingdom.

ATTACK

For the moment, Antony pretended to negotiate, sending an embassy to demand the return of Crassus' eagles and any Roman prisoners still held by the Parthians. Phraates could not risk damaging his own prestige by making such a concession, but Antony wanted to convince the king that hostilities were unlikely in the immediate future. Then Antony concentrated a substantial part of his army – probably most of the legions and auxiliary cavalry – and marched to Zeugma on the Syrian bank of the Euphrates. This suggested that he planned to threaten and perhaps invade Mesopotamia, just as Crassus had done. Phraates duly concentrated the royal army ready to meet this attack.

Antony may have always intended this to be a deception, but even if he still planned to invade from Armenia the route from Zeugma via Edessa was shorter at around 500 miles. The Parthians had not mustered quickly enough to block Crassus' initial invasion and perhaps the Romans hoped to slip by before the enemy concentrated. Yet Phraates was quick, or Antony was late, and the route was closed. Instead, the Roman army marched north, looping around into Armenia to rendezvous with most of the allied contingents and quite probably the forces led by Canidius. (An extra problem in judging the size of the army during this campaign is the uncertainty over whether the figures in our sources refer to simply Antony's men, the entire field army or all the troops within the wider theatre of operations. It seems quite probable that some troops remained in Syria, if only to preserve the illusion that the main army was there, although this is not mentioned in any of the accounts.)[11]

The move wrong-footed the Parthians, but it was a long march. The precise route cannot now be established – Plutarch claimed the soldiers had to cover 1,000 miles – and it was a huge detour compared to the quicker route, which the Parthians controlled. As a result, it was well into summer before the Roman army was ready on the borders of Armenia. Later, it was suggested that Antony ought to have waited until the next year, resting his men. This would have given Phraates time to prepare his defence, squandering any advantage gained by the deception and rapid outflanking march. It would

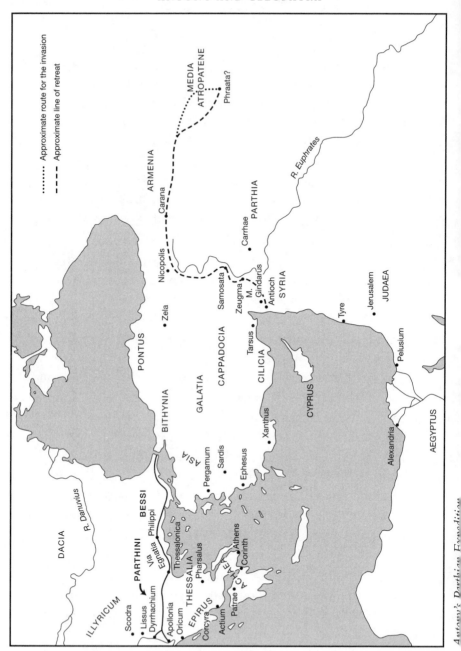

········· Approximate route for the invasion
– – – – Approximate line of retreat

MEDIA ATROPATENE

Phraata?

ARMENIA

Carana

Nicopolis

R. Euphrates

PARTHIA

Carrhae

Samosata

Zeugma
M. Gindarus
Antioch SYRIA

Zela

PONTUS

Tarsus

CILICIA

Tyre

Jerusalem JUDAEA

Pelusium

CAPPADOCIA

GALATIA

BITHYNIA

Xanthus

CYPRUS

Pergamum

Sardis

Ephesus

ASIA

Alexandria

AEGYPTUS

R. Danuvius

DACIA

BESSI

PARTHINI

Via Egnatia Philippi

Thessalonica

THESSALIA

Pharsalus

Athens
Corinth

ACHAEA

ILLYRICUM

Scodra

Lissus
Dyrrhachium

Apollonia
Oricum

EPIRUS

Corcyra

Actium

Patrae

Antony's Parthian Expedition

also have meant that Antony himself would have achieved no tangible result from a season's campaigning. He still believed that he could achieve more before the weather rendered campaigning impossible. Philippi had not been decided until late October. It was the first of his gambles.[12]

Antony pressed on, leading the combined army into Media. The king of this region was also called Artavasdes, like the king of Armenia. Antony targeted the royal city of Phraata – the location of which is not now identifiable – which contained his treasury and the royal household with his wives and children. Its capture would have been a serious blow to the king's prestige and perhaps forced Artavasdes of Media to defect. Phraates IV, like all Parthian monarchs, ruled a disparate collection of lesser kings and powerful aristocrats, who might readily change sides if it no longer seemed in their interest to support him.[13]

Boldness, speed of movement and surprise were hallmarks of Antony's style of war-making, but he must already have been aware that they were harder to achieve on a grand scale. The Parthians had long since realised that the threat to Mesopotamia was a feint. Phraates ordered his army to re-form in Media. It would take time for them to move there, and longer still to prepare sufficient supplies to support them. Artavasdes of Media was the first to bring his own forces to meet the attack on his lands, but he was soon joined by other contingents. Then Phraates himself arrived and, although it was not the custom for a Parthian king to lead his army in person, he closely supervised the campaign.

Phraata was deep inside Media and Antony's column made frustratingly slow progress through country that lacked good roads. This was in spite of the fact that the Romans kept to the plains around the river – favourable ground for the Parthian cavalry if these put in an appearance. Most awkward of all were the 300 wagons carrying the siege train and heavy baggage. Draught oxen are slow, plodding along at no more than 2–2.5 mph for at best seven or eight hours a day, and will be lucky to make 60 miles in a week if they are to be kept fit enough to continue working. Wheeled transport tends to become even more difficult to move if the terrain is even a little broken. At every obstacle a traffic jam would develop, taking hours to sort out and more time for the waiting vehicles and troops to catch up.[14]

The heavy train could not move any faster, so Antony decided to leave it behind and press on with the bulk of the fighting troops and only lighter equipment and limited food supplies. He would hurry to Phraata and perhaps be able to terrify the defenders into submission or take the city by a sudden assault. Two of his least experienced legions and some allied contingents were left to guard the train as it followed behind at its own pace. In Gaul, Caesar had routinely led out the best of his legions, leaving raw troops to guard his heavy baggage and stores. Yet the latter had always been left in a strongly fortified camp or behind the walls of a town. They had never been allowed to wander on their own with such weak protection, even in Gaul, where the enemy was far less mobile than the Parthians. This was a second, even greater gamble.[15]

Antony reached Phraata, but the defenders failed to be overawed by the size of his army. He was forced to begin a formal siege, setting the soldiers to building a mound that was intended to be higher than the wall and allow them to shoot down at the defenders. The Romans seem to have brought some light artillery with them and had plenty of soldiers armed with missiles. Yet progress was slow and until the heavy equipment arrived there was little prospect of taking the city.

Phraates' scouts located the Roman heavy train and reported on the weakness of its escort. Seizing the opportunity, Phraates despatched a strong force of cavalry to intercept it. By this time the convoy was probably only a few days away from the main Roman force. The escort's commander sent word to Antony asking for rescue. He may also have hoped for assistance from Artavasdes of Armenia's contingent, but in the aftermath of the campaign the king was accused of failing to offer support. The Parthians attacked and quickly overwhelmed the two legions. Such a large convoy would have been difficult to protect for a force of this size. The Roman escort was wiped out and its commander killed. King Polemo of Pontus – one of the monarchs whose power Antony had greatly increased in the last years – was amongst the prisoners. The siege equipment was burnt, the transport animals, vehicles and supplies carried off or destroyed.

When he heard of the threat, Antony took a strong force away from the siege of Phraata and force-marched it to rescue the baggage train. He arrived to find only corpses and the ash and debris of destruction. Phraata continued to hold out and without the irreplaceable siege train there was very little prospect of taking it. Capitulation seemed extremely unlikely, now that a substantial Parthian army was operating in the area. More immediately, Antony had also lost the greater part of his reserves of food. Foraging parties were extremely vulnerable unless sent out in great strength. Casualties began to mount as a succession of small columns were caught and destroyed by the Parthian horse archers. Artavasdes of Armenia had already decided to lead his own contingent home.[16]

Antony decided to take yet another gamble. Leaving only a skeleton force to protect his siege lines, he led ten legions, three cohorts of praetorian guard and all his cavalry on a march through the surrounding countryside. At the very least, they were to gather food and forage, but the hope was that the Parthians would be drawn into fighting a battle. A clear battlefield victory could easily change the course of the campaign, forcing King Phraates to retreat or seek terms and perhaps breaking the will of the defenders of the city of Phraata.[17]

A strong Parthian force was soon shadowing the Roman column on the first day of its march. The enemy did not attack, impressed by the discipline of Antony's men, each formation keeping in place to offer mutual support. The Roman commander pretended to retreat, marching his men close in front of the wide crescent formed by the enemy, who continued simply to observe. Orders had been issued for the units in the column to wheel into line and attack as soon as Parthians were close enough for the legionaries to charge them. Trumpets sounded to give the signal and the Roman army surged into the attack, the legionaries shouting and banging their weapons against their shields to frighten the enemy horses. The onslaught panicked the enemy, but as the Parthian horsemen fled it proved difficult for the Romans to catch them. Perhaps the order had been given too soon. More probably the enemy cavalry were difficult to catch unless they were strongly committed to an attack, as in the battles against Ventidius. The Romans killed eighty men and captured a mere thirty.

Antony had failed to get the decisive battle he needed. On the next day he led his troops back to Phraata and the enemy showed their continued confidence by harassing the Roman column every yard of the way. In the meantime – or perhaps just after his dispirited men had returned – the defenders of the city launched a sally. The legionaries stationed as outposts panicked and the enemy was able to reach the Roman mound and do some damage to the siege works. Antony ordered the units involved to be decimated, executing one in ten and feeding the survivors with a ration of barley rather than wheat. As supplies grew shorter, this last measure may have extended to the army as a whole.[18]

It was now well into autumn and the Romans were making no progress in the siege. Food was running short for both sides and Phraates realised that he would soon find it difficult to keep the semi-feudal contingents within the Parthian army together. Like Antony before him, he now chose to deceive his opponent. Attacks on Roman foraging parties were deliberately reduced. Parthian patrols were encouraged to talk to their opponents – perhaps especially the allied contingents – praising their courage and speaking of the king's desire for an end to hostilities. It was just what the Romans and their commander wanted to hear. An embassy was sent to the Parthian camp. Dio provides a vivid portrait of Phraates sitting on a golden throne to receive them, all the while toying with a strung composite bow – a symbol of continuing hostilities. An unstrung bow was a sign of peace. A renewed plea for the return of Crassus' standards and prisoners was brusquely refused, but the Romans were assured that if they now retreated, then they would not be pursued. The truce was limited. The defenders of Phraata sallied out again and destroyed the Roman siege works and there were further attacks on foragers.

Perhaps Antony and his senior officers believed, or wanted to believe, the king's pledge. In many ways it did not matter. If Phraata had fallen they might have captured enough food to supply the troops and spend the winter in Media. It had not, and an undefeated enemy army hovered menacingly around them. Staying where they were offered no prospect of success and a strong chance of utter disaster. The decision was made to retreat to Armenia. Antony was unwilling to make a speech informing the army of the new orders and instead delegated the task to Domitius Ahenobarbus, the former ardent Republican whose son was now betrothed to Antony's elder daughter by Octavia. Given the size of the army, it is likely that the speech had to be made several times, unless it was simply addressed to a gathering of the centurions and other officers, who then passed the essence on to their men. Many of the soldiers were moved by their commander's evident shame about his bad decisions. Antony remained popular.[19]

RETREAT

Withdrawing in the face of the enemy is one of the more difficult manoeuvres for any army. When that enemy is far more mobile, the risk of serious loss, even disaster, becomes all the greater. Antony decided not to use the same route taken during the advance. A Mardian, who had managed to survive the massacre of the heavy train, advised him that the country was too open. It would be better to stick closer to the hill country, passing villages and fields not already stripped bare. The man had already given proof of loyalty and now willingly submitted to riding in chains and under escort as he guided the column.

The Mardian may have been right to say that King Phraates had no intention of giving the Romans safe passage, or perhaps Antony's change of route made him suspect treachery. On the third day's march there were signs that the enemy had deliberately broken a dam and flooded one section of road. Antony re-formed the army into an *agmen quadratum* – a rectangular formation where the remaining baggage was kept in the middle and surrounded on all sides by formed troops ready to deploy into battle order. They were in the process of doing this when the first Parthian patrols appeared.

The enemy cavalry were soon streaming into the attack, trying to overwhelm the Romans before they could complete the new deployment. Antony's light infantry engaged them, but were eventually forced to withdraw behind the shelter of his legionaries. Finally, a formed charge by Gallic auxiliary cavalry drove off the main body of Parthians. There were no more attacks for the remainder of the day. Overnight, Antony and his officers made sure that the whole army was familiar with its places in the new formation. Strict orders were given for any cavalry counter-attack to be limited, so that no unit could be lured away from the main army and isolated – the fate of Crassus' son Publius and his Gallic horsemen at Carrhae.[20]

For four days the Romans kept to the plan. Progress was slow, for the formation was cumbersome, but although there was a steady trickle of casualties, they were able to inflict similar losses on the enemy. Horse archers relied on speed to make themselves less of a target and that reduced the effective range of their bows if they wanted to hit an enemy formation, let alone an individual. Archers and slingers on foot had a longer effective range than bowmen on horseback. Sling bullets had the added advantage that they were difficult to see in flight and could cause concussion if they struck a helmet, making even armour no certain protection.[21]

There was frustration at the slow pace and passive defence, prompting an officer named Flavius Gallus to ask permission to form a special force of skirmishers and cavalry. Antony was persuaded by the promise that he would hurt the enemy more seriously. On the next day Gallus achieved a local success at the rear of the column, but then followed up until he was too far away from the nearest legionaries to gain any support. As his men and horses grew tired, the Parthians closed around him, but Gallus remained confident or simply stubborn and refused the order to withdraw. Reinforcements were sent up in dribs and drabs by Canidius Crassus, not enough to make any real difference and so just adding to the scale of the potential disaster. Eventually, a counter-attack by the *Third* Legion and the arrival of Antony himself leading troops from the advance guard, drove the enemy back and allowed the detachment to return to the safety of the army. Gallus had four arrows in his body and would die in the coming days.

Arrows were more likely to wound than to kill outright, and the action had substantially added to the number of wounded men in the army. Plutarch says 5,000 wounded were rescued and 3,000 men killed. Antony visited the injured, tearfully taking their hands, as soldiers asked him not to worry and assured him that things would work out as long as he was in charge. Dramatic displays of emotion were quite acceptable in Roman society and he had been with the army long enough to win their affection and trust. When he made a formal speech to the troops on the next day, the response was enthusiastic, with some of the troops who had been beaten 'begging him' to decimate them. Dio claims that many men were ready to desert and only held back because they had seen the Parthians shoot down anyone who tried to surrender. Phraates' men did not have enough food to take too many prisoners, so there may have been a practical reason for this as well as the desire to spread terror.[22]

The Parthians were even more encouraged by their success and their army had grown as Phraates sent the royal troops to join the next attacks. Plutarch says there were 40,000 men in the enemy camp, but it seems unlikely that the Romans had an accurate count either at the time or later. With their mobility, and the need of the Romans to stay in formation, the Parthians could always be sure of a local superiority in numbers whenever they attacked. They were surprised to see the column once again marching in good order. Even so they quickly began to launch probing attacks, which grew larger and more frequent as the day progressed. At one point, the horse archers drew so close to some legionaries that the latter formed the famous testudo – front rank kneeling behind their shields and those in the rear holding their overlapping shields over their heads. The movement in the ranks as they took up the formation was seen as a sign of disorder and imminent flight. The enthusiastic horse archers charged home, for fleeing infantry were at the mercy of men on horseback. They were surprised when the legionaries proved steady and eager to fight at close quarters. More than usual were caught and killed when the horse archers turned to flee.[23]

For a while the enemy was deterred, but the food situation was becoming desperate. Many pack and draught animals had died or were now being used to transport the substantial numbers of wounded. This was good for morale, but the health of the remaining soldiers was also suffering. Small quantities of wheat changed hands at an exorbitant rate. The soldier's ration was normally issued unprepared, but there were now very few handmills left to grind the grain into flour. Men scrabbled desperately to find edible herbs and vegetables, and some fell ill and died as a result of these experiments. Men continued to perish even though the Parthian attacks had slackened a little.[24]

King Phraates again showed himself willing to negotiate and tried to persuade the Romans to turn onto an easier, lowland route, promising that they would be merely observed by the locals and not attacked. Antony received a message from Monaeses claiming that this was a trap. Apart from gratitude for Antony's past generosity, the former exile may not have been keen on the king winning such an overwhelming victory and so cementing his hold on power. The Mardian guide echoed these suspicions, and Velleius tells a story of one of Crassus' legionaries who was still in captivity, but somehow managed to slip across to the Roman outposts and warn them of the treachery. Antony ordered the army to move out under cover of darkness, in the hope of gaining some breathing space from the pursuit, and stuck to the more difficult route. The soldiers were ordered to carry water, so that there would be no need to halt and distribute this. The principle was sound, but by this time many had no vessel suitable for carrying.[25]

The Romans marched a thirsty 30 miles, but were caught by the Parthians before the day was too far advanced. Some were so desperate that in spite of warnings they drank from a polluted stream and were prostrated by stomach cramps as Antony rode amongst them, begging them to keep going until the next river. That night, discipline broke down altogether. What was left of the baggage train – and some officers seem to have still possessed substantial personal equipment and luxuries – was plundered and men murdered for their money. Dellius, the probable source for the surviving accounts, was with the army and said that at this time Antony even warned one of his bodyguards that he might need help to commit suicide.[26]

Order was eventually restored at daylight. They moved on and again fought off a series of Parthian attacks. It was the last day of fighting, as the pursuit was then abandoned. In a few days' time

Antony's men reached the River Artaxes, the border with Armenia, twenty-seven days after they had left Phraata. Plutarch says that when Antony paraded his army he found that he had lost 20,000 infantry and 4,000 cavalry, which does not seem to include the legions wiped out with the heavy baggage train. Armenia was an ally, but for the moment the lacklustre performance of its king was overlooked.

The army's ordeal was not yet over. It was now late autumn and there was not enough food available to permit the soldiers to spend the winter until they had marched a considerable distance into Armenia. They had to keep moving, marching through the mountainous country in the teeth of snowstorms. Plutarch says another 8,000 men died of exhaustion, disease and exposure. As ever with numbers in our ancient sources, some caution is required. Velleius says that a quarter of his legionaries perished in the expedition and a third of the camp followers, along with virtually all the baggage. A loss of between one-quarter and one-third of Antony's entire army seems plausible, and fewer than half of these had fallen to enemy action. The bulk of the survivors can only have been exhausted and many probably in poor health. On top of the human casualties were the animals, lost with the heavy train or on the long march home. Horses, mules and oxen will tend to break down before men, or may simply be eaten when food supplies run out. Finally, there were the lost wagons and specialised equipment from the siege train. For the moment, Antony's army was crippled, incapable of launching another major operation and needing time to recover.[27]

Damage to his prestige would be even harder to repair. The Parthian War was supposed to bring him glory and wealth. Unlike Crassus, Antony had survived and brought away more than half of his army. Yet the Romans expected victory, not simply survival or feats of endurance. There was plenty of scope for criticising Antony's generalship. The initial plan seems to have been unclear about the objectives and how to achieve them. At best, it was probably too ambitious given the time scale, while the decision to let the siege train and heavy baggage follow on behind was predictably disastrous. Mistakes could be forgiven and excused if the outcome of the war was successful. Good Roman generals paraded their luck, since in the end it was winning that counted.

Antony had not won and clearly failed in all of his objectives. No territory had been taken and not only had no eagles or captives been recovered, but the Parthians had also gained fresh trophies of victory. He stayed with his army until the troops were safely back in billets in Syria. His personal courage had been exemplary throughout the campaign and he had shared the danger and the hardship with his men. Antony was still popular, but then so was Lord Raglan in the British Army he led so badly in the Crimea. A general needs to be far more than just physically brave to do his job well. Antony had failed in the one field of endeavour most central to the identity of a Roman aristocrat.[28]

His men safe, Antony hurried to the coast of Syria and sent for Cleopatra.

[XXV]

QUEEN OF KINGS

Antony chose an obscure location for his rendezvous with Cleopatra. Leuce Come – literally, 'the white port' – lay between Berytus (modern-day Beirut) and the old Phoenician city of Sidon. Both of the latter were substantial cities, but instead of going to them he waited in what was little more than a village. Perhaps he was afraid that the Parthians would take advantage of his retreat to counter-attack into Syria and so felt the major cities were more attractive targets to the enemy. Yet it was probably December 36 BC or January 35 BC by the time he reached the coast and at such a season a major raid was unlikely. Apart from that, the walls of somewhere like Tyre were far more likely to offer safety than a small place like Leuce Come.

More probably he chose such a minor port because this was not to be a great occasion of ceremony and pomp, but a private reunion – or at least as private as was possible when a Roman triumvir met such an important client monarch. He instructed her to bring money and supplies for his troops, so that there was an element of business, but if that had been the main issue there was no need for him to summon the queen in person. That need was personal.

Antony was mentally and physically exhausted. In less than a year he had travelled well over 2,000 miles, prosecuted a siege and fought a succession of skirmishes and other engagements. During the retreat, he had driven himself hard to keep his army going and had at least once seriously contemplated suicide. As commander, he had made the key decisions and was responsible for their disastrous consequences. He had failed, and this failure would overshadow the rest of his life.

Cleopatra offered a chance to forget this for a while. Antony could rely on her to be lively, entertaining and uncritical company. She would listen when he wanted to talk and her comments would be plausibly encouraging. They could feast and celebrate, continuing to live 'inimitable' lives, as well as making love. The queen was a mistress who needed to keep his backing. It is also hard to believe that there was not at least a degree of genuine love on both sides. Most important of all, Cleopatra was not Roman. With her, Antony could pretend to be a Hellenistic ruler, or Hercules or Dionysus if he preferred. He did not have to be the Roman noble who had fallen short of the military prowess so important to his class.

Antony waited impatiently for his lover to arrive. Plutarch talks of him wandering restlessly and getting up in the middle of meals to go and look out to sea in the hope of spotting her ships. He began to drink even more heavily as the days stretched into weeks and Cleopatra had not arrived. There is no hint that she deliberately delayed. It was only a matter of months since she had given birth to their third child together, a boy given the name Ptolemy Philadelphus. The name was a reminder of the second king of her line, who had presided over the empire at its greatest extent. Perhaps Cleopatra had not yet recovered from the birth and did not feel immediately able to travel. As importantly, the summons was unexpectedly urgent and preparations needed to be made. Antony wanted money and clothes for his ragged army. Obtaining ten thousand or more tunics or pairs of boots inevitably took time, as did obtaining sufficient coin in the right sort of denomination to be issued as pay to the soldiers, and both were bulky to transport.

When Cleopatra eventually arrived, she brought considerable quantities of clothing, but less money than Antony had requested. It may not have been available in the time and, in any case, he still had substantial reserves of his own. The troops were paid – quite probably a generous bounty in addition to their normal salary, for the legions had become accustomed to such things in the last decade or so. Antony was accused of telling his men that the money was a generous gift from Cleopatra, even though it was not. His spirits certainly recovered now that the queen was with him. Soon, they both went back to Alexandria.[1]

AND THEN THERE WERE TWO

Much had changed since Antony had set out for Armenia. In 36 BC Octavian launched a major offensive against Sextus Pompey. Lepidus had helped, bringing his own forces from Africa to invade Sicily. Sextus showed some of his old skill, and his men their usual courage, but this time they were outclassed. Agrippa had spent a year creating a larger and very well-trained navy, which included the 120 warships loaned to his colleague by Antony. He won the first battle of the year. Sextus soon struck back, defeating Octavian. However, he could not prevent both Octavian and Lepidus from landing armies in Sicily. Much of the island was soon overrun. There were some 300 ships on each side at the decisive battle fought off Cape Naulochus. Octavian watched from the shore as Agrippa virtually destroyed the Pompeian fleet, making use of a newly invented device called the *harpax*, which made it easier to grapple the enemy vessels. Once held, they could be boarded and captured. Agrippa had bigger vessels carrying larger numbers of legionaries acting as marines and so was always likely to win such encounters.[2]

Sextus' power was broken and he fled. Lepidus chose this moment to try and regain the power and prominence he had once enjoyed. Perhaps he hoped to dispose of Octavian altogether, or at least renegotiate their alliance. Lepidus assumed control of the combined armies in Sicily. The details are a little unclear and much clouded by propaganda, but there is no doubt that it was all quickly over. The young Caesar went into Lepidus' camp in person. The legionaries now defected to him, just as they had flocked to join Antony's men in 43 BC. Lepidus was stripped of his powers as triumvir, but allowed to live out the remainder of his life in comfortable retirement. It was a display of clemency reminiscent of Julius Caesar and unlike the savagery of the proscriptions. Lepidus remained *Pontifex Maximus*, although he cannot have actually performed the role in practice. Only when he died, more than twenty years later, did Octavian – by now having assumed the name Augustus – assume the priesthood. From then on, it remained the prerogative of the emperors until the collapse of the Western Empire in the fifth century AD, when it passed to the pope, who still holds the title.[3]

Octavian celebrated an ovation for the defeat of Sextus, just as Crassus had once performed this lesser ceremony to mark his victory over Spartacus. At one point, Octavian himself had freed large numbers of slaves to provide manpower for the fleet, but his propaganda painted Sextus as the leader of runaway slaves rebelling against the natural order. Thousands of prisoners were crucified in another reminder of Spartacus. It was claimed that they were former slaves whose previous owners could not be found. Perhaps this was true, although more important was the propaganda message denying that this was another civil war. Instead, it was a matter of restoring order, of dealing with a pirate and not the son of Pompey the Great.[4]

It was still a success, which contrasted strongly with Antony's defeat in Media. The latter's despatches to the Senate concealed the scale of the losses and painted some of the skirmishes as great victories. For the moment, at least in public, Octavian and his associates did not question the truth of Antony's version. Rumour would have flourished anyway, for no doubt many of his officers wrote their own versions of events. At the very least, it was soon clear that the expedition had made few, if any, tangible gains.[5]

Octavia travelled to Athens in the spring of 35 BC, intent on joining her husband. She brought with her 2,000 praetorians and also a substantial quantity of money, supplies and draught animals. Appian also mentions a unit of cavalry. Around the same time, Octavian sent back to Antony the ships he had borrowed at Tarentum. Only seventy remained, reflecting the heavy losses in the struggle with Sextus. The promised legionaries – whether two legions or 20,000 men – were not included. Plutarch thought that Octavian sent his sister with less than the pledged aid as a deliberate provocation and modern commentators have been inclined to agree. If Antony welcomed his wife, then he could be seen to accept without question whatever assistance his triumviral colleague chose to grant. More probably he would be insulted and might rebuff the well-respected Octavia. Scorning a Roman wife in favour of a mistress who was not only foreign, but royal, was bound to damage Antony's reputation.[6]

Yet it was natural enough for Octavia to go again to Athens, bringing aid to her husband, and everything she brought – including the praetorians – was presented as a personal gift from her, not from her brother. It would have been a strange thing to stop her. On the other hand, in the past she had never gone further east than Athens. Antony sent word telling her to remain in the city, since he planned to campaign once again. A Roman wife was not supposed to follow her husband to war itself. He accepted the gifts she brought, although he was understandably – and no doubt publicly – annoyed by the failure of her brother to fulfil his promises. Octavian's lack of support was a convenient thing for Antony to blame as an excuse for his own mistakes. More soldiers are very unlikely to have made any major difference to the outcome of the expedition in 36 BC.

Nor would they have been of much immediate use in the following summer. The remnants of his army had not had enough time to recover from the hardships of the retreat. In particular, the cavalry mounts must have been in poor shape and the mounted arm was of vital importance in any operation against the Parthians. Even more serious were the losses in baggage animals and wagons, and those brought by Octavia are unlikely to have made up for these. Without transport a major offensive was simply impossible. Fortunately, the enemy had fallen to bickering over the spoils of their recent victory. Artavasdes of Media sent messengers to Antony offering alliance against the Parthian king.[7]

There seemed to be an opportunity for limited operations, suitable for his currently limited resources, when Antony was suddenly forced to deal with a wholly unexpected threat. Sextus Pompey had fled eastwards and landed in the province of Asia. At first he offered alliance with Antony against Octavian. Then, hearing of the disaster in Media, he seems to have decided either that the eastern triumvir was vulnerable or perhaps that it was better to negotiate from a position of strength. Sextus began enrolling legions of his own. After a brief campaign he was suppressed by the nearest governors and executed. It is unclear whether or not Antony himself gave this order. Octavian would later contrast his own generosity to Lepidus with his colleague's summary killing of Sextus. Yet it is difficult to imagine that he would not have killed Pompey's son if Sextus had fallen into his hands, and it would certainly have been hard to reconcile with the concerted effort to portray him as a pirate. Nor was there any real incentive for Antony to spare him. At the time Octavian publicly celebrated the execution in Rome.[8]

Faced with these distractions, and with the bulk of his army still exhausted, Antony achieved very little before the autumn made campaigning impractical. He may still have been very tired himself. Cleopatra was with him for much of the year, either in Alexandria or afterwards probably in Antioch. Plutarch says that she feared Octavia and was reluctant to let her lover spend the winter with his wife. Antony responded to affection and, although she was Octavian's sister, Octavia was a similar age to the queen, was clever and widely considered beautiful. Her love for her husband may well also have been genuine and her sense of duty was clearly very strong. Therefore, Cleopatra was supposed to have worked on Antony, showing utter delight when he was with her and 'letting' him catch glimpses of her quickly hidden tears when he was not. She deliberately lost weight, while her courtiers, and quite possibly some of his Roman friends whom she had taken care to cultivate, spoke to him of her utter devotion.[9]

Cleopatra relied on Antony to hold on to power. Love may well have grown, whether or not it was there from the start. Together they had had three children, and there were very few men indeed whom Cleopatra could see as her equal and so a worthy companion as well as a lover. Genuine passion probably fuelled the political dependency. Antony had left her for years in 40 BC, returning to Italy and a new wife. At some point he was bound to return to Rome and the heart of the Republic, which had given him power. If he joined Octavia, then this could well happen sooner rather than later and remove his direct support from the queen. The Roman wife was a dangerous rival.

She was also a reminder to her husband of his recent failure. If Antony joined her, then he renewed the close connection with her brother, but more than that would once again become fully the Roman senator. His administrative reorganisation of the east had generally been successful, renewing and sometimes improving on the work of Pompey. Yet unlike Pompey he could not boast of genuine victories. Nor was there any prospect of fighting another campaign on the same scale – and with as good a chance of success – for several years. His career had gone badly wrong and that was not a pleasant thought. This truth would have been much harder to ignore in the company of Octavia, and so would the knowledge that her brother was bound to capitalise on his weakness.

It was not a very attractive prospect, in contrast to staying with Cleopatra, who was a much more pleasant and encouraging companion. With her he could live pleasantly and try to forget about the future. Perhaps it was also easier to believe that he could do something to repair the damage of his defeat. Antony sent word to Octavia telling her to return to Rome. Like a good Roman wife she obeyed and returned to their house – the property once owned by Pompey the Great. She continued to use her influence on behalf of Antony's friends. Rumour said that her brother suggested that she divorce her husband, but that she staunchly refused.[10]

It was probably a minor concern to Octavian, since he was very busy. From 35 to 33 BC he led three consecutive campaigns in the Balkans, fighting against several Illyrian tribes. Caesar had himself planned to campaign in the area, so perhaps there was an echo of the great commander in his choice. There were also defeats to avenge and lost standards to recapture, for Antony's old commander Gabinius had lost an army there back in 47 BC. The region was also near the border with the territory governed by Antony, and so a useful place to demonstrate the strength of his forces against any potential rival, including his colleague. Yet the main reason was the same as the one that had led Antony to attack the Parthians. Octavian wanted to prove himself a proper servant of the Republic and win the glory of defeating foreign enemies. In his case, even his victories over other Romans were tainted by rumours of cowardice and weakness.

In the campaigns that followed he took good care now to appear as heroic as possible, managing to get injured during an assault on a town. (It was probably not through direct enemy action, but the enemy was certainly close.) Like Antony he ordered at least one cohort to be decimated. There are other stories of his exemplary punishments that may date to these operations – for instance, having centurions stand at attention outside his tent. Sometimes a man's belt was undone, so that the long military tunic fell almost to his ankles and so looked unmartial and perhaps even feminine. They might also be made to hold up a piece of turf or a measuring pole. Barely thirty by the time the campaigns were over, Octavian wanted to establish a reputation as a stern commander in the traditional mould, a man who personified the *virtus* expected of a Roman aristocrat. Awarded a triumph, he chose to postpone it and busy himself with working on the Republic's behalf.[11]

The spoils of victory were pumped into rebuilding Rome. Octavian began a series of major projects and others were undertaken by other successful generals, many of them close associates. There was a spate of temple building, and the Regia and several basilicas were restored. Rome also for the first time acquired a permanent stone amphitheatre, while Asinius Pollio gave it a public library – something Caesar had planned, but not had time to create. In later life Augustus would boast that he 'found Rome brick, and left it marble'. (He did not mean the incredibly strong, oven-fired red bricks visible today in so many of Rome's great monuments, for this was an innovation of the imperial period. Under the Republic cheap and simple mud bricks were one of the commonest building materials.)

The transformation of the city really began in these years. As important as the monuments themselves was the work and incomes provided for the inhabitants of Rome. Little construction work was ever done by slaves and these projects were important job creation schemes. A good deal of the improvements were highly practical. Agrippa became aedile in 33 BC, an extraordinarily junior post for a man who had been consul in 37 BC, but since he was technically still too young to hold either office this was a minor breach of tradition. He took on the task of improving the city's water supply and drainage system, and was remembered for sailing through the sewers in a boat to inspect them properly. Inspection was followed by a long programme of work. Agrippa repaired existing aquaducts and added a new one, the Aqua Julia, and made '700 cisterns, 500 fountainheads ... 130 water towers'. Rome was not only to be beautiful, but also functional and a better place in which to live. The spoils of victory were to benefit the Roman people.[12]

THE DONATIONS

In 34 BC Antony finally achieved a little revenge for the disaster in Media. He was still not in a position to seriously harm Phraates IV, and instead turned his attention to King Artavasdes of Armenia, the ally accused of letting the Romans down. In a limited operation Armenia was overrun and Artavasdes was taken prisoner, probably seized under cover of negotiations. Dellius had been the delegate chosen to negotiate with the king. The Romans found such methods acceptable if they helped to resolve a conflict, so in itself this was not too damaging an accusation. Yet in the end this was a minor operation, achieving victory over a recent ally with very little fighting. There was little glory in such a success, certainly nowhere near enough to balance the earlier failure. The operation was also not complete, since the Armenian nobility proclaimed the king's son as king, who was able to escape to Parthia.

Antony strengthened Rome's position in the border kingdoms by securing Armenia for the time being. Around this time the alliance with Artavasdes of Media was also strengthened, when Antony and Cleopatra's son Alexander Helios was betrothed to the king's daughter. Both were still young children, so the marriage could not meaningfully take place for at least a decade, but it was a pledge for the future. In many ways a more surprising wedding actually occurred a few years later when Antony married his eldest daughter Antonia to Pythodorus of Tralles, a wealthy and influential aristocrat from Asia Minor. Presumably he already had – or was given – Roman citizenship, but it remained an extremely unorthodox alliance for a senator's daughter. It is generally assumed that this Antonia was the offspring of his second marriage to his own cousin, also named Antonia, although perhaps it is possible that she was the child of his first wife, the freedman's daughter Fadia. Even more than his formal recognition of his children with Cleopatra, this went a stage further than previous emulation of Hellenistic royalty by Roman commanders. Antony is said to have boasted that founding dynasties from his own bloodline set him alongside his ancestor

Hercules and that the best thing about Rome's dominance was what they gave to the provincial peoples.[13]

The capture of Artavasdes was the biggest success Antony himself had enjoyed since Philippi seven years earlier. That in itself suggests his lack of personal focus on military adventures. Time and again he had felt called away to deal with crises in the west, as the triumvirate threatened to break apart. His visits to Italy and the need in the previous year to deal with Sextus Pompey were all important concerns, and yet it does contrast very strongly with the ruthlessly single-minded approach to campaigning of Pompey and Caesar, and indeed many less famous Roman commanders. These interruptions had certainly hindered preparations for the attack on Parthia and probably contributed to its rushed start and muddled conduct.

The Armenian victory was a small one, but it was all that he had had for such a long time and Antony decided to celebrate on a grand scale. What followed soon became deeply controversial and the reality of what happened smothered in hostile propaganda, so that the whole truth is probably impossible to establish. Antony had decided to spend another winter in Alexandria and entered into the city in a grand procession. Once again he appeared as Dionysus – Bacchus or Liber Pater, the 'Free Father' to the Romans. The triumvir rode in a Bacchic carriage and wore a wreath of ivy, a robe of saffron and gold, as well as the buckskins associated with the god, and carried his sacred wand, known as the *thrystus*. None of this was new, and it was a more tactful way of displaying power to a Hellenistic audience, appearing as a personification of the great god of celebration and victory and not as a blatantly Roman overlord.[14]

Artavasdes walked in the procession, along with many other prisoners. The king was in chains, but in deference to his rank these were symbolic and made of precious metal – silver or gold, depending on the source. The column followed a route into the city, past cheering crowds, and eventually was received by Cleopatra, sitting on a golden throne on a lavishly decorated platform within the traditions of Ptolemaic spectacle. This was probably in front of the Serapeion, the great temple to Serapis, the god created by the Ptolemies. Artavasdes and the Armenian nobles were said to have refused to salute or bow to the queen, in spite of every effort to persuade or intimidate them.[15]

Octavian's allies soon painted the parade as a triumph in all but name and thus a mockery of one of the Romans' most ancient and revered rituals. A triumph could only be held at Rome and end with a sacrifice to Capitoline Jupiter. The victory was for Rome and the Roman people, granted by Rome's gods. It could not be transferred to a foreign city and marked with foreign rituals, worst of all centred around a foreign monarch.

Antony is very unlikely to have intended the ceremony to be a triumph. Some of the Roman rituals had their origin in Dionysiac processions, which added to the similarities and made it easier to criticise. It was surely intended for a Hellenistic audience, although it also reflected his own love of theatre. He could enjoy his success, before spending another pleasant winter in Alexandria. His continuing power would no doubt have secured him a real triumph had he returned to Rome, but everyone would have known that this was a sham. On top of that he had no intention of returning to Italy yet, before he had achieved a genuinely major victory, or at the very least further built up his wealth and the influence this gave him. A Hellenistic display, much like the formal entry of any great king into a city, advertised his power throughout the region and his sympathy for the local culture.

There seems to have been a similar motive behind the even more bizarre ceremony held a few days later. It occurred in the great gymnasium of Alexandria, that most Hellenistic institution of the largest Greek city in the world. Later it became known as the Donations of Alexandria, but it is unclear how Antony and Cleopatra would have described the event. It is not certain how he was dressed, but his lover appeared as the New Isis, so was probably clad in the black robes of the goddess. The Roman triumvir and Ptolemaic queen sat side by side on golden thrones. In front of them, and a little lower down, the thirteen-year-old Caesarion, the six-year-old twins Alexander and Cleopatra Selene and the two-year-old Ptolemy Philadelphus occupied smaller thrones.

Antony formally pronounced Cleopatra and Caesarion rulers of Egypt, Cyprus and part of Syria. Alexander Helios was named king

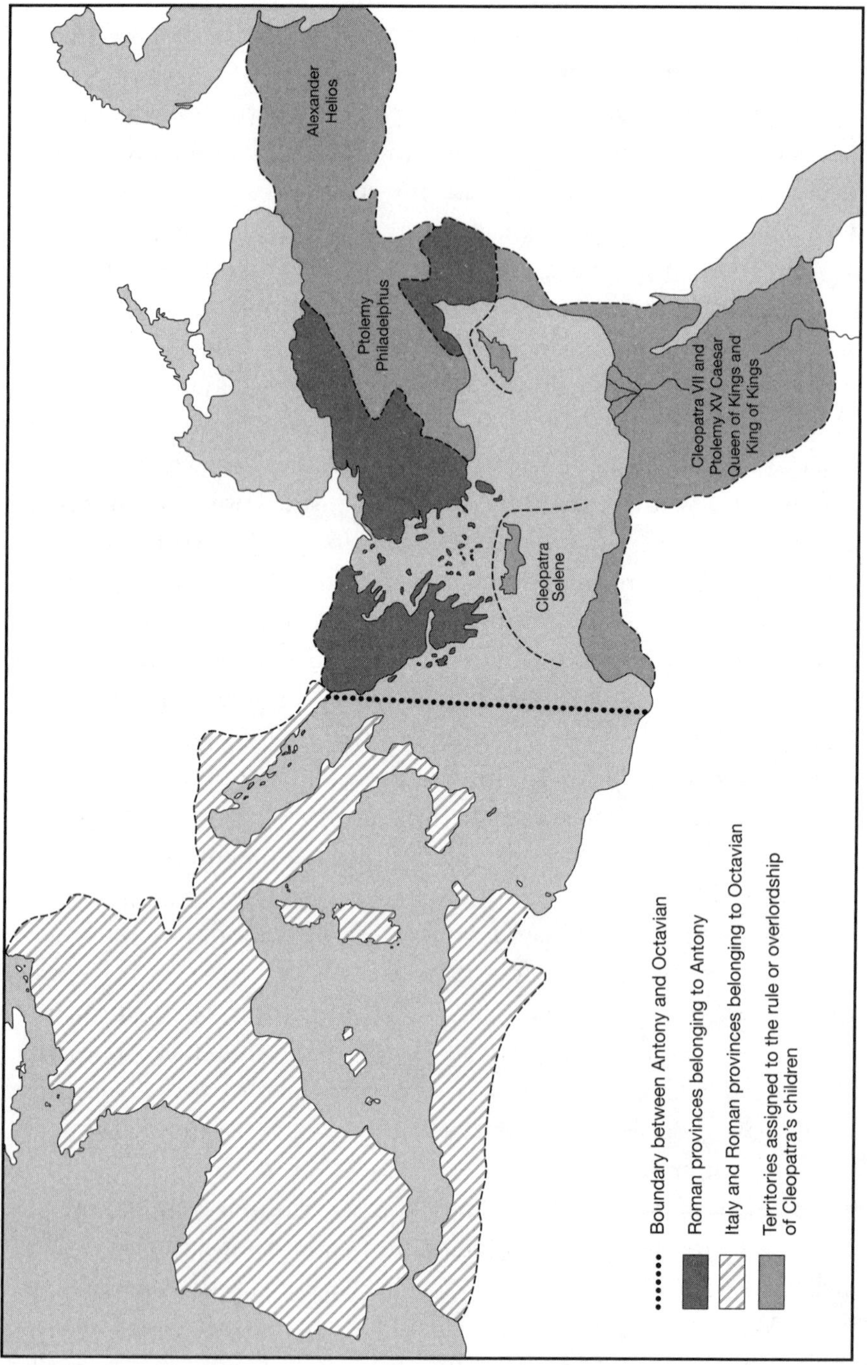

Alexander
Helios

Ptolemy
Philadelphus

Cleopatra VII and
Ptolemy XV Caesar
Queen of Kings and
King of Kings

Cleopatra
Selene

•••••• Boundary between Antony and Octavian

Roman provinces belonging to Antony

Italy and Roman provinces belonging to Octavian

Territories assigned to the rule or overlordship
of Cleopatra's children

The Donations of Alexandria

of Armenia, Media and Parthia, while his twin sister was given rule of Cyrenaica and Libya. Ptolemy was granted the rest of Syria, Phoenicia and Cilicia. The infant was dressed up in Macedonian military cloak and boots and wore a traditional hat topped by a royal diadem. Alexander Helios wore a version of Median royal costume, with a much more eastern royal tiara. Their mother was also named 'Queen of Kings, whose sons are kings' and variations of these slogans soon began to appear on coins and official documents.

Cleopatra's superiority over her children was confirmed, for even her co-ruler Caesarion was seated below her and received no new titles. Dio claims that Antony formally proclaimed the boy as the son of Caesar. If this was so, then he made no attempt to have him made a citizen or legitimised in Roman law. The Ptolemaic tradition allowed the existing monarch to mark out any of his or her children as co-ruler and rightful successor, regardless of age or details of parentage. Therefore Caesarion did not need to have a declared father to hold power. However, the fame of Caesar as father could do no harm and, if it was rarely mentioned within Egypt, it is possible that it was more important in their other territories.[16]

Yet in practical terms the most striking thing about the Donations is how little difference they made to anything. Media remained an allied kingdom under its own monarch and the Parthians were not about to give up their independence to accept the rule of a small boy with no claim whatsoever to rule there. Roman provinces and allied communities given to the children continued to run their affairs as they had done before the ceremony. Alexander and Ptolemy were supposedly given bodyguards of Armenians and Macedonians respectively, at least for the day of the ceremony itself. They were not given guardians or regents, nor any machinery of government created around them.

The Donations were marvellous theatre, popular with the Alexandrian crowd who liked a good show and no doubt highly enjoyable for Antony and Cleopatra themselves. They were well within the traditions of Ptolemaic celebrations and demonstrated the queen's dominance through the support of her Roman lover. What is much less clear is how Antony hoped to benefit from them. Perhaps he felt that the promise of future rule suggested long-term stability for the settlement he was creating in the eastern Mediterranean. Promise was the most it could be, since nothing was actually changed by the ceremony and, in any event, the inclusion of Parthia gave everything an air of fantasy. It was if Antony was pretending to be a real conqueror, so far taken in by his own propaganda to believe (or to want to believe) himself truly a Dionysus, Hercules or Alexander the Great.

For Octavian it provided splendid ammunition to blacken his colleague's name. Antony appeared deluded and was acting like a monarch, freely giving provincial and allied territory won by the legions to his children at the behest of a foreign queen. Antony's allies in the Senate are supposed to have suppressed his own report on the campaign and the ceremonies, since it was so discreditable to him. For little or no gain, he damaged himself badly in Rome and Italy in general. Even at the time, many people struggled to understand just what Antony planned for the future. He and Octavian were still triumvirs, although the second five-year term for the triumvirate was due to expire at the end of 33 BC. The big question was when and how did Antony plan to return home?

[XXVI]

'IS SHE MY WIFE?'

On 1 January 34 BC Antony had become consul for the second time. It was nine years since the end of his first consulship, so this was almost the decade that law decreed should pass before holding a magistracy again. That rule had anyway been breached so many times that it was scarcely worth comment. It was far rarer for a consul not to be in Rome when he assumed office, although Marius and Caesar had both done this. More disturbing was his resignation at the end of a single day, showing the minor importance of the Republic's supreme magistracy to a man with Antony's power. Consuls now rarely served for the entire year, but none had chosen to resign within twenty-four hours. In spite of his absence and the extreme brevity of his tenure, the year was still officially known as the consulship of Marcus Antonius and Lucius Scribonius Libo.[1]

In 39 BC Antony and Octavian had drawn up a list of consuls for the next eight years, including the suffect consuls who would replace them once they resigned. There were four such men in 34 BC, for the first pair also resigned before the year was complete. In this way more loyal followers were rewarded, receiving the dignity of consular status, the precedence this brought in senatorial debate and the prospect of a suitably important provincial command. Octavian would similarly take up and resign the consulship on 1 January 33 BC, and there were no fewer than six suffect consuls in the remainder of that year.

This figure was in turn dwarfed by the sixty-seven praetors the triumvirs had appointed in 38 BC. Their lack of respect for the traditional magistracies was blatant and yet it is equally clear that both the triumvirs and their followers still valued the prestige these posts brought. There were also numerous irregularities, ignoring age restrictions and other conventions. One praetor resigned his office in favour of his son. One quaestor was recognised as a runaway slave by his former master. Another escaped slave was discovered serving as praetor. Slaves were usually executed by crucifixion, but this terrible punishment was thought inappropriate for anyone who had served as a praetor, however illegally. Therefore the court decreed that the man should be given his freedom, and then be thrown to his death from the Tarpeian Rock. Antony and Octavian had awarded themselves a joint consulship for 31 BC. Interestingly, it was over a year after their triumviral power was supposed to lapse. Perhaps they planned that both of them would be in Rome by this time, so that their alliance could be renewed or renegotiated.[2]

Antony had certainly not turned his back on Rome, for all that he enjoyed the trappings of monarchy in the Greek world. He seems to have been genuinely fond of Alexandria and at some point he served as *gymnasiarch* there, just as he had done in Athens. Yet although he publicly acknowledged his children by Cleopatra, greater prominence was given to Marcus Antonius Antyllus, his teenage son by Fulvia. A series of silver coins was issued showing Antony on one side and the boy on the other.[3]

Although Octavia looked after his other Roman children, Antyllus seems to have been in the east with his father during these years. In Alexandria he enjoyed both the company of learned men and something of the lavish lifestyle of the royal court. Plutarch's grandfather's friend Philotas knew the boy during these years and told stories of his quick wit and generous nature. On one occasion Antyllus gave him the gold cups that they had just used for a feast – an interesting echo of Cleopatra's visit to Tarsus. Philotas was worried that the lad might get into trouble for making such a costly gift. Yet when the servants came to present him with the vessels and get a receipt for them, they assured him that Mark Antony's son could give away as much gold as he liked. They did replace the vessels with their value in money, since some were antiques and so might be missed by his father.[4]

Elsewhere, Plutarch tells another story of Antony's own generosity, when he promised a man the gift of 250,000 denarii. One of his personal slaves was apparently concerned that his master did not realise how substantial a sum this was and so laid out all the coins to show their number. When informed what the money was for, Antony claimed to be shocked, since he had thought the gift was bigger, and immediately ordered the sum to be doubled.[5]

Antony's taste for spectacular expenditure long pre-dated his years in the east, but was fully indulged while he was with Cleopatra. Grand wagers were a common feature of the royal court during these years. The most famous incident occurred some time between 34 and 32 BC, and centred on the famed luxury of the Ptolemaic court and Antony's own obsession with expensively rare and exotic foods. The queen is supposed to have sneered at the fare he was serving and promised that on the next day she would show him a banquet costing no less than 2.5 million denarii. Yet when the meal came he was unimpressed by the food she gave her guests, for this seemed nothing unusual by their recent standards. Cleopatra – our source Pliny does not name her, but dismisses her as an 'impertinent royal tart' – merely laughed when Antony claimed that he had won the wager. The food was a mere preliminary and she alone would consume the 2.5 million denarii feast. Enjoying his confusion, the queen ordered the final course to be served. This dessert was as lavish as the earlier courses, but she herself was given a single bowl, filled with *acetum*, the sour, vinegar-like wine issued to soldiers as part of their ration and usually a drink for the poor. Reaching up, Cleopatra took off one of her pearl earrings – the pair were famous for their size and quality – and dropped it into the bowl. The pearl dissolved into a slush and she drank the mixture. Lucius Munatius Plancus, who had the task of deciding who won the bet, quickly declared the queen the victor and stopped her from repeating the process with the other pearl.[6]

Pearls had become highly fashionable as jewellery at Rome in the last generation or so. In 59 BC Julius Caesar had given his mistress Servilia a pearl that cost 1.5 million denarii, and so was of similar quality to Cleopatra's earrings. It was even rumoured that he had invaded Britain hoping to find a plentiful supply of good pearls. Nor was dissolving pearls in sour wine and drinking the mixture altogether unknown, for we hear of one wealthy young Roman doing the same, in a story spread by one of Horace's poems. It is impossible to know whether Cleopatra was aware of this incident or came up with the idea on her own. In latter years the Emperor Caligula, a descendant of Antony, would copy the practice, a mark both of his eccentricity and extravagance.[7]

Most modern commentators have been sceptical about the possibility of dissolving a pearl in vinegar and attempts to repeat Cleopatra's trick have invariably failed. The acid in the liquid does soften pearls and dissolve crushed pearls, but appears to take a very long time to do this. The value of such experiments is anyway limited, since we do not know the size or consistency of the pearl earrings. These may well have been smaller than modern expectation. Nor should we necessarily insist that Cleopatra's bowl was filled only with sour wine. Other substances might accelerate the chemical reaction and the philosophers of the Museum had for generations specialised in using their knowledge to perform spectacular, apparently miraculous tricks to grace royal occasions. The pearl did not need to vanish altogether, but dissolve enough to be no longer of value and easy to both consume and keep down. Pliny does not suggest that she simply swallowed the earring to retrieve it later. The precious object had to be permanently destroyed to make the wager meaningful.[8]

Munatius Plancus is elsewhere described as one of the leading flatterers of the queen from amongst Antony's Roman followers. He clearly felt that this would also win the triumvir's favour. It is said that he went so far as to perform a dance during one of the feasts, acting the part of the sea god Glaucus, his naked skin painted blue and wearing a false fish's tail. This was scarcely the behaviour expected of a former consul. A few aristocratic Roman men were known to be proud of their skill in dancing, but Cicero had probably reflected the general feeling when he said, 'No sane man ever dances while sober.'[9]

Sobriety is unlikely to have been a conspicuous feature of Antony and Cleopatra's intimates. Antony had always been a heavy drinker and it seems likely that this had only increased, especially after the disappointment and stress of the Parthian expedition. He may well have been an alcoholic and choosing to associate himself with Hercules and Dionysus meant revering deities famed for drink and festivities. The latter was important to the Ptolemies, and Cleopatra wore a ring carrying the inscription 'Drunkenness' (*Methe* in Greek). The female attendants of Dionysus, the Maenads, were supposed to be in a permanent state of ecstatic frenzy, induced not by alcohol, but the mere presence of the god. Probably the ring celebrated this. We cannot say whether the sources accusing her of frequent inebriation were true or simply propaganda. It may well have been difficult to spend a lot of time in Antony's company without sharing at least to some degree in his heavy drinking.[10]

The circle surrounding Antony and Cleopatra included performers from the Greek east. We hear of one man who seems to have specialised in erotic dances, and there was also the 'Parasite' mentioned earlier. Yet apart from the queen herself, only Romans were treated as close advisers by Antony, and certainly only Romans were given important commands as well as other major responsibilities. Plancus, Dellius and Canidius were just a few of the senators amongst the triumvir's close companions and key agents.[11]

In 2000 a papyrus that contained an ordinance passed by Cleopatra in 33 BC (or 'Year Nineteen which is also Year Four') was identified, prompting considerable excitement because the last word may be in the queen's own handwriting – *ginestho* ('let it be so' in Greek). The main content received little attention outside scholarly circles, but is highly instructive:

> We have granted to Publius Canidius and his heirs the annual exportation of 10,000 artabas of wheat [approximately 300 tons] and the annual importation of 5,000 Coan amphoras of wine without anyone exacting anything in taxes from him or any other expense whatsoever. We have also granted tax exemption on all the land he owns in Egypt. ... Let it be written to those to whom it may concern, so that knowing it they can act accordingly.[12]

Canidius had clearly been given extensive estates by the queen and the income he gained was to be free of any royal levy. His agents were also allowed to import and sell wine within Egypt without paying any duty. Antony's other senior followers no doubt also did well from her generosity. Cleopatra needed Roman backing and for the last few years that had meant keeping Antony's favour. To ensure this she exploited her kingdom for the benefit of the triumvir and his henchmen. Earlier Ptolemies had been just as generous in granting land and tax-free wealth to powerful aristocrats. Now the important beneficiaries were all Roman and there is no indication that any of these men planned to settle permanently within her realm. Their families, much of their property and their ultimate political ambitions all lay in Italy. There is no good indication that Antony felt any differently. He was in the east to build wealth and power to enhance his position within the Republic.

'WHY HAVE YOU CHANGED?'

The stories of the excess and debauchery of Antony and Cleopatra's inner circle no doubt grew with the telling as they travelled to Italy. The mood in Rome was usually uneasy while waiting for powerful men to return after a long spell in the provinces. People had been very nervous awaiting Pompey's return from his eastern campaigns and similar fears over what Caesar might do had helped to create the civil war in 49 BC. Octavian managed to visit Rome on several occasions during his Illyrian wars and had been in Italy for most of the last decade. He bore the brunt of any discontent and resentment, for instance from dispossessed Italian farmers and dissatisfied veterans, but had managed to deal with each crisis in turn. The defeat of Sextus Pompey had ended the long sequence of civil war and there was cautious optimism that this might be permanent. There was certainly no appetite amongst the wider population for a renewal of conflict. Poets like Horace and Virgil helped to express this mood, encouraged by Octavian's close associate Maecenas.[13]

Antony gained no fresh honours from the Senate after 37 BC, but his colleague was far more visible. A year later Octavian had been awarded the same sacrosanct status given to the tribunes of the plebs. This was a high honour. In 35 BC the same status was extended to Livia and Octavia, who were also given public statues and the right to run their own affairs and finances without the need for a male guardian. These were unprecedented honours for women. This made Antony's curt instructions for his wife to return to Italy all the more shocking and rendered her obedience and continued care for his house, children and friends especially poignant.[14]

Octavian and Antony competed for prestige and dominance. It was natural for Roman aristocrats to behave in this way and perhaps inevitable that, once all other rivals had gone, the two most powerful men in the state would turn against each other. By 33 BC the rivalry was becoming steadily more open, although as yet neither side launched a direct attack on the other. Instead, it was a question of contrasts. Octavian had beaten Sextus Pompey. His successes in Illyria were small scale, but genuine, unlike Antony's failure in Media. Antony countered, mainly through his supporters in Rome, but also it seems through letters that were readily made public, and spoke of Octavian's personal failings. At Philippi he had been 'ill' and absent. In the final confrontation with Sextus Pompey, the young Caesar had again been prostrate with sickness – or was it fear?

Roman political invective had always been personally abusive and often obscene. As usual there was very little attention to specific policies and the heart of the matter was character. Both men had provided their rival with plenty of good material. Yet in the main the hostile stories about Octavian concerned the past – his cruelty during the proscriptions, or his dressing as Apollo at the notorious feast. A favourite target for the unquestionably aristocratic Antony was his rival's family and time and again the alleged obscurity and demeaning professions of his father and grandfather were hurled at Octavian. It was only at this point that Caesarion began to matter in Rome. Here was a genuine son of Caesar, and it did not matter that he was a foreigner and a bastard, for there was no attempt to make the teenager a figurehead in Roman politics. It was merely a useful – and highly embarrassing – way of reminding everyone that the 'son of the divine Julius' was of humble birth and only one of the Julii Caesares by adoption. Adoption was taken seriously by the Romans, but Octavian's position was vulnerable because he had not been adopted while Caesar was alive and posthumous adoption was legally very questionable. It was probably now that Octavian commissioned one of Caesar's close associates to write a pamphlet denying that the boy was Caesar's child, while Antony proclaimed that the dictator had publicly acknowledged the baby.[15]

Although Antony lost in the long run, many stories about Octavian were set down in these years and so survived to be repeated by later authors, giving him a small posthumous victory. Years before, Cicero's *Philippics* had begun the blackening of Antony's reputation and memory, and now these slurs were reinforced. Many of the attacks were exaggerated, but there were too many truths behind them to prevent serious damage. Attacked as a drunkard, Antony responded by publishing his only known work of literature, entitled *On His Drinking* (*de sua ebrietate*). It has not survived, but presumably he denied some of the excesses, or at least maintained that alcohol had never impaired his judgement or actions. Yet the fact that he felt it necessary to defend himself against the charge at all showed that the damage had already been done. (Caesar had been laughed at for taking a public oath denying his alleged affair with King Nicomedes. People mocked the dictator whether or not they believed the story.)[16]

Sexual excess accompanied the stories of Antony's alcoholic excess. Too much of either was seen as weakness, betraying the stern *virtus* expected of a Roman senator. Praise of Octavia for her virtue, and also her beauty, highlighted her husband's mistreatment of her. Yet the affair with Cleopatra was far too public to deny and so instead, Antony tried to pass it off lightly, writing an open letter to Octavian. The style was blunt, deliberately crude and overtly manly:

> Why have you changed? Is it because I'm screwing the queen? Is she my wife? Have I just started this or has it been going on for nine years? How about you – is it only [Livia] Drusilla you screw? Congratulations, if when you read this letter you have not been inside Tertulla or Terentilla, Rufilla or Salvia Titiseniam, or all of them. Does it really matter where or in whom you dip your wick?[17]

'Is she my wife?' – the Latin *uxor mea est* could equally be the statement, 'She *is* my wife.' Only the context as part of a series of quick-fire questions suggests that it is not only a question, but that the implicit answer is also: 'No, she is not.' Yet Antony did not deny the affair, and indeed stressed that it had already lasted for nine years.

His position was weak from the start, for the best he could hope for was the belief that Octavian's behaviour was no better than his own. Octavian might be an enthusiastic adulterer, but he had no single mistress and at least his lovers were Roman. Antony circulated other stories, of how the young Caesar's friends hunted out women for him, even stripping respectable girls and married women for inspection as if they were slaves. It was even claimed that at one dinner he had taken a senator's wife into another room and when they rejoined her husband and the rest of the company, she was blushing and looking dishevelled.[18]

This was certainly not respectable behaviour for a Roman, although the cuckolding of other senators did match the exploits of Caesar. In addition, Octavian was still an adolescent, while Antony was in his fifties, by which time a man was expected to behave with more decorum. Taking many lovers was bad, but it was worse for a Roman man to have one mistress, worse still to appear to be dominated by her and unforgivable that she was foreign and royal. This was the most damning charge, that Antony had become so unmanned by his passion for Cleopatra that he obeyed her and made decisions on major issues according to her whims. The grants of land, the allegations of delaying the Parthian War to stay with her and, most of all, the Donations of Alexandria suggested an Antony manipulated by his lover to the point where he was no longer acting in the best interests of the Republic. Even his own propaganda could be turned against him. Hercules, too, had been brought low by a woman, when Omphale made him wear a dress and perform household tasks such as spinning. It is unlikely to be coincidental that depictions of this story appear in the art of the period.[19]

Octavian was in Rome, in a city enjoying peace and the visible signs of rebuilding and physical renewal, much of it undertaken by him or his close associates. He was far better placed to influence public opinion. Senators were one audience, but so were the local aristocracies of the towns and cities of Italy. It was difficult for a distant Antony to compete, especially since his achievements in the east were so limited. He does seem to have administered the region reasonably well, but such things were rarely a great source of popularity with a Roman audience. In the long run he could not hide the scale of the disaster in Media – especially when Octavian and his allies no longer helped to suppress the news – or the meagreness of his subsequent successes.

In the spring of 33 BC, Antony had concentrated the bulk of his legions on the Euphrates, ready for a fresh intervention in the affairs of Parthia and its neighbouring kingdoms. After some minor operations, he changed his mind. Once again, his eye was on Italy and the struggle with Parthia would take second place to defending his position in Rome itself. Canidius was ordered to march the army over 1,000 miles to the Ionian coast of Asia Minor, ready to cross the sea to Greece. There was no external threat to that region requiring such a large concentration of troops. Unless he was planning to return at last to Italy, bringing with him his soldiers, perhaps to march in a triumph, or at least to be discharged and given land, then this move can only be seen as a threat to Octavian. Antony did complain that Octavian was not providing sufficient land for his veterans and it may be that he had future distributions in mind. His colleague sent the ironic reply that surely he could give them land from his eastern 'conquests'.[20]

At the very least, Antony escalated the conflict by transferring his legions westwards. The timing of this move is all too readily forgotten since it is easier to trace the build-up of Octavian's propaganda towards the eventual war. Neither man seems to have been very reluctant to fight, but the wider population hated the thought of a renewal of civil war, so both were eager to let the other provoke the conflict. The triumvirate lapsed on 31 December 33 BC. Antony ignored this and continued to use the title. Octavian pretended to retire into private life. Both kept control of their armies and provinces.[21]

On 1 January 32 BC, Domitius Ahenobarbus became consul with Caius Sosius as colleague. Both men were supporters of Antony, a coincidence that may not have been significant when the triumvirs had nominated consuls back in 39 BC. The consuls took precedence in alternate months and Ahenobarbus began the year, presiding over meetings of the Senate. Antony had sent them an account of his reorganisation of the eastern provinces, which included the grants of land to Cleopatra and her children. He wanted the Senate's endorsement, even though his powers as triumvir already conferred legality on his actions. Ahenobarbus thought the document too inflammatory, with its formal statement of the Donations, and so suppressed it.

In February, Sosius took over and immediately launched a direct attack on Octavian. The measures he proposed were vetoed by a tribune before a vote could be taken. It was an interesting survival of earlier politics, although it is unclear who inspired the veto. Sosius may have felt that simply making the statements was enough to damage Octavian. On the other hand, the latter may have been genuinely worried. Even if the measures were not passed, and it was unlikely that they would be, it was a considerable blow to his prestige and *auctoritas* to have them mentioned in the first place.[22]

The 'retired' triumvir was not present, but he summoned the Senate to another meeting, although legally he no longer had the power to do this. Octavian arrived, escorted by soldiers and guarded by friends whose 'concealed' daggers were visible. He took his seat between the two consuls, thus marking his superiority, and proceeded to defend himself. Ahenobarbus and Sosius fled from Rome after this meeting, going straight to Antony, who by this time was again in Athens. By letter, and the voices of a few adherents, he was able to continue the battle of accusations with Octavian. Apart from the personal denigration, he returned to familiar complaints. Octavian was blamed for both deposing Lepidus and then taking all of the latter's troops and territory under his own control. His failure to deliver the promised soldiers was another charge. Octavian countered by saying that Antony had not shared the spoils of his own victories, but the main attack remained personal. The Roman commander had been corrupted by Cleopatra – there were even stories that she used magic potions to enslave him.[23]

Munatius Plancus chose this moment to defect from Antony and join Octavian. He was an ex-consul, and with him came his nephew who was a consul designate, but there are no other recorded defections by senators at this time. Plancus gave a speech in the Senate accusing Antony of a long list of crimes and abuses of power. Not everyone was impressed and an old rival drily commented, 'Antony must have done a great many things to make *you* leave him!' Far more damaging was the report that the two men had witnessed Antony's will, now deposited in the Temple of Vesta at the heart of the Forum, and that its provisions were shocking.[24]

The six Vestal Virgins composed Rome's only female priesthood and were figures of great respect. The head of the order refused Octavian's demand to be given the will, since this would have been an unprecedented breach of law and custom. However, he went into the temple and read the document, before removing it and having it – or more probably, carefully chosen sections – read out at a public meeting. In it Antony formally recognised Caesarion as the dictator's son and also gave legacies to his own children by Cleopatra. This last was illegal, since a citizen could not make a non-citizen his heir. There must have been mention of Antyllus and his other Roman children, but it suited Octavian's purpose to ignore such normal clauses. Finally, even if Antony were to be in Rome when he died, his remains were to be sent to be interred alongside Cleopatra.

None of our ancient sources suggests that the will was a forgery, although plenty of modern scholars have assumed this. There was certainly a will, and the odds are that Octavian was simply selective in his use of it. Antony had already publicly acknowledged his children by Cleopatra and proclaimed Caesarion as Caesar's son, so in that sense there was nothing new in repeating these statements. His legacies to the children raise many questions, since he could not have been unaware that these were illegal. Perhaps he planned to give them citizenship or simply assumed that as triumvir anything he did was legal. Yet it is notable that Antony could imagine dying in Rome, away from Cleopatra.[25]

That was not the impression people received. Octavian encouraged rumours that Antony and Cleopatra planned to rule the Republic as a personal empire, moving the capital to Alexandria – an echo of one of the accusations made against Caesar. The arrogance of the queen was stressed. She was said to have adopted a favoured oath, saying, 'as surely as I shall dispense justice on the Capitol'. It did not matter that this contradicted the stories of Antony preferring Alexandria to Rome, wanting to rule from the Egyptian city and be buried there. The important thing was to convince Romans of

Cleopatra's pride and the danger she posed. Old prejudices against Greeks, easterners in general, royalty and powerful women interfering in the affairs of state all made the audience highly receptive to this message. To emphasise his own patriotism, Octavian began construction of a grand mausoleum on the Campus Martius.[26]

There was no enthusiasm for another civil war and so Octavian marginalised Antony. He was merely a dupe, a weak man who had ceased to be a Roman and could no longer refuse his mistress anything. Stories of him washing her feet to honour a bet, of reading love letters while conducting public business and of trailing after her litter like a puppy all reinforced the image, even if they were untrue. Cleopatra was the danger, hence the vitriol of poets directed against her, savaging her character and bemoaning that a Roman commander and Roman legionaries 'served' such a mistress.[27]

Instead of a new civil war, Octavian gave Italy a great cause. Rome's Republic faced the dire threat of a foreign ruler who wished to crush their freedom. It was a better pretext for war and people willingly chose to believe it as far as was necessary, since it was unrealistic to stop Antony and Octavian from fighting each other. Yet they would not fight against Antony but Cleopatra, not against Roman legions but an eastern host who worshipped strange, animal-headed gods. Communities throughout Italy took an oath of personal loyalty to Octavian. A few of Antony's veteran colonies were exempted, but none showed any desire to fight on his behalf. Some senators fled to join him. Octavian later claimed that more than 700 chose to serve with him. The Senate was at most 1,000 strong at this time, and quite possibly smaller. Many of the remainder went to Antony, although it was most likely fewer than the 300 often alleged as having done. Some may have been too elderly to take an active role, while others chose neutrality. The most famous of these was Asinius Pollio, who said that he would 'stand apart from your quarrel and be a spoil of the victor'.[28]

Antony's active supporters in the Senate were heavily outnumbered. Some were desperate, including the last survivors from Caesar's murderers, who obviously could not hope for reconciliation with Octavian. One of these men, Cassius of Parma, produced a string of vitriolic pamphlets attacking the young Caesar. He was accused of planning to marry his only daughter Julia to the king of the Getae from the Balkans to cement his Illyrian victories – clearly a reaction to disapproval of Antonia's marriage to Pythodorus of Tralles. Even wilder was the allegation that Octavian had planned to divorce Livia and marry the king's daughter instead.[29]

What Antony had actually done was, or at least seemed, a lot more damaging than anything it could be claimed his rival had merely considered. By 32 BC, it was clear that Antony had lost the political struggle. The propaganda war would continue, but it had not gone well for him so far and things were unlikely to improve. His only hope was now to win the real war of armies and fleets.

[XXVII]

WAR

Antony and Cleopatra spent most of the winter of 33–32 BC at Ephesus, as his troops mustered on the coast of Asia Minor. It was the first time she had not wintered in Alexandria for many years. In the spring the slow process began of ferrying the army across to Greece. It could not be rushed, so Antony and Cleopatra made a leisurely journey, stopping at the island of Samos, where they celebrated a festival of theatre, music and dance dedicated to Dionysus. Performers came from all over the Greek world to compete for prizes, while the triumvir and the queen feasted in their usual extravagant style. As a reward, Antony gave the guild of performers a grant of property and special rights in the city of Priene in Asia Minor.[1]

His generosity was less obvious to the wider population of the eastern Mediterranean, as once again they were called upon to support the war effort of one side in a Roman civil war. Heavy contributions of money, supplies and other resources were required from every provincial and allied community. Antony's subordinates were not gentle in the enforcement of these demands. On the island of Cos, groves of trees sacred to Aesculapius, the god of healing, were chopped down to be used for shipbuilding on the command of Decimus Turullius, one of Caesar's assassins. Manpower was also demanded. Antony needed craftsmen to make ships and all the other equipment needed for the army and the fleet. On top of that he needed rowers and sailors to crew the vessels, and soldiers to serve in the army. Denied access to the recruiting grounds of Italy, many of his legionaries were provincials, hastily granted citizenship when they were enrolled in the legions. Most seem to have been conscripts.[2]

Cleopatra contributed a vast sum of money to fund the war. Plutarch says it amounted to 20,000 talents, twice the sum her father had promised to Gabinius in 55 BC. Like the rest of the east, her kingdom was squeezed to support Antony's war effort. In addition she contributed 200 vessels to the fleet of 500 warships and some 300 merchantmen that her lover was assembling. Some of the warships were large, built in the grand tradition of the Ptolemaic navy, and it is probable that many of the merchant vessels were large grain ships. It was the biggest fleet her kingdom had formed for several generations – the ships used against Caesar in the Alexandrian War were smaller, more suitable for the confined fighting within the harbours and less numerous. Cleopatra does seem to have provided crews as well as the ships themselves, but how many of these men came from Egypt – or her wider realm – is unclear. She paid them, but many seem to have been recruited by press gangs from anywhere they could be found.[3]

Willingly contributing ships and money to back her lover, Cleopatra was already benefiting from Antony's gratitude as he seized statues and other artworks from temples and presented them to her. One of Octavian's allies accused him of presenting her with 200,000 scrolls from the Library at Pergamum. The story may be an invention, or at least the number exaggerated, although her family's long-standing appetite for acquiring new volumes for Alexandria's Library was well known.[4]

After Samos, the couple went to Athens and were there at the latest by the early summer. If Cleopatra really did accompany her father into exile, then she had been to the city before, more than twenty years earlier, but this was certainly her first visit as an adult. Antony's longest visit in recent years had been the months spent there with Octavia, when the Athenians had taken care to honour both the triumvir and his wife. Now, they were equally eager to secure his favour by honouring his mistress. Her statue dressed in the robes of Isis – or perhaps a statue of the goddess deliberately made to resemble the queen's features – was set up by the city. Cleopatra responded by staging and paying for some of the round of musical and dramatic performances that were ordered here as on Samos. A formal delegation of the leaders of the city, including

Antony himself who had been made an honorary citizen, came to the house she occupied, where he made a speech listing the special privileges the council had granted her.

Ahenobarbus and Sosius had probably joined Antony before he left Asia Minor. Other news from Rome continued to reach him. In Athens he finally decided to divorce Octavia, a clear indication that he felt the breach with her brother was serious and perhaps irreconcilable. Graffiti appeared on one of Antony's statues – 'Octavia and Athena to Antony: take your things and go!', referring to his earlier sacred marriage to the goddess of the city. The first phrase was in Greek, the second the traditional Latin formula of divorce – *res tuas tibi habe* – which rather suggests that the wag was one of his Roman followers.[5]

We do not know whether now or at some earlier stage Antony and Cleopatra contracted a formal marriage. This would not have been legal under Roman law, unless he had granted her citizenship. None of the main narrative sources claims that the couple did marry, although Plutarch could be taken to imply this. The poet Virgil, writing not too many years after their death, does make outraged mention of Antony's 'Egyptian wife', but otherwise the claim is only made in much later, and generally unreliable, sources. It is difficult to believe that Octavian would not have flung the charge against him if any form of wedding had taken place. We cannot be sure, which makes the ambiguity of Antony's own words – *uxor mea est*, 'Is she my wife?' or 'She is my wife'– all the more frustrating. The debate is often complicated by modern attitudes to marriage and partnerships. The truth is that we simply do not know what either Antony or Cleopatra thought about such things, and what they did or did not do.[6]

What we do know is that Cleopatra accompanied Antony, and from the beginning it seems to have been accepted that she would stay with him even if, or when, war broke out. Other client monarchs were also with him and if they did not contribute as much money or as many ships to the war effort, several brought strong contingents of troops. Polemo had been left to watch the frontier with Parthia, for Antony had stationed very few of his own troops to guard against any renewal of war in that theatre. Herod was sent to deal with the king of the Nabataean Arabs, whose loyalty was in question and who had stopped paying the rent for the lands leased from Cleopatra. She also sent one of her own Greek officers, presumably with a force of mercenaries, to co-operate with the Judaean king, but the campaign achieved little. It was claimed that she simply wanted Herod out of the way and less able to win Antony's favour.[7]

The other rulers to serve with Antony were all male and most would lead their soldiers in person. Cleopatra was Antony's lover and spent far more time close beside him, both when he conducted official business and when he relaxed and celebrated. She received public honours far greater than any awarded to the other kings and clearly possessed greater influence over him. Domitius Ahenobarbus was the only Roman in Antony's entourage who refused to address her as 'Queen', still less as 'Queen of Kings', and instead called her by name. He was not the only one who was unhappy with her very public presence, which did so much to aid Octavian's propaganda campaign focusing on her control of Antony. In 32 BC there were still a number of senators in Italy who remained sympathetic. Antony was generous with money to reinforce their loyalty and win more adherents, but his close association with the queen was politically disastrous.[8]

Plutarch tells us that a senator called Geminius – perhaps Caius Geminius – travelled from Italy to see Antony, probably during the months Antony spent at Athens. Cleopatra is supposed to have distrusted him, suspecting that he hoped to reconcile Antony to Octavia. She arranged for him to be seated at feasts away from her lover and that the senator should be made the butt of some of the jokes and pranks common at the court. Geminius remained patient and finally was asked to present his case during one banquet. Claiming that it would be better to wait until everyone was fully sober, he nevertheless said that the most important message was that Antony must send the queen away. The triumvir flew into a rage and Cleopatra was delighted, supposedly saying that it was good that Geminius had admitted the truth without the need for torture – something to which a senator should never be subject. Geminius left and the queen remained at her lover's side. Whether or not the story is true, it reflects the growing disquiet of many of Antony's men. Monarchs were acceptable only if they were clearly subordinate.[9]

Some of his Roman followers spoke up in favour of the queen's continued presence. Canidius argued that Cleopatra was one of the most able and experienced monarchs in all the eastern Mediterranean. She had contributed so much to the campaign, and it would be dangerous for the morale of the naval contingent she had supplied if their queen was sent away. Plutarch claims that he was bribed and the papyrus recording the tax exemptions granted to him do testify to Cleopatra's generosity. Perhaps he was also inclined to adopt a different stance to Ahenobarbus and others out of sheer competitiveness. Yet it is quite possible that he genuinely believed the queen's presence to be a good thing, whether in its own right or because of the influence she had on Antony.

Most modern scholars have been inclined to agree with Canidius' claim that Cleopatra needed to remain to foster the morale of the sailors in her warships. Given that many of these seem to have been reluctant conscripts, this is highly unlikely. Even less probable is the idea that she inspired the many recruits from the Hellenistic provinces included amongst the legions and fleet, and that these men were somehow fighting against the Romans. An oracle foretelling the conquest of Rome by the east is the only evidence cited in support of this claim, but there is no good reason to date the document to this period. That many provincials hated the Romans is unsurprising. Roman imperialism was brutal, the decisions of the Roman authorities often arbitrary and many of their governors savage in their exploitation of conquered and allied peoples. Antony was more tactful in his respect for Greek sensibilities, but was no less exploitative, especially as he prepared for the confrontation with Octavian. He did not offer an alternative to Roman rule, merely a slightly softer version. The conflict was a Roman civil war. Only Octavian tried to portray it as a struggle between east and west.[10]

Antony wanted Cleopatra beside him. Her money and her ships were of great use, but his need for her companionship was greater still. Antony enjoyed luxury, something his lover was good at providing in inventive ways, and needed affection and flattery, at which she excelled. She made him feel better and either this blinded him to just how politically damaging her presence was or persuaded him that this price was worth paying. Philippi was now ten years ago and since then his only major operation had ended in disaster. It is hard to avoid the conclusion that Antony had lost much of his confidence and assurance on the retreat from Media. Perhaps he no longer believed that he could function without Cleopatra staying close to him.

She may well have sensed this and felt that it was not safe to let him go to war on his own. Cleopatra had become ruler of an expanded realm through Antony's generosity. If he lost the war, then she too might lose all that she had gained. To this end she committed the resources of her kingdom to support him. It was understandable if she also wanted to be close at hand, to help secure victory in any other way that she could, if only through advising Antony. Cleopatra had very little military experience, but it is not clear that she realised this and may have felt that at least she could help her lover to be decisive and resolute in prosecuting the war. Perhaps she did help in the planning, for moving and feeding such a large army and fleet was a major project.

There was another reason for her presence. Tension had been high between Octavian and Antony on several occasions in the past and yet they had pulled back from the brink of war and come to a settlement. This might well happen again, and if it did, then Cleopatra needed to make sure that her own interests were secure. She did not wish to become an acceptable loss, permitting Antony to return peacefully to Rome and the heart of the Republic. Whether or not such a fear was realistic, it was entirely understandable.[11]

Politics mingled with passion. Both Antony and Cleopatra were ambitious, and neither had survived the dangerous worlds of the Ptolemaic court and Rome's fractured Republic without a strong streak of ruthless self-interest. For a combination of reasons he wanted her beside him and she also felt that this was important. The decision played into Octavian's hand, as he whipped up fervour against the foreign queen and her Roman puppet who threatened Italy itself. By the late summer he was ready. Reviving – or quite possibly inventing – an archaic ritual, he acted as a fetial priest and presided over a sacrifice in the Temple of Bellona, the war god.

Taking a spear dipped in the blood of a sacrificial animal, Octavian hurled it into a patch of earth symbolically representing Egypt. War had been declared by the Roman Republic against Cleopatra. Nothing was said of Antony, although everyone knew that the real fight was actually against him, and that the former allies were fighting for supremacy.[12]

[XXVIII]

ACTIUM

Neither side was ready to fight and, apart from that, it was late in the campaigning season. Antony was subsequently criticised for not invading Italy immediately, for Octavian had not gathered all of his forces and was facing opposition as he introduced extraordinary taxes to raise money for the war. Although Octavian had plenty of soldiers, and a fleet experienced and confident after the defeat of Sextus Pompey, he was very short of funds. He was not yet ready for war, but nor could he afford to let the conflict last too long. As usual, both sides were promising generous bonuses to their legionaries. Antony minted a series of coins showing a war galley on the face, with the eagle and two *signa* standards on the reverse and listing the name of one of the units in his army.[1]

The combination of warship and army standards emphasised that this war would be fought on both land and sea. Antony had added three more legions to the sixteen brought by Canidius, but even our sources suggest that these formations were below strength. In addition, he had allied foot soldiers, some of them armed with bows, slings and other missiles, and a strong force of cavalry. Plutarch claims that he had altogether 100,000 infantry and 12,000 cavalry. Octavian had a similar force of cavalry and some 80,000 infantry. Some of his legions remained to garrison the provinces and Antony had also left a smaller proportion of his own troops behind, including a force of four legions to defend Cyrenaica. Plutarch credited Octavian with only 250 warships, but other sources suggest that the figure was larger and he may have had nearer 400.

The figures given for the totals of warships may well be accurate, but as usual the figures for the armies look suspiciously like rounded up totals based on a number of legions assumed to be at full theoretical strength. The totals are probably too large. Nevertheless, the armies were clearly very big by Roman standards, even if most of the legions were substantially under strength. It is quite possible that as many soldiers were involved in this campaign as had fought in the rival armies at Philippi. Both in 31 BC and at Philippi the opposing commanders relied more on numbers than subtlety. From the beginning they faced serious logistical challenges, as they operated at the upper limit of force size feasible for the Romans' military and logistic systems.[2]

It did not help that the military and naval forces were unbalanced. The oared warships employed by both sides carried exceptionally large crews in proportion to their size, since their main motive power came from the teams of rowers. A quinquereme ('five') carried 280 rowers and twenty deck crew. (Most warships had three banks of oars. They were named after the team of rowers needed to operate one set of three oars. Therefore a 'five' had a team of five men, two sitting at the highest bench wielding one oar, two more on the middle bench to use the middle oar, and finally one sitting on the lowest bench to row the lowest oar. A 'five' was a standard warship, but bigger vessels, such as 'sixes', 'eights' and 'tens' were also in use.) There was very little space to carry food and water even to feed this crew. If battle was expected the larger warships could take on board 100 or so soldiers for a short period – ideally, just the day of battle itself. They could not carry this many men for any distance, and certainly not with the food, tents and other equipment they would need to operate. There was absolutely no question of their carrying significant numbers of cavalry mounts and pack and baggage animals.[3]

Antony had 300 transport ships. These had to bring regular convoys of grain and other food, much of it travelling from Egypt to Greece, for it was impossible in the long term to supply so many soldiers and sailors from locally available stocks. Some of the ships, especially the larger vessels, would always be needed for this task. That left even fewer to transport soldiers, animals, short-term reserves of food and fodder, and equipment. Antony could not hope to carry his entire army in a single convoy, and probably it would require several. It certainly seems to have taken a while to ferry the legions across the Aegean in the spring and summer of 32 BC. Any invasion of Italy would have to take place in several stages and this would make it more difficult for his warships to protect the convoys. The vagaries of the weather added another uncertainty. Any vessels lost to enemy action or storm would not be available for future convoys, in addition to the actual losses of men and *matériel* killed or captured with them.[4]

It was late in the summer of 32 BC before Antony's forces had concentrated on the western coast of Greece, and he and Cleopatra took up residence at Patrae on the Gulf of Corinth. The weather in the autumn and winter months was less likely to be good and that argued against an immediate attack. In addition, the east coast of Italy has few natural ports and past experience had shown that it was difficult to take Brundisium or Tarentum. Antony decided against an immediate invasion. He was not in a rush, unlike Octavian whose finances were stretched almost to breaking point.

Apart from better weather, the difficulties of transporting and landing an army in Italy would be just as serious when the spring arrived. By the end of the year it was clear that he planned to let Octavian come to him. Antony would wait in Greece, hoping to harry the enemy's convoys as they crossed the Adriatic. We do not have a figure for the merchant vessels available to Octavian, but it is probable that he faced similar problems to Antony and would not be able to carry his army across at once. At least in the beginning, the advantage ought to be with Antony, whose forces should significantly outnumber the enemy. There was also a political element. Invading Italy with Cleopatra at his side would alienate any potential supporters there.

Modern scholars have generally applauded Antony's plan as sensible and the only practical option. Yet it is worth remembering that this was the same strategy adopted unsuccessfully by Pompey in 48 BC and Brutus and Cassius in 42 BC. On both of those occasions, the defenders had enjoyed a greater naval superiority than Antony now possessed and yet this had failed to prevent the attacker from landing sufficient troops to prevail – if narrowly in 48 BC. Sulla had won a civil war from Greece, but only by using it as a base from which to invade Italy. Defensive strategies did not work well in Rome's civil wars, for they immediately handed the initiative over to the enemy. It created an impression of passivity and weakness, which made it unlikely to convince waverers to join. Once again, Antony was losing the political battle.[5]

There were also practical difficulties in implementing such a strategy. The coastline of Greece offers abundant natural harbours and is dotted with islands, many of which were potential landing bases. Geography encouraged Antony to spread his forces out to cover as wide an area as possible. The constant problem of feeding the sailors, soldiers and animals over winter also made it desirable to disperse them. Antony spread his ships and land forces from Methone in the south of the Peloponnese to the island of Corcyra in the north. Further north, he stationed no significant forces on the coast of Epirus. Probably the largest concentration of ships was at Actium, where the Gulf of Ambracia offered an extensive natural harbour. Substantial stores were massed there to supply these squadrons and the position was fortified. High towers, probably containing artillery, guarded the mouth of the bay.[6]

The campaigns in 48 BC and 42 BC had been fought in the north, in Macedonia and Thessaly. Antony abandoned this area and the main route of the Via Egnatia. Perhaps he was inviting Octavian to land there, confident that there would then be sufficient time to concentrate his own forces and confront and destroy the enemy. Yet at the moment Antony's defenders were spread dangerously thinly along a coastline where armies could not move rapidly. For the winter this was not much of a risk, and he and Cleopatra settled down to pass these months pleasantly at Patrae, waiting to see what Octavian would do in the spring. There were some diplomatic exchanges. Octavian asked Antony to withdraw from the coast and permit him to land, promising that they would then fight the decisive battle within five days. Antony replied by challenging his younger opponent to single combat. Neither proposal was serious, but they were intended as proof of confidence.[7]

CONTACT WITH THE ENEMY

On 1 January 31 BC Octavian became consul for the third time, with Marcus Valerius Messalla Corvinus as colleague. Antony had been stripped of the consulship awarded to him back when the triumvirate was secure. Octavian again had formal power as a magistrate of the Republic. Antony continued to call himself triumvir, although he promised to lay down his power once he had achieved victory. At first he said this would be two months after the war was won, but Dio claims that friends persuaded him that there would be much work to do and so he ought to wait for six months. Octavian held legal *imperium* and that was some advantage. A far greater one was the utterly loyal assistance of his old friend, Agrippa, by now a gifted general and one of the finest admirals Rome ever produced.[8]

With winter barely over, Agrippa attacked, striking at Methone. It was Antony's southernmost outpost, somewhat isolated from the rest of his forces. To get there Agrippa had to sail further than the northern route. This was always a risk in war galleys, whose range was limited by the difficulty of carrying much food and water for the crew. If he had been repulsed, or badly delayed by the weather, he could easily have got into serious difficulties. The gamble paid off. Antony's men were not prepared and the harbour town was swiftly overrun. The enemy ships were destroyed or captured and one of their commanders, the exiled King Bogud of Mauretania, was amongst the dead. Octavian and Agrippa now had a base on the Greek coast.[9]

Antony had expected the main attack to come in the north, but instead the enemy had struck in the south. Wrong-footed, he was thrown further off balance when Agrippa launched a succession of raids along the Greek coast, reaching as far as Corcyra. In the confusion, Octavian crossed the Adriatic in the north and began landing the army at Panormus, a little to the north of Corcyra. As far as we can tell, each of his convoys went unmolested by Antony's squadrons and soon the bulk of his troops were safely in Greece. He occupied Corcyra, which had been abandoned by Antony's garrison in the confusion caused by Agrippa's raids. Octavian marched south along the coast, his ships raiding ahead of the army.

Antony reacted slowly, and he and Cleopatra tried to present a façade of calm. Perhaps it was genuine and they were still confident of inevitable victory given the size of their forces and their belief in Antony's own talent. Dio makes him boast of his generalship in a speech to his men: 'you are the kind of soldiers that could win even without a good leader, and ... I am the kind of leader that could prevail even with poor soldiers'. When news arrived that Octavian had occupied a town in Epirus called Torone (meaning 'ladle'), she joked that why should they worry 'if Octavian is sitting on the ladle' – the word was also slang for penis. Antony began to react to the invasion, but his forces were widely dispersed and would take time to concentrate.[10]

Octavian's target was Actium, and although he was unable to surprise the squadrons there, he managed to occupy the hill – today known as Mikalitzi – which dominated the peninsula forming the northern entrance to the Gulf of Ambracia. Antony arrived soon afterwards, having moved up from Patrae and camped on the southern side of the bay. For the moment he had only an advance guard and so declined the enemy's offer of battle. As more of his soldiers arrived, his confidence grew and he established a second smaller camp on the north side of the bay, close to Octavian's position. Antony then deployed his men in battle order, but the enemy refused to commit to battle now that they had lost their advantage in numbers.

Octavian's hilltop position, reinforced by earthworks connecting it to the sea and offering protection to his ships, was too strong to risk a direct assault. It was also considerably better placed than Antony's main camp, which lay in low-lying, waterlogged ground, rife with mosquitoes. Disease became a serious problem, with so many soldiers and sailors concentrated in a small area. Probably the main culprits were malaria, dysentery and other stomach complaints. Men fell sick and many died. Desperate measures were taken to conscript more rowers for the fleet, and perhaps these suffered especially badly. Paid less than legionaries, and probably fed less well, such recent recruits were unlikely to take readily to the discipline of the camp, where in ideal circumstances care was taken to regulate hygiene, especially in the digging of latrines. Disease and desertion whittled away at Antony's strength.

The stand-off extended from spring into summer. Octavian sent some raiding parties into northern Greece, but failed to draw off any significant enemy force to deal with them. Instead, Antony began work on a line of fortifications behind Mikalitzi Hill, hoping to deny Octavian's men access to the River Louros, which provided their only source of fresh water. A series of skirmishes was fought to control this position, mostly by cavalry while the infantry worked. Octavian's men won all the major encounters and it proved impossible for Antony's men to maintain the blockade.[11]

Agrippa continued to range along the coast. Just south of the entrance to the Gulf of Ambracia lay the island of Leucas – the 'White Promontory', named after the high limestone cliffs along one of its shores. Agrippa destroyed the Antonian squadron based there and captured the island. This made it much harder for Antony's reinforcements and supplies to reach Actium by sea. It also provided a better anchorage for Octavian, whose ships might have suffered badly in the preceding months if luck had turned against him and a major storm had blown up.

An even more startling blow came shortly afterwards when Agrippa captured Patrae, then Corinth itself. More of Antony's ships and stores were taken, but as importantly the enemy now dominated the waters around the west coast of Greece. The supply route bringing grain from Egypt was effectively severed, destroying one of the main props for his strategy. Food ran short in Antony's camp at Actium, which in turn worsened the damage done by disease. Orders were sent out to confiscate food from the cities of Greece. Plutarch's great-grandfather recalled how his home city of Chaeronea was forced to provide grain. There were nowhere near enough animals to transport the heavy sacks and so the citizens were compelled to carry them on their backs, urged on by blows from Antony's men.[12]

By late summer the situation for Antony at Actium was only getting worse, and for a while he considered marching away from the coast and taking the war inland. Dellius and a Thracian nobleman were sent to Macedonia and Thrace to recruit new contingents of auxiliaries and also to explore this possibility. It would have meant abandoning the ships in the harbour, unless these could break out. Antony for a while also led a force inland. Encouragement came when Sosius managed to attack an isolated squadron of enemy ships and defeat them, but on the way back he was caught by Agrippa and badly beaten. The blockade remained in place. Antony returned to Actium, but was himself beaten in another cavalry action. Plutarch claims that at one point he narrowly avoided capture by an ambush set by Octavian's men.[13]

Morale plummeted in Antony's camp and a visible sign was the abandonment of the smaller camp. The entire army withdrew to the original, highly unhealthy site. The situation looked desperate and the troops despaired of his ability to do anything to change this. Domitius Ahenobarbus left in a small rowing boat and joined Octavian, but was already ill and died soon afterwards. Antony made the same gesture Caesar had done to Labienus, by sending Ahenobarbus' baggage after him. Dellius – who had in the past twice managed to quit a losing cause before the end came – also left. He claimed that Cleopatra was plotting against him, because he had joked about the poor quality of the wine served at a feast, compared to the 'best Falernian' vintages drunk at the table of Sarmentus. The latter was a freed slave, famed for his good looks and willingness to exploit them, who had risen to the equestrian order and become an intimate of Maecenas, and through him of Octavian.[14]

As well as a number of senators, client monarchs also began to change sides. Octavian was joined by the rulers of Paphlagonia and Galatia, the latter bringing 2,000 cavalrymen with him. Increasingly distrustful and suspicious of his subordinates, Antony ordered the execution of a senator and an Arab king, as well as other unnamed men. By the end of August it was clear that nothing was to be gained by remaining where he was. His army and fleet were dwindling. There were now barely enough crew to man some 230–240 warships and many of the rowers were recent conscripts.[15]

The legions had also suffered, but remained a formidable force, and Canidius argued that it was best to abandon the fleet and move

inland. Antony disagreed and decided to break out by sea, leaving
Canidius to march the army to safety. Ancient sources saw this as
part of his obsession for Cleopatra. Some of the ships were hers and,
most importantly, her treasury was probably too bulky to carry away
over land. Modern scholars tend to strain every nerve to justify
Antony's decision, the most optimistic arguing that he still hoped
to win a decisive battle at sea, while most simply see the breakout
as the best option of continuing the war. A few realistically point
out that he had already lost the campaign. For other Romans, there
could be no doubt that Antony failed as a commander at Actium.
A good Roman general never gave in and rallied as much of his
force as possible, leading them away to renew the conflict at a
later stage. This was the *virtus* expected of a Roman aristocrat.
Abandoning his army, in the hope that a subordinate would lead
them in an escape, was against all the values of his class.

Bad weather delayed the breakout for several days. All of the ships
that could not be crewed were burnt. It was sensible to prevent them
from falling into enemy hands, but was also a clear sign of desperation
and despair. Cleopatra with some sixty or so ships remained in
reserve, carrying her money and courtiers. The remainder were
formed into three squadrons, with the left wing commanded by
Sosius, the centre by Antony supported by Marcus Insteius and
Marcus Octavius – a distant relative of Octavian who had also fought
for Pompey against Julius Caesar – and the right by Gellius Publicola.
Cleopatra's ships, and probably some or all of the others, carried
sails on board. This was unusual, since oars were the only effective
way of controlling a galley in battle and masts were usually left
onshore because of their bulk and encumbrance. It is harder to know
whether the crews knew that the aim was to break out and not to
fight. This was certainly kept secret from the legions to be left
onshore. Some of these men were put on board the ships to act as
marines, but their comrades were to be abandoned.

By this time Octavian had around 400 ships, some of them
captured during the last months. Antony had a number of very large
galleys – 'tens' and 'eights', although the bulk of his fleet were 'fives'
and 'sixes' – giving him a slight advantage, but nowhere near enough
to offset the enemy's superiority in numbers. Even more import-

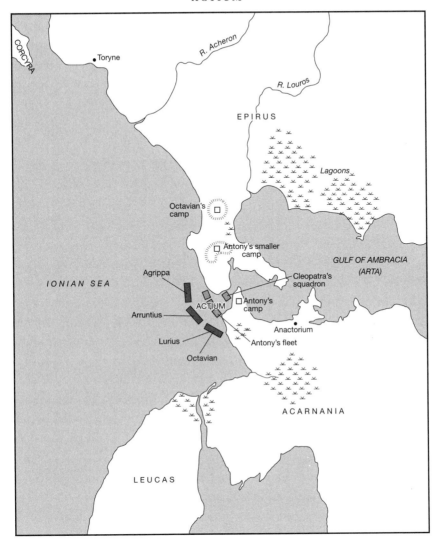

The Battle of Actium

antly, many of Agrippa's crews had years of experience – as vital for teams of rowers to perform effectively as for captains to control their vessels. They deployed in a shallow arc facing the enemy, with Agrippa on the left, Lucius Arruntius in command of the centre and Marcus Lurius on the right. Octavian was also on the right and would share the danger with his men, but wisely left control of the battle to Agrippa.[16]

On 2 September 31 BC Antony's fleet came out of the Gulf of

Ambracia. They formed up, and then the two sides faced each other for several hours. Neither wanted to fight too close inshore. Agrippa wanted the enemy to come further out, so that his more numerous ships would be able to envelop the enemy line. He seems to have dissuaded Octavian from an unlikely plan of letting the enemy through and then hitting them from the rear. Antony faced the problem of getting past the island of Leucas. For this he needed to wait for the afternoon, when usually a wind picked up blowing north-north-west. To outpace the enemy, Antony's ships would need the wind behind them and enough room to clear Leucas. This meant that they needed to be some distance out to sea when the wind changed to the right direction.[17]

Halfway through the day the wind began to veer and Antony at last gave the signal for a general advance. Agrippa still wanted more sea room, so instructed his own ships to back water, rowing away from the enemy. Only once he was satisfied that there was space to threaten the enemy's flanks, did he give the signal to attack. The opposing fleets closed and then the fighting broke down into contests between one or two ships on either side. Ramming was rarely very effective against the bigger galleys used by both sides. More effective were missiles fired from the deck and from the raised towers carried in battle by most warships, and by boarding. Larger ships could be dealt with if attacked by more than one smaller vessels.

Agrippa struggled to envelop the enemy right and Antony's squadron commander Publicola moved away from the centre to prevent this. The Antonian ships eventually formed a rough line at an angle to the rest of their fleet as they tried to fend off Agrippa. In the centre, large gaps had opened as these manoeuvres took place. At this point, Cleopatra's squadron hoisted sail and headed for this space. Once they were far enough out to take advantage of the wind, they began to move too fast to ram or board, for at these speeds ships did not manoeuvre quickly. However, more importantly they were moving too fast for the enemy to have much chance of intercepting them.

Antony saw them go and left his flagship – one of the great 'tens' – and transferred by rowing boat to a smaller 'five', which presumably had not yet been engaged or was otherwise in better shape. This, too, hoisted sail and followed the queen. Some of his other warships were able to go with him. Agrippa's ships were not carrying masts and sails so had little chance of catching them, apart from the need to keep fighting the remaining enemy vessels. Only two ships were intercepted and taken, and perhaps some seventy to eighty galleys managed to escape with Antony and Cleopatra. At least two-thirds of the fleet was left behind. Fighting continued for some time, although the scale and intensity of the combat is hotly debated.[18]

Octavian's propaganda exaggerated the ferocity of the struggle to overcome Antony's larger ships. There certainly was some fighting and the stories of Agrippa's crews using burning projectiles to set fire to the enemy vessels appear in several sources and are probably true. Plutarch says that there were 5,000 casualties, but is not explicit as to whether these were combined losses for both sides, or only those suffered by Antony's fleet. Most scholars, as usual inclined to be bloodthirsty, see this as a low figure, and this convinces them that the fighting was limited. That is possible, although it is equally possible that in a battle fought not far from the shore many crews of sunken ships were saved from drowning – we read, for instance, that Sextus Pompey had an organised rescue service using small boats.[19]

Some of Antony's warships were sunk or burnt. Others eventually surrendered. A significant number backed water and re-entered the Gulf of Ambracia. Agrippa's men may have let them go, feeling it was not worth taking casualties to destroy ships that were still under a blockade, which they were incapable of breaking. Canidius led the army inland, but supplies would soon run short and there was nowhere for them to go. Even if they had reached the coast some-where away from the enemy, there were no ships to evacuate them. These were Antony's legions. They did not fight for a cause, but for a general who had rewarded them generously in the past and promised more in the future. Now, that commander had abandoned them and there was no reason for them to suffer and die on his behalf. In spite of Canidius, army officers began to negotiate with Octavian, who was generous. Several legions were preserved, the soldiers from the remainder were either posted to serve in one of his legions or, if they were due for discharge, were to be given land as part of his veteran settlement. Canidius fled.[20]

Antony had abandoned the bulk of his fleet at Actium. The army he left behind had changed sides within a week. All that remained was a third of his fleet, and the legionaries serving on board as marines. These were only a small minority of his legionaries and the number may have been less if Cleopatra's vessels had not been reinforced in this way. The queen's treasure had been saved, but neither this nor all the revenue she might extract from her kingdom in future would be able to replace the legions and fleet he had lost.

It may well have made sense to get the queen and her money away from the blockade at Actium. Yet there was no need for Antony to follow her if that was the sole aim of the battle. It is unlikely that even his presence could have allowed his outnumbered warships to defeat the enemy. Yet the remainder of the fleet might have withdrawn to the harbour in better order, saving more of the crews and the embarked legionaries. If Antony in person had led the army away from the coast then the soldiers were far more likely to have remained loyal. There was even the remote possibility that he could have fought and won a decisive battle to turn the campaign around, just as Caesar had done at Pharsalus. If not, then he might just have managed to withdraw. At the very least he would have put up a struggle, refusing to admit defeat in a properly Roman way.

Instead, Antony fled, having sacrificed the lives of some of his men to make his escape and leaving the rest to their fate. Worse still, he had run to be with his mistress. Some sources later blamed her for treachery, claiming that the cowardly eastern woman had been willing to abandon even her own lover to escape herself. This was mere propaganda, for it is clear – not least from the fact that the ships were carrying masts and sails – that the manoeuvre was premeditated. What is less clear is whether the intention was for the entire fleet to escape, or whether they were simply to create a path for Cleopatra and her squadron. The former seems more likely. If the latter was consciously planned, then Mark Antony had already effectively conceded defeat in the struggle with Octavian.

Cleopatra, or whoever actually led the squadron, in fact displayed considerable coolness rather than panic in waiting for the right moment and then finding the gap in the battle lines. This required some courage, but it remains true that in every respect Antony and

Cleopatra's plan was self-centred. They saved their own skins – and her treasure – without apparently giving any thought to the men they left behind, the soldiers and sailors enlisted to fight and perhaps die on their behalf.[21]

At Actium, Antony failed to display the courage and military skill – the *virtus* – expected of a Roman senator. With the utter assurance of an aristocrat, Antony had never felt any particular need to obey conventions. He was an Antonius, and nothing would change that or mean that it was not his right to be one of the great leaders of the Republic. In the past he had often displayed courage, even if he was far less experienced and capable as a commander than his own myth-making suggested and posterity has believed. At Actium he abandoned fleet and army to escape. This alone would have been enough to doom him, discrediting him forever in the eyes of his peers. It seemed to confirm all that Octavian's propaganda had been saying about him, a man so enslaved that he was as emasculated in spirit as Cleopatra's eunuchs were physically.

Antony's cause was broken, with no reason left beyond personal obligation for any Roman to rally to his cause. In practical terms he had lost the great army and fleet he had assembled and had no realistic chance of replacing them. The war was over and Antony had lost. It was only a question of time before the end came.

[XXIX]

'A Fine Deed'

Cleopatra's men sighted Antony's quinquereme following them and she ordered them to make a signal of recognition. Probably they slowed and he was able to come on board. His mood was grim and he refused to speak to his lover. The pause in their flight seems to have allowed some enemy ships to catch up. These were of a type known as Liburnians, which were small, but fast. For a while his energy returned and Antony boldly faced about to meet them. One ship was lost, but the pursuit was also broken. Afterwards, he is supposed to have sat alone at the prow of the queen's ship. Plutarch, who tells the story, says that he did not know whether Antony was consumed with shame or rage. On the third day they landed at one of the southernmost points of the Peloponnese. Cleopatra's two closest attendants, probably her maids Charmion and Iras, managed to persuade him to join her. The lovers talked, ate together and slept together for the remainder of the journey. They were joined by some transport ships and also a few more galleys that had managed to escape from Actium, and perhaps this encouraged Antony. He took the money carried aboard one of the transports and gave generous gifts to his remaining followers.

They sailed to the North African coast, landing at Paraetonium (modern-day Mersa Matruh), some 200 miles west of Alexandria, where they separated. Cleopatra went back to her capital city, while Antony looked to rally his only remaining army of any significance. Four legions had been left in Cyrenaica under the command of Lucius Pinarius Scarpus – a great-nephew of Julius Caesar, who had been mentioned as a minor heir in the dictator's will. It was a very modest force to set against the armies of Octavian, who controlled a much larger army than Antony even before he had enlisted the latter's legions left behind in Greece. Pragmatically, Pinarius now changed sides, declaring allegiance to Octavian and executing the handful of his officers who resisted. The vast majority had no great desire to die for a lost cause. When the news reached Antony, his companions had to restrain him from killing himself.[1]

Cleopatra remained far more determined. When her ships sailed into the Great Harbour at Alexandria, their prows were garlanded and musicians played. There was probably always ceremony when one of the Ptolemies entered or left the city, but in this case these were symbols of victory. Confident that news of Actium would not have preceded her, the queen took up residence in her palace. Yet she knew that her position was weak and promptly ordered the execution of many prominent Alexandrian aristocrats before any tried to challenge her. They were killed and their property confiscated. Much of her war chest must already have been spent to fund the campaign, and it was clear that nothing could be achieved without substantial money. Gold and other treasures were levied from the survivors and also taken from her country's many temples. Artavasdes of Armenia, kept prisoner since 34 BC, was also executed, perhaps in an effort to please the king of Media and so secure his support, or possibly to take his remaining treasure. A late and rather questionable source claims that priests from southern Egypt now offered to fight for her. For some this is taken as a sign of her widespread popularity amongst Egyptians. If it in fact occurred, the fear generated by her recent purge would have provided as strong an incentive.[2]

Antony came to Alexandria, but once again sank into depression. A mole extended into the great harbour, from a point near the temple to Poseidon. Antony either converted an existing royal house built on the end of this or had a new structure built onto it. Giving up for the moment on being Dionysus or Hercules, he aped a famous – and semi-mythical – Athenian named Timon, who lived virtually as a hermit, lamenting his sorrows and loathing his fellow citizens. (Shakespeare's *Timon of Athens* was later inspired by the stories told of this man.) For a while Antony indulged himself in self-pity and bitterness, living in relative, although no doubt fairly comfortable, solitude.[3]

There was opportunity for such theatrical displays, because in the aftermath of Actium Octavian had not launched a concerted pursuit. The immediate priority had been to deal with the Antonian fleet and the legions left behind. After the latter defected, Antony ceased to be a serious military threat. It was more important to secure Greece. Very quickly the various communities sent representatives to make their peace with the victor. The inhabitants of Charonea had been about to make another trek, carrying grain to Antony's camp, when news arrived of Actium. They stayed at home and divided the stockpiled grain amongst themselves.[4]

Octavian was generous to most of the communities of Greece and the eastern provinces. Some were again called upon to give money or art treasures to another Roman leader to gain his support. Antony's appointees to the thrones of the eastern kingdoms all switched sides in the months after Actium. Herod was one of the last, and sent the royal regalia to Octavian, before presenting himself in person. It was important to keep the provinces and allied kingdoms stable and, apart from that, the men appointed by Antony had generally done all that the Romans required of them. They had obeyed him because he had represented Roman authority throughout the region. None saw any reason to lose power and perhaps their lives now that his strength was broken. Nor did any see the civil war as a chance to throw off the Roman yoke, any more than they had done in previous Roman conflicts.[5]

In the middle of winter, at a time when sea travel was normally avoided, Octavian hurried back to Italy to deal with a crisis. There was continued discontent over the taxes he had raised for the war and, in response, he now drastically reduced his demands. Maecenas claimed to have discovered and suppressed a plot to seize power led by Lepidus' son, who was promptly executed. More serious was discontent amongst soldiers due for discharge. Now that he had taken on responsibility for Antony's nineteen legions in addition to his own forces, this task was massive in scale, but the veterans were impatient at any delay. Octavian had to appease the mutineers in person, but he needed money to fund the generous land allocations he had just promised. Seizing the wealth of Egypt became all the more pressing.[6]

THE LAST STRUGGLES

Cleopatra was far more active than her lover: she ordered the construction of ships at one of the ports on the Red Sea coast and some of her existing vessels were dragged overland from the Nile to join them. The labour involved was massive, adding to the already major task of moving her treasury to the port. From there she – and presumably Antony – could sail away, with enough wealth to ensure their comfort and sufficient courtiers and mercenaries to protect them. They might live in luxurious exile or even carve out a small kingdom in India. Perhaps she even dreamed of returning from exile, as she had done almost two decades before. For these plans her money was spent and the toil of her subjects expended. It was not to be, however. King Malchus – the Nabataean ruler whose lands Antony had ceded to Cleopatra – had little love for the queen and a natural desire to ingratiate himself with Octavian. Malchus attacked and burned the ships before the project was complete.

Cleopatra had not left Alexandria and was able to coax Antony into rejoining her in the palace. Canidius arrived to tell of the loss of the army and there was continued news of defections. There were still moments of optimism and grand plans. They may have considered sailing to Spain in the hope of reviving the war there. Unlikely though this sounds, one of Octavian's officers was busy building fortified positions on the Spanish coast. It was probably too great a distance to travel without secure bases en route and, for whatever reason, the idea was abandoned.[7]

Antony was happy to revel in luxury once more. Cleopatra arranged a grand celebration for his birthday on 14 January 30 BC. He was fifty-three. She let her own birthday pass in far more modest fashion, eager to focus attention on him and rebuild his confidence. The queen was thirty-nine. Their society of 'Inimitable Livers' was disbanded and instead they formed a new club – 'the Sharers in Death'. The name was inspired by a play, telling of lovers who believed that their deaths were certain, although on the stage the story ended in a last minute reprieve.[8]

The state of mind of both Antony and Cleopatra in the winter and spring of 30 BC is harder to judge and no doubt their moods swung. Both had survived apparently hopeless situations in the past and perhaps this encouraged them to cling on to hope now. The queen is supposed to have taken an interest in poisons, allegedly watching tests on condemned prisoners to see how quickly and reliably they died and the degree of pain and discomfort involved. Death was another form of escape, but neither of them was inclined to rush to that fate or to fail to explore other possibilities. Cleopatra made arrangements for Caesarion to be sent with treasure and an escort to India, doing on a smaller scale what she planned for all of them.[9]

Caesarion was now about sixteen, and in a public festival Antony and Cleopatra celebrated his coming of age. He was enrolled in the ephebeia at the gymnasium, a quintessentially Greek ceremony. At the same time Antyllus, who was about fourteen or fifteen, also became formally a man, donning the *toga virilis*. It was seen as a promise that even if Antony and Cleopatra should die, then their heirs were ready as adults to take over their power. In particular, the promotion of Caesarion was intended to assure her subjects that the regime was stable. Perhaps it was also hoped that there would be more chance of his being allowed to remain as king if he was already firmly established.[10]

Both Antony and Cleopatra repeatedly and independently wrote and sent messengers to Octavian in an effort to bargain. She assured him of her loyalty to Rome and at some point copied Herod's gesture of sending the royal regalia, including the throne, sceptre and diadem. No doubt there were generous gifts and the promise of far greater wealth if either she or her children were permitted to keep some or all of her kingdom. Antony employed a friendlier version of his bluff style, now hearty in talking of their former friendship and amorous adventures they had shared in the past. He offered to go into retirement, asking permission to live in Athens if he was not allowed to stay with Cleopatra in Alexandria.

Octavian made no concrete offer to either of them, at least publicly, although Dio claims that he secretly promised Cleopatra her kingdom if she killed Antony. Much of the negotiation was done by freedmen from their respective households, although Antony also sent Antyllus on one occasion. The youth brought gold, which Octavian took, before sending the boy on his way without making any concrete proposal to carry to his father. It is interesting that Antony and Cleopatra chose to contact their enemy independently, and that he preferred to reply in the same way. In his case, Octavian clearly hoped to encourage suspicion between the lovers that the other might make a separate deal.

One of Octavian's representatives to the queen was a freedman called Thrystus, a man of charm and clear diplomatic skill. He was granted long private audiences with Cleopatra, prompting a mistrustful Antony to have him flogged and sent back to Octavian. Antony said that if the latter wanted to respond he could always give Hipparchus a whipping – referring to one of his own freedmen who had long since defected to the enemy. On another occasion he sent a different type of present, his envoys bringing a captive Turullius, last but one of Caesar's assassins. The prisoner was sent to Cos and executed there, both for the murder and his desecration of the sacred grove.[11]

Antony had little to offer, apart from voluntary retirement and a quick completion of a war that in any event could not last very long. His armies had dwindled away and the only group to declare open allegiance to him was a force of gladiators at Cyzicus in Asia Minor. Condemned to die in the arena, these men seem to have hoped to be turned into soldiers and win their freedom from Antony. Eventually they were suppressed and, although promised life by their captors, they were treacherously executed. Lepidus had been allowed to live, although the recent conspiracy involving his son may have made Octavian question the wisdom of this. Antony had always been a stronger figure and he had two Roman sons, one of whom had just come of age. To spare his beaten opponent would have been a great display of clemency, but also a gamble.[12]

Cleopatra was better placed. Octavian needed to draw on the wealth of her kingdom, and she was in a position to make this easier for him. If she chose to resist, then in the short term she could also rob him of the revenue he desperately needed to provide for his veterans. Since her return to Alexandria, the queen had gathered a great deal of the readily accessible wealth of the kingdom. Much of this she stored in the mausoleum she was preparing for herself – the location is unknown, but it was near a great temple to Isis. Combustible material was piled inside the tomb, so that the building and its treasure could easily be destroyed if she issued the order. Even if the precious metals could be retrieved, it would take time before they could be restored to usable form. The preparations were not kept secret. Cleopatra was preparing for her death at the same time as she bargained for life.[13]

In the summer of 30 BC Octavian attacked Egypt from two directions. An army came along the coast from Cyrenaica in the west, supported by a fleet. It included the four formerly Antonian legions and probably some of Octavian's own troops. The whole force was under the command of Caius Cornelius Gallus, a descendant of Gallic aristocrats who had been brought into public life by Caesar. Octavian himself advanced from Syria in the east, marching overland to Pelusium along the traditional invasion route. Antony had whatever legionaries had been carried on board the ships from Actium, along with whatever forces had been stationed in Egypt or had been raised since his return. At most he is unlikely to have been able to muster a force equivalent to a couple of legions and auxiliaries, along with a small navy.[14]

Antony first confronted the force approaching from the west, hoping to persuade his men to return to their former allegiance. Gallus is supposed to have had his trumpeters sound a fanfare to blot out the words. Antony attacked and was repulsed, then Gallus managed to lure the enemy ships into attacking the harbour and trapped them there. Antony and the remnants of his forces withdrew. In the meantime, Pelusium had fallen, apparently without a fight. Dio claims that Cleopatra had betrayed the fortress to the enemy. The commander of her garrison there was named Seleucus and Plutarch says that she had this man's wife and children executed for his failure. This may have been genuine anger, an attempt to quash the rumour or even to conceal her involvement.[15]

Coming back from his defeat, Antony bumped into Octavian's vanguard and was able to rout some cavalry. He had archers shoot arrows into the enemy camp, each with a message tied to the shaft, offering the soldiers 1,500 denarii each if they came over to his side.

None did. Even so, Antony returned to Alexandria – the action had been fought on the outskirts of the city – and without bothering to take off his armour, embraced Cleopatra and kissed her in suitably Homeric fashion. One of his cavalrymen had distinguished himself in the skirmish and Antony presented the man to the queen, who rewarded him with a helmet and cuirass decorated with gold. Perhaps the soldier was one of the bodyguard of Gauls he had given to her some years before. Whatever his background, he deserted to the enemy that night.[16]

'The Sharers in Death' held a last feast that night. It was lavish in scale, but tearful, with Antony talking openly of his desire for an heroic death – scarcely an encouraging topic for the night before a battle. Overnight, it was said people heard music and chants, just like one of the Dionysiac processions so favoured by the two lovers. The sound seemed to leave the city, as if the god was abandoning it. The Greeks and Romans were inclined to believe that the deities associated with a place left before a disaster. The Roman army regularly performed a ceremony intended to welcome the gods of a besieged city into new homes freshly prepared for them by the besiegers.[17]

Antony had planned an ambitious combined attack for the following day, 1 August 30 BC. It would begin with warships attacking the enemy fleet and this would be followed by an assault on land. There was no realistic chance of victory, or at least not of any success that might actually turn the tide of the war. This may explain what happened next. Antony watched as his warships closed with the enemy, but was amazed to see them stop and raise their oars out of the water, a gesture of surrender. Closer to him, his cavalry followed their example, choosing this moment to defect. His infantry – less able to move quickly, less sure of each other's mood or truly loyal – remained. They attacked and were quickly beaten. Antony returned to the palace and Plutarch claims that he was yelling out that the queen had betrayed him. Dio simply states that Cleopatra had ordered the ships' captains to defect.

Most of the ships to escape from Actium were hers. Some may have been lost in the attempt to reach the Arabian coast, but any built to replace them were constructed and crewed at her expense.

In most respects the naval squadrons were hers rather than Antony's and so it is certainly possible that she had arranged their defection in secret negotiations. Most modern historians dismiss this as propaganda aimed at blackening her reputation. They may be right, and the truth in such cases was unlikely to have been widely known even at the time. However, there was absolutely nothing to be gained by fighting. Possessing the fleet gave a bargaining counter and giving it up could well have been a gesture of faith. Unconditional surrender either then or in the past months meant simply trusting to the mercy of the conqueror. Cleopatra hoped to persuade Octavian to make her a deal and that meant conceding slowly, demonstrating both her capacity and willingness to be of assistance. Giving up Pelusium, and later ordering the surrender of her fleet, would make sense as gestures, making Octavian's conquest easier and less costly in lives. These would be coldly pragmatic decisions, but they were certainly not impossible ones.[18]

Cleopatra was a survivor who had clung on to power for almost twenty years amidst all the intrigues of the Ptolemaic court and the chaos of Roman civil wars. It would have been out of character for her to despair and it is clear that she had not yet done so. She might be able to save something of her own power, or if not then secure the position of some or all of her children. Caesarion was vulnerable after the emphasis on his paternity in the struggle with Octavian, but he had already been sent away on the long journey that should eventually take him to India. Her children by Antony might well be more acceptable to the young Caesar, and the Romans liked to employ client rulers. Their father may already have been beyond salvation.

'CONQUERED VALIANTLY BY A ROMAN'

While Antony's army dissolved around him, Cleopatra went to her mausoleum. It was a two-storey structure, with a single door and one or more large windows on the upper storey. Construction work was not yet complete and there were ropes and other building equipment for raising and placing the stone blocks still around it.

She went inside, accompanied only by her two maids and a eunuch. Mechanisms were sprung, dropping into the doorway a stone barrier to close the entrance permanently. Sealed in with her treasure, the queen obviously did not expect her lover to join her. Both Plutarch and Dio say that she told her courtiers to tell Antony that she was dead.[19]

He believed the report and his anger against her turned to sorrow and a desire to join his lover in death. Plutarch makes him regret that the queen had been the first to take this courageous step, so that he – the great commander – had to follow her example. Retiring to his chamber and taking off his armour, he asked a slave to help him do the job, just as Brutus and Cassius had done. Although this generation of Roman aristocrats had become so enamoured of suicide, most still realised that it was a difficult thing to do cleanly and quickly. Even the determined Cato had not succeeded at his first attempt. On the retreat from Media, Plutarch says that Antony had asked one of his bodyguards to perform the task. His choice now was different and fell on an attendant named Eros, who had already been told to prepare for this final service to his master. Taking Antony's sword as if to guide and give force to the thrust, instead the slave ran himself through.

Inspired by this gesture, Mark Antony then stabbed himself in the stomach, slumping back to lie on a couch. Either there were others in the room or they were attracted by the noise. Antony regained consciousness and begged them to help him die. None would, and some or all of them then fled. Plutarch says that at this point Cleopatra sent one of her scribes to have Antony brought to her, although does not explain how she knew what he had done. Dio claims that the cries of his attendants had made the queen look out from a window in the mausoleum. Someone saw her and told Antony, who realised that his lover was not dead. He tried to rise, collapsed from the exertion, then ordered them to carry him to her.

The door to the mausoleum was sealed and so they used some of the builders' ropes to raise him on a bed up to the window, Cleopatra and her servants pulling hard to lift his weight. After a struggle, they brought him into the tomb and laid him out. After this effort she is supposed to have wept loudly, tearing her clothes and striking and scratching her own chest in grief. Antony begged her to be calm, then asked for wine and drank. It may have hastened the end and he died soon afterwards, with the queen beside him. Plutarch has him say that his end was a good one for a 'Roman, conquered valiantly by a Roman', but it is hard to know how anyone could have known what he said. These were good dying words, both for Octavian's propaganda and for those Romans who cherished Antony's reputation.

At best his suicide had been a series of misunderstandings, but since both our main sources report that some of the confusion was deliberately created by Cleopatra, then it is hard not to believe that she planned to separate her own fate from that of Antony. The report of her death was bound to make him react. He might flee from Alexandria, although with another invader to the west it would have been hard for him to go anywhere but to the south, and there was little chance of his rallying support there. Perhaps he would surrender or let himself be captured, suffering imprisonment or execution as Octavian saw fit. Most likely he would do what he did and take his own life. Cleopatra knew him as well as anyone and must have guessed how he would react. She did not kill her lover, and most certainly had not in the past months stooped to murder, although admittedly Antony's Roman friends would most likely have reacted violently had she done so. Yet the false message made it likely that he would take his own life, or leave, or be killed in some other manner.[20]

Whichever action he took, Antony would be out of the way and leave her to negotiate her own settlement with Octavian. For it is clear that Cleopatra had no intention of being a 'Sharer in Death', at least for the moment, and she was to survive him by more than a week. Ensconced in her mausoleum, surrounded by her treasure and the means to destroy it, she had a few cards left to play. That does not mean that her grief for Antony was any less real, even if – perhaps especially if – it was tinged with an element of guilt through having to sacrifice him so that there was a chance for her and any of her children to survive with dignity and perhaps power. Cleopatra mourned her lover and she and her attendants did their best to treat the body properly. There was nothing she could have done to save him.

Octavian entered Alexandria with more show than actual use of force. He summoned the population to a public meeting in the gymnasium. There, he addressed them in Greek. Unlike Antony and most Romans of his class, he was not entirely comfortable in the language, in part because his education had been cut short by Caesar's murder. He assured the Alexandrians of good treatment and brought before them a philosopher named Areius, whom he planned to use as a local representative. The inhabitants of the city did not respond with the enthusiasm they had kept for Antony, but there was certainly general relief.[21]

Antony's suicide in turn relieved Octavian of having to deal with him and the stigma likely to follow his execution. He could afford to be magnanimous and put on a display of grief, reading Antony's letters to his senior staff and speaking of their past friendship. Cleopatra and her treasure presented a problem, even if they were not a threat to his victory. Whatever contact and secret negotiation had occurred, either no agreement had been struck or she was not yet prepared to rely on his good faith. Octavian sent an equestrian named Caius Proculeius along with a freedman to the mausoleum to speak to the queen. In Plutarch's account of his death, Antony is supposed to have told her that she could trust Proculeius, although once again it is hard to know how the author could have obtained this information. None of the witnesses wrote an account of what happened, although it is possible that they did tell others about what had happened in the days before they died. Proculeius and the queen spoke, but she refused to come out and he returned to report to Octavian.

Next, Proculeius returned with Cornelius Gallus and it was the latter who led the negotiations. As on the earlier occasion, she did not come to the window, but shouted through the sealed door. While Gallus kept her attention, Proculeius and two slaves put a ladder up against the side of the building and climbed in through the window. Going down to the ground floor, they grabbed hold of Cleopatra, thwarting her attempt to stab herself with a knife. The eunuch died in the struggle, perhaps of snakebite or poison, but the queen and her maids were taken as prisoners back to the palace.[22]

Cleopatra was given permission to attend to the funeral arrangements for her dead lover, a task that several prominent Romans and other client rulers are said to have requested. Romans, and especially the aristocracy, in the first century BC generally cremated the dead and then interred the ashes in a tomb. Antony's body does not seem to have been burned, but was embalmed and probably placed in a coffin. Alexander the Great had been mummified, and so were many of the Ptolemies, at least from the second century BC onwards. However, the full process took seventy days, and could not have been completed before Cleopatra herself was dead.[23]

From grief, and an infection in the cuts she had given herself with her own nails, Cleopatra fell ill, developing a fever and refusing to eat. She was treated by her doctor, Olympus, who later wrote an account of her last days, which was used by Plutarch. He said that the queen had lost the will to live, but then rallied a little when told that Octavian wished to see her, perhaps unwillingly because it was said that he threatened to harm her children.

Dio and Plutarch present the encounter in dramatically different ways. The former has Cleopatra dressed to look at once pitiful and beautiful – much as she had first met Caesar. She reclined on an elaborately decorated couch in a grand apartment, surrounded by pictures and busts of Caesar, with his letters clutched to her bosom. When Octavian entered, she rose to greet him, not the proud queen, but the respectful and open suppliant. Her talk was mainly of Caesar and she read extracts from his letters, pausing sometimes to weep and then kiss the papyrus. Dio has Octavian refuse to look at the beautiful petitioner when he replied, but simply assure her that her life was not in danger. The queen went down on her knees to beg, but could get no more than this, even when she begged him to let her join Antony in death. Propaganda emphasised that the virtuous Octavian was not to be seduced like Caesar and Antony, but in reality the situations were so different that this was never likely.

Plutarch's account of Cleopatra's final days is a good deal more sympathetic, and indeed far warmer than his portrayal of the rest of her life. He depicts her wearing only a tunic or shift, her hair dishevelled and lying on a mattress of plain straw. Yet perhaps his version is not so different in that he also maintained her looks were still striking. Plutarch's Cleopatra pleaded that she had had no choice but to obey Antony and that the guilt was his. Octavian is supposed to have patiently disproved all her arguments.

Both our sources make it clear that they discussed her wealth, Cleopatra listing her property in some detail. A royal attendant named Seleucus – presumably not the general of the same name, but someone equally keen to win Roman approval – spoke out to say that she was omitting many valuable items. Plutarch says Cleopatra grabbed the man by the hair and repeatedly struck his face. Then she explained that she was keeping aside some of her most precious jewellery to present as gifts to Livia and Octavia. Dio also says that she hoped to win favour from Octavian's wife and sister and that she offered to sail to Rome. Imaginations were doubtless given free rein in both accounts of this dramatic encounter. Yet there is nothing implausible in the claims that Cleopatra was willing to try charm, pathos, flattery, the musical qualities of her voice and the force of her looks and personality to persuade the conqueror. It was only sensible to employ every means still left to her.[24]

The meeting ended with little resolved. Octavian was determined to take her to Rome to be led in triumph and believed that the meeting had reassured her and restored her willingness to live. It is doubtful that at any point he or anyone else suggested that she be executed at the end of the triumph. This had never been done to a woman and, even with male leaders, this ritual was not always followed. Yet it was probably also clear that although her life would be spared she would not be permitted any power. Comfortable exile, perhaps in Italy or just possibly somewhere in the Greek world, was the extent of his mercy. Octavian had also pointedly not promised to let any of her children rule as monarchs. He would soon annex Egypt, but it was to be a province different from any other, virtually run as a personal possession of Octavian and his successors. It was vital for him to exploit its resources directly and equally important to prevent any rival from ever controlling them.

Cleopatra was disappointed. The most she could take away from the meeting was the satisfaction of convincing the Roman leader that she would not try to take her own life. Retirement held no appeal for her, especially since she was denied the satisfaction of passing power to her children. The prospect of being led as a captive along the Via Sacra for the amusement of the Roman mob repelled her. Plutarch claims that a sympathetic young aristocrat on Octavian's staff secretly let her know that she must undergo this ordeal. She decided to kill herself.[25]

Some scholars have speculated that, in spite of his attempts to keep the queen alive, it was actually more convenient for Octavian to let her die or even have her killed. Therefore the guard placed over her was loose enough to give Cleopatra every chance to commit suicide. The example of Arsinoe, who won the Roman crowd's pity when she was led in Caesar's triumph, is cited. It is possible that a similar reaction was feared, but given that Cleopatra was much older and had been portrayed so strongly as Rome's enemy, then it was far from certain. As a famous captive she would grace Octavian's triumph and for the rest of her life be a visible sign of his clemency. On balance, it is more likely that he wanted to keep her alive. It would surely have been possible for her to be killed 'accidentally' in the confusion of Antony's defeat had he wanted this – at least once her treasure was secured.[26]

The precise method of the suicide tends to be discussed at great, even excessive length, to the extent that it sometimes overbalances far more important episodes in her life. Our ancient sources were clearly unsure over precisely what happened and it is therefore highly improbable that we can solve every detail of the mystery. If the bite of a snake was the method used, then people have speculated about the precise species of asp or viper, and then wondered how many animals would be required to kill both Cleopatra and her two maids. The most likely candidate is the Egyptian cobra, which can grow to 6 feet and so would have been harder to conceal, especially if two or three were needed. Plutarch tells a story of a snake being smuggled into the royal chamber, concealed in a basket of figs, whereas in Dio's version it was a basket of flowers. Both report other versions and other sources of poison – for instance, a hollow pin that Cleopatra wore in her hair and which contained a fatal poison. The substance may have been snake venom collected at an earlier time. Strabo talks of a poisonous ointment.[27]

The broad details are more certain. On 10 August 30 BC Cleopatra probably went to visit Antony's corpse one last time. Presumably it was still in her mausoleum and the entrance to this had now been opened, if only to remove the treasure. None of our sources suggests that the queen and her attendants had to climb a ladder to get in and out again. Returning to the palace she bathed, dressed once more in royal finery and with only Charmion and Iras for company, took a sumptuous last meal. Earlier she had sent a letter to Octavian, confident that it would not arrive in time for him to stop her.

Cleopatra then killed herself. One of the sources reported faint scratches or punctures to her arm and this was the only visible mark on her. Whether made by the fangs of a snake or by the point of a pin is unknown. If she did use a cobra, then its venom can cause convulsions in the latter stages. Her attendants took care to lie their mistress down on a couch, keeping her body, clothes and jewellery as immaculate as possible. After that they too took poison in some form, allowing themselves to be bitten by snakes or drinking or otherwise ingesting a fatal substance. By the time Octavian had received the letter and sent men to the royal chamber, Iras was already dead, lying at the feet of the queen. The dying Charmion was struggling to make last minute corrections to Cleopatra's royal diadem.

Plutarch says that one of the men angrily called to her that this was a fine thing. 'Truly a fine deed, becoming a queen descended from so many kings,' Charmion replied, and then collapsed and died. Whether or not the story is true, it was a fittingly theatrical final scene for Cleopatra's story.[28]

CONCLUSION: HISTORY
AND THE GREAT ROMANCE

All attempts to revive the queen failed. Octavian ordered special snake handlers known as Psylli to be brought, since these were credited with being able to suck poison from wounds. He was said to be angry, but treated the body with all due respect. Cleopatra was interred alongside Antony in the mausoleum she had built. Octavian was more scornful of earlier Ptolemies. He paid a visit to the tomb of Alexander, not simply looking at the corpse within the crystal sarcophagus, but reaching inside to touch it, and accidentally snapped off part of the nose. When asked if he would like to see the tombs of Cleopatra's family, he said that he had come to see a king and not a load of corpses.[1]

Based on the well-established tradition of entertaining visiting Roman dignitaries, he was also asked if he wanted to see the Apis bull. Octavian was not interested, saying that he worshipped 'gods and not cattle'. He was far more concerned to gather as much gold and other treasure as possible, a task made easier by Cleopatra's energetic fund-raising since her return from Actium. Dio says that he did not need to commit sacrilege by confiscating property from the temples.

He may have received additional 'gifts' from the temple cults. Plutarch claims that Antony's statues were destroyed, but a man named Archibus paid 1,000 talents to Octavian to protect the images of the queen. Many of these would have been carved onto temples and their destruction likely to cause wider damage to the physical structure and prestige of these shrines. Some doubt the story altogether, but others suggest that the man was a representative of one of the priestly cults. Even if that is so, the gesture need not be an indication of particular fondness for Cleopatra. Octavian wanted money, and it was better for the temples and more convenient for him if this was 'willingly' given rather than taken. The temple cults would also naturally hope to prove as useful to the new Roman occupiers just as they been to the Ptolemies.

Apart from treasure there were other trophies. Two ancient obelisks were taken to Rome, one to form the gnomon of a giant sundial constructed by Octavian. (Today it stands in the Piazza di Montecitorio. The other is in the Piazza San Giovanni in Laterano.) On a smaller scale, the pearl earring that survived Cleopatra's trick with vinegar was split into two and placed in the ears of the statue of the queen in the temple of Venus Genetrix. Some suggest that the statue itself came to Rome as part of Octavian's spoils, rather than being set up in Caesar's day.[2]

Antony and Cleopatra were not the only victims of their defeat. Canidius was executed, as was Cassius of Parma, the last survivor of Caesar's assassins. Rather more of Antony's closest followers managed to change sides before it was too late and at the very least saved their lives. Sosius, the consul of 32 BC who had led the attack on Octavian in the Senate and later commanded the left wing of the fleet at Actium, surrendered and was well treated. Marcus Licinius Crassus, grandson of Caesar's ally, defected somewhat earlier and was rewarded with the consulship in 30 BC. Munatius Plancus did well out of the new regime and after a long life was interred in a monumental mausoleum, which stands to this day at Gaeta on the coast of Italy. It was said that many of Octavian's closest companions in the years to come were men who had once followed Antony.[3]

Antyllus did not long survive his father. The teenager, who had only a few months before becoming a man, was dragged from the shrine to Caesar built by Cleopatra in Alexandria. He was beheaded on Octavian's orders. His tutor had betrayed him and then stolen a valuable gem the youth wore as a pendant. The jewel was discovered hidden in the tutor's belt and he was crucified.[4]

Caesarion was also betrayed by his tutor on the journey to the Red Sea. The man's name was Rhodion, and he either sent word to their pursuers or actually lured his charge back to Alexandria. Caesarion was immediately murdered. Areius the philosopher is supposed to have urged Octavian to give this order, changing a passage of the *Iliad* to declare that 'there can be too many Caesars'. (In the original, Odysseus controlled a meeting of the Greeks who were inclined to abandon the war with Troy by physical force, and telling them, 'Surely not all of us Achaians can be as kings here. Lordship for many is no good thing. Let there be one ruler, one king ... to watch over his people.'[5])

On 1 January 29 BC Octavian became consul for the fourth time. Between 13 and 15 August he celebrated three triumphs. The first was for his victories in Illyricum, which he had deferred in 34 BC. The second was for Actium and the third for the capture of Alexandria. An effigy of Cleopatra – and probably pictures as well – was carried as part of the procession. She was depicted with two snakes. This makes it clear that the story of the queen dying from a snakebite was already current and given official support. On the other hand, other forms of poison would have been more difficult to represent. Horace had written: 'Now is the time for drinking, now stamp the earth in dance' in a poem celebrating the defeat of Rome's enemy. Yet later in the same piece he spoke of the queen's courage in taking her own life. Attitudes towards Cleopatra were already changing. The Romans admired courage, even in an enemy – or at least in a defeated enemy.[6]

Also included in the triumph were Alexander Helios and Cleopatra Selene, now aged about eleven, and perhaps the seven-year-old Ptolemy Philadelphus. The latter is not mentioned by name, but apart from Antyllus and Caesarion none of Antony's or Cleopatra's other children was harmed. All were raised in the household of Octavia. Antyllus' younger brother Iullus Antonius enjoyed considerable favour until he was involved in the scandal surrounding Octavian's daughter Julia in 2 BC. It may in fact have been an attempted coup, and certainly the punishments were severe. Julia was exiled. Iullus and a number of other young men from prominent senatorial families were executed. Cleopatra Selene was in due course married to King Juba II of Mauretania. (He was the son of Juba I of Numidia and as a boy had also walked as a prisoner when Caesar celebrated his African triumph in 45 BC.) Her two remaining brothers may have accompanied her to live in the royal court. Juba and Cleopatra Selene's son Ptolemy succeeded to the kingdom, until he was deposed and executed by Emperor Caligula, who was himself Antony's great-grandson.[7]

Caligula was the first of three emperors to be descended from Mark Antony, through the younger Antonia, his second child with Octavia. When Caligula was murdered, he was succeeded by his uncle – and Antony's grandson – Claudius. The latter was followed by another of Antony's great-grandsons, this time through the elder Antonia, who married the son of Lucius Domitius Ahenobarbus, the man who had defected before Actium. His name was Nero and he proved himself to be one of the least capable men ever to hold imperial power at Rome, although perhaps his love of music and display owed something to his ancestor.

With Nero's suicide, the Julio-Claudian line of emperors established by Octavian/Augustus came to an end. His creation, the system of imperial rule known as the Principate, would endure for another two centuries, and emperors would rule from Italy until the fifth century and from Constantinople until the fifteenth century. The man who defeated Antony and Cleopatra was Rome's first emperor, whose reforms fundamentally altered the state. His success was not inevitable. Only thirty-two when Antony and Cleopatra killed themselves, no one would have guessed that he would live on and continue to dominate for another forty-four years. Indeed, given his continuing poor health and bouts of apparently life-threatening illness, his survival was all the more amazing. Octavian became Augustus, and over a long time and after a number of changes of direction, he shaped the system that would govern the empire in the height of its success.

We cannot know how different things would have been if Antony had won, or simply outlived his rival. At no point in his career did Antony suggest strong commitment to any particular reforms. All of his legislation as consul and triumvir was designed first and foremost to bring tangible advantage to himself and his close allies. He does not appear to have wanted to change the state, but simply to have as much power and wealth as possible. In this Antony's ambitions were highly traditional, even if his methods were extreme. The same could be said of many senators in the last decades of the Republic.

As an adult, Cleopatra's first concern was always to stay in power. The greatest threats came from her own family and those in the court willing to support them. Arsinoe and her two brothers were disposed of, but she did not live long enough for her own children to challenge her position. The grants of land made to her by Antony, culminating in the Donations, offered a way of maintaining her dominance, becoming 'Queen of Kings' and so on a higher level than her offspring. Her survival and this elevation were achieved solely through Roman support.

Julius Caesar's critics claimed – and perhaps genuinely believed – that he wanted to become a king, and the only real model for kingship was that of the Hellenistic world. Some saw Cleopatra as encouraging his desire, but the evidence makes this unlikely. Caesar was dictator, held supreme power, which he clearly intended to keep, and this was enough to prompt his murder. There is scarcely much more evidence to support the allegations of Octavian's propaganda that Antony and Cleopatra planned some form of joint rule. Her supposed boast of giving judgement on the Capitol and his alleged plan of moving the centre of rule from Rome to Alexandria are just some of the contradictions in the charges made against them. Antony kept Cleopatra at his side in the civil war. That attested to her importance to him, but was a serious political mistake. He had done nothing to promote her position more formally in a Roman context.

If either Antony or Cleopatra wanted to rule as king and queen of a Roman empire – and this does seem unlikely – then such a plan was utterly unrealistic. Caesar had been murdered for far less, and although since then people had been forced to accept that power lay with the commanders of the strongest armies, they were certainly not ready to accept open monarchy. Octavian toned down some of the grander projects and symbols of his power in the next decade or so. These were far less provocative than the presence of a foreign queen at the side of the man who controlled Rome. If Antony and Cleopatra had won the civil war and tried to rule as monarchs, then they would have failed. He would certainly have been murdered and she might also have perished. Indeed, it is hard to believe that Antony would have survived in the long run even if he had tried to exercise power in a more traditionally Roman way. Subtlety was never his strongpoint and he too readily paraded his power. Opinion at Rome was not yet ready for this. Octavian would take care to veil the reality of his sole power behind a façade of tradition.

Antony's career reflected the great advantages enjoyed by the established nobility at Rome. He was raised to expect a place at the centre of the Republic and his birth gave him so many advantages that at least some eminence was assured, assuming that he lived long enough. This was true in spite of the heavy debts he inherited from his father and accumulated on his own. The record of his uncle, Caius Antonius Hybrida, is instructive. He was expelled from the Senate in 70 BC and yet managed to become consul in 63 BC. Exiled in the civil war, he nevertheless returned to Rome and public life. Established families like the Antonii had a strong network of clients and connections, bolstered by past favours and the promise of more in the future. They also had the added advantage that their name was well known.

It was because he was an Antonius that Caesar was so ready to promote Antony's career. Few *nobiles* joined Caesar in Gaul and even fewer sided with him in 49 BC. Men like Antony were valuable for their name and connections as much or more than any personal ability. The deputies Caesar employed to control Italy in his absence were all men from established families. In the confusion of civil war, Antony gained responsibilities far greater than would normally have been possible for a man of his age, however eminent his family. Luck also played a part. In 44 BC Antony was consul, making him the most senior magistrate when the dictator was murdered. He had immediate power, and the promise of a province and army in the near future. Combined with his name and family connections, this provided the basis for his dominance for the next thirteen years.

None of this had much to do with exceptional talent. Antony began his career with considerable advantages and made the most of his opportunities. In 44 BC he exploited his position as consul to the full, building up his power and influence. Personally brave, he enjoyed considerable success in small-scale engagements, but that was also true of many senators. In more senior positions he proved an adequate subordinate officer to Caesar, but in independent commands Antony failed more often than he succeeded. He was beaten in 43 BC and survived only through the political manoeuvring that created the triumvirate. At Philippi he proved the most able of the four senior commanders, but since none of the others displayed any real skill this achievement should not be exaggerated. Had Brutus been a better general, he might well have turned his success in the First Battle of Philippi into a decisive victory, while Antony was caught up in the details of storming Cassius' camp. The invasion of Media was a disaster caused largely by his own mistakes. In 31 BC he let the enemy take and keep the initiative, and his only achievement was to break out from the blockade, abandoning two-thirds of his fleet and virtually all of his army.

Antony was not a very good general, in spite of his own public image and the portrayal of him in our ancient sources and modern myth. His political rise allowed him to amass huge resources of men and supplies massed for the attack on Parthia, but he proved incapable of using them well. On its own, a large army is no guarantee of victory. The failure in Media was the turning point in his career. He achieved very little in the years that followed. It is tempting to see him in these years as suffering some sort of mental and emotional breakdown – today we might speak of post traumatic stress disorder – and probably declining into alcoholism, as he struggled to cope with his defeat.

There was nothing in his past career to expect a more competent performance in 31 BC, and yet his behaviour seems so exceptionally lethargic that it again reinforces the picture of a man broken in spirit, and in turn indecisive or rash. Perhaps Cleopatra sensed this and that was one of the reasons she wished to stay beside him in the hope of strengthening his resolve. Yet she was no commander, and while they were able to concentrate a grand navy and army in Greece, they do not seem to have known how to use these forces to achieve victory. In a way, this would bring us closer to Octavian's propaganda, which painted Antony as controlled by the queen. The difference would be that Cleopatra was not the cause of Antony's weakness, but the source of whatever strength he had left. The evidence can support this interpretation, but then it can equally support other views. We simply do not have enough information to understand the emotional state and motives of Antony, Cleopatra or any of the major figures in their story. We can only look at what happened.

In spite of his shaky start, Octavian was by this time better able to play the part of a general than Antony. More importantly, he had Agrippa to make the key decisions and actually lead the soldiers and sailors in battle. The skill with which Octavian won the propaganda war has frequently been noted; the degree to which he and Agrippa so far outstripped Antony's military talent is usually ignored. In 31 BC Antony was outclassed and outmanoeuvred in every important respect. He had resources to match his opponent, but failed to use them anywhere near as well.

Mark Antony had risen to be one of the most powerful men in the Roman world through his family background, joining Caesar and sharing his success, and the chance that placed him at the centre of things when the latter was murdered. He showed some skill as a politician and administrator, but had only limited ability as a soldier. Like the overwhelming majority of politicians throughout history, Antony's rise owed little to conspicuous talent and far more to good connections, luck and the ardent desire for power, position and wealth. In this respect his career was traditional, and the same was true of his ambitions. This again made him very different to Octavian. The latter could easily have died young or been defeated and utterly discredited by Sextus Pompey. Antony was ready for war – or at the very least for a demonstration of force – against his triumviral colleague by 33 BC. Yet he had not used his time in the east at all well to prepare himself for this conflict.

Cleopatra was more intelligent, and certainly far better educated, than Antony. It is harder to say whether she was more able in other respects. Her political ability was enough to keep her in power for two decades, through harnessing Roman support. We do not really know how popular she was within her kingdom, whether in Alexandria with its mixed population, amongst the Greek community or with the various sections of the wider Egyptian people. Roman force restored her after her exile and kept her in power, just as it had done for her father. Rome dominated the Mediterranean world and this brings us back to one of the basic facts about Cleopatra's life with which we began. In terms of power and political importance, she was never the equal of Caesar or Antony, or indeed of any Roman senator. Her Roman supporters – and most of all her two lovers – kept her on the throne and added to her territory. She could not have achieved this on her own.

Cleopatra was the last of the Ptolemies to rule from Alexandria, since Caesarion cannot really be counted as ruling in his own right. Her kingdom was the last of the great powers created in the break-up of Alexander the Great's empire, and in that sense her death marked the end of an era. Yet the rise of Rome had occurred over a long period and was already clearly unstoppable by the time she was born. Cleopatra did not try to resist Rome, but accepted its power and tried best to make use of it.

Antony was the last man to challenge the dominance of Octavian. His death marked the beginning of another new era, the rule of Rome by emperors – three of whom would be his descendants. Later tradition, fuelled by a senatorial class nostalgic for their former political dominance, at times cast him as closer in spirit to Brutus and Cassius on the basis that he had opposed Octavian just as they had murdered Caesar. Such claims make little sense. As triumvir, Antony shared supreme power equivalent to that of a dictator and was unaccountable either to the Senate or Popular Assemblies. There is no doubt that he would also have taken exclusive dictatorial powers if he had been able to seize them. Antony did not fight and lose against Octavian for any vision of the Republic, but for personal supremacy.[8]

As much as anything else it was the drama of Antony and Cleopatra's suicides that helped to fuel the fascination with them, which persists to this day. Their stories grew, and over the centuries were embellished so that the truth began to be buried. Cleopatra became the far larger figure, more famous and more important in a way she had never been in life. Today an image of Cleopatra probably owes more to Elizabeth Taylor than the Ptolemaic queen, but is instantly recognisable, whether on screen or as a fancy dress costume. Antony lags behind, rarely mentioned unless in the same breath as Cleopatra.

This is not the place to trace the long cultural history of Antony and Cleopatra, for that is a major theme in itself and has already been dealt with in other books. Here, the focus has been exclusively on the Antony and Cleopatra of history, of what we know, and do not know, and sometimes what we guess. Fiction and drama freely invent and alter, but in the simple history there was ambition, pride, cruelty, ruthlessness, jealousy, deceit, savagery and passion enough. Neither Antony nor Cleopatra lived a quiet life. They will continue to fascinate, their story being retold and reinvented by each new generation. The same is almost as true of their most famous fictional portrayal, as new productions of Shakespeare's play adopt different styles and presentations. Nothing any historian could say will ever stop this process, nor should it.[9]

The history is there for those who care to look and, as we have seen, the sources contain many gaps and difficulties of interpretation. It is unlikely that these will ever be filled and the mysteries will remain. There will be fresh archaeological discoveries, but these are unlikely to add more than small details to our picture of the world. The underwater excavations on the site of Alexandria have produced a great quantity of artefacts, although since the city was occupied for so many centuries only a small proportion date to the first century BC, let alone have any direct connection with Cleopatra. Yet such is the appeal of her name and story that people will continue to hunt for places more intimately linked to the queen and her Roman lover.

Recently, one team has claimed to be close to finding the mausoleum in which Antony and Cleopatra were interred – a story that rapidly made the newspapers and television news reports. Nothing has come of this so far, and such a find seems unlikely. It is true that such a discovery might provide much new information, although this would inevitably be mainly personal and not in any way alter our understanding of the politics of the time. Even so, as an historian, any new discoveries would be of interest. Yet in the main, I cannot help hoping that the excavators are unsuccessful. Neither Antony nor Cleopatra enjoyed much peace in their lives (although it is of course arguable whether or not they deserved more or less than they experienced). It would seem a shame if their remains ended up on display to crowds of tourists, or even examined, stored and catalogued in a museum basement. Both Cleopatra and Antony separately expressed the wish to be laid to rest next to the other. Better to let them stay like that, in the tomb that she began and was completed after their suicides.

FAMILY TREES

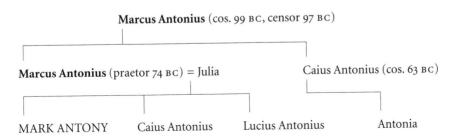

Marcus Antonius (cos. 99 BC, censor 97 BC)

Marcus Antonius (praetor 74 BC) = Julia   Caius Antonius (cos. 63 BC)

MARK ANTONY   Caius Antonius   Lucius Antonius   Antonia

MARK ANTONY'S MARRIAGES AND CHILDREN

Wife	Her Fate	Children
Fadia	Unknown	'children' mentioned by Cicero, unclear how many or what happened to them
Antonia, daughter of Caius Antonius (cos. 63 BC)	divorced c. 47 BC	**Antonia,** later married to Pythodorus of Tralles
Fulvia	died c. 40 BC	**Marcus Antonius ANTYLLUS,** executed 30 BC **Iullus Antonius,** executed 2 BC
Octavia	divorced 32 BC died 11 BC	**Antonia Major,** grandmother of Emperor Nero **Antonia Minor,** mother of Emperor Claudius, grandmother of Emperor Caligula

MARK ANTONY'S CHILDREN WITH CLEOPATRA

1 Alexander Helios, born 40 BC
2 Cleopatra Selene, born 40 BC
3 Ptolemy Philadelphus, born 36 BC

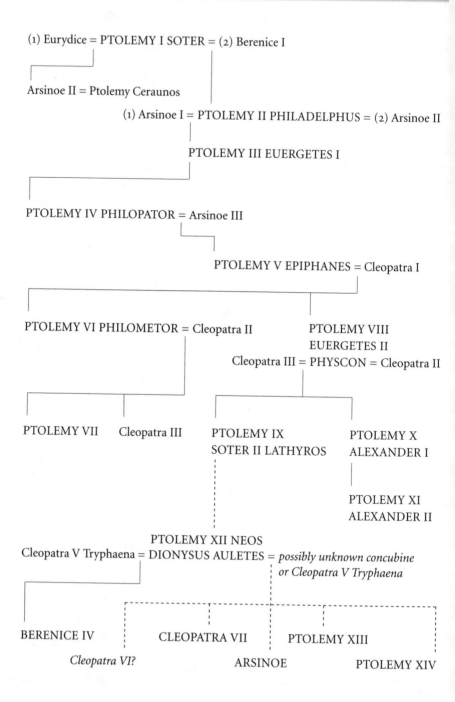

SIMPLIFIED FAMILY TREE OF THE PTOLEMIES

(1) Eurydice = PTOLEMY I SOTER = (2) Berenice I

Arsinoe II = Ptolemy Ceraunos

(1) Arsinoe I = PTOLEMY II PHILADELPHUS = (2) Arsinoe II

PTOLEMY III EUERGETES I

PTOLEMY IV PHILOPATOR = Arsinoe III

PTOLEMY V EPIPHANES = Cleopatra I

PTOLEMY VI PHILOMETOR = Cleopatra II   PTOLEMY VIII
EUERGETES II
Cleopatra III = PHYSCON = Cleopatra II

PTOLEMY VII   Cleopatra III   PTOLEMY IX   PTOLEMY X
SOTER II LATHYROS   ALEXANDER I

PTOLEMY XI
ALEXANDER II

PTOLEMY XII NEOS
Cleopatra V Tryphaena = DIONYSUS AULETES = *possibly unknown concubine
or Cleopatra V Tryphaena*

BERENICE IV   CLEOPATRA VII   PTOLEMY XIII

Cleopatra VI?   ARSINOE   PTOLEMY XIV

398

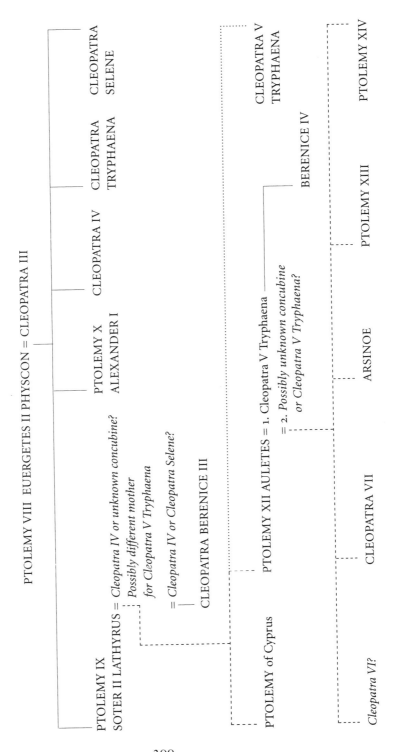

CLEOPATRA AND HER IMMEDIATE ANCESTORS

PTOLEMY VIII EUERGETES II PHYSCON = CLEOPATRA III

PTOLEMY IX
SOTER II LATHYRUS = *Cleopatra IV or unknown concubine?*
Possibly different mother
for Cleopatra V Tryphaena
= *Cleopatra IV or Cleopatra Selene?*

CLEOPATRA BERENICE III

PTOLEMY X
ALEXANDER I

CLEOPATRA IV

CLEOPATRA
TRYPHAENA

CLEOPATRA
SELENE

PTOLEMY of Cyprus

PTOLEMY XII AULETES = 1. Cleopatra V Tryphaena
= 2. *Possibly unknown concubine*
or Cleopatra V Tryphaena?

CLEOPATRA V
TRYPHAENA

BERENICE IV

Cleopatra VI?

CLEOPATRA VII

ARSINOE

PTOLEMY XIII

PTOLEMY XIV

PTOLEMY VI, PTOLEMY VIII AND THE TWO CLEOPATRAS

PTOLEMY V EPIPHANES = CLEOPATRA I

PTOLEMY VI
PHILOMETOR = CLEOPATRA II

PTOLEMY VIII
EUERGETES II PHYSCON = CLEOPATRA II
= CLEOPATRA III

CLEOPATRA II

Ptolemy Memphites?

Ptolemy Eupator

PTOLEMY VII
NEOS PHILOPATOR

CLEOPATRA III

Cleopatra Thea

PTOLEMY IX
SOTER II LATHYRUS

PTOLEMY X
ALEXANDER I

CLEOPATRA IV

CLEOPATRA
TRYPHAENA

CLEOPATRA
SELENE

CHRONOLOGY

753 BC	Traditional date for foundation of Rome by Romulus.
509	Expulsion of Rome's last king, Tarquinius Superbus, and the creation of the Republic.
332–321	Alexander the Great visits Egypt and founds Alexandria.
323	Death of Alexander the Great. Ptolemy I becomes satrap of Egypt.
305–304	Ptolemy I declares himself king.
305–283/282	**Reign of Ptolemy I Soter**
282	Death of Ptolemy I, accession of Ptolemy II.
282–246	**Reign of Ptolemy II Philadelphus**
273	Ptolemy II sends ambassadors to Rome, establishing friendly relations and encouraging trade.
246	Death of Ptolemy II.
246–221	**Reign of Ptolemy III Euergetes I**
221	Death of Ptolemy III.
221–204	**Reign of Ptolemy IV Philopator**
217	Ptolemy IV defeats Seleucids at the Battle of Raphia.
205	First Macedonian War between Rome and Philip V of Macedon ends in a peace treaty.
204	Death of Ptolemy IV.
204–181/180	**Reign of Ptolemy V Epiphanes**
201	Rome wins the Second Punic War with Carthage.
197	Romans defeat King Philip V of Macedon at the Battle of Cynoscephale.
196	Second Macedonian War between Rome and Philip V ends in his defeat. Rosetta Stone set up recording decree of Ptolemy V.
189	Rome defeats the Seleucid Antiochus III in the Syrian War at the Battle of Magnesia.
181/180	Death of Ptolemy V.
180–164	**First reign of Ptolemy VI Philometor**
170–163	**First reign of Ptolemy VIII Euergetes II Physcon as co-ruler**

168	Rome defeats Perseus of Macedon in the Third Macedonian War at the Battle of Pydna. His kingdom is dissolved. Roman embassy forces Antiochus IV to withdraw his army from Egypt.
164	Ptolemy VI flees to Rome and appeals unsuccessfully to the Senate.
163	Ptolemy VIII flees to Rome and appeals unsuccessfully to the Senate.
163–145	**Second reign of Ptolemy VI Philometor**
163–145	Ptolemy VIII controls Cyrenaica.
154	Ptolemy VIII tries to occupy Cyprus, but is captured and returned to Cyrenaica.
146	Third Punic War ends with destruction of Carthage.
145	Ptolemy VI killed intervening in civil war in Syria.
145/144	**Reign of Ptolemy VII Neos Philopator**
145/144	Ptolemy VII murdered by Ptolemy VIII.
145–116	**Second reign of Ptolemy VIII Euergetes II Physcon**
123–122	Tribunates and death of Caius Sempronius Gracchus.
116–101	**Reign of Cleopatra III Euergetis**
116–107	**First reign of Ptolemy IX Philometor Soter II Lathyrus with Cleopatra III**
113	Marcus Antonius (Antony's grandfather) elected quaestor. He is tried and exonerated on a charge of seducing a Vestal Virgin.
107–103/102	**First reign of Ptolemy X Alexander I with Cleopatra III**
107–106	Ptolemy IX forced out of Egypt, and gains, loses and re-takes Cyprus.
104–100	Five successive consulships for Caius Marius, who campaigns against and defeats the migrating Cimbri and Teutones.
103/102	Cleopatra III expels Ptolemy X from Egypt.
102–100	Marcus Antonius serves as praetor and governs Cilicia, where he campaigns successfully against pirates and is awarded a triumph.
101	Ptolemy X returns to Alexandria and murders Cleopatra III.
101–87	**Second reign of Ptolemy X Alexander I with Cleopatra Berenice**
100	Political violence in Rome as the tribune Saturninus is suppressed. Birth of Julius Caesar.
99	Consulship of Marcus Antonius.
97–93	Censorship of Marcus Antonius and Lucius Valerius Flaccus.
91–88	The Social War, the last great rebellion by Rome's Italian allies.

88	Sulla marches his legions on Rome and seizes the city.
87	Marius occupies Rome. Marcus Antonius murdered. Ptolemy X expelled from Alexandria. Ptolemy X killed in naval battle.
87–81/80	**Second reign of Ptolemy IX Philometor Soter II Lathyrus**
83 (or 86)	Birth of Mark Antony.
83–81	Sulla returns from the east and wins the civil war, making himself dictator.
81/80	Death of Ptolemy IX. For some months Cleopatra Berenice (daughter of Ptolemy IX and niece and widow of Ptolemy X) is sole ruler.
81/80	**Reign of Cleopatra Berenice**
80	Ptolemy XI (son of Ptolemy X), returns to Egypt. He marries and then murders Cleopatra Berenice.
80	**Reign of Ptolemy XI Alexander II**
80	Ptolemy XI killed by mob. Ptolemy XII (illegitimate son of Ptolemy IX) seizes power.
80–58	**First reign of Ptolemy XII Auletes**
78	Unsuccessful coup of the consul Marcus Aemilius Lepidus (father of the triumvir).
74	Marcus Antonius (father of Antony) serves as praetor and is given an extraordinary command against the pirates.
73–71	Slave rebellion in Italy led by Spartacus, eventually suppressed by Crassus.
72	Marcus Antonius defeated by the pirates. He is ironically dubbed Creticus, but dies before returning to Rome.
71 or later?	Antony's mother Julia marries Publius Cornelius Lentulus Sura and Antony is raised in his house.
70	Consulship of Pompey and Crassus. Censors expel Lentulus and Antony's uncle, Caius Antonius, from the Senate.
69	Birth of Cleopatra.
63	Conspiracy of Catiline. Lentulus arrested and executed by Cicero after the Senate has passed the *senatus consultum ultimum*.
59	First consulship of Julius Caesar and dominance of the first triumvirate, his alliance with Pompey and Crassus. Ptolemy XII recognised as king and friend of the Roman people after paying them a heavy bribe.
58	Tribunate of Clodius. Roman annexation of Cyprus and suicide of Ptolemy (younger brother of Ptolemy XII). Ptolemy XII flees Alexandria and goes to Rome. His daughter Berenice IV is appointed queen.

58–55	**Reign of Berenice IV**
57	Aulus Gabinius made proconsul of Syria. He recruits Antony to command some or all of his cavalry.
57–56	Gabinius and Antony campaign in Judaea.
55	Second consulship of Pompey and Crassus. Ptolemy XII Auletes persuades Gabinius to restore him to his throne. Antony plays a conspicuous role in the expedition to Egypt. Auletes is restored and executes Berenice IV.
55–51	**Second reign of Ptolemy XII Auletes**
54	Crassus appointed proconsul of Syria and begins invasion of Parthia. Gabinius returns to Rome and is tried on several charges and eventually forced into exile. Late in the year Antony joins Caesar in Gaul.
53	Crassus defeated and killed by Parthians at Carrhae. Antony goes to Rome to campaign for election to the quaestorship. Elections delayed by political violence. Antony attempts to kill Clodius.
52	Clodius murdered. Pompey made sole consul to restore order. Antony elected quaestor. He returns to Gaul and serves at the siege of Alesia.
51	Death of Ptolemy XII Auletes. He is initially succeeded by Cleopatra ruling alone. Antony commands a legion during punitive expeditions in Gaul.
51–49/48	**First reign of Cleopatra VII**
50	Cleopatra forced to accept her brother Ptolemy XIII as co-ruler. Antony returns to Rome to seek election as augur and as tribune. Tribunate of Curio. Political tension heightens as his enemies attempt to have Caesar recalled from Gaul and prevent him from going straight into a second consulship. Antony becomes augur and tribune elect.
49	Antony's tribunate. The Senate passes the *senatus consultum ultimum*. Antony, his colleague, Cassius and Curio flee Rome and hurry to Caesar. Caesar invades Italy to start civil war. Antony serves with Caesar as he overruns Italy. Pompey retreats to Greece. Antony left as tribune with propraetorian *imperium* to administer Italy. Caesar defeats Pompeian forces in Spain. Curio takes Sicily, but is killed in Africa.
49/48	Cleopatra flees from Egypt and raises an army.
48	Caesar's second consulship. He leads invasion of Macedonia. Several months later he is joined by Antony and reinforcements. They are repulsed at Dyrrachium, but win a decisive victory at Pharsalus. Cleopatra leads invasion of Egypt, but is confronted by Ptolemy XIII's army. Pompey

arrives in Egypt and is murdered. Caesar arrives, demands
money and declares that he will arbitrate in the dispute
between the siblings. Caelius and Milo rebel in Italy and are
killed.

48–47 Alexandrian War. Brief rule of Arsinoe. Death of Ptolemy
XIII. Arsinoe captured and taken to Rome. Cleopatra rules
jointly with younger brother Ptolemy XIV. In his absence,
Caesar made dictator for a year, with Antony as his Master
of Horse. The latter administers Italy. Caesar and Cleopatra
cruise the Nile. Birth of Caesarion.

48–30 **Second reign of Cleopatra VII**

47 Tribunate of Dolabella. Senate passes the *senatus consultum
ultimum*, but only when Antony brings troops into Rome
is the tribune suppressed. Caesar returns after Zela campaign.

46 Caesar's third consulship, with Lepidus as colleague. Antony
holds no formal office and perhaps out of favour. Dolabella
taken by Caesar to Africa. Caesar wins African War at
Thapsus. He is made dictator for ten years, with Lepidus as
Master of Horse. Cleopatra and Ptolemy XIV visit Rome
and their rule is formally recognised. Caesar celebrates four
triumphs. Arsinoe appears in the Egyptian triumph.

45 Caesar's fourth consulship. Caesar wins Spanish War at
Munda and returns to celebrate triumph. Antony publicly
restored to favour and named as consul for the next year.
Caesar made dictator for life. Twenty-four-hour consulship
of Caninius Rebilus on 31 December.

45/44 Cleopatra and Ptolemy XIV visit Rome again.

44 Caesar consul for the fifth time with Antony as colleague.
In February, Antony plays a controversial role at the
Lupercal. Caesar is murdered on 15 March. Dolabella
becomes colleague. Antony rallies crowd against
conspirators at Caesar's funeral. Cleopatra returns to Egypt.
Death/murder of Ptolemy XIV. Ptolemy Caesarion made
co-ruler with Cleopatra VII. Antony seeks to build up own
power on the basis of Caesar's notebooks. Cicero begins to
deliver the *Philippics*. Octavian arrives in Rome and accepts
Caesar's legacy. Antony goes to Cisalpine Gaul and besieges
Decimus Brutus at Mutina.

43 Octavian joins the consuls Hirtius and Pansa to defeat
Antony, who retreats into Transalpine Gaul. Hirtius killed
in battle and Pansa dies of wounds. Brutus seizes power in
Macedonia and arrests Caius Antonius. Cassius seizes power
in Syria. Dolabella defeated and commits suicide. Antony

and Lepidus join forces. Octavian made consul in November. Octavian joins Antony and Lepidus to form the triumvirate. Decimus Brutus captured and executed. Caius Antonius is executed in reprisal. The triumvirs occupy Rome and begin proscriptions. Cicero is one of the victims.

42 Julius Caesar deified. Both sides prepare for war. Cleopatra's subordinate in Cyprus aids Cassius, but the queen unsuccessfully attempts to take a squadron of ships to join the triumvirs. The two battles of Philippi are fought in October. Cassius and Brutus defeated and commit suicide. Antony placed in charge of the eastern provinces. Octavian returns to Italy. Power of Sextus Pompey steadily grows, allowing him to blockade Italy.

41 Antony levies taxes and appoints leaders throughout the east. Herod and his brother made tetrarchs in Judaea. Antony summons Cleopatra to Tarsus and they become lovers. Lucius Antonius consul and begins to agitate against Octavian. Arsinoe executed at Ephesus.

41–40 Antony and Cleopatra winter in Alexandria. Perusine War breaks out in Italy, with Lucius Antonius and Fulvia rallying Antony's veterans and dispossessed farmers against Octavian. Antony's commanders fail to intervene effectively and Lucius is besieged in Perusia. He surrenders and is sent to govern Spain, where he dies. Fulvia and Antony's mother Julia flee to Athens.

40 Cleopatra gives birth to the twins, Alexander Helios and Cleopatra Selene. Parthians and their ally Labienus invade and occupy Syria. Labienus invades Asia Minor. Parthians support an attack on Judaea. Hyrcanus deposed. Herod escapes to Egypt, but declines offer of employment from Cleopatra. He goes to Rome. Antony travels to Athens, where he repudiates Fulvia. He sails to Italy and is joined by the Republican Domitius Ahenobarbus. They are refused admission to Brundisium and begin a siege. Reluctance of soldiers to fight each other encourages negotiation and leads to the Treaty of Brundisium. Lepidus marginalised. Octavian and Antony renew their alliance and the latter marries Octavia.

39 Negotiations with Sextus Pompey to relieve the blockade of Italy lead to the Peace of Misenum.

39–38 Antony and Octavia spend winter in Athens. Ventidius Bassus defeats Labienus and the Parthian prince Pacorus in a series of battles, reconquering Asia and Syria.

38	Octavian marries Livia. Renewal of conflict between Octavian and Sextus Pompey. Sextus wins two sea battles. Antony comes to Italy for a meeting, but Octavian fails to turn up. Antony goes to the east and takes over siege of Samosata, which eventually surrenders.
37	Antony again travels to Tarentum. This time negotiations occur and result in the Pact of Tarentum. Antony returns to the east, but sends the pregnant Octavia back to Italy. He appoints several client kings, including Herod, Polemo, Archelaus and Amyntas of Galatia. Antony summons Cleopatra to Antioch and they renew their affair.
36	Sextus Pompey wins another victory, but is then decisively beaten at Naulochos. Lepidus attempts to seize control of Sicily and is deposed, his legions defecting to Octavian. Antony leads disastrous expedition to Media. Cleopatra gives birth to Ptolemy Philadelphus. Antony returns to the Mediterranean coast and summons Cleopatra.
35	Sextus Pompey flees to Asia and is killed. Antony spends winter in Alexandria. Octavia arrives with praetorians and supplies for the army. These are taken, but she is told to return to Italy.
35–33	Octavian campaigns in the Balkans.
34	Antony consul for the second time, but remains in the east and resigns after a day. Antony leads small expedition to Armenia and captures King Artavasdes, probably through treachery. He is taken back to Alexandria and led in a Dionysiac procession into the city. The Donations of Alexandria occur soon afterwards.
33	Octavian consul for the second time, but resigns after a day. Agrippa is aedile and continues his extensive building and amenities programme in Rome. Octavian and his supporters begin more open criticism and attacks on Antony. Antony's army concentrates on the Euphrates, but then he orders it to march to Asia Minor and begins to concentrate his forces in Greece. Antony and Cleopatra spend winter in Ephesus. Powers of the triumvirate formally lapse at end of the year. Octavian pretends to obey this. Antony ignores it and continues to use the title, but talks of laying it down in the future.
32	Domitius Ahenobarbus and Sosius consuls and begin attacks on Octavian. He replies and they flee to Antony. Antony and Cleopatra visit Samos and then Athens. Antony divorces Octavia. Munatius Plancus defects to Octavian. Octavian

takes Antony's will from the Temple of Vesta and has it read publicly. The communities of Italy take an oath of personal loyalty to Octavian. War declared on Cleopatra. Antony and Cleopatra station their forces along the western coast, with their headquarters at Patrae.

31 Octavian consul for the third time. Agrippa captures Methone and then raids as far as Corcyra. Octavian lands in Epirus and moves south to threaten Actium. Antony concentrates at Actium, but comes under blockade after Agrippa captures Leucas, Patrae and Corinth. Antony attempts to break out on 2 September, resulting in the Battle of Actium. Most of his fleet and all his army are abandoned and soon defect or are captured. Antony's legions in Cyrenaica defect to Octavian. He and Cleopatra return to Alexandria. Octavian returns to Italy to deal with mutinous troops and other unrest.

30 Octavian invades Egypt from the east, while Cornelius Gallus invades from the west. Antony's forces defect or are defeated. He kills himself on 1 August. Cleopatra captured by Octavian and there is a period of negotiation. She kills herself on 10 August. Antyllus dragged from the Caesareum and killed. Caesarion betrayed and killed.

29 Octavian returns to Rome and becomes consul for the fourth time. He celebrates three triumphs. Antony and Cleopatra's children are amongst the prisoners in the Egyptian triumph.

27 Octavian given the name Augustus.

*c.*20 King Juba II of Mauretania marries Cleopatra Selene.

13 Death of Lepidus.

12 Octavian becomes *Pontifex Maximus*. Death of Agrippa.

2 Julia exiled. Iullus executed.

14 AD Death of Augustus.

37–41 Reign of Caligula.

40 King Ptolemy of Mauretania (son of Juba and Cleopatra Selene) executed by Caligula.

41–54 Reign of Claudius.

54–68 Reign of Nero.

GLOSSARY

Aedile: The aediles were magistrates responsible for aspects of the day-to-day life of the city of Rome, including the staging of a number of annual festivals. Usually held between the quaestorship and the praetorship, there were fewer aediles than praetors and the post was not a compulsory part of the **cursus honorum**.

Antigonid: The dynasty founded by Antigonus Gonatus controlled Macedonia from the second quarter of the third century BC. Only the Ptolemies and Seleucids rivalled the power of the Antigonids amongst the Successor kingdoms. The last king was deposed by the Romans after his defeat in the Third Macedonian War in 168 BC.

Aquilifer: The standard-bearer who carried the Legion's standard (aquila), a silver or gilded statuette of an eagle mounted on a staff.

Auctoritas: The prestige and influence of a Roman senator. *Auctoritas* was greatly boosted by military achievements.

Augur: One of the most important priestly colleges at Rome, the fifteen augurs were appointed for life. Their most important responsibility was the supervision of the correct observation and interpretation of the auspices, taken regularly as part of Roman public life. Mark Antony became an augur in 50 BC. During his dictatorship, Julius Caesar added a sixteenth member to the college.

Auxilia (auxiliaries): The non-citizen soldiers recruited into the army during the Late Republican were known generally as auxiliaries or supporting troops.

Ballista: A two-armed torsion catapult capable of firing bolts or stones with considerable accuracy. These were built in various sizes and most often used in sieges.

409

Cataphract: Heavily armoured cavalryman often riding an armoured horse. These formed an important component of the Parthian army.

Centurion: Important grade of officers in the Roman army for most of its history; centurions originally commanded a century of eighty men. The most senior centurion of a legion was the *primus pilus*, a post of enormous status held only for a single year.

Century (centuria): The basic sub-unit of the Roman army, the century was commanded by a centurion and usually consisted of eighty men.

Cleruchy (pl. cleruchies): Originally, cleruchs had been soldiers given land (literally, a *kleros* or field) by the Ptolemies and other Successor kings in return for military service. By Cleopatra's day the system had long since decayed. Cleruchies became purely hereditary, passing to daughters as well as sons, and the obligation to serve in the army was forgotten.

Cohort (cohors): The basic tactical unit of the legion, consising of six centuries of eighty soldiers with a total strength of 480.

Comitia Centuriata: The Assembly of the Roman people that elected the most senior magistrates, including the consuls and praetors. It was divided into 193 voting groups of centuries, membership of which was based on property registered in the census. The wealthier members of society had a highly disproportionate influence on the outcome. Its structure was believed to be based on the organisation of the early Roman army.

Comitia Tributa: The Assembly of the entire Roman people, including both patricians and plebians. It was divided into thirty-five voting tribes, membership of which was based on ancestry. It had power to legislate and was presided over by a consul, praetor or curule aedile. It also elected men to a number of posts, including the quaestorship and curule aedileship.

Concilium Plebis: The Assembly of the Roman plebs, whether meeting to legislate or elect certain magistrates such as the tribunes of the plebs. Patricians were not allowed to take part or attend. The people voted in thirty-five tribes, membership of which was based on ancestry. This assembly was presided over by the tribunes of the plebs.

Consul: The year's two consuls were the senior elected magistrates of the Roman Republic and held command in important campaigns. Sometimes the Senate extended their power after their year of office, in which case they were known as proconsuls.

Curia: The Curia (Senate House) building stood on the north side of the Forum Romanum and had traditionally been built by one of the kings. Sulla restored it, but it was burnt down during the funeral of Clodius. As dictator Caesar began work on a new curia. Even when the building was in good condition, on some occasions the Senate could be summoned to meet in other buildings for specific debates.

Cursus honorum: The term given to the career pattern regulating public life. Existing legislation dealing with age and other qualifications for elected magistracies was restated and reinforced by Sulla during his dictatorship.

Demotic: By the Ptolemaic period, Demotic was the form of the Egyptian language used in everyday speech and for writing in cursive script as opposed to hieroglyphics.

Dictator: In times of extreme crisis a dictator was appointed for a six-month period during which he exercised supreme civil and military power. Later victors in civil wars, such as Sulla and Julius Caesar, used the title as a basis for more permanent power.

Dioecetes: The *dioecetes* was the senior financial official of the Ptolemaic king, tasked with overseeing the collection and distribution of all taxes, levies and the product of royal lands.

Ephebe: Adolescent males in Greek cities underwent a process of state-supervised training at the gymnasium. This was mainly concerned with physical fitness, but often included elements of more specifically military training.

Epistrategos: Originally a military post, by Cleopatra's day the *epistrategos* was the civil governor of the Thebiad. Weakness of central government granted this official considerable freedom of action.

Equites (sing. Eques): The 'knights' were the group with the highest property qualification registered by the census. From the time of the Gracchi they were given a more formal public role as jurors in the courts, an issue that became extremely contentious.

Fasces (sing. Fascis): An ornamental bundle of rods some 5 feet long, in the middle of which was an axe. They were carried by **lictors** and were the most visible symbols of a magistrate's power and status.

Forum Romanum: The political and economic heart of the city of Rome that lay between the Capitoline, Palatine, Quirinal and Velian hills. Public meetings were often held either around the **Rostra**, or at the eastern end of the Forum. The **Concilium Plebis** and **Comitia Tributa** also usually met in the Forum to legislate.

Gladius: A Latin word meaning sword, gladius is conventionally used to describe the *gladius hispaniensis*, the Spanish sword that was the standard Roman sidearm until well into the third century AD. Made from high-quality steel, this weapon could be used for cutting, but was primarily intended for thrusting.

Hasmonaean: In the second century BC, Judaea successfully rebelled against the Seleucids. An independent kingdom was created, ruled by the Hasmonaean dynasty. Antony and Octavian eventually installed Herod the Great in place of the old royal family.

Imperium: The power of military command held by magistrates and pro-magistrates during their term of office.

Kinsman: The most senior courtiers at the Ptolemaic court were granted the status of 'kinsmen'.

Lagid: Alternative name for the dynasty founded by Ptolemy I, who was the son of Lagus.

Legatus (pl. Legati): A subordinate officer who held delegated **imperium** rather than exercising power in his own right. *Legati* were chosen by a magistrate rather than elected.

Legion (Legio): Originally a term meaning levy, the legions became the main unit of the Roman army for much of its history. In Caesar's day the theoretical strength of a legion was around 4,800–5,000 men. The effective strength of a legion on campaign, however, was often much lower.

Lictor: The official attendants of a magistrate who carried the **fasces**, which symbolised his right to dispense justice and inflict capital and corporal punishment. Twelve lictors attended a consul, while a dictator was normally given twenty-four.

Magister Equitum: Second-in-command to the Republican **dictator**, the Master of Horse traditionally commanded the cavalry, since the dictator was forbidden to ride a horse.

Nome: The nomes were the basic administrative regions of Ptolemaic Egypt.

In each region an official known as the nomarch controlled agricultural production.

Nomenclator: A specially trained slave whose task was to whisper the names of approaching citizens, permitting his master to greet them in a familiar way. Such a slave normally accompanied a canvassing politician.

Ovatio (ovation): A lesser form of the **triumph**, in an ovation the general rode through the city on horseback rather than in a chariot.

Pilum (pl. pila): The heavy javelin that was the standard equipment of the Roman legionary for much of Rome's history. Its narrow head was designed to punch through an enemy's shield, the long thin shank then giving it the reach to hit the man behind it.

Pontifex Maximus: The head of the college of fifteen pontiffs, one of three major priesthoods monopolised by the Roman aristocracy. The pontiffs regulated the timing of many state festivals and events. The *Pontifex Maximus* was more chairman than leader, but the post was highly prestigious.

Praetor: Praetors were annually elected magistrates who under the Republic governed the less important provinces and fought Rome's smaller wars.

Praetorian cohort: The praetorians in this period were carefully selected and splendidly equipped soldiers drawn from the legions. Each general was entitled to raise a single cohort of praetorians, but in the course of the civil wars Antony came to control several of these formations, taken over from his subordinates.

Prefect (praefectus): An equestrian officer with a range of duties, including the command of units of allied or auxiliary troops.

Quaestor: Magistrates whose duties were primarily financial, quaestors acted as deputies to consular governors and often held subordinate military commands.

Rostra: The speaker's platform in the Forum from which politicians addressed public gatherings.

Saepta: The voting area on the Campus Martius where the various assemblies met to hold elections.

Satrap: The Persian kings had administered their empire by appointing satraps to control each region. Alexander the Great retained the system, and after his

413

death men like Ptolemy I were appointed as satraps. Most subsequently used this as a basis for declaring themselves kings.

Scorpion: The light bolt-shooting **ballista** employed by the Roman army both in the field and in sieges. They possessed a long range, as well as great accuracy and the ability to penetrate any form of armour.

Seleucid: The dynasty founded by Seleucus in the conflicts following Alexander the Great's death was based in Syria. Conflict was frequent between the Seleucids and the Antigonids in Macedonia and Ptolemies in Egypt to control the lands between their kingdoms. Defeated by Rome in 189 BC, the Seleucids nevertheless remained strong until the later years of the second century BC. Parthia rebelled and became independent in the late third century, and by the first century BC controlled much of the old Seleucid Empire. The last Seleucid king, Antiochus XIII, was deposed by Pompey in 64 BC.

Signifer: The standard-bearer who carried the standard (*signum*) of the century.

Strategos (pl. strategoi): Although the word means 'general', by Cleopatra's day the *strategoi* were essentially civilian officials who had replaced the nomarchs in control of the nomes, relegating the later to agricultural administration.

Subura: The valley between the Viminal and Esquiline hills was notorious for its narrow streets and slum housing.

Talent: The actual size of this Greek measurement of weight – and by extension money – varied considerably, from *c.*57–83 lb. It is rarely clear from our sources who employ the term which standard was in use.

Testudo: The famous tortoise formation in which Roman legionaries overlapped their long shield to provide protection to the front, sides and overhead. It was most often used during assaults on fortifications.

Thebiad: The region around the capital of Thebes, the ancient capital of the Upper Kingdom of Egypt. It consisted of seven nomes.

Tribune of the plebs: Although holding a political office without direct military responsibilities, the ten tribunes of the plebs elected each year were able to legislate on any issue. During the later years of the Republic many ambitious generals, such as Marius, Pompey and Caesar, enlisted the aid of tribunes to secure important commands for themselves.

Tribuni aerarii: The group registered below the equestrian order in the census. Relatively little is known about them.

Tribunus militum (military tribune): Six military tribunes were elected or appointed to each Republican legion, one pair of these men holding command at any one time.

Triumph: The great celebration granted by the Senate to a successful general took the form of a procession along the Via Sacra, the ceremonial main road of Rome, displaying the spoils and captives of his victory and culminated in the ritual execution of the captured enemy leader. The commander rode in a chariot, dressed like the statues of Jupiter, a slave holding a laurel wreath of victory over his head. The slave was supposed to whisper to the general, reminding him that he was mortal.

Triumvir: In 43 BC, Antony, Lepidus and Octavian were named as *triumviri rei publicae constituendae* (board of three to reconstitute the state) by the *Lex Titia* proposed by a tribune and passed by the **Concilium Plebis**. The triumvirate was granted dictatorial powers, initially for five years.

Uraeus: The snake-shaped headband worn at times by the Ptolemies as a symbol of monarchy. Double uraei are typical, probably symbolising the two kingdoms of Egypt. Triple uraei appear on some images identified as Cleopatra, but the precise significance of this is unclear.

Vexillum: A square flag mounted crosswise on a pole, the *vexillum* was used to mark a general's position and was also the standard carried by a detachment of troops. A general's *vexillum* seems usually to have been red.

ABBREVIATIONS

Appian, *BC* = Appian, *Civil Wars.*

Broughton, *MRR* 2 = Broughton, T., & Patterson, M., *The Magistrates of the Roman Republic*, Vol. 2 (1951).

Caesar, *BC* = Caesar, *The Civil Wars.*

Caesar, *BG* = Caesar, *The Gallic Wars.*

CAH² IX = Crook, J., Lintott, A., & Rawson, E. (eds.), *The Cambridge Ancient History* 2nd edn, Vol. IX: *The Last Age of the Roman Republic, 146–43 BC* (1994).

CAH² X = Bowman, A., Champlin, E., & Lintott, A. (eds.), *The Cambridge Ancient History* 2nd edn, Vol. X: *The Augustan Empire, 43 BC–AD 69* (1996).

Cicero, *ad Att.* = Cicero, *Letters to Atticus.*

Cicero, *ad Fam.* = Cicero, *Letters to his Friends.*

Cicero, *ad Quintum Fratrem* = Cicero, *Letters to his Brother Quintus.*

Cicero, *Agr.* = Cicero, *Orationes de Lege Agraria.*

Cicero, *De reg. Alex. F.* = Cicero, fragment from the *Oration Concerning the King of Alexandria.*

Cicero, *Verrines* = Cicero, *Verrine Orations.*

CIG = *Corpus Inscriptionum Graecarum.*

CIL = *Corpus Inscriptionum Latinarum.*

De vir. Ill. = the anonymous *De viris illustribus.*

Dio = Cassius Dio, *Roman History.*

Galen, *Comm. In Hipp. Epid., CMG* = Kühn, C., *Galenus Medicus* (1821–1833), supplemented by Diels, H. et al. (1918–).

Gellius, *NA* = Aulus Gellius, *Attic Nights.*

ILS = Dessau, H. (ed.), *Inscriptiones Latinae Selectae* (1892–1916).

Josephus, *AJ* = Josephus, *Jewish Antiquities.*

Josephus, *BJ* = Josephus, *The Jewish War.*

JRA = *Journal of Roman Archaeology.*

JRS = *Journal of Roman Studies.*

Livy, *Pers.* = Livy, *Roman History: Periochae.*

OGIS = Dittenberger, W., *Orientis Graeci Inscriptiones Selectae* (1903–1905).

PIR¹ = Kelbs, E., et al., *Prosopographia Imperii Romani* (1933–).

Pliny, *Epistulae* = Pliny the Younger, *Letters.*
Pliny, *NH* = Pliny the Elder, *Natural History.*
Quintilian = Quintilian, *Training in Oratory.*
RIB = Collingwood, R., & Wright, R., *Roman Inscriptions in Britain* (1965–).
Sallust, *Bell. Cat.* = Sallust, *The Catilinarian War.*
Sallust, *Bell. Jug.* = Sallust, *The Jugurthine War.*
SEG = Roussel, P., Tod, M., Ziebarth, E., & Hondius, J. (eds.), *Supplementum Epigraphicum Graecum* (1923–).
Serv. = Servius.
Strabo, *Geog.* = Strabo, *Geography.*
Valerius Maximus = Valerius Maximus, *Memorable Doings and Sayings.*
Velleius Paterculus = Velleius Paterculus, *Roman History*.

BIBLIOGRAPHY

Books

Adcock, F., *The Roman Art of War under the Republic* (1940).

Ashton, S., *The Last Queens of Egypt* (2003).

Ashton, S., *Cleopatra and Egypt* (2008).

Austin, M., *The Hellenistic World from Alexander to the Roman Conquest: A Selection of Ancient Sources in Translation* (1981).

Austin, N., & Rankov, B., *Exploratio: Military and Political Intelligence in the Roman World from the Second Punic War to the Battle of Adrianople* (1995).

Badian, E., *Publicans and Sinners* (1972).

Bagnall, R., & Frier, B., *The Demography of Roman Egypt* (1994).

Barrett, A., *Livia: First Lady of Imperial Rome* (2002).

Beard, M., *The Roman Triumph* (2007).

Bernard, A., *Alexandrie des Ptolémées* (1995).

Bernard, A., *Alexandrie la Grande* (1998).

Bianchi, R., *Cleopatra's Egypt: Age of the Ptolemies* (1988).

Bingen, J., *Hellenistic Egypt: Monarchy, Society, Economy, Culture* (2007).

Bowman, A., *Egypt after the Pharaohs: 332 BC–AD 642 – from Alexander to the Arab conquest* (1986).

Broughton, T., & Patterson, M., *The Magistrates of the Roman Republic*, Vol. 2 (1951).

Brunt, P., *Italian Manpower 225 BC–AD 14* (1971).

Burnstein, S., *The Reign of Cleopatra* (2004).

Carter, J., *The Battle of Actium: The Rise and Triumph of Augustus Caesar* (1970).

Cartledge, P., *Alexander the Great: The Hunt for a New Past* (2004).

Chauveau, M., *Egypt in the Age of Cleopatra* (trans. Lorton, D.) (2000).

Crawford, M., *Roman Republican Coinage* (1974).

Cunliffe, B., *Greeks, Romans and Barbarians: Spheres of Interaction* (1988).

Dixon, N., *On the Psychology of Military Incompetence* (1994).

Dixon, S., *The Roman Mother* (1988).

Dunand, F., & Zivie-Coche, C., *Gods and Men in Egypt 3000 BCE to 395 BCE* (trans. Lorton, D.) (2002).

Ellis, W., *Ptolemy of Egypt* (1994).

Empereur, J-Y., *Alexandria Rediscovered* (1998).

Evans, R., *Gaius Marius* (1994).

Finneran, N., *Alexandria: A City and Myth* (2005).

Fletcher, J., *Cleopatra the Great: The Woman Behind the Legend* (hardback 2008, paperback 2009).

Fraser, P., *Ptolemaic Alexandria*, 3 Vols. (1972).

Gabba, E., *The Roman Republic, the Army and the Allies* (trans. Cuff, P.) (1976).

Gelzer, M., *Caesar* (trans. Needham, P.) (1968).

Goddio, F., *L'Égypte Engloutie: Alexandrie* (2002).

Goddio, F., with Bernard, A., Bernard, E., Darwish, I., Kiss, Z., & Yoyotte, J., *Alexandria: The Submerged Royal Quarters* (1998).

Goldsworthy, A., *The Roman Army at War 100 BC–AD 200* (1996).

Goldsworthy, A., *In the Name of Rome* (2003).

Goldsworthy, A., *Caesar: The Life of a Colossus* (2006).

Grant, M., *Cleopatra* (1972).

Green, P., *Alexander to Actium: The Historical Evolution of the Hellenistic Age* (1990).

Grenfell, B., Hunt, A., et al. (eds.), *The Oxyrhynchus Papyri* (1898–).

Grimal, P., *Love in Ancient Rome* (1986).

Grimm, G., *Alexandria: Die erste Königsstadt der hellenistischen Welt* (1998).

Gruen, E., *Roman Politics and the Criminal Courts, 149–78 BC* (1968).

Gruen, E., *The Last Generation of the Roman Republic* (1974).

Gruen, E., *The Hellenistic World and the Coming of Rome*, Vol. 2 (1984).

Gwynn, A., *Roman Education* (1926).

Hamer, M., *Signs of Cleopatra: History, Politics, Representation* (1993).

Hardy, E., *The Catilinarian Conspiracy in its Context: A Re-study of the Evidence* (1924).

Hölbl, G., *A History of the Ptolemaic Empire* (trans. Saavedra, T.) (2001).

Hopkins, K., *Conquerors and Slaves* (1978).

Hughes-Hallett, L., *Cleopatra: Queen, Lover, Legend* (1990, reprinted with new afterword 2006).

Jeffrey Tatum, W., *The Patrician Tribune: Publius Clodius Pulcher* (1999).

Keaveney, A., *Sulla: The Last Republican* (1982).

Keppie, L., *The Making of the Roman Army* (1984).

Kleiner, D., *Cleopatra and Rome* (2005).

Lampela, A., *Rome and the Ptolemies of Egypt: The Development of their Political Relations 273–80 BC* (1998).

Lane Fox, R., *The Classical World: An Epic History from Homer to Hadrian* (2006).

Lewis, N., *Greeks in Ptolemaic Egypt: Case Studies in the Social History of the Hellenistic World* (1986).

Lintott, A., *The Constitution of the Roman Republic* (1999).

Marrou, H., *A History of Education in Antiquity* (1956).

Matyszak, P., *Mithridates the Great: Rome's Indomitable Enemy* (2008).

Mayor, A., *The Poison King: The Life and Legend of Mithridates* (2009).

Meier, C., *Caesar* (trans. McLintock, D.) (1996).

Millar, F., *The Crowd in the Late Roman Republic* (1998).

Mitchell, T., *Cicero: The Ascending Years* (1979).

Mitchell, T., *Cicero: The Senior Statesman* (1991).

Morrison, J., & Coates, J., *Greek and Roman Oared Warships* (1996).

Mouritsen, H., *Plebs and Politics in the Late Roman Republic* (2001).

Murray, W., & Petsas, P., *Octavian's Campsite Memorial for the Actian War*, Transactions of the American Philosophical Society 79. 4 (1989), pp. 133–134.

Osgood, J., *Caesar's Legacy: Civil War and the Emergence of the Roman Empire* (2006).

Parkin, T., *Demography and Roman Society* (1992).

Pelling, C. (ed.), *Plutarch: Life of Antony* (1988).

Pitassi, M., *The Navies of Rome* (2009).

Pomeroy, S., *Women in Hellenistic Egypt* (1984).

Powell, A., *Virgil the Partisan: A Study in the Re-integration of Classics* (2008).

Preston, D., & Preston, M., *Cleopatra and Antony* (2008).

Rawson, B., *Children and Childhood in Roman Italy* (2003).

Rawson, E., *Cicero* (1975).

Rice, E., *Cleopatra* (1999).

Rice Holmes, T., *The Roman Republic and the Founder of the Empire*, 3 Vols. (1923–1928).

Rich, J., *Declaring War in the Roman Republic in the Period of Transmarine Expansion* (1976).

Roberts, A., *Mark Antony: His Life and Times* (1988).

Roth, J., *The Logistics of the Roman Army at War (264 BC–AD 235)* (1999).

Roymans, N., *Tribal Societies in Northern Gaul: An Anthropological Perspective*, Cingula 12 (1990).

Saller, R., *Personal Patronage in the Early Empire* (1982).

Samuel, A., *From Athens to Alexandria: Hellenism and Social Goals in Ptolemaic Egypt* (1983).

Scheidel, W., *Measuring Sex, Age, and Death in the Roman Empire: Explorations in Ancient Demography*, JRA Supplementary Series 21 (1996).

Scheidel, W., *Death on the Nile: Disease and the Demography of Roman Egypt* (2001).

Schürer, E., Vermes, G., & Millar, F., *The History of the Jewish People in the Age of Jesus Christ*, Vol. 1 (1973).

Seager, R., *Pompey the Great* (2nd edn, 2002).

Shaw, I. (ed.), *The Oxford History of Ancient Egypt* (2000).

Sheppard, S., *Actium: Downfall of Antony and Cleopatra*, Osprey Campaign Series 211 (2009).

Sherk, R., *Roman Documents from the Greek East* (1969).

Sherwin-White, A., *Roman Foreign Policy in the East 168 BC to AD 1* (1984).
Shipley, G., *The Greek World after Alexander 323–30 BC* (2000).
Southern, P., *Mark Antony* (1998).
Southern, P., *Antony and Cleopatra* (hardback 2007, paperback 2009).
Stockton, D., *Cicero: A Political Biography* (1971).
Syme, R., *The Roman Revolution* (1939, paperback 1960).
Taylor, L., *Party Politics in the Age of Caesar* (1949).
Taylor, L., *Roman Voting Assemblies: From the Hannibalic War to the Dictatorship of Caesar* (1966).
Thompson, D., *Memphis under the Ptolemies* (1988).
Treggiari, S., *Roman Marriage* (1991).
Tyldesley, J., *Cleopatra: Last Queen of Egypt* (hardback 2008, paperback 2009).
Walbank, F., *The Hellenistic World* (3rd edn, 1992).
Walker, S., & Higgs, P. (eds.), *Cleopatra of Egypt: From History to Myth* (2001).
Walker, S., & Ashton, S. (eds.), *Cleopatra Reassessed* (2003).
Ward, A., *Marcus Crassus and the Late Roman Republic* (1977).
Watson, G., *The Roman Soldier* (1969).
Weigel, R., *Lepidus: The Tarnished Triumvir* (1992).
Welch, K., & Powell, A. (eds.), *Sextus Pompeius* (2002).
Weinstock, S., *Divus Julius* (1971).
Yazetz, Z., *Julius Caesar and his Public Image* (1983).
Zanker, P., *The Power of Images in the Age of Augustus* (trans. Shapiro, A.) (1988).

Articles

Badian, E., 'The Early Career of A. Gabinius (cos. 58 BC)', *Philologus* 103 (1958), pp. 87–99.
Bagnall, R., 'Greeks and Egyptians: Ethnicity, Status and Culture', in Bianchi, R. (ed.), *Cleopatra's Egypt: Age of the Ptolemies* (1988), pp. 21–25.
Bennett, C., 'Cleopatra Tryphaena and the Genealogy of the Later Ptolemies', *Ancient Society* 28 (1997), pp. 39–66.
Bradley, K., 'Wet-nursing at Rome: A Study in Social Relations', in Rawson, B. (ed.), *The Family in Ancient Rome* (1986), pp. 201–229.
Carson, R., 'Caesar and the Monarchy', *Greece and Rome* 4 (1957), pp. 46–53.
Clarysee, W., 'Greeks and Egyptians in the Ptolemaic Army and Administration', *Aegyptus* 65 (1985), pp. 57–66.
Clarysee, W., 'Ethnic Diversity and Dialect among the Greeks of Egypt', in Verhoogt, A., & Vleeming, S. (eds.), *The Two Faces of Graeco-Roman Egypt: Greek and Demotic and Greek-Demotic Texts and Studies Presented to P. W. Pestman* (1998), pp. 1–13.
Erskine, A., 'Culture and Power in Ptolemaic Egypt: The Museum and Library of Alexandria', *Greece & Rome* 42 (1995), pp. 38–48.
Fraser, P., 'Mark Antony in Alexandria – A Note', *JRS* 47 (1957), pp. 71–74.

Gabba, E., 'The Perusine War and Triumviral Italy', *Harvard Studies in Classical Philology* 75 (1971), pp. 139–160.

Goudchaux, G., 'Cleopatra's Subtle Religious Strategy', in Walker, S., & Higgs, P. (eds.), *Cleopatra of Egypt: From History to Myth* (2001), pp. 128–141.

Goudchaux, G., 'Was Cleopatra Beautiful? The Conflicting Answers of Numismatics', in Walker, S., & Higgs, P. (eds.), *Cleopatra of Egypt: From History to Myth* (2001), pp. 210–214.

Goudchaux, G., 'Cleopatra the Seafarer Queen: Strabo and India', in Walker, S., & Ashton, S. (eds.), *Cleopatra Reassessed* (2003), pp. 109–111.

Grimm, G., 'Alexandria in the Time of Cleopatra', in Walker, S., & Ashton, S. (eds.), *Cleopatra Reassessed* (2003), pp. 45–49.

Gruen, E., 'P. Clodius: Instrument or Independent Agent?', *Phoenix* 20 (1966), pp. 120–130.

Gruen, E., 'Cleopatra in Rome: Facts and Fantasies', in Braund, D., & Gill, C. (eds.), *Myths, History and Culture in Republican Rome: Studies in Honour of T. P. Wiseman* (2003), pp. 257–274.

Hammond, N., 'The Macedonian Imprint on the Hellenistic World', in Green, P. (ed.), *Hellenistic History and Culture* (1993), pp. 12–37.

Harrington, D., 'The Battle of Actium: A Study in Historiography', *Ancient World* 9. 1–2 (1984), pp. 59–64.

Huzar, E., 'Mark Antony: Marriages vs. Careers', *The Classical Journal* 81. 2 (1986), pp. 97–111.

Johansen, F., 'Portraits of Cleopatra – Do They Exist?' in Walker, S., & Ashton, S. (eds.), *Cleopatra Reassessed* (2003), pp. 75–77.

Johnson, J., 'The Authenticity and Validity of Antony's Will', *L'Antiquité Classique* 47 (1978), pp. 494–503.

Kennedy, D., 'Parthia and Rome: Eastern Perspectives', in Kennedy, D. (ed.), *The Roman Army in the East, JRA* Supplement 18 (1996), pp. 67–90.

Keppie, L., 'A Centurion of *Legio Martia* at Padova?', *Journal of Roman Military Equipment Studies* 2 (1991), pp. 115–121 (also published as Keppie, L., *Legions and Veterans: Roman Army Papers 1971–2000* (2000), pp. 68–74.

Keppie, L., 'Mark Antony's Legions', in Keppie, L., *Legions and Veterans: Roman Army Papers 1971–2000* (2000), pp. 75–96.

Lintott, A., 'P. Clodius Pulcher – Felix Catilina', *Greece and Rome* 14 (1967), pp. 157–169.

Lintott, A., 'Electoral Bribery in the Roman Republic', *JRS* 80 (1990), pp. 1–16.

Maehler, H., 'Alexandria, the Mouseion, and Cultural Identity', in Hirst, A., & Silk, M. (eds.), *Alexandria, Real and Imagined* (2004), pp. 1–14.

Mendels, D., 'The Ptolemaic Character of Manetho's *Aegyptica*', in Verdin, H., Schepens, G., & De Keyser, E. (eds.), *Purposes of History: Proceeding of the International Colloquim – Leuven, 24–26 May 1988* (1990), pp. 91–110.

Millar, F., 'Triumvirate and Principate', *JRS* 63 (1973), pp. 50–67.

Murray, W., 'The Development and Design of Greek and Roman Warships (399–30 BC)', *JRA* 12 (1999), pp. 520–525.

Purcell, N., 'Literate Games: Roman Urban Society and the Game of *Alea*', *Past & Present* 147 (1995), pp. 3–37.

Rankov, B., 'The Second Punic War at Sea', in Cornell, T., Rankov, B., & Sabin, P. (eds.), *The Second Punic War: A Reappraisal* (1996), pp. 49–56.

Rathbone, D., 'Villages, Land and Population in Graeco-Roman Egypt', *Proceedings of the Cambridge Philological Society* 36 (1990), pp. 103–142.

Rathbone, D., 'Ptolemaic to Roman Egypt: The Death of the Dirigiste State?', in Lo Cascio, E., & Rathbone, D. (eds.), *Production and Public Powers in Classical Antiquity* (2000), pp. 44–54.

Rawson, E., 'Caesar's Heritage: Hellenistic Kings and their Roman Equals', *JRS* 65 (1975), pp. 148–159.

Ray, J., 'Alexandria', in Walker, S., & Higgs, P. (eds.), *Cleopatra of Egypt: From History to Myth* (2001), pp. 32–37.

Ray, J., 'Cleopatra in the Temples of Upper Egypt: The Evidence of Dendera and Armant', in Walker, S., & Ashton, S. (eds.), *Cleopatra Reassessed* (2003), pp. 9–11.

Rundell, W., 'Cicero and Clodius: The Question of Credibility', *Historia* 28 (1979), pp. 301–328.

Salmon, E., 'Catiline, Crassus, and Caesar', *American Journal of Philology* 56 (1935), pp. 302–316.

Salway, B., 'What's in a Name? A Survey of Roman Onomastic Practice from 700 BC–AD 700', *JRS* 84 (1994), pp. 124–145.

Scott, K., 'The Political Propaganda of 44–30 BC', *Memoirs of the American Academy in Rome* 11 (1933), pp. 7–49.

Seaver, J., 'Publius Ventidius: Neglected Roman Military Hero', *The Classical Journal* 47 (1952), pp. 275–280 and 300.

Siani-Davies, M., 'Ptolemy XII Auletes and the Romans', *Historia* 46 (1997), pp. 306–340.

Syme, R., 'The Allegiance of Labienus,' *JRS* 28 (1938), pp. 113–125.

Tait, J., 'Cleopatra by Name', in Walker, S., & Ashton, S. (eds.), *Cleopatra Reassessed* (2003), pp. 3–7.

Tarn, W. 'The Bucheum Stelae: A Note', *JRS* 26 (1936), pp. 187–189.

Tchernia, A., 'Italian Wine in Gaul at the End of the Republic', in Garnsey, P., Hopkins, K., & Whittaker, C. (eds.), *Trade in the Ancient Economy* (1983), pp. 87–104.

Thompson, D., 'Cleopatra VII: The Queen in Egypt', in Walker, S., & Ashton, S. (eds.), *Cleopatra Reassessed* (2003), pp. 31–34.

Tyrell, W., 'Labienus' Departure from Caesar in January 49 BC', *Historia* 21 (1972), pp. 424–440.

Ullman, B., 'Cleopatra's Pearls', *The Classical Journal* 52. 5 (Feb. 1957), pp. 193–201.

van Minnen, P., 'An Official Act of Cleopatra (with a Subscription in her Own Hand)', *Ancient Society* 30 (2000), pp. 29–34.

van Minnen, P., 'A Royal Ordinance of Cleopatra and Related Documents', in Walker, S., & Ashton, S. (eds.), *Cleopatra Reassessed* (2003), pp. 35–44.

Walker, S., 'Cleopatra's Images: Reflections of Reality', in Walker, S., & Higgs, P. (eds.), *Cleopatra of Egypt: From History to Myth* (2001), pp. 142–147.

Walker, S., 'Cleopatra VII at the Louvre', in Walker, S., & Ashton, S. (eds.), *Cleopatra Reassessed* (2003), pp. 71–74.

Welch, K., 'Caesar and his Officers in the Gallic War Commentaries', in Welch, K., & Powell, A. (eds.), *Julius Caesar as Artful Reporter: The War Commentaries as Political Instruments* (1998), pp. 85–110.

Winnicki, J., 'Carrying off and Bringing Home the Statues of the Gods', *Journal of Juristic Papyrology* 24 (1994), pp. 149–190.

Yakobson, A., 'Petitio et Largitio: Popular Participation in the Centuriate Assembly of the Late Republic', *JRS* 8 (1992), pp. 32–52.

NOTES

INTRODUCTION

[1] Plutarch, *Caesar* 15 for the figures of 1 million dead and as many enslaved during the Gallic campaigns.

[2] Quote from P. Green, *Alexander to Actium: The Historical Evolution of the Hellenistic Age* (1990), p.664.

[3] In just the last few years, several biographies of Cleopatra were published, including J. Tyldesley, *Cleopatra: Last Queen of Egypt* (hardback 2008, paperback 2009), J. Fletcher, *Cleopatra the Great: The Woman Behind the Legend* (hardback 2008, paperback 2009) and the briefer S. Ashton, *Cleopatra and Egypt* (2008), which followed on from the same author's *The Last Queens of Egypt* (2003). Other recent offerings include S. Burnstein, *The Reign of Cleopatra* (2004), and E. Rice, *Cleopatra* (1999). There were also two biographies of the couple: D. Preston & M. Preston, *Cleopatra and Antony* (2008), which notably reversed the usual order of their names to emphasise Cleopatra, and P. Southern, *Antony and Cleopatra* (hardback 2007, paperback 2009), which was based on earlier individual biographies of the couple by the same author. There have been no biographies dedicated to Antony since P. Southern, *Mark Antony* (1998), and A. Roberts, *Mark Antony: His Life and Times* (1988), and books devoted to Cleopatra have always been far more common. The same is true of TV documentaries.

[4] R. Syme, *The Roman Revolution* (1939, paperback 1960) remains one of the most important studies of this period. Writing as fascist dictators in Germany and Italy threatened a new World War, he had little taste for Octavian. This encouraged a generosity in his treatment of Antony – 'the frank and chivalrous soldier', Syme (1960), p.104.

[5] For general studies of the Hellenistic period, see F. Walbank, *The Hellenistic World* (3rd edn, 1992), G. Shipley, *The Greek World after Alexander 323–30 BC* (2000), and Green (1990).

[6] Both Tyldesley and Fletcher are Egyptologists, and naturally develop these threads more strongly and in greater detail than Greek or Roman elements. For instance, note the allusions to Hatshepsut, who ruled as a female pharaoh in the fifteenth century BC, in Tyldesley (2009), pp.45, 121, Fletcher (2008), pp.43, 82–83, 86, and the particular concern for traditional iconography. This in itself is no bad thing and particularly valuable to Classicists who lack knowledge of earlier Egyptian history. The danger is that it comes to dominate the narrative of Cleopatra's own times and culture. Ashton

425

has more of a background in Classics, but openly chose to emphasise the Egyptian aspects of the queen, feeling that these had been neglected, and wanted 'to consider her as a ruler of Egypt, not as a Greek monarch' – Ashton (2008), p.3, cf. p.1. Her study focused in particular on representations of the queen in art.

[7] P. van Minnen, 'An Official Act of Cleopatra (with a Subscription in her Own Hand)', *Ancient Society* 30 (2000), pp.29–34.

[8] Plutarch, see the excellent commentary provided by C. Pelling (ed.), *Plutarch: Life of Antony* (1988).

[9] The comment was made by W. Tarn, in S. Cook, F. Adcock & M. Charlesworth (eds.), *The Cambridge Ancient History*, Vol. X: *The Augustan Empire 44 BC–AD 70* (1934, reprinted with corrections 1952), p.111–'For Rome, who had never condescended to fear any nation or people, did in her time fear two human beings; one was Hannibal, and the other was a woman.'

I THE TWO LANDS

[1] An Egyptian priest named Manetho drew up the list of pharaohs as part of a history he wrote in Greek at the request of Ptolemy II. It survives only in fragments quoted in much later sources, see D. Mendels, 'The Ptolemaic Character of Manetho's *Aegyptica*', in H. Verdin, G. Schepens & E. De Keyser, *Purposes of History: Proceeding of the International Colloquim – Leuven, 24–26 May 1988* (1990), pp.91–110. For earlier Egyptian history in general, a useful introduction is I. Shaw (ed.), *The Oxford History of Ancient Egypt* (2000).

[2] For claims about the size of Egypt's population, see Josephus, *BJ* 2. 385, Diodorus Siculus 1. 31. 6–9, with R. Bagnall & B. Frier, *The Demography of Roman Egypt* (1994), T. Parkin, *Demography and Roman Society* (1992), W. Scheidel, *Measuring Sex, Age, and Death in the Roman Empire: Explorations in Ancient Demography, JRA* Supplementary Series 21 (1996), and D. Rathbone, 'Villages, Land and Population in Graeco-Roman Egypt', *Proceedings of the Cambridge Philological Society* 36 (1990), pp.103–142.

[3] See F. Dunand & C. Zivie-Coche, *Gods and Men in Egypt 3000 BCE to 395 CE* (trans. D. Lorton) (2002), esp. pp.197–199.

[4] Plutarch, *Caesar* 11, Suetonius, *Caesar* 7. 1–2, and Dio 37. 52. 2.

[5] P. Green, *Alexander to Actium: The Historical Evolution of the Hellenistic Age* (1990), pp.3–7, and F. Walbank, *The Hellenistic World* (3rd edn with amendments, 1992), pp.29–45.

[6] For discussion and sources see Green, (1990), pp.3–20.

[7] J. Bingen, *Hellenistic Egypt: Monarchy, Society, Economy, Culture* (2007), p.24.

[8] For Ptolemy I's career see W. Ellis, *Ptolemy of Egypt* (1994); on language see W. Clarysee, 'Ethnic Diversity and Dialect among the Greeks of Egypt', in A. Verhoogt & S. Vleeming (eds.), *The Two Faces of Graeco-Roman Egypt: Greek and Demotic and Greek-Demotic Texts and Studies Presented to P. W. Pestman* (1998), pp.1–13.

[9] For introductory discussion of what happened at Siwah see P. Cartledge, *Alexander the Great: The Hunt for a New Past* (2004), pp.265–270.

[10] Walbank, (1992), pp.108–110.

[11] W. Scheidel, *Death on the Nile: Disease and the Demography of Roman Egypt* (2001), pp.184–248.

[12] R. Bagnall, 'Greeks and Egyptians: Ethnicity, Status and Culture', in R. Bianchi (ed.), *Cleopatra's Egypt: Age of the Ptolemies* (1988), pp.21–25, N. Lewis, *Greeks in Ptolemaic*

Egypt: Case Studies in the Social History of the Hellenistic World (1986), pp.26–35, 69–87 and 124–154; the soldier's will, see W. Clarysee, 'Greeks and Egyptians in the Ptolemaic Army and Administration', *Aegyptus* 65 (1985), pp.57–66, esp. 65.
[13] Lewis (1986), pp.104–123, and Clarysee (1985), pp.57–66.

II THE 'SHE-WOLF': ROME'S REPUBLIC

[1] A. Lampela, *Rome and the Ptolemies of Egypt: The Development of their Political Relations 273–80 BC* (1998), pp.50–51, E. Gruen, *The Hellenistic World and the Coming of Rome*. Vol. 2 (1984), pp.672–719, esp. 673–678, and P. Green, *Alexander to Actium: The Historical Evolution of the Hellenistic Age* (1990), pp.146 and 231.
[2] Gruen (1984), pp.674–677.
[3] F. Walbank, *The Hellenistic World* (3rd impression, 1992), pp.228–240. There was brief reluctance on the part of the Roman people to vote for war so soon after the end of the Second Punic War. This reluctance was quickly overcome, see Livy 31. 5–9.
[4] Polybius 1. 1. 5 (Loeb translation by W. Paton (1922)).
[5] On the development of the army see L. Keppie, *The Making of the Roman Army* (1984), pp.14–63, and in general F. Adcock, *The Roman Art of War under the Republic* (1940), P. Brunt, *Italian Manpower 225 BC–AD 14* (1971), and E. Gabba, *The Roman Republic, the Army and the Allies* (trans. P. Cuff) (1976).
[6] E. Badian, *Publicans and Sinners* (1972).
[7] For the economic impact of imperialism see K. Hopkins, *Conquerors and Slaves* (1978); on the wine trade see B. Cunliffe, *Greeks, Romans and Barbarians: Spheres of Interaction* (1988), pp.59–105, esp. p.74, N. Roymans, *Tribal Societies in Northern Gaul: An Anthropological Perspective*, Cingula 12 (1990), pp.147–167, and A. Tchernia, 'Italian Wine in Gaul at the End of the Republic', in P. Garnsey, K. Hopkins & C. Whittaker (eds.), *Trade in the Ancient Economy* (1983), pp.87–104.
[8] Plutarch, *Tiberius Gracchus* 9 (Penguin translation by I. Scott-Kilvert (1965)).
[9] Catullus 10; Cicero, *Verrines* 1. 40.
[10] See M. Beard, *The Roman Triumph* (2007) for a detailed discussion of triumphs, emphasising in particular the variations in ritual.

III THE PTOLEMIES

[1] For spear-won land and the nature of Hellenistic kingship see P. Green, *Alexander to Actium: The Historical Evolution of the Hellenistic Age* (1990), pp.5, 187, 194, 198 and 367, and N. Hammond, 'The Macedonian Imprint on the Hellenistic World', in P. Green (ed.), *Hellenistic History and Culture* (1993), pp.12–37.
[2] See J. Bingen, *Hellenistic Egypt: Monarchy, Society, Economy, Culture* (2007), pp.15–30, esp. 18–19; for stories that Philip was his father see Curtius 9. 8. 22, Pausanius 1. 6. 2.
[3] R. Bianchi, *Cleopatra's Egypt: Age of the Ptolemies* (1988), pp.29–39, F. Dunand & C. Zivie-Coche, *Gods and Men in Egypt 3000 BCE–395 BCE* (trans. D. Lorton) (2002), pp.197–341, esp. pp.199–210, N. Lewis, *Greeks in Ptolemaic Egypt: Case Studies in the Social History of the Hellenistic World* (1986), pp.4–5, and M. Chauveau, *Egypt in the Age of Cleopatra* (trans. D. Lorton) (2000), pp.37–39, 100–109; on the return of objects taken by the Persians see J. Winnicki, 'Carrying off and Bringing Home the Statues of the Gods', *Journal of Juristic Papyrology* 24 (1994), pp.149–190.
[4] Diodorus Siculus 20. 100. 3–4, with Green (1990), pp.32–33.

[5] In general see A. Erskine, 'Culture and Power in Ptolemaic Egypt: The Museum and Library of Alexandria', *Greece & Rome* 42 (1995), pp.38–48, and G. Shipley, *The Greek World after Alexander 323–30 BC* (2000), p.243; on the aggressive acquisition of books see Galen, *Comm. In Hipp. Epid. iii, CMG* 5. 10. 2. 1, pp.78–79.

[6] See Shipley (2000), p.139.

[7] For Arsinoe in general see S. Pomeroy, *Women in Hellenistic Egypt* (1984), pp.14–20, and Bingen (2007), pp.30–31.

[8] Polybius 5. 34. 1–11, 15. 25. 1–33.13.

[9] Polybius 5. 107. 1–3, and in general Shipley (2000), pp.203–205.

[10] M. Austin, *The Hellenistic World from Alexander to the Roman Conquest: A Selection of Ancient Sources in Translation* (1981), p.227.

[11] Polybius 15. 20. 1–2.

[12] Polybius 29. 27. 1–11, Livy 45. 12. 3–8.

[13] Green (1990), pp.442–446.

[14] Green (1990), pp.537–543, Pomeroy (1984), pp.23–24, and Chauveau (2000), pp.14–16.

[15] Polybius 34. 14. 1–7, Strabo, *Geog.* 17. 1. 12.

[16] Lewis (1986), pp.15–20 and 29–30, A. Samuel, *From Athens to Alexandria: Hellenism and Social Goals in Ptolemaic Egypt* (1983), pp.110–117, and Shipley (2000), pp.232–234; for the Potter's Oracle see S. Burnstein, *The Reign of Cleopatra* (2004), pp.142–143.

[17] See Green (1990), pp.158–160.

[18] Diodorus 33. 28b.1–3, Athenaeus 6. 273a.

IV THE ORATOR, THE SPENDTHRIFT AND THE PIRATES

[1] On childbirth in this period see B. Rawson, *Children and Childhood in Roman Italy* (2003), esp. pp.99–113; for an especially poignant tombstone see that of 'Ertola, properly called Vellibia, who lived most happily four years and sixty days' from Corbridge, which is decorated with a child-like carving of the little girl playing with a ball, *RIB* 1181. There was also a tradition of very specific ages, even for adults, on tombstones in some parts of Italy.

[2] For a general survey of the significance of Roman names see B. Salway, 'What's in a Name? A Survey of Roman Onomastic Practice from 700 BC–AD 700', *JRS* 84 (1994), pp.124–145, esp. pp.124–131.

[3] Cicero, *Brutus* 138–141 (Loeb translation).

[4] Valerius Maximus 3. 7. 9, 6. 8. 1, and see E. Gruen, *Roman Politics and the Criminal Courts, 149–78 BC* (1968), pp.127–132.

[5] For Mithridates and his wars with Rome see P. Matyszak, *Mithridates the Great: Rome's Indomitable Enemy* (2008), and A. Mayor, *The Poison King: The Life and Legend of Mithridates* (2009).

[6] For Marius' career see A. Goldsworthy, *In the Name of Rome* (2003), pp.113–136, and for more detail R. Evans, *Gaius Marius* (1994); for Sulla see A. Keaveney, *Sulla: The Last Republican* (1982).

[7] Appian, *BC* 1. 72, Plutarch, *Marius* 44, Valerius Maximus 8. 9. 2.

[8] Valerius Maximus 9. 2. 2 (Loeb translation by D. Shackleton Bailey); heads displayed on the Rostra by Marius see Livy, *Pers.* 80.

⁹ It has sometimes been suggested that Antony was born in 86 BC, but the evidence is not convincing; 83 BC is now universally accepted.

¹⁰ Plutarch, *Sulla* 31; on the proscriptions see Keaveney (1982), pp.148–168, Appian, *BC* 1. 95, and Velleius Paterculus 2. 31. 3–4.

¹¹ Plutarch, *Sulla* 38.

¹² Plutarch, *Antony* 1, with C. Pelling (ed.), *Plutarch: Life of Antony* (1988), pp.117–120, Sallust, *Histories* 3. 3.

¹³ P. Asconius 259, cf. Plutarch, *Lucullus* 5–6.

¹⁴ Velleius Paterculus 2. 31. 4.

¹⁵ On the shortages of supply for Pompey in war with Sertorius see Plutarch, *Sertorius* 21; on the pirate wars see Cicero, 2 *Verrines* 2. 2. 8, 3. 213–216, Livy, *Pers.* 97, Sallust, *Histories* 3. 4–7, most readily accessible in *Sallust: The Histories: Volume 2* (translation by P. McGushin) (1994), pp.64–70 and 122–125.

¹⁶ Cicero, *Philippics* 2. 44.

V THE OBOE PLAYER

¹ P. Green, *Alexander to Actium: The Historical Evolution of the Hellenistic Age* (1990), pp.480–496, G. Shipley, *The Greek World after Alexander 323–30 BC* (2000), pp.346–350, F. Walbank, *The Hellenistic World* (1992), pp.189–190, and M. Chauveau, *Egypt in the Age of Cleopatra* (trans. D. Lorton) (2000), pp.176–177.

² In general see G. Hölbl, *A History of the Ptolemaic Empire* (trans. T. Saavedra) (2001), pp.204–214, and D. Thompson in *CAH²* IX (1994), pp.310–317; for the inscription see Hölbl (2001), p.204, fn. 121.

³ Hölbl (2001), pp.210–211, *CAH²* IX (1994), pp.316–317.

⁴ For thorough discussion see C. Bennett, 'Cleopatra Tryphaena and the Genealogy of the Later Ptolemies', *Ancient Society* 28 (1997), pp.39–66, esp. 43–45.

⁵ A Ptolemy referred to as boy (*puer*) by Cicero, *De reg. Alex.* F9, see discussion in Bennett (1997), pp.47 and 48–51, who argues that this does not refer to Ptolemy XII.

⁶ Sulla sent his quaestor, Lucius Licinius Lucullus, see Plutarch, *Lucullus* 2. 2–3. 3.

⁷ A visit of a senator in 112 BC is described in some detail in *Tebtunis Papyrus* I. 33, see Hölbl (2001), p.207.

⁸ Cicero, *Agr.* 1. 1, 2. 41–42, *CAH²* IX (1994), p.316; Ptolemy Euergetes II had already willed Cyrene to Rome in 155 BC, although this is not mentioned by any literary source and is known to us through an inscription, *SEG* 9. 7.

⁹ Cicero, *Verrines* 2. 4. 61–68.

¹⁰ Hölbl, (2001), pp.223–225, *CAH²* IX (1994), pp.318–319.

¹¹ The 'young butcher', Valerius Maximus 6. 2. 8; for Pompey's early career in general see R. Seager, *Pompey the Great* (2002), pp.20–39.

¹² See Plutarch, *Crassus* 2–3, and A. Ward, *Marcus Crassus and the Late Roman Republic* (1977), pp.46–57.

¹³ For the campaign against the pirates see Appian, *Mithridatic Wars* 91–93, Plutarch, *Pompey* 26–28, and A. Goldsworthy, *In the Name of Rome* (2003), pp.164–169.

¹⁴ Goldsworthy (2003), pp.169–179.

¹⁵ For gifts to Pompey see Josephus, *AJ* 14. 35, Appian, *Mithridates* 114 and Pliny, *NH* 33. 136; on the attempt to annex Egypt see Plutarch, *Crassus* 13, Suetonius, *Caesar* 11 and Dio 37. 9. 3–4; Ward (1977), pp.128–135, M. Gelzer, *Caesar* (1968), pp.39–41.

[16] Cicero, *Agr.* 2. 43, Hölbl (2001), pp.224–225, and for more detail on the Rullan land bill see Gelzer (1968), pp.42–45, D. Stockton, *Cicero: A Political Biography* (1971), pp.84–91, T. Rice Holmes, *The Roman Republic and the founder of the Empire*, Vol. 1 (1928), pp.242–249, and Ward (1977), pp.152–162.

[17] Seager (2002), pp.75–85.

[18] On the triumvirate and consulship see A. Goldsworthy, *Caesar: The Life of a Colossus* (2006), pp.158–181.

[19] Suetonius, *Caesar* 54. 3, with M. Siani-Davies, 'Ptolemy XII Auletes and the Romans', *Historia* 46 (1997), pp.306–340, esp. 315–316.

[20] A. Sherwin-White, *Roman Foreign Policy in the East 168 BC to AD 1* (1984), pp.268–270, who is sceptical as to whether Cyprus yielded much money in the short term to Rome.

[21] On attitudes to Romans and the cat incident see Diodorus Siculus 1. 83. 1–9, 1. 44. 1; in general see Siani-Davies (1997), pp.317–322, and Hölbl (2001), pp.225–227.

[22] *CAH²* IX (1994), pp.319–320.

[23] Bennett (1997), pp.63–64.

[24] Bennett (1997), pp.57–65; for alternative views see *CAH²* IX (1994), p.319, accepting Cleopatra VI as a sister, and Hölbl (2001), p.227, and Green (1990), pp.650, 901, n. 21 where the co-ruler is her mother; cf. Hölbl (2001), p.223, asserting that Cleopatra's mother was an Egyptian concubine, M. Grant, *Cleopatra* (1972), pp.3–4, accepting that her mother was Cleopatra V Tryphaena, and J. Bingen, *Hellenistic Egypt: Monarchy, Society, Economy, Culture* (2007), pp.52–53, arguing that Cleopatra's mother was a concubine, but not Egyptian.

[25] Strabo, *Geog.* 17. 1. 11 (Loeb translation).

[26] For Cleopatra's possible visit to Italy see G. Goudchaux, 'Cleopatra's Subtle Religious Strategy', in S. Walker & P. Higgs (eds.), *Cleopatra of Egypt: From History to Myth* (2001), pp.128–141, esp. 131–132, backed by Grant (1972), pp.15–16.

VI ADOLESCENT

[1] Plutarch, *Antony* 2, 20.

[2] See S. Dixon, *The Roman Mother* (1988), *passim*, but esp. pp.13–70; on Cornelia see Plutarch, *Tiberius Gracchus* 1. Some have suggested that it was Ptolemy VI, rather than Physcon, who proposed to her.

[3] Tacitus *Dialogues* 28. 6 (Loeb translation by Sir W. Peterson, revised M. Winterbottom (1970), p.307).

[4] Cicero, *Orator* 120; on breastfeeding see K. Bradley, 'Wet-nursing at Rome: A Study in Social Relations', in B. Rawson, *The Family in Ancient Rome* (1986), pp.201–229; on childhood in general see B. Rawson, *Children and Childhood in Roman Italy* (2003), esp. pp.99–113, and on the mother's role and that of nurses see Dixon (1988), pp.104–167; on education see H. Marrou, *A History of Education in Antiquity* (1956), pp.229–291, A. Gwynn, *Roman Education* (1926), esp. pp.1–32; Cicero, *de Re Publica* 4. 3.

[5] For an introduction to the client system see R. Saller, *Personal Patronage in the Early Empire* (1982); for boys accompanying fathers as they went about their business see Gellius, *NA* 1. 23. 4, Pliny, *Epistulae* 8. 14. 4–5, and on importance of father's influence from age of seven see Quintilian 2. 2. 4, and comments in Marrou (1956), pp.231–233.

[6] Rawson (2003), pp.153–157.

[7] Cicero, *Brutus* 138–145, 296, *Orator* 18, 132; Antonius' refusal to write down his speeches, Cicero, *pro Cluentio* 140.

[8] Plutarch, *Antony* 2, 4.

[9] On the expulsions from the Senate in 70 BC see T. Broughton, *The Magistrates of the Roman Republic*, Vol. 2 (1952), pp.126–127.

[10] For the importance of the Liberalia festival see Ovid, *Fasti* 3. 771–788; on the sacrifice to Iuventus see Dionysius of Halicarnassus 4. 15. 5; on the ceremonies associated with adopting the *toga virilis* in general see Rawson (2003), pp.142–144.

[11] Cicero, *pro Caelio* 28–30. Even if Cicero exaggerates, he clearly expected his audience to have some sympathy with this view.

[12] Sallust, *Bell. Cat.* 12. 1–2 (Loeb translation).

[13] Cicero, *In Catilinam* 2. 22 (Loeb translation by C. MacDonald (1977), p.91); Hercules, see Plutarch, *Antony* 4. On the Julii's descent from Venus see Velleius Paterculus 2. 41. 1, and Suetonius, *Caesar* 6. 1; for Caesar's style see Suetonius, *Caesar* 45. 3.

[14] Plutarch, *Antony* 2.

[15] Plutarch, *Pompey* 2.

[16] P. Grimal, *Love in Ancient Rome* (1986), pp.112–115 and 226–237, and S. Treggiari, *Roman Marriage* (1991), esp. pp.105–106, 232–238, 253–261, 264, 270–275 and 299–319.

[17] Sallust, *Bell. Cat.* 25.

[18] Suetonius, *Caesar* 47, 50. 1–52.

[19] Cicero, *Philippics* 2. 44.

[20] Cicero, *Philippics* 2. 45–46, Plutarch, *Antony* 2.

[21] See Sallust, *Bell. Cat.* 23. 5–24. 1. For Cicero's career and election to the consulship see E. Rawson, *Cicero* (1975), T. Mitchell, *Cicero: The Ascending Years* (1979), esp. pp.93ff., and D. Stockton, *Cicero: A Political Biography* (1971), esp. pp.71–81; for attitudes to Antonius, see Plutarch, *Cicero* 11.

[22] For Catiline see Sallust, *Bell. Cat.* 15. 1–5, with E. Salmon, 'Catiline, Crassus, and Caesar', *American Journal of Philology* 56 (1935), pp.302–316, esp. 302–306; E. Hardy, *The Catilinarian Conspiracy in its Context: A Re-study of the Evidence* (1924), pp.12–20; T. Rice Holmes, *The Roman Republic*, Vol. 1 (1928), pp.234–235.

[23] Sallust, *Bell. Cat.* 14. 1–7, 16. 1–4.

[24] Sallust, *Bell. Cat.* 59. 3.

[25] Sallust, *Bell. Cat.* 31. 4–48. 2, Rice Holmes (1928), pp.259–272, Stockton (1971), pp.84–109.

[26] Plutarch, *Antony* 2; on the provinces see Cicero, *In Pisonem* 5, cf. *Pro Sestio*.8.

[27] Sallust, *Bell. Cat.* 59. 4; see also E. Gruen, *The Last Generation of the Roman Republic* (1974), pp.287–289.

[28] Cicero, *Philippics* 2. 3–4.

[29] Cicero, *ad Att.* 2. 19.

[30] On Clodius see Plutarch, *Antony* 2, Cicero, *Philippics* 2. 48, with W. Jeffrey Tatum, *The Patrician Tribune: Publius Clodius Pulcher* (1999), esp. pp.70 and 235–236, A. Lintott, 'P. Clodius Pulcher – Felix Catilina', *Greece and Rome* 14 (1967), pp.157–169, W. Rundell, 'Cicero and Clodius: The Question of Credibility', *Historia* 28 (1979), pp.301–328, and E. Gruen, 'P. Clodius: Instrument or Independent Agent?', *Phoenix* 20 (1966), pp.120–130.

VII THE RETURN OF THE KING

[1] Dio 39. 12. 1–3, Strabo, *Geog.* 17. 1. 11, with P. Green, *Alexander to Actium: The Historical Evolution of the Hellenistic Age* (1990), pp.649–650, and M. Grant, *Cleopatra* (1972), pp.16–19.

[2] Plutarch, *Cato the Younger 6*, 35–36; Sallust, *Bell. Jug.* 35. 10 for quote; for Cicero's comment about Cato see Cicero, *ad Att.* 2. 1.

[3] Dio 39. 13. 1–14. 4, Cicero, *pro Caelio* 23–24, with E. Gruen, *The Last Generation of the Roman Republic* (1974), pp.305–309.

[4] R. Seager, *Pompey the Great* (2002), pp.111–112, Plutarch, *Pompey 49*, Cicero, *ad Fam.* 1. 1–8.

[5] Dio 39. 57. 1–2, Strabo, *Geog.* 17. 1. 11; see also M. Siani-Davies, 'Ptolemy XII Auletes and the Romans', *Historia* 46 (1997), pp.306–340, esp. 323–327, Green (1990), pp.650–652, and G. Hölbl, *A History of the Ptolemaic Empire* (trans. T. Saavedra) (2001), pp.225–229.

[6] See E. Badian, 'The Early Career of A. Gabinius (cos. 58 BC)', *Philologus* 103 (1958), pp.87–99.

[7] Plutarch, *Antony 3*, with C. Pelling (ed.), *Plutarch: Life of Antony* (1988), pp.120–122.

[8] Josephus, *BJ* 1. 160–178, *AJ* 14. 27–104, with E. Schürer, G. Vermes & F. Millar, *The History of the Jewish People in the Age of Jesus Christ*, Vol. 1 (1973), pp.233–242 and 267–269.

[9] Plutarch, *Antony 3*, Dio 39. 57. 2–58. 3, Cicero, *Philippics 2. 48, pro Rabirio Postumo* 19–20, with A. Sherwin-White, *Roman Foreign Policy in the East 168 BC to AD 1* (1984), pp.271–279 for more detail.

[10] Appian, *BC* 5. 8.

[11] Plutarch, *Antony 4*, with Pelling (1988), pp.123–126; on Gabinius see Gruen (1974), pp.322–331.

VIII CANDIDATE

[1] Dio 39. 59. 160. 4, 62. 1–63. 5, R. Seager, *Pompey the Great* (2002), pp.123–125 and 128–130, E. Gruen, *The Last Generation of the Roman Republic* (1974), pp.323–327.

[2] Plutarch, *Crassus 16*, Dio 39. 39. 3–8, with T. Rice Holmes, *The Roman Republic*, Vol. 2 (1923), pp.147–148.

[3] For a summary of the campaign see T. Wiseman in *CAH²* IX, pp.402–403.

[4] Cicero, *Philippics 2. 48*; Cicero, *ad Quintum Fratrem* 3. 1. 15 for Gabinius' arrival in Rome.

[5] Caesar, *BG* 7. 65; for a discussion of Caesar's legates see Gruen (1974), pp.114–118.

[6] Pliny, *NH* 7. 92, Suetonius, *Caesar 54*, 71, Plutarch, *Caesar 17*.

[7] Caesar first refers to Antony as a legate in Caesar, *BG* 7. 31, but in *BG* 8. 2 and subsequently he is a quaestor.

[8] For officers in Gaul see K. Welch, 'Caesar and his Officers in the Gallic War Commentaries', in K. Welch & A. Powell (eds.), *Julius Caesar as Artful Reporter: The War Commentaries as Political Instruments* (1998), pp.85–110; on the public thanksgiving see Caesar, *BG* 4. 38, Dio 39. 53. 1–2, and on the expedition in general see A. Goldsworthy, *Caesar: The Life of a Colossus* (2006), pp.278–292.

[9] For a narrative of these operations see Goldsworthy (2006), pp.293–314.

[10] Cicero, *Philippics* 2. 49 on Caesar's support for his candidature.

[11] Cicero, *Philippics* 2. 21, 49.

[12] On the death of Clodius see Wiseman in *CAH²* IX, pp.405–408, Rice Holmes (1923), pp.164–167.

[13] Seager (2002), pp.133–139.

[14] For discussions of elections see L. Taylor, *Party Politics in the Age of Caesar* (1949), esp. pp.50–75, and *Roman Voting Assemblies: From the Hannibalic War to the Dictatorship of Caesar* (1966), esp. pp.78–106, A. Lintott, 'Electoral Bribery in the Roman Republic', *JRS* 80 (1990), pp.1–16, F. Millar, *The Crowd in the Late Roman Republic* (1998), H. Mouritsen, *Plebs and Politics in the Late Roman Republic* (2001), esp. pp.63–89, and A. Yakobson, 'Petitio et Largitio: Popular Participation in the Centuriate Assembly of the Late Republic', *JRS* 8 (1992), pp.32–52.

[15] Cicero, *Philippics* 2. 50, *ad Att.* 6. 6. 4, 7. 8. 5, *ad Fam.* 2. 15. 4; for an account of the rebellion of 53–52 BC see Goldsworthy (2006), pp.315–342; on favours shown to Vercingetorix by Caesar see Dio 40. 41. 1, 3.

[16] Antony did not leave Rome until after Milo's trial, see Asconius 41 C; on Lucius Caesar as Legate in Transalpine Gaul see Caesar, *BG* 7. 65.

[17] Caesar, *BG* 7. 81.

[18] Caesar, *BG* 8. 2; for an account of these operations see Goldsworthy (2006), pp.343–353.

[19] Caesar, *BG* 8. 24, 38.

[20] Caesar, *BG* 8. 46–48; cf. 8. 23 for the murder attempt against him.

IX 'THE NEW SIBLING-LOVING GODS'

[1] Caesar, *BC* 1. 4.

[2] Caesar, *BC* 3. 110, Valerius Maximus 4. 1. 15, Cicero, *pro Rabirio Postumo* 34.

[3] Cicero, *pro Rabirio Postumo* 20, 34; Plutarch, *Pompey* 78. For Italians/Romans serving with the armies of client kings, examples include Rufus and Gratus commanding parts of Herod the Great's army in 4 BC, see Josephus, *BJ* 2. 52, 58, 63, with E. Schürer, G. Vermes & F. Millar, *The History of the Jewish People in the Age of Jesus Christ*, Vol. 1 (1973), pp.362–364.

[4] Caesar, *BC* 3. 110; on legionary pay see Suetonius, *Caesar* 26, with discussion in G. Watson, *The Roman Soldier* (1969), pp.89–91; see also M. Siani-Davies, 'Ptolemy XII Auletes and the Romans', *Historia* 46 (1997), pp.306–340, esp. 338–339.

[5] Cicero, *pro Rabirio Postumo* 4–7, 19–29.

[6] Cicero, *pro Rabirio Postumo* 38–42; on the royal bureaucracy in general see D. Rathbone, 'Ptolemaic to Roman Egypt: The Death of the Dirigiste State?', in E. Lo Cascio & D. Rathbone (eds.), *Production and Public Powers in Classical Antiquity* (2000), pp.44–54, M. Chauveau, *Egypt in the Age of Cleopatra* (trans. D. Lorton) (2000), pp.72–95, and J. Bingen, *Hellenistic Egypt: Monarchy, Society, Economy, Culture* (2007), pp.157–205.

[7] P. Green, *Alexander to Actium: The Historical Evolution of the Hellenistic Age* (1990), pp.156–158, J. Tyldesley, *Cleopatra: Last Queen of Egypt* (2009), p.81; on the Pharos see P. Fraser, *Ptolemaic Alexandria*, Vol. 1 (1972), pp.17–20.

[8] Strabo, *Geog.* 17. 1. 9–10, Chauveau (2000), pp.61–62.

[9] Strabo, *Geog.* 17. 1. 8, J. Ray, 'Alexandria', in S. Walker & P. Higgs (eds.), *Cleopatra of Egypt: From History to Myth* (2001), pp.32–37, and G. Grimm, 'Alexandria in the Time

of Cleopatra', in S. Walker & S. Ashton (eds.), *Cleopatra Reassessed* (2003), pp.45–49; on the Museum and Greek culture see also H. Maehler, 'Alexandria, the Mouseion, and Cultural Identity', in A. Hirst & M. Silk (eds.), *Alexandria, Real and Imagined* (2004), pp.1–14.

[10] Green (1990), pp.317–318.

[11] For Alexandria in general see Fraser (1972), *passim*, A. Bernard, *Alexandrie la Grande* (1998), and *Alexandrie des Ptolémées* (1995), G. Grimm, *Alexandria: Die erste Königsstadt der hellenistischen Welt* (1998), N. Finneran, *Alexandria: A City and Myth* (2005), pp.9–88, J-Y. Empereur, *Alexandria Rediscovered* (1998), F. Goddio, *L'Égypte Engloutie: Alexandrie* (2002), F. Goddio, with A. Bernard, E. Bernard, I. Darwish, Z. Kiss & J. Yoyotte, *Alexandria: The Submerged Royal Quarters* (1998), and Chauveau (2000), pp.100–134.

[12] In general see D. Thompson, *Memphis under the Ptolemies* (1988), esp. pp.3–31, G. Hölbl, *A History of the Ptolemaic Empire* (trans. T. Saavedra) (2001), pp.271–293.

[13] M. Grant, *Cleopatra* (1972), p.20, citing *CIG* 4926, Hölbl (2001), pp.222–223, Green (1990), pp.649–650.

[14] Caesar, *BC* 3. 108.

[15] Hölbl (2001), p.230, and Bingen (2007), p.66; the expression occurs in the inscription *OGIS* 2. 741 dated to 31 May 52 BC.

[16] Bingen (2007), pp.67–68.

[17] Bingen (2007), pp.66–67.

[18] On her appearance see Grant (1972), pp.65–67, E. Rice, *Cleopatra* (1999), pp.95–102, Walker & Higgs (2001), esp. S. Walker, 'Cleopatra's Images: Reflections of Reality', pp.142–147, and G. Goudchaux, 'Was Cleopatra Beautiful? The Conflicting Answers of Numismatics', pp.210–214, and also in Walker & Ashton (2003), esp. S. Walker, 'Cleopatra VII at the Louvre', pp.71–74, and F. Johansen, 'Portraits of Cleopatra – Do They Exist?', pp.75–77.

[19] Dio 42. 34. 3–5 (Loeb translation by E. Cary (1916), p.169); Plutarch, *Antony* 27 (Oxford translation by R. Waterfield).

[20] Lucan, *Pharsalia* 10. 127–143; *Candida Sidonio perlucent pectora filo, quod Nilotis acus impressum pectine serum, solvit et extenso laxavit stamina velo*, 10. 140–142.

[21] These were *Cleopatra: Portrait of a Killer* (Lion TV) shown on BBC television in the UK, and an episode on Cleopatra from the series *Egypt Unwrapped* (Atlantic TV) shown on Channel 5 in the UK.

[22] See J. Fletcher, *Cleopatra the Great: The Woman Behind the Legend* (2008), p.87, and Walker & Higgs (2001), pp.314–315, n. 325.

X TRIBUNE

[1] Caesar, *BG* 8. 50.

[2] Cicero, *De Divinatione* 1. 30–33, 2. 70–83.

[3] E. Gruen, *The Last Generation of the Roman Republic* (1974), pp.484–485 on this election; in general see A. Lintott, *The Constitution of the Roman Republic* (1999), pp.182–190.

[4] See Lintott (1999), pp.121–128.

[5] Broughton, *MRR* 2, pp.258–259; Caesar, *BG* 8. 50.

[6] On the fears surrounding the return of Pompey in 62 BC see R. Seager, *Pompey the*

Great (2002), pp.74–79; on the wider story of the years building up to the civil war in 49 BC see M. Gelzer, *Caesar* (trans. P. Needham) (1968), pp.169–194, C. Meier, *Caesar* (trans. D. McLintock) (1996), pp.330–348, and A. Goldsworthy, *Caesar: The Life of a Colossus* (2006), p.358–379 for fuller accounts with references.

[7] On the virtues of Cornelia see Plutarch, *Pompey* 55.

[8] Suetonius, *Caesar* 30. 3.

[9] On Crassus and the reluctance of anyone to prosecute him see the discussion in A. Ward, *Marcus Crassus and the Late Roman Republic* (1977), p.78, cf. Plutarch, *Crassus* 7.

[10] Caelius' quote from Cicero, *ad Fam.* 8. 8. 9.

[11] Suetonius, *Caesar* 29. 1, Plutarch, *Caesar* 29, *Pompey* 58, Dio 40. 60. 2–3, Appian, *BC* 2. 26, Valerius Maximus 9. 1. 6, Velleius Paterculus 2. 48. 4; on revolving theatres see Pliny, *NH* 36. 177; on Caelius' belief in Curio's planned opposition to Caesar see Cicero, *ad Fam.* 8. 8. 10, moderated at 8. 10. 4.

[12] Quotation from Cicero, *ad Fam.* 8. 11. 3; for the earlier debate see Velleius 2. 48. 2–3, Plutarch, *Pompey* 57, *Caesar* 30, *Cato the Younger* 51, and Dio 40. 62. 3; for discussion see Seager (2002), p.144, and Gelzer (1968), pp.178–181.

[13] Cicero, *ad Fam.* 8. 11. 1.

[14] Appian, *BC* 2. 28, with a slightly different version in Plutarch, *Pompey* 58, cf. Dio 60. 64. 1–4.

[15] Caesar, *BC* 1. 1–4.

[16] Cicero, *ad Fam.* 16. 11. 2, *ad Att.* 8. 11d.

[17] On Antony's appearance and style of oratory see Plutarch, *Antony* 2, 4; on Pompey's comments and Cicero's reaction see Cicero, *ad Att.* 7. 8, where he specifically refers to Antony as a quaestor and not as tribune, and also *ad Fam.* 16. 11. 3; on Antony vomiting his words see Cicero, *ad Fam.* 12. 2.

[18] Caesar, *BC* 1. 5, Dio 41. 1. 1–3. 4, Appian, *BC* 2. 32–33.

[19] For a more detailed discussion of the crossing of the Rubicon see Goldsworthy (2006), pp.377–379, and for the ancient sources see Suetonius, *Caesar* 31–32, Plutarch, *Caesar* 32, and Appian, *BC* 2. 35; Suetonius, *Caesar* 30. 4 for the quotation.

[20] Caesar, *BC* 1. 8, Appian, *BC* 2. 33.

[21] Cicero, *Philippics* 2. 22, cf. Plutarch, *Antony* 6, with C. Pelling (ed.), *Plutarch: Life of Antony* (1988), pp.130–131.

[22] Caesar, *BC* 1. 11; for a more detailed account of the Italian campaign see Goldsworthy (2006), pp.385–391.

[23] Cicero, *ad Att.* 9. 7C.

[24] Caesar, *BC* 1. 8.

[25] Quote from Cicero, *ad Att.* 9. 10. 2.

[26] Caesar, *BC* 1. 32–33, Dio 41. 15. 1–16. 4 for the meeting of the Senate; Caesar, *BC* 1. 32–33, Dio 41. 17. 1–3, Appian, *BC* 2. 41, Plutarch, *Caesar* 35, Pliny, *NH* 33. 56 and Orosius 6. 15. 5 for the confrontation with the tribune; for a more detailed account see Goldsworthy (2006), pp.391–397.

[27] Cicero, *ad Att.* 10. 4.

[28] Cicero, *ad Att.* 10. 8A, *Philippics* 2. 56–58, and Broughton *MRR* 2, p.260 for full references.

XI QUEEN

[1] M. Grant, *Cleopatra* (1972), p.54, and G. Hölbl, *A History of the Ptolemaic Empire* (trans. T. Saavedra) (2001), pp.231–232.

[2] J. Bingen, *Hellenistic Egypt: Monarchy, Society, Economy, Culture* (2007), pp.66–68, and J. Tyldesley, *Cleopatra: Last Queen of Egypt* (2009), pp.39–46.

[3] See W. Tarn, 'The Bucheum Stelae: A Note', *JRS* 26 (1936), pp.187–189 for the quotation, and the belief that Cleopatra was present; Tyldesley (2009), p.41–42, expresses a measure of doubt over Cleopatra's actual participation, while Grant (1972), pp.46–47, and J. Fletcher, *Cleopatra the Great: The Woman Behind the Legend* (2008), pp.88–91, accept her actual involvement in the ceremonies.

[4] See G. Goudchaux, 'Cleopatra's Subtle Religious Strategy,' in S. Walker & P. Higgs, *Cleopatra of Egypt: From History to Myth* (2001), pp.132–133.

[5] 'She was indeed queen of Egypt' quote from D. Thompson in *CAH²* IX, p.321, who also accepts Cleopatra's presence at the enthronement of the Buchis bull.

[6] Cicero, *pro Rabirio Postumo* 8. 20.

[7] Suetonius, *Julius Caesar* 20. 2; for discussion of this see A. Goldsworthy, *Caesar: The Life of a Colossus* (2006), pp.164–175.

[8] Valerius Maximus 4. 1. 15 (Loeb translation by D. Shackleton Bailey), and cf. Caesar, *BC* 3. 110. Central control of the Roman army in this period was often weak. When Cicero took over in Cilicia he discovered that three cohorts out of his two legions were missing, and it was some time before they were located and brought back under control, see Cicero, *ad Fam.* 3. 6. 5.

[9] Translation from *Select Papyri: Volume II Official documents* (Loeb translation by A. Hunt & C. Edgar, 1974), pp.57–58.

[10] Bingen (2007), pp.69–70, Grant (1972), pp.49–51, Hölbl (2001), p.231, and D. Thompson, 'Cleopatra VII: The Queen in Egypt', in S. Walker & S. Ashton (eds.), *Cleopatra Reassessed* (2003), pp.31–34, esp. 32.

[11] Caesar, *BC* 3. 4–5; the Egyptian ships seem to have remained under Cnaeus Pompey's command, Caesar, *BC* 3. 40.

[12] Plutarch, *Antony* 25, and Lucan, *Pharsalia* 5. 58–64, with Grant (1972), pp.51–52, and Hölbl (2001), p.232.

[13] Malalas 9. 279, Strabo, *Geog.* 17. 1. 11, Appian, *BC* 2. 84.

[14] See Walker & Higgs (2001), p.234.

[15] Caesar, *BC* 3. 110.

[16] Caesar, *BC* 3. 103–104, Plutarch, *Pompey* 77, Appian, *BC* 84.

XII CIVIL WAR

[1] Plutarch, *Pompey* 63–4.

[2] For the campaign in Sicily and Africa, Plutarch, *Cato the Younger* 53. 1–3, Caesar, *BC* 2. 23–44.

[3] For Caesar's followers a 'rabble' see Cicero, *ad Att.* 9. 18; for Cicero's accusation that Antony did nothing to aid Caius Antonius' recall from exile see Cicero, *Philippics* 2. 56.

[4] On the allegiance of consulars see R. Syme, *The Roman Revolution* (1960), pp.61–62; Suetonius, *Caesar* 72, on rewarding even bandits if they were faithful to him.

[5] Cicero, *Philippics* 2. 58.

[6] Cicero, *ad Att.* 10. 10; see also Plutarch, *Antony* 6.

[7] Plutarch, *Antony* 6, 9.

[8] Plutarch, *Antony* 9; in general see Cicero, *ad Fam.* 9. 26, *ad Att.* 10. 10, Serv. on E10 *De vir. Ill.* 82. 2. Cicero's distaste only became public in the *Philippics* 2. 58, 69, 77; in general see P. Grimal, *Love in Ancient Rome* (1986), pp.222–237.

[9] Cicero, *ad Att.* 10. 13, Plutarch, *Antony* 9, and Pliny, *NH* 8. 55.

[10] For Cicero's attitude in these months see D. Stockton, *Cicero: A Political Biography* (1971), pp.251–265, and T. Mitchell, *Cicero: The Senior Statesman* (1991), pp.232–261.

[11] Cicero, *ad Att.* 10. 10 on writing frequently to Antony; the quote is from *ad Att.* 10. 8a.

[12] Cicero, *ad Att.* 10. 10.

[13] On the mutiny see Appian, *BC* 2. 47, Dio 41. 26. 1–35. 5, and Suetonius, *Caesar* 69.

[14] See Cicero, *ad Att.* 9. 9. 3; for Servilius see *CAH²* IX, p.431, Dio 41. 36. 1–38. 3, Caesar, *BC* 3. 1–2, Plutarch, *Caesar* 37, Appian, *BC* 2. 48, with M. Gelzer, *Caesar* (trans. P. Needham) (1968), pp.220–223.

[15] Caesar, *BC* 3. 2–8, Dio 41. 39. 1–40. 2, 44. 1–4, Appian, *BC* 2. 49–54, Plutarch, *Caesar* 37.

[16] Caesar, *BC* 3. 8, 14–18.

[17] Appian, *BC* 2. 50–59, Plutarch, *Caesar* 65, *Antony* 7, Dio 41. 46. 1–4; Caesar, *BC* 3. 25 admits to a belief that his subordinates were slow and had not taken advantage of every opportunity.

[18] Caesar, *BC* 3. 24.

[19] Caesar, *BC* 3. 39–44, Dio 41. 47. 1–50. 4, Appian, *BC* 2. 58–60; for 'veterans of exceptional courage' see Caesar, *BG* 8. 8.

[20] Caesar, *BC* 3. 45–46.

[21] Caesar, *BC* 3. 45–53, Plutarch, *Caesar* 39, Appian, *BC* 2. 60–61, Suetonius, *Caesar* 68. 3–4.

[22] Caesar, *BC* 3. 61–70, Plutarch, *Caesar* 39, Appian, *BC* 2. 62.

[23] Caesar, *BC* 3. 71–75, Appian, *BC* 2. 63–64, Dio 41. 51. 1.

[24] Caesar *BC* 3. 77–81, Plutarch, *Caesar* 41, Appian, *BC* 2. 63, Dio 41. 51. 4–5.

[25] Caesar, *BC* 3. 72, 82–83, Cicero, *ad Fam.* 7. 3. 2; Plutarch, *Cato the Younger* 55, *Pompey* 40–41, Appian, *BC* 2. 65–67, Dio 41. 52. 1; in general for Pompey's strategy and attitude see R. Seager, *Pompey the Great* (2002), pp.157–163 and 166–167.

[26] Caesar, *BC* 3. 86–99, Appian, *BC* 2. 78–82, Plutarch, *Caesar* 42–47, and also Dio 41. 58. 1–63. 6; on Antony's role see Plutarch, *Antony* 8, Cicero, *Philippics* 2. 71.

[27] Caesar, *BC* 3. 94, 102–103, Plutarch, *Pompey* 76.

XIII CAESAR

[1] Caesar, *BC* 3. 103–104, Plutarch, *Pompey* 77–80, Appian, *BC* 2. 84–86, Dio 42. 3. 1–4. 5, and R. Seager, *Pompey the Great* (2002), p.168.

[2] Plutarch, *Pompey* 80, *Caesar* 48, Dio 42. 8. 1–3; for a much more cynical view see Lucan, *Pharsalia* 9. 1010–1108.

[3] Caesar, *BC* 3. 106, *Alexandrian War* 69, Dio 42. 7. 1–8. 3; Caesar's cavalry bodyguard, *BC* 1. 41.

[4] Caesar, *BC* 3. 110, with M. Grant, *Cleopatra* (1972), pp.61–63, P. Green, *Alexander to Actium: The Historical Evolution of the Hellenistic Age* (1990), pp.664–665, and G. Hölbl,

A *History of the Ptolemaic Empire* (trans. T. Saavedra) (2001), p.233.

⁵ Quote from Caesar, *BC* 3. 107; for the money see Plutarch, *Caesar* 48.

⁶ Plutarch, *Caesar* 48, Dio 42. 34. 1–2.

⁷ Plutarch, *Caesar* 48, Dio 42. 34. 3.

⁸ Plutarch, *Caesar* 49, Dio 42. 34. 4–35. 1, and on the claim that Cleopatra bribed Ptolemy's guards see Lucan, *Pharsalia* 10. 5–8; for some of the modern discussions see Grant (1972), pp.63–64, J. Tyldesley, *Cleopatra: Last Queen of Egypt* (2009), pp.53–58, E. Rice, *Cleopatra* (1999), pp.33–35, J. Fletcher, *Cleopatra the Great: The Woman Behind the Legend* (2008), pp.100–112, and E. Gruen, 'Cleopatra in Rome: Facts and Fantasies', in D. Braund & C. Gill (eds.), *Myths, History and Culture in Republican Rome: Studies in Honour of T. P. Wiseman* (2003), pp.257–274, esp. 264–266.

⁹ Quotes from Dio 52. 34. 3 & 5 (Loeb translation by E. Cary).

¹⁰ On Caesar's womanising see A. Goldsworthy, *Caesar: The Life of a Colossus* (2006), pp.84–89.

¹¹ For Caesar's receding hairline see Suetonius, *Caesar* 45. 2.

¹² Caesar, *BC* 3. 108, Plutarch, *Caesar* 49, Dio 42. 35. 1–6.

¹³ For the mistreatment of the city of Salamis on Cyprus by Roman businessmen representing Brutus, see T. Mitchell, *Cicero: The Senior Statesman* (1991), pp.223–224, with references to the relevant letters of Cicero.

¹⁴ Caesar, *BC* 3. 109, Dio 42. 37. 1–3.

¹⁵ Caesar, *BC* 3. 111–112, *Alexandrian War* 1–3, Dio 42. 12. 1–4, 38. 1–4.

¹⁶ Plutarch, *Caesar* 49, Dio 42. 39. 2, Appian, *BC* 2. 90.

¹⁷ Caesar, *Alexandrian War* 4, Dio 42. 39. 1.

¹⁸ Caesar, *Alexandrian War* 13.

¹⁹ Caesar, *Alexandrian War* 5–22, Plutarch, *Caesar* 49, Dio 42. 40. 1–6, Suetonius, *Caesar* 64, Appian, *BC* 2. 90.

²⁰ Caesar, *Alexandrian War* 24.

²¹ Caesar, *Alexandrian War* 26–32, Dio 42. 41. 1–43. 4, Josephus, *AJ* 14. 8. 12, *BJ* 1. 187–192.

²² Caesar, *Alexandrian War* 33, Dio 42. 35. 4–6, 44. 1–45. 1, Suetonius, *Caesar* 52. 1, Appian, *BC* 90; for the bemused attitude of scholars to this cruise see Grant (1972), pp.79–82, Tyldesley (2009), pp.98–100, Fletcher (2008), pp.125–153, M. Gelzer, *Caesar* (trans. P. Needham) (1968), pp.255–259, and also C. Meier, *Caesar* (1995), pp.408–410 and 412.

XIV MASTER OF HORSE

¹ Dio 42. 17. 1–20. 5.

² Dio 42. 21. 1–2 with Broughton, *MRR* 2, p.272; Cicero, *Philippics* 2. 25 claims that Caesar did not know of Antony's appointment, but this seems unlikely.

³ Cicero, *Philippics* 2. 61–63, Plutarch, *Antony* 9; for *On his Drinking* see Pliny, *NH* 14. 148.

⁴ Dio 42. 27. 3–28. 4.

⁵ See D. Stockton, *Cicero: A Political Biography* (1971), pp.263–268, and T. Mitchell, *Cicero: The Senior Statesman* (1991), pp.262–266 with references.

⁶ Dio 42. 27. 3.

[7] Caesar, *BC* 3. 20–22, Dio 42. 22. 1–25. 3; Caelius' last letter to Cicero is Cicero, *ad Fam.* 8. 17.

[8] Dio 42. 29. 1–4, Plutarch, *Antony* 9, with C. Pelling (ed.), *Plutarch: Life of Antony* (1988), pp.136–140, Appian, *BC* 2. 92.

[9] Dio 42. 50. 1–55. 3, Appian *BC* 2. 92–94, Plutarch, *Caesar* 51, Suetonius, *Caesar* 70, Frontinus, *Strategemata* 1. 9. 4.

[10] R. Weigel, *Lepidus: The Tarnished Triumvir* (1992), pp.30–34.

[11] Dio 48. 38. 2–3.

[12] Cicero, *Philippics* 2. 64–69, 72–74, 78, Plutarch, *Antony* 10, Dio 45. 28. 1–4.

[13] Suetonius, *Caesar* 50. 2.

[14] Plutarch, *Antony* 10, Cicero, *Philippics* 2. 69, 99.

[15] Plutarch, *Antony* 10, claims that there was a breach between Caesar and Antony. M. Gelzer, *Caesar* (trans. P. Needham) (1968), pp.261–262, is inclined to see this as serious. R. Syme, *The Roman Revolution* (1960), p.104, doubts this.

[16] Plutarch, *Antony* 10–11, Cicero, *Philippics* 2. 75–78.

XV NOT KING, BUT CAESAR

[1] Cicero, *ad Att.* 14. 20. 2.

[2] Tacitus, *Histories* 4. 55, Dio 66. 3. 1, 16. 1.

[3] Suetonius, *Caesar* 52. 2, Plutarch, *Caesar* 49; however, note also Plutarch, *Antony* 52, which suggests that the boy was not born until after Caesar's death; for discussions see M. Grant, *Cleopatra* (1972), pp.83–85.

[4] Suetonius, *Caesar* 52. 1, and for discussion see E. Gruen, 'Cleopatra in Rome: Fact and Fantasies', in D. Braund & C. Gill (eds.), *Myths, History and Culture in Republican Rome: Studies in Honour of T. P. Wiseman* (2003), pp.257–274, esp. 258–260 and 267–270.

[5] Dio 53. 19. 1–20. 4, Appian, *BC* 2. 101, and Grant (1972), pp.85–86, 260, n. 13, including the much later source claiming that Ganymede was one of the captives.

[6] Suetonius, *Caesar* 52. 1.

[7] Suetonius, *Caesar* 76. 3.

[8] Suetonius, *Caesar* 52. 1.

[9] Suetonius, *Caesar* 44. 1–2, Pliny, *NH* 18. 211, Plutarch, *Caesar* 59, Macrobius, *Saturnalia* 1. 14. 2–3, T. Rice Holmes, *The Roman Republic*, Vol. 3 (1923), pp.285–287, M. Gelzer, *Caesar* (1968), p.289, and Z. Yazetz, *Julius Caesar and his Public Image* (1983), pp.111–114.

[10] Dio 43. 42. 3, 44. 1–3.

[11] Dio 43. 14. 7, 44. 1–46. 4, Cicero, *ad Att.* 12. 47. 3, 45. 3, *ad Fam.* 6. 8. 1, 6. 18. 1, Suetonius, *Caesar* 41. 2, 76. 1; see also R. Carson, 'Caesar and the Monarchy', *Greece and Rome* 4 (1957), pp.46–53, E. Rawson, 'Caesar's Heritage: Hellenistic Kings and their Roman Equals', *JRS* 65 (1975), pp.148–159, and S. Weinstock, *Divus Julius* (1971), esp. pp.200–206.

[12] Dio 43. 50. 3–4, Suetonius, *Caesar* 42. 1, 81, *Tiberius* 4. 1, Plutarch, *Caesar* 57–58, Strabo, *Geog.* 8. 6. 23, 17. 3. 15, Appian, *Punic History* 136, Cicero, *ad Fam.* 9. 17. 2, 13. 4, 13. 5, 13. 8; also Yazetz (1983), pp.137–149, E. Rawson, *CAH²* IX, pp.445–480, and Rice Holmes (1923), pp.320–324. For Cicero receiving unwarranted thanks from provincials see Cicero, *ad Fam.* 9. 15. 4.

[13] Suetonius, *Caesar* 77, 79. 2, Dio 44. 10. 1, Appian, *BC* 2. 108.

[14] Dio 44. 11. 1–3, Appian, *BC* 2. 109, Plutarch, *Caesar* 61, *Antony* 12, Cicero, *Philippics* 2. 84–87, *De Divinatione* 1. 52, 119, Suetonius, *Caesar* 79. 2; see also Weinstock (1971), pp.318–341.

[15] Dio 43. 51. 1–2, 44. 1. 1, Appian, *BC* 2. 110, 3. 77, Plutarch, *Caesar* 58, Velleius Paterculus 2. 59. 4, Suetonius, *Caesar* 44. 3.

[16] Cicero, *Philippics* 2. 79–82, Plutarch, *Antony* 11.

[17] Cicero, *ad Att.* 13. 40. 1.

[18] Suetonius, *Caesar* 77.

[19] See R. Syme, *The Roman Revolution* (1960), pp.56–59; Caesar's comment is in Cicero, *ad Att.* 14. 1. 2; for the Salamis episode see, for example, *ad Att.* 6. 2.

[20] Dio 43. 10. 1–13. 4, Appian, *BC* 2. 98–99, Plutarch, *Cato the Younger* 56. 4, 59. 1–73. 1.

[21] Cicero, *ad Att.* 12. 21. 1, 13. 40. 1, 46, 51. 1, *Orator* 10, 35, Plutarch, *Cato the Younger* 11. 1–4, 25. 1–5, 73. 4, *Cicero* 39. 2, *Caesar* 3. 2, Suetonius, *Caesar* 56. 5, with Gelzer (1968), pp.301–304, Rice Holmes (1923), p.311, and D. Stockton, *Cicero: A Political Biography* (1971), p.138.

[22] Syme (1960), p.69; on Cassius see Cicero, *ad Att.* 5. 21.

[23] Dio 44. 14. 3–4, Plutarch, *Brutus* 18; Appian, *BC* 3. 98; on Trebonius and Antony see Plutarch, *Antony* 13.

[24] For discussion see A. Goldsworthy, *Caesar: The Life of a Colossus* (2006), pp.500–510.

[25] Suetonius, *Caesar* 52. 3, 83. 2.

[26] Appian, *BC* 2. 102, Dio 51. 22.3, with Gruen (2003), pp.259 and 270–272.

[27] Cicero, *ad Att.* 15. 15. 2.

[28] Plutarch, *Caesar* 66, *Brutus* 17, *Antony* 13, Dio 44. 19. 1–5, Appian, *BC* 2. 117, Suetonius, *Caesar* 82. 1–3.

XVI CONSUL

[1] Appian, *BC* 2. 118, Plutarch, *Antony* 14–15, Dio 44. 20. 1–22. 3.

[2] J. Osgood, *Caesar's Legacy: Civil War and the Emergence of the Roman Empire* (2006), p.29.

[3] Cicero, *Philippics* 2. 28; R. Syme, *The Roman Revolution* (1960), pp.97–103.

[4] Appian, *BC* 2. 120–123.

[5] Appian, *BC* 2. 123–136, Dio 44. 22. 3–34. 7; Osgood (2006), pp.12–14, Syme (1960), pp.102–103 and 107, D. Stockton, *Cicero: A Political Biography* (1971), pp.280–282, T. Mitchell, *Cicero: The Senior Statesman* (1991), pp.289–291, and E. Rawson in *CAH*² IX, pp.468–470.

[6] For Lepidus' legion see Appian, *BC* 2. 118, 126, with P. Brunt, *Italian Manpower 225 BC–AD 14* (1971), p.477.

[7] Consul and Antonius, see Cicero, *Philippics* 2. 70; on Antony see Syme (1960), pp.105–106.

[8] Plutarch, *Antony* 14, *Brutus* 20, Dio 44. 35. 1–52. 3, Appian, *BC* 2. 137–148, Suetonius, *Caesar* 84. 2, with Osgood (2006), pp.12–13, and Syme (1960), pp.98–99.

[9] Rawson in *CAH*² IX, p.470, Osgood (2006), pp.14–16 and 30.

[10] Appian, *BC* 3. 2–3, 36, Cicero, *ad Att.* 14. 15, Syme (1960), pp.99.

[11] Appian, *BC* 3. 2–8, Dio 44. 53. 1–7, 45, with Syme (1960), pp.109–111 and 115–116, Rawson in *CAH²* IX, pp.470–471, and Osgood (2006), p.30.

[12] Cicero, *Philippics* 2. 92–100, *ad Att.* 14. 12.

[13] Cicero, *ad Att.* 14. 13, 13a and 13b.

[14] Cicero, *Philippics* 1. 20.

[15] Dio 44. 53. 6–7, with Syme (1960), p.109, Mitchell (1991), pp.292–293, and Osgood (2006), pp.35 and 40.

[16] Cicero, *ad Att.* 14. 8, 20, with M. Grant, *Cleopatra* (1972), pp.95–96, J. Tyldesley, *Cleopatra: Last Queen of Egypt* (2009), p.108, and J. Fletcher, *Cleopatra the Great: The Woman Behind the Legend* (2008), pp.213–214.

[17] Suetonius, *Caesar* 83. 1–2, *Augustus* 8. 1–2, Appian, *BC* 2. 143, Pliny, *NH* 35. 21, Dio 45. 1. 1–6. 3, with Syme (1960), pp.112–115.

[18] Suetonius, *Caesar* 83, Cicero, *ad Att.* 14. 11 and 12, with Osgood (2006), pp.31–32; for the quote, Cicero, *Philippics* 13. 24.

[19] Syme (1960), pp.115–122.

[20] Plutarch, *Brutus* 21, Suetonius, *Caesar* 88, and *Augustus* 10, Pliny, *NH* 2. 93–94, Dio 45. 6. 4–8. 4, with Osgood (2006), pp.21–22 and 40–41.

[21] Syme (1960), pp.115–116, and Brunt (1971), pp.477–483.

[22] Stockton (1971), pp.286–287 and 319–320, and Osgood (2006), pp.32–33.

XVII 'One of Three'

[1] R. Syme, *The Roman Revolution* (1960), pp.123–124, D. Stockton, *Cicero: A Political Biography* (1971), pp.292–294, T. Mitchell, *Cicero: The Senior Statesman* (1991), pp.295–306, and J. Osgood, *Caesar's Legacy: Civil War and the Emergence of the Roman Empire* (2006), pp.41–42.

[2] Cicero, *ad Fam.* 12. 3 (SB 345).

[3] Appian, *BC* 3. 31, 40–45, Dio 45. 12. 1–13. 5, Cicero, *Philippics* 3. 4, 6, 38–39, 4. 5–6, with Osgood (2006), pp.47–50; for a discussion of *Legio Martia* and a possible tombstone of one of its centurions see L. Keppie, 'A Centurion of *Legio Martia* at Padova?', *Journal of Roman Military Equipment Studies* 2 (1991), pp.115–121 = L. Keppie, *Legions and Veterans: Roman Army Papers 1971–2000* (2000), pp.68–74.

[4] On the raising of legions see P. Brunt, *Italian Manpower 225 BC–AD 14* (1971), p.481.

[5] Appian, *BC* 3. 46, Dio 45. 13. 5, with Syme (1960), pp.126–127; on Antony's popularity see Plutarch, *Antony* 4.

[6] Quote from Cicero, *ad Fam.* 11. 4 (Loeb translation by Shackleton Bailey, SB 342); Sallust, *Bell. Cat.* 56. 1–3, describes the creation of the officers and organisation for two legions, which were then filled up with recruits as men and equipment became available.

[7] Osgood (2006), p.50.

[8] Syme (1960), pp.127–150 and 162–171, Stockton (1971), pp.295–316, Mitchell (1991), pp.301–315.

[9] Cicero, *Philippics* 11. 5–10, Appian, *BC* 3. 26, Dio 47. 29. 1–6.

[10] Cicero, *Philippics* 5. 3, 4, 25, 31, 8. 27, Appian, *BC* 3. 63, with E. Rawson in *CAH²* IX, pp.478–479.

[11] Appian, *BC* 3. 50–51, Cicero, *Philippics* 8. 1, 25–28, 33, with Syme (1960), pp.167–173, Stockton (1971), p.308, and Mitchell (1961), pp.312–316.

[12] Cicero, *ad Fam.* 11. 21. 1; on the legions see Brunt (1971), p.481.

[13] Dio 46. 36. 3–5, Pliny, *NH* 10. 110.

[14] For accounts of Forum Gallorum see Cicero, *ad Fam.* 10. 30; for Servius Sulpicius Galba's account see Appian, *BC* 66–70, Dio 46. 37. 1–7, with Osgood (2006), pp.51–55, and L. Keppie, *The Making of the Roman Army* (1984), pp.115–118.

[15] Appian, *BC* 3. 71–76, Dio 46. 38. 1–41. 5, with Syme (1960), pp.173–177, Stockton (1971), pp.318–323, and Mitchell (1991), pp.316–319; see Suetonius, *Augustus* 10. 4 for an heroic story of Octavian carrying a legion's eagle to rally the men at the battle outside Mutina.

[16] Plutarch, *Antony* 18, Appian, *BC* 3. 80–84, Dio 46. 38. 6–7, with Syme (1960), pp.178–179, and Brunt (1971), pp.481–484; for Caesar not shaving until he had avenged his men see Suetonius, *Caesar* 67. 2.

[17] Appian, *BC* 3. 85–95, Dio 46. 39. 1–49. 5, with Syme (1960), pp.181–188, Stockton (1971), pp.329–331, and Mitchell (1991), pp.319–322.

[18] Plutarch, *Antony* 19–21, Appian, *BC* 3. 96–4. 46. 50. 1–56. 4, with Syme (1960), pp.188–191, Osgood (2006), pp.57–61, and Rawson in *CAH*² IX, pp.485–486.

[19] Plutarch, *Antony* 19–20, Appian, *BC* 4. 5–30, 37, Dio 57. 1. 1–14. 5, with Syme (1960), pp.190–196, and Osgood (2006), pp.62–82; Plutarch, *Antony* 20 (Oxford translation, modified) for quote.

XVIII GODDESS

[1] Cicero, *ad Att.* 14. 8, and quotes from *ad Att.* 15. 15.

[2] For instance, M. Grant, *Cleopatra* (1972), pp.95–97, on Cicero's troubled relationships with women and most Greeks.

[3] Josephus, *AJ* 15. 39, *Against Apion* 2. 58, Porphyry, *Fragments of Greek Historians* 260, and for a papyrus mentioning Ptolemy XIV in late July see B. Grenfell, A. Hunt et al. (eds.), *The Oxyrhynchus Papyri* (1898–), 14. 1629, with Grant (1972), pp.97–98, J. Tyldesley, *Cleopatra: Last Queen of Egypt* (2009), pp.109–110, and J. Fletcher, *Cleopatra the Great: The Woman Behind the Legend* (2008), pp.214–215.

[4] Strabo, *Geog.* 14. 6. 6, with P. Green, *Alexander to Actium: The Historical Evolution of the Hellenistic Age* (1990), p.669. Strabo says that Antony gave the rule of Cyprus to Cleopatra and Arsinoe, but that this arrangement was abandoned when he lost power. Since Arsinoe was dead long before Antony lost the civil war with Octavian, his loss of power can only refer to the period from late 44–43 BC.

[5] Appian, *BC* 3. 78, 4. 59, 5. 8, Dio 47. 28. 3, with P. Brunt, *Italian Manpower 225 BC–AD 14* (1971), p.480.

[6] Appian, *BC* 4. 60–62, Dio 47. 26. 3–30. 7.

[7] Appian, *BC* 4. 63.

[8] Appian, *BC* 4. 8–9, 61, 63, 74, 82, Dio 47. 31. 5, with Grant (1972), pp.100–105, and Tyldesley (2009), pp.143–144.

[9] J. Bingen, *Hellenistic Egypt: Monarchy, Society, Economy, Culture* (2007), pp.72–74.

[10] Appian, *BC* 4. 61, Pliny, *NH* 5. 58, Seneca, *Naturales Quaestiones* 4. 2, with D. Thompson, 'Cleopatra VII: The Queen in Egypt', in S. Walker & S. Ashton (eds.), *Cleopatra Reassessed* (2003), pp.31–34, esp. 33; for Alexandria's Jews see Josephus, *Against Apion* 2. 60.

[11] *CIL Suppl.* No. 6583 = *OGIS* 129, with Thompson (2003), p.33.

[12] P. van Minnen, 'A Royal Ordinance of Cleopatra and Related Documents', in

Walker & Ashton (2003), pp.35–44, and Grant (1972), p.100, citing *OGIS* 194, and Tyldesley (2009), p.141 for Callimachus.

[13] See J. Tait, 'Cleopatra by Name', in Walker & Ashton (2003), pp.3–7, esp. p.4, and J. Ray, 'Cleopatra in the Temples of Upper Egypt: The Evidence of Dendera and Armant', in Walker & Ashton (2003), pp.9–11, G. Goudchaux, 'Cleopatra's Subtle Religious Strategy', in S. Walker & P. Higgs (eds.), *Cleopatra of Egypt: From History to Myth* (2001), pp.128–141, G. Hölbl, *A History of the Ptolemaic Empire* (trans. T. Saavedra) (2001), pp.271–285 and 289–293, Grant (1972), pp.99–100, and Tyldesley (2009), pp.121–122 and 125–126.

[14] Plutarch, *Of Isis and Osiris*, with discussion in Tyldesley (2009), pp.113–118, Grant (1972), pp.117–120, Goudchaux (2001), pp.130–131 and 133–137, and Hölbl (2001), pp.289–293.

[15] Grant (1972), pp.103–105, and Tyldesley (2009), pp.144–145; S. Burnstein, *The Reign of Cleopatra* (2004), p.21, rather overstates Octavian's suspicion of Caesarion at this stage.

XIX VENGEANCE

[1] Dio 47. 8. 3–4.

[2] Cornelius Nepos, *Atticus* 9. 3–7.

[3] Plutarch, *Cicero* 48–49, *Antony* 20, Appian, *BC* 4. 19.

[4] Cornelius Nepos, *Atticus* 10. 4. 4 for the quote (Loeb translation by J. Rolfe).

[5] See Appian, *BC* 4. 40, Dio 47. 7. 4–5, 8. 5.

[6] For an interesting discussion of the impact of the proscriptions, their presentation and the role of Octavian see A. Powell, *Virgil the Partisan: A Study in the Re-integration of Classics* (2008), pp.55–62, 68–69. For an extreme version of the exoneration of Octavian at the expense of Antony and Lepidus see Velleius Paterculus 2. 66. 67. 4; on Sextus Pompey's rescue of refugees see Appian, *BC* 4. 36; on large number of books devoted to the theme of the proscriptions see Appian, *BC* 4. 16.

[7] Appian, *BC* 4. 31, Dio 47. 17. 2–4, with J. Osgood, *Caesar's Legacy: Civil War and the Emergence of the Roman Empire* (2006), pp.82–83.

[8] Appian, *BC* 4. 31–34, with Osgood (2006), pp.84–88.

[9] Dio 47. 16. 1–5.

[10] Appian, *BC* 4. 63–82, Dio 47. 32. 1–35. 6, Josephus, *AJ* 14. 271–276, *BJ* 1. 218–222, with Osgood (2006), pp.88–94.

[11] Dio 47. 25. 3, and for examples M. Crawford, *Roman Republican Coinage* (1974), pp.498–508.

[12] R. Syme, *The Roman Revolution* (1960), pp.149–161, Powell (2008), pp.51–75; for criticism of Octavian's refusal to honour the *pietas* of others see Suetonius, *Augustus* 13. 1–2.

[13] For example, Appian, *BC* 4. 100–101; *BC* 5. 17 provides a detailed discussion of soldiers' attitudes, cf. Cornelius Nepos, *Eumenes* 8. 2.

[14] Appian, *BC* 4. 88, 108; for discussion, but generally accepting a high estimate, see P. Brunt, *Italian Manpower 225 BC–AD 14* (1971), pp.485–488.

[15] Dio 47. 39. 1, contrasting with Appian, *BC* 4. 137; for Tiberius see Velleius Paterculus 2. 113.

[16] For this scale of reward see Appian, *BC* 4. 100.

[17] Appian, *BC* 4. 3.

[18] Appian, *BC* 4. 82, 86–87.

[19] Appian, *BC* 4. 101–106, Plutarch, *Brutus* 37–38.

[20] Appian, *BC* 4. 107–108, Plutarch, *Brutus* 39–40.

[21] As an example of legionaries being dismayed by the loss of their baggage, see Caesar, *BG* 5. 33, contrasted with better discipline at *BG* 5. 43 by a different legion.

[22] For the various versions of Octavian's behaviour see Plutarch, *Brutus* 41, *Antony* 22, Dio 47. 41. 3–4, 46. 2, Velleius Paterculus 2. 70. 1, Suetonius, *Augustus* 13. 1, Pliny, *NH* 7. 147, with brief discussion in Syme (1960), pp.204–205, Osgood (2006), pp.95–96, and Powell (2008), p.106.

[23] For the first battle see Appian, *BC* 4. 109–114, Plutarch, *Brutus* 40–45, Dio 47. 42. 1–47. 1.

[24] Appian, *BC* 4. 115–124, Plutarch, *Brutus* 45–48, Dio 47. 47. 2–48. 3.

[25] Appian, *BC* 4. 125–131, Plutarch, *Brutus* 49–52, Dio 47. 48. 1–49. 4.

[26] On Brutus' head see Suetonius, *Augustus* 13. 1, Dio 47. 49. 2; in general Suetonius, *Augustus* 13. 1, Plutarch, *Antony* 22, Appian, *BC* 4. 135, Velleius Paterculus 2. 86. 2. A useful survey of the different versions of Antony's and Octavian's behaviour can be found in K. Scott, 'The Political Propaganda of 44–30 BC', *Memoirs of the American Academy in Rome* 11 (1933), pp.7–49, esp. 21–23.

[27] Gellius, *NA* 3. 9. 1–6.

XX DIONYSUS AND APHRODITE

[1] Plutarch, *Antony* 23, Suetonius, *Augustus* 13. 3, Appian, *BC* 5. 3, Dio 48. 3. 1.

[2] See R. Syme, *The Roman Revolution* (1960), pp.206–207.

[3] Appian, *BC* 5. 3, with P. Brunt, *Italian Manpower 225 BC–AD 14* (1971), pp.488–495.

[4] Plutarch, *Antony* 23, *Brutus* 24.

[5] Plutarch, *Antony* 24, Appian, *BC* 5. 4–6.

[6] Plutarch, *Brutus* 30, *Antony* 24.

[7] Appian, *BC* 5. 7, Dio 49. 32. 3; for Octavian's verse see Martial, *Epigrams* 11. 20.

[8] Josephus, *AJ* 14. 314–316, and 14. 301–312 (quotes from Loeb translation); see also J. Osgood, *Caesar's Legacy: Civil War and the Emergence of the Roman Empire* (2006), pp.105–106.

[9] E. Schürer, G. Vermes & F. Millar, *The History of the Jewish People in the Age of Jesus Christ*, Vol. 1 (1973), pp.277–279.

[10] 'No mean city', from Acts 21. 39.

[11] M. Grant, *Cleopatra* (1972), p.111, referring to Strabo, *Geog.* 14. 1. 23; confirming the rights of the temple at Ephesus see R. Sherk, *Roman Documents from the Greek East* (1969), no. 57.

[12] Plutarch, *Antony* 25; on Dellius see Syme (1960), p.214; p.265 cites Strabo, *Geog.* 11. 13. 3, where it is noted that Dellius wrote an account of Antony's expedition to Media.

[13] Plutarch, *Antony* 26 (Oxford translation by R. Waterfield).

[14] P. Green, *Alexander to Actium: The Historical Evolution of the Hellenistic Age* (1990), p.663 for quote.

[15] Plutarch, *Antony* 26–27, Appian, *BC* 5. 1, 8–9, Dio 48. 24. 2, with Grant (1972), pp.111–118, G. Hölbl, *A History of the Ptolemaic Empire* (trans. T. Saavedra) (2001), pp.240–241, J. Tyldesley, *Cleopatra: Last Queen of Egypt* (2009), pp.149–152, and J. Fletcher, *Cleopatra the Great: The Woman Behind the Legend* (2008), pp.235–241.

[16] Plutarch, *Antony* 25.

[17] Josephus, *AJ* 15. 89, Appian, *BC* 5. 9, Dio 48. 24. 2. I am very grateful to Dr Dorothy King for pointing out to me the problems of associating the tomb at Ephesus with Arsinoe, or indeed the Ptolemies at all, on the basis of a supposed similarity to the Pharos, and also for providing me with a copy of her unpublished PhD thesis, D. King, 'The Sculptural Decoration of the Doric Order, ca. 375–31 BC' (King's College London, 2000).

[18] Plutarch, *Antony* 28–29, Appian, *BC* 5. 11; for Arsinoe III helping to lead the Ptolemaic army at Raphia see Polybius 5. 83. 3; the importance of horses and hunting to the Greek and Roman aristocracies is well brought out in R. Lane Fox, *The Classical World: An Epic History from Homer to Hadrian* (2006), *passim*.

[19] Plutarch, *Antony* 29.

[20] For the importance of dice (*alea*), and the associations with decadence and poor character for Romans in this era see N. Purcell, 'Literate Games: Roman Urban Society and the Game of *Alea*', *Past & Present* 147 (1995), pp.3–37; for the self-dubbed 'Parasite' see *OGIS* 195, discussed in P. Fraser, 'Mark Antony in Alexandria – A Note', *JRS* 47 (1957), pp.71–74.

[21] Plutarch, *Antony* 28.

[22] Athenaeus, *Epitome* 4. 147 ff., citing Socrates of Rhodes for the feasts at Tarsus; on golden chamber pots see Pliny, *NH* 33. 49.

[23] Plutarch, *Antony* 29.

XXI CRISIS

[1] J. Osgood, *Caesar's Legacy: Civil War and the Emergence of the Roman Empire* (2006), pp.108–151.

[2] On the Perusine War see Appian, *BC* 5. 12–51, Dio 48. 5. 1–14. 6, Plutarch, *Antony* 30, Velleius Paterculus 2. 74–76, with discussions in E. Gabba, 'The Perusine War and Triumviral Italy', *Harvard Studies in Classical Philology* 75 (1971), pp.139–160, R. Syme, *The Roman Revolution* (1960), pp.207–212, Osgood (2006), pp.152–172, and C. Pelling in *CAH²* X, pp.14–17.

[3] Appian, *BC* 5. 52–53, Dio 48. 5. 2–3, 16. 3.

[4] Appian, *BC* 5. 52.

[5] Plutarch, *Antony* 30, Appian, *BC* 5. 51, 54–55, 59.

[6] Appian, *BC* 5. 55, Velleius Paterculus 2. 76.

[7] Appian, *BC* 5. 56–66, Dio 48. 28. 1–30. 2, with Syme (1960), pp.129, 216–217, 242 and 253–255, and Pelling in *CAH²* X, pp.17–20.

[8] See Osgood (2006), pp.188–201, Syme (1960), pp.217–220; for Antony's guilt over his treatment of Fulvia see Appian, *BC* 5. 59.

[9] Appian, *BC* 5. 67–68, Dio 48. 31. 1–6.

[10] Appian, *BC* 5. 69–74, Dio 48. 36. 1–38. 3, Velleius Paterculus 2. 77, Plutarch, *Antony* 32, with Syme (1960), pp.221–222, Osgood (2006), pp.205–207, and A. Powell, *Virgil the Partisan: A Study in the Re-integration of Classics* (2008), pp.190–191.

[11] Plutarch, *Antony* 33, Appian, *BC* 5. 76, Dio 48. 39. 2, Seneca, *Suasoriae* 1. 6, with M. Grant, *Cleopatra* (1972), pp.129–130.

[12] Osgood (2006), pp.225–231, quote from p.229, and F. Millar, 'Triumvirate and Principate', *JRS* 63 (1973), pp.50–67.

XXII INVASION

[1] Dio 49. 32. 4, Plutarch, *Antony* 36.

[2] See in general E. Huzar, 'Mark Antony: Marriages vs. Careers', *The Classical Journal* 81. 2 (1986), pp.97–111, esp. p.98 for Fadia and the children, referring to Cicero, *ad Att.* 16. 11. 1 for the implication that the latter had died.

[3] On Labienus' father see R. Syme, 'The Allegiance of Labienus', *JRS* 28 (1938), pp.113–125, and W. Tyrell, 'Labienus' Departure from Caesar in January 49 BC', *Historia* 21 (1972), pp.424–440; on the son see Dio 48. 24. 4–25. 1.

[4] Dio 48. 26. 5, with R. Syme, *The Roman Revolution* (1960), p.223, and discussion of the campaign and its context in D. Kennedy, 'Parthia and Rome: Eastern Perspectives', in D. Kennedy (ed.), *The Roman Army in the East, JRA* Supplement 18 (1996), pp.67–90, esp. 77–81.

[5] For discussion of Roman and Parthian armies see A. Goldsworthy, *The Roman Army at War 100 BC–AD 200* (1996), pp.60–68, Kennedy (1996), pp.83–84; on the execution of the victorious commander at Carrhae see Plutarch, *Crassus* 32.

[6] Kennedy (1996), pp.79–81, J. Osgood, *Caesar's Legacy: Civil War and the Emergence of the Roman Empire* (2006), pp.185, 225–228; for Hybreas see Strabo, *Geog.* 14. 2. 23–24.

[7] Josephus, *AJ* 14. 330–369, *BJ* 1. 248–273, with Osgood (2006), pp.185–186, E. Schürer, G. Vermes & F. Millar, *The History of the Jewish People in the Age of Jesus Christ*, Vol. 1 (1973), pp.278–286.

[8] Josephus, *AJ* 14. 370–376, *BJ* 1. 274–279.

[9] Appian, *BC* 5. 92, Dio 48. 41. 7, 49. 2–3, with Syme (1960), pp.222–223 and 230–231, and Osgood (2006), pp.245 and 251.

[10] Dio 48. 39. 2–41. 6, 49. 19. 1–20. 5, Plutarch, *Antony* 34, Gellius, *NA* 15. 4, Frontinus, *Strategems* 1. 1. 6, 2. 2. 5, 2. 5. 36–37, and on Crassus, Plutarch, *Crassus* 31–33, with Kennedy (1996), pp.80–81, and Osgood (2006), pp.255 and 280–281; on Ventidius' career see J. Seaver, 'Publius Ventidius: Neglected Roman Military Hero', *The Classical Journal* 47 (1952), pp.275–280 and 300.

[11] On the failure of Octavian to meet Antony at Tarentum see Appian, *BC* 4. 78–80; on Sextus Pompey see Osgood (2006), pp.202–205 and 242–243, C. Pelling in *CAH*² X, pp.24–25, K. Welch & A. Powell (eds.), *Sextus Pompeius* (2002), *passim*, and A. Powell, *Virgil the Partisan: A Study in the Re-integration of Classics* (2008), pp.16–19, 97–100.

[12] Plutarch, *Antony* 34.

[13] See F. Millar, 'Triumvirate and Principate', *JRS* 63 (1973), pp.50–67, esp. 51 and 53, and Pelling in *CAH*² X, pp.67–68.

[14] Appian, *BC* 5. 93–95, Plutarch, *Antony* 35, with Pelling in *CAH*² X, pp.24–27, and P. Brunt, *Italian Manpower 225 BC–AD 14* (1971), p.502.

[15] Syme (1960), pp.129 and 231, Osgood (2006), pp.298–300.

[16] Josephus, *BJ* 1. 282–357, *AJ* 14. 377–491, Dio 49. 22. 6.

[17] Dio 49. 23. 2–5, Plutarch, *Antony* 37, with Kennedy (1996), p.81.

[18] Suetonius, *Augustus* 62. 2, Velleius Paterculus 2. 75, with Syme (1960), pp.228–229, Osgood (2006), pp.231–232, and for more detail on her family and the marriage see A. Barrett, *Livia: First Lady of Imperial Rome* (2002), pp.3–27.

[19] Suetonius, *Caius* 23.

[20] Suetonius, *Augustus* 70, with comments in K. Scott, 'The Political Propaganda of 44–30 BC', *Memoirs of the American Academy in Rome* 11 (1933), pp.7–49, esp.30–32, and Powell (2008), p.74.

XXIII 'LOVER OF HER FATHERLAND'

[1] Plutarch, *Antony* 36.
[2] Josephus, *AJ* 15. 23–31.
[3] Dio 49. 3–5, with C. Pelling in *CAH²* X, pp.28–30, and R. Syme, *The Roman Revolution* (1960), pp.259–261.
[4] Plutarch, *Antony* 36, Dio 49. 32. 5, Strabo, *Geog.* 14. 669, 671, with M. Grant, *Cleopatra* (1972), pp.135–141, G. Hölbl, *A History of the Ptolemaic Empire* (trans. T. Saavedra) (2001), p.242, and J. Tyldesley, *Cleopatra: Last Queen of Egypt* (2009), pp.162–164.
[5] Josephus, *AJ* 15. 88–, 91–96, with Hölbl (2001), p.242 and p.254, n. 103.
[6] On the titles and their implications see J. Bingen, *Hellenistic Egypt: Monarchy, Society, Economy, Culture* (2007), pp.57–62 and 74–79, contrasting with D. Thompson in *CAH²* IX, p.321, and 'Cleopatra VII: The Queen in Egypt', in S. Walker & S. Ashton (eds.), *Cleopatra Reassessed* (2003), pp.31–34.
[7] Thompson (2003), pp.31–34, argues that the 'homeland' was primarily, but not exclusively, Egypt, but Bingen (2007), pp.57–62 and 74–79, is more convincing. Thompson's examples of the queen taking a personal interest in the welfare of a range of groups within Egypt does not seem more than the practical measures of a monarch wishing to remain in power.
[8] G. Goudchaux, 'Cleopatra the Seafarer Queen: Strabo and India', in Walker & Ashton (2003), pp.109–111; introduction of a type of cabbage from Rhodes, Athenaeus 9. 369; for failure to innovate see D. Rathbone, 'Ptolemaic to Roman Egypt: The Death of the Dirigiste State?', in E. Lo Cascio & D. Rathbone (eds.), *Production and Public Powers in Classical Antiquity* (2000), pp.44–54, esp. 46–51.
[9] S. Walker & P. Higgs (eds.), *Cleopatra of Egypt: From History to Myth* (2001), p.234, ns. 218–222.
[10] Josephus, *AJ* 15. 31–67, with E. Schürer, G. Vermes & F. Millar, *The History of the Jewish People in the Age of Jesus Christ*, Vol. 1 (1973), pp.296–297.
[11] Josephus, *AJ* 15. 96–103. Josephus dates this encounter to 34 BC, but it may equally have occurred before Antony's first Parthian expedition at the start of 36 BC.
[12] Josephus, *BJ* 1. 397.
[13] Rathbone (2000), pp.44–54.

XXIV 'INDIA AND ASIA TREMBLE': THE GRAND EXPEDITION

[1] For example, Plutarch, *Antony* 34, Dio 49. 21. 2, and Tacitus, *Germania* 38, with C. Pelling in *CAH²* X, p.31, fn. 142.
[2] J. Osgood, *Caesar's Legacy: Civil War and the Emergence of the Roman Empire* (2006), pp.303–305.
[3] For Caesar's planned expedition see Dio 43. 51. 1–2, 44. 1. 1, Appian, *BC* 2. 110, 3. 77, Plutarch, *Caesar* 58, Velleius Paterculus 2. 59. 4, Suetonius, *Caesar* 44. 3, and T. Rice Holmes, *The Roman Republic*, Vol. 3 (1923), pp.326–327; on the operations against the Albani and Iberi see A. Sherwin-White, *Roman Foreign Policy in the East 168 BC–AD 1*

(1984), pp.307–308. Publius Canidius Crassus was no relation of Marcus Licinius Crassus, Caesar's ally.

[4] Plutarch, *Antony* 37.

[5] Appian, *BC* 2. 110, Velleius Paterculus 2. 82. 1–2; for discussion see P. Brunt, *Italian Manpower 225 BC–AD 14* (1971), pp.503–504, Sherwin-White (1984), p.311, fn. 37, and L. Keppie, 'Mark Antony's Legions', in L. Keppie, *Legions and Veterans: Roman Army Papers 1971–2000* (2000), pp.75–96.

[6] Josephus, *AJ* 14. 449, *BJ* 1. 324 for legions 'recently levied in Syria'.

[7] Plutarch, *Antony* 38; for supply in general see J. Roth, *The Logistics of the Roman Army at War (264 BC–AD 235)* (1999), *passim*.

[8] For Roman military intelligence in general see N. Austin & B. Rankov, *Exploratio: Military and Political Intelligence in the Roman World from the Second Punic War to the Battle of Adrianople* (1995), *passim*, but esp. p.73.

[9] Plutarch, *Antony* 37–38, Livy, *Pers.* 130 for criticism of Antony.

[10] For discussions of Parthian armies see the sources cited in chapter 22, n. 6.

[11] Dio 49. 25. 1, Plutarch, *Antony* 38, with Pelling in *CAH²* X, p.32.

[12] Plutarch, *Antony* 38, Strabo, *Geog.* 11. 13. 3–4, and Frontinus, *Strategemata* 1. 1. 6 on the route through Zeugma, with Sherwin-White (1984), pp.308–311.

[13] Plutarch, *Antony* 38, Dio 49. 25. 3.

[14] Plutarch, *Antony* 38, with Sherwin-White (1984), pp.311–315, and for the paces of draught and pack animals see A. Goldsworthy, *The Roman Army at War 100 BC–AD 200* (1996), pp.287–296.

[15] Dio 49. 25. 2, Velleius Paterculus 2. 82. 2.

[16] Plutarch, *Antony* 38, Dio 49. 25. 3–26. 1.

[17] Plutarch, *Antony* 39. This incident is the basis for the assumption that he must have had more than the thirteen legions claimed by Velleius. The logic is that with two destroyed in the convoy, and ten led out in this operation, the remaining one legion would have been inadequate to guard the siege lines at Phraata. This is conjecture, and in any case ignores the possibility that elements of the ten legions also remained behind. In the end we simply do not know.

[18] Plutarch, *Antony* 39, Dio 49. 26. 1–27. 1, with Sherwin-White (1984), p.318.

[19] Plutarch, *Antony* 40, Dio 49. 27. 2–28. 1.

[20] Plutarch, *Antony* 41–42, *Crassus* 25.

[21] For a discussion of missile weapons and effectiveness see Goldsworthy (1996), pp.183–190, 228–229 and 232–235.

[22] Plutarch, *Antony* 42–43, Dio 49. 29. 1.

[23] Plutarch, *Antony* 44–45, Dio 49. 29. 2–4.

[24] Plutarch, *Antony* 45.

[25] Velleius Paterculus 2. 82. 2.

[26] Plutarch, *Antony* 46–48.

[27] Plutarch, *Antony* 49–51, Velleius Paterculus 2. 82. 3. Dio 49. 31. 1–3, with Sherwin-White (1984), pp.320–321. Livy, *Pers.* 130, also claims that 8,000 men died 'in storms' during the march through Armenia, but does not give a figure for overall casualties. He also accuses Antony of ordering the march so that he could winter with Cleopatra.

[28] See N. Dixon, *On the Psychology of Military Incompetence* (1994), for an interesting discussion of Raglan and other unsuccessful leaders.

XXV QUEEN OF KINGS

[1] Plutarch, *Antony* 51, Dio 49. 31. 4. M. Grant, *Cleopatra* (1972), p.149, suggests that Leuce Come was chosen in case the Parthians had invaded Syria.

[2] Appian, *BC* 5. 96–122; for summaries and more detailed references see C. Pelling in *CAH²* X, pp.34–35, J. Osgood, *Caesar's Legacy: Civil War and the Emergence of the Roman Empire* (2006), pp.298–303, and R. Syme, *The Roman Revolution* (1960), pp.230–231.

[3] Appian, *BC* 5. 122–126, 131, Dio 49. 11. 2–12. 5, 15. 3, Velleius Paterculus 2. 80. 1–4, with Syme (1960), pp.232–233.

[4] Appian, *BC* 5. 131; on the use of slaves in Octavian's fleet see Suetonius, *Augustus* 16. 1, Dio 47. 17. 4, 48. 49. 1, 49. 1. 5, the last passage implying that they were given freedom on discharge.

[5] Dio 49. 32. 1–2, Velleius Paterculus 2. 82. 3.

[6] Plutarch, *Antony* 53–54, Appian, *BC* 5. 95, 138, Dio 49. 33. 3–4, with Grant (1972), pp.150–153, Osgood (2006), p.336, and Syme (1960), p.265.

[7] Plutarch, *Antony* 52, 54, Dio 49. 33. 1–2.

[8] Dio 49. 17. 1–18. 7, 50. 1. 4, Appian, *BC* 5. 127, 133–144, Velleius Paterculus 2. 79. 5.

[9] Plutarch, *Antony* 53. The passage tends to be summarily dismissed by modern biographers of Cleopatra, for example, Grant (1972), p.152, J. Tyldesley, *Cleopatra: Last Queen of Egypt* (2009), pp.165–166, and J. Fletcher, *Cleopatra the Great: The Woman Behind the Legend* (2008), pp.272–273. However, just because there were strong political reasons for Antony to rebuff Octavia does not necessarily mean that there was not also genuine – perhaps even extreme – emotion involved as well.

[10] Plutarch, *Antony* 54.

[11] Appian, *Illyrian Wars* 16–28, Dio 49. 34. 1–38. 4, and the useful summary by E. Gruen in *CAH²* X, pp.171–174; for the punishments see Dio 49. 38. 4, Suetonius, *Augustus* 24. 2.

[12] Suetonius, *Augustus* 28. 3, Pliny, *NH* 36. 121, and for discussion see N. Purcell in *CAH²* X, pp.782–789.

[13] Plutarch, *Antony* 36, 52–53, Dio 49. 33. 1–3, 39. 1–40. 2, Syme (1960), p.262, citing *PIR¹*, P 835.

[14] Plutarch, *Antony* 54, Dio 49. 40. 3–4, Velleius Paterculus 2. 82. 3–4, with comments in Grant (1972), pp.161–162, and Pelling in *CAH²* X, p.40.

[15] Dio 49. 40. 4.

[16] Plutarch, *Antony* 54, Dio 49. 41. 1–6, with Pelling in *CAH²* X, pp.40–41, Osgood (2006), pp.338–339, Grant (1972), pp.162–175, J. Bingen, *Hellenistic Egypt: Monarchy, Society, Economy, Culture* (2007), pp.78–79, G. Hölbl, *A History of the Ptolemaic Empire* (trans. T. Saavedra) (2001), pp.244–245, Tyldesley (2009), pp.168–169, Fletcher (2008), pp.274–276, and M. Chauveau, *Egypt in the Age of Cleopatra* (trans. D. Lorton) (2000), p.27.

XXVI IS SHE MY WIFE?

[1] Dio 49. 39. 1.

[2] Dio 47. 15. 2–3, 48. 43. 2, 49. 43. 6–7; runaway slaves as magistrates, 48. 34. 5.

[3] Dio 50. 5. 1; on coins of Antyllus, see M. Crawford, *Roman Republican Coinage* (1974), p.543.

[4] Plutarch, *Antony* 28, and cf.; for the story told of Antony's father see Plutarch, *Antony* 1.

[5] Plutarch, *Antony* 4.

[6] Pliny, *NH* 9. 119–121; for another alleged wager see Plutarch, *Antony* 58, although in 59 he was sceptical of the truth of some of the stories he lists, and see also Pliny, *NH* 21. 122.

[7] Horace, *Satires* 2. 3. 239–42, Valerius Maximus 9. 1. 2, Pliny, *NH* 9. 122; Suetonius, *Caligula* 37. 1, and cf. his wife who wore emeralds and pearls to the value of 10 million denarii and carried the receipts around to prove it, Pliny, *NH* 9. 117; for Servilia see Suetonius, *Caesar* 50. 2, and for Britain, Suetonius, *Caesar* 47.

[8] The fullest discussion is to be found in B. Ullman, 'Cleopatra's Pearls', *The Classical Journal* 52. 5 (Feb. 1957), pp.193–201.

[9] Velleius Paterculus 2. 83. 1–2, with J. Osgood, *Caesar's Legacy: Civil War and the Emergence of the Roman Empire* (2006), pp.276–280; on dancing, see Cicero, *Pro Murena* 13.

[10] Horace, *Odes* 1. 37. 14, Propertius 3. 11, Plutarch, *Roman Questions* 112, *Moralia* 291A, with M. Grant, *Cleopatra* (1972), pp.178–179.

[11] Seneca, *Moralia* 87. 16, with Grant (1972), p.179; for the 'Parasite' see ch. 20, fn. 19.

[12] P. van Minnen, 'An Official Act of Cleopatra with a Subscription in her Own Hand', *Ancient Society* 30 (2000), pp.29–34, with P. van Minnen, 'A Royal Ordinance of Cleopatra and Related Documents', in S. Walker & S. Ashton (eds.), *Cleopatra Reassessed* (2003), pp.35–44, esp.40–41.

[13] For discussion of the mood of the times see Osgood (2006), pp.298–349.

[14] Dio 49. 15. 5–6, 38. 1.

[15] For discussions of the propaganda war, see K. Scott, 'The Political Propaganda of 44–30 BC', *Memoirs of the American Academy in Rome* 11 (1933), pp.7–49, esp. 33–49, Osgood (2006), pp.335–349, C. Pelling in *CAH²* X, pp.40–48, and R. Syme, *The Roman Revolution* (1960), pp.276–278; Suetonius, *Caesar* 52. 2 on the pamphlet written by Caius Oppius denying that Caesarion was Caesar's son.

[16] Pliny, *NH* 14. 148; Caesar and the public oath, Dio 43. 20. 4.

[17] Suetonius, *Augustus* 69. 2; praise for Octavia's beauty led J. Fletcher, *Cleopatra the Great: The Woman Behind the Legend* (2008), p.256, to suggest that this was in direct contrast to Cleopatra's carefully presented looks and hairstyles.

[18] Suetonius, *Augustus* 69. 1.

[19] Plutarch, *Comparison between Antony and Demetrius* 4, with Grant (1972), p.188, and Pelling in *CAH²* X, p.43; on Hercules and Omphale see P. Zanker, *The Power of Images in the Age of Augustus* (trans. A. Shapiro) (1988), pp.57–65, and esp. 58–60.

[20] Plutarch, *Antony* 55–56, Dio 49. 44. 3, 50. 1. 1–2. 2.

[21] Dio 50. 2. 4, with Pelling in *CAH²* X, pp.67–68.

[22] Dio 49. 41. 4, 50. 2. 2–4.

[23] Dio 50. 2. 5–7; on magic potions see Dio 49. 34. 1, and Josephus, *AJ* 15. 93.

[24] Velleius Paterculus 2. 83. 3.

[25] Plutarch, *Antony* 58, Suetonius, *Augustus* 17. 1, Dio 50. 3. 1–4. 1, with J. Johnson, 'The Authenticity and Validity of Antony's Will', *L'Antiquité Classique* 47 (1978), pp.494–503. The latter suggests that Antony may have employed a form of the military will, which in later periods permitted soldiers to name non-citizens as heirs. Caesar

introduced an early form of this, but its details are unknown, making this no more than a possibility.

[26] Suetonius, *Caesar* 79. 3, Dio 50. 5. 4.

[27] Plutarch, *Antony* 58–59, Horace, *Epodes* 9. 11–16, on the shame of Romans serving a foreign queen and her eunuchs, and Propertius 3. 11 on the threat Cleopatra posed.

[28] Velleius Paterculus 2. 86. 3 for Asinius Pollio; on the oath see *The Res Gestae of the Divine Augustus* 25. 2–3, Suetonius, *Augustus* 17. 2, with discussion in Osgood (2006), pp.357–368; Syme (1960), p.278, fn. 3, claims that more than 300 senators went to Antony, and his authority is one of the main reasons this figure is so often repeated as fact rather than inference.

[29] Suetonius, *Augustus* 63. 2.

XXVII WAR

[1] Plutarch, *Antony* 56–57, M. Grant, *Cleopatra* (1972), pp.193–197.

[2] In general, Plutarch, *Antony* 56, with J. Osgood, *Caesar's Legacy: Civil War and the Emergence of the Roman Empire* (2006), pp.370–371; Valerius Maximus 1. 1. 19, Dio 51. 8. 3 for Turullius.

[3] Plutarch, *Caesar*, 48, *Antony* 56, 61–62, with C. Pelling (ed.), *Plutarch: Life of Antony* (1988), pp.266–267 and 270–271.

[4] Plutarch, *Antony* 58, who says that most of the stories were not believed.

[5] Seneca, *Suasoriae* 1. 6, cf. Plutarch, *Antony* 57, with Pelling (1988), pp.258–259.

[6] Plutarch, *Comparison between Demetrius and Antony* 1 and 4 seem to imply a marriage, not suggested at *Antony* 31, 53; for discussion of the question see Pelling (1988), pp.219–220, R. Syme, *The Roman Revolution* (1960), pp.261, 274, 277 and 280, and G. Hölbl, *A History of the Ptolemaic Empire* (trans. T. Saavedra) (2001), p.244. Livy, *Pers.* 131 claims that after the Donations of Alexandria in 34 BC Antony began to treat Cleopatra like a wife, but does not actually say a formal marriage occurred. Late sources claiming a marriage include Eutropius 7. 6. 2, Orosius 6. 19. 4, and Athenaeus, *Deipnosophists* 4. 147; Virgil, *Aeneid* 8. 688 – *sequiturque nefas Aegyptia coniunx*; for a range of views see J. Tyldesley, *Cleopatra: Last Queen of Egypt* (2009), pp.169–170, J. Fletcher, *Cleopatra the Great: The Woman Behind the Legend* (2008), pp.264–265, who argues for a marriage as early as 37 BC, and Grant (1972), p.186.

[7] Josephus, *AJ* 15. 108–120, Plutarch, *Antony* 61, with Pelling (1988), pp.267–268, and Grant (1972), pp.196 and 272, n. 51.

[8] Velleius Paterculus 2. 84. 2.

[9] Plutarch, *Antony* 56, 59, with Pelling (1988), p.263.

[10] Plutarch, *Antony* 56, with Pelling (1988), pp.255–256, and *CAH²* X, pp.50–51, Grant (1972), pp.195–196, Tyldesley (2009), pp.173–174, and on resentment of Rome in the east see Osgood (2006), pp.340–344.

[11] Plutarch, *Antony* 56–57, 59.

[12] Dio 50. 4. 1–6. 1, Livy 1. 32 for a detailed account of the ceremony written after Octavian had revived it; see also J. Rich, *Declaring War in the Roman Republic in the Period of Transmarine Expansion* (1976), pp.56–58 and 104–107.

XXVIII ACTIUM

[1] Plutarch, *Antony* 58, Dio 50. 9. 1–22 argues that Antony planned a quick offensive,

but lost heart when he mistook some enemy patrol ships for the whole fleet; Livy, *Pers.* 132 claims Antony planned and prepared an invasion of Italy, but does not say why it did not occur, merely stating that Octavian crossed to Epirus; on the impact of taxation and the mood of Italy see J. Osgood, *Caesar's Legacy: Civil War and the Emergence of the Roman Empire* (2006), pp.368–370.

[2] On the forces see Plutarch, *Antony* 61, with C. Pelling (ed.), *Plutarch: Life of Antony* (1988), pp.266–269, Dio 50. 6. 2–6 gives no numbers, for discussion see P. Brunt, *Italian Manpower 225 BC–AD 14* (1971), pp.500–507, and J. Carter, *The Battle of Actium: The Rise and Triumph of Augustus Caesar* (1970), pp.188–189 and 202–203.

[3] On the crew of a quinquereme see Polybius 1. 26. 7, and see also J. Morrison & J. Coates, *Greek and Roman Oared Warships* (1996), pp.259–260, 270–272 and 312–317, with the review by W. Murray, 'The Development and Design of Greek and Roman Warships (399–30 BC)', *JRA* 12 (1999), pp.520–525, esp. 523–524, where it is argued that ramming was an important, perhaps the main, tactic of the largest galleys; see also M. Pitassi, *The Navies of Rome* (2009), esp. pp.191–197.

[4] Dio 50. 9. 3, Plutarch, *Antony* 56.

[5] Pelling (1988), pp.259–260, and *CAH*² X, pp.52 and 55, M. Grant, *Cleopatra* (1972), pp.197–198, and R. Syme, *The Roman Revolution* (1960), pp.294–295.

[6] Dio 50. 9. 3 noted that both strategy and supply encouraged Antony to disperse his forces; on the preparations at Actium see Dio 50. 12. 7–8.

[7] Dio 50. 9. 5–6; Plutarch, *Antony* 62 has a variation of this story, claiming that Octavian offered to withdraw from the coast of Italy and let Antony land unmolested.

[8] Dio 50. 10. 1.

[9] Dio 50. 11. 3; for insights into problems of long-range operations in the Roman period, see B. Rankov, 'The Second Punic War at Sea', in T. Cornell, B. Rankov & P. Sabin (eds.), *The Second Punic War: A Reappraisal* (1996), pp.49–56, esp. 49–52.

[10] Plutarch, *Antony* 62, with Pelling (1988), pp.271–272, for the double meaning of 'ladle'; Dio 50. 11. 4–12. 3, and 50. 17. 2 for the quote, taken from the Loeb translation by E. Cary.

[11] Plutarch, *Antony* 63, Dio 50. 12. 4–13. 4, with Pelling in *CAH*² X, pp.55–56, Osgood (2006), pp.372–373, and Carter (1970), pp.203–213. A well-illustrated account of the campaign is provided in S. Sheppard, *Actium: Downfall of Antony and Cleopatra*, Osprey Campaign Series 211 (2009).

[12] Dio 50. 13. 5, Velleius Paterculus 2. 84. 2, Plutarch, *Antony* 68.

[13] Plutarch, *Antony* 63, Dio 50. 13. 5–14. 4.

[14] Plutarch, *Antony* 59, 63, Velleius Paterculus 2. 84. 2, Dio 50. 13. 6, 14. 3, with Osgood (2006), pp.372–373, and Syme (1960), p.296, on the defections; see Osgood (2006), pp.263–264 for the career of Sarmentus, who also appears in Horace, *Satires* 1.

[15] Dio 50. 13. 7–8.

[16] On numbers see Pelling (1988), pp.276–277, W. Murray & P. Petsas, *Octavian's Campsite Memorial for the Actian War*, Transactions of the American Philosophical Society 79. 4 (1989), pp.34–57, 95–114 and 133–134.

[17] See Carter (1970), pp.213–227.

[18] Pliny, *NH* 32. 2 tells a bizarre story of Antony's flagship being halted in the water by a small fish gripping onto its hull.

[19] For the battle see Plutarch, *Antony* 64–66, 68, Dio 50. 14. 4–35. 6, with Osgood

(2006), pp.374–375 and 380–382, Grant (1972), pp.206–215, and Pelling (1988), pp.278–289, and D. Harrington, 'The Battle of Actium – a Study in Historiography', *Ancient World* 9. 1–2 (1984), pp.59–64.

[20] Plutarch, *Antony* 68, Dio 51. 1. 4–3. 1, Velleius Paterculus 2. 85. 5–6, with L. Keppie, *The Making of the Roman Army* (1984), pp.134–136.

[21] Plutarch, *Antony* 66; Josephus, *Against Apion* 2. 59 is the earliest author to accuse Cleopatra of treachery, and is followed by Dio 50. 33. 1–5.

XXIX 'A FINE DEED'

[1] Dio 51. 1, 5, and Plutarch, *Antony* 67, 69 with C. Pelling (ed.), *Plutarch: Life of Antony* (1988), pp.285–287, 289, including discussions of the similarities to his account of Pompey's escape from Pharsalus; on forces see P. Brunt, *Italian Manpower 225 BC–AD 14* (1971), pp.500–507, where it is argued that even if Octavian did not have many more legions than Antony, these were significantly larger in size; on Pinarius see R. Syme, *The Roman Revolution* (1960), pp.128 and 266.

[2] Dio 51. 5. 2–5, Josephus, *Against Apion* 2. 58; on the music and garlands when her ships entered the harbour see the comment in G. Goudchaux, 'Cleopatra's Subtle Religious Strategy', in S. Walker & P. Higgs (eds.), *Cleopatra of Egypt: From History to Myth* (2001), pp.128–141, esp. 140; J. Tyldesley, *Cleopatra: Last Queen of Egypt* (2009), p.181, doubts the executions on the implausible basis that Cleopatra needed the support of the Alexandrians; J. Fletcher, *Cleopatra the Great: The Woman Behind the Legend* (2008), p.297, suggests the temples willingly gave the queen their treasures; M. Grant, *Cleopatra* (1972), pp.217–218 and p.275, n. 7, on the priests of Upper Egypt. The source is Pseudo-Acro's commentary on Horace, *Odes* 1. 37, 23.

[3] Strabo, *Geog.* 17. 1. 9, Plutarch, *Antony* 69–70, with Pelling (1988), pp.291–293, and G. Grimm, 'Alexandria in the Time of Cleopatra', in S. Walker & S. Ashton (eds.), *Cleopatra Reassessed* (2003), pp.45–49, esp. 49.

[4] Plutarch, *Antony* 68.

[5] Plutarch, *Antony* 71, Dio 51. 2. 1–6, 4. 1, 5. 1, Josephus, *AJ* 15. 183–198; in general see J. Osgood, *Caesar's Legacy: Civil War and the Emergence of the Roman Empire* (2006), pp.375–378 and 385–390.

[6] Dio 51. 3. 1–4. 8.

[7] See Pelling (1988), pp.289–291, and Osgood (2006), pp.387–388, citing *ILS* 2672 for fortifications on the Spanish coast.

[8] Dio 51. 6. 3–7. 1, Plutarch, *Antony* 69, who says that Antony was fifty-three and Cleopatra thirty-nine when they died. Since the ancients did not have a zero, this would imply that each was in fact a year younger. However, their probable dates of birth make this unlikely. Plutarch, *Antony* 71, with Pelling (1988), pp.295–296.

[9] Plutarch, *Antony* 71.

[10] Plutarch, *Antony* 71, Dio 51. 6. 1–2.

[11] Dio 51. 6. 4–8. 7, Plutarch, *Antony* 72–73, with Pelling (1988), pp.297–300.

[12] Dio 51. 7. 2–7, Josephus, *AJ* 15. 195.

[13] Plutarch, *Antony* 74.

[14] For Gallus, see Syme (1960), pp.75 and 252–253.

[15] Dio 51. 9. 1–6, Plutarch, *Antony* 74, with Pelling (1988), p.300.

[16] Dio 51. 10. 1–4, Plutarch, *Antony* 74.

[17] Plutarch, *Antony* 75, with Pelling (1988), pp.302–304.

[18] Dio 51. 10. 4–5, Plutarch, *Antony* 76; see Grant (1972), pp.222–223, who doubts treachery and sees the defections as due to the hopelessness of the situation.

[19] Plutarch, *Antony* 76, Dio 51. 10. 5–7, with Grimm (2003), pp.48–49, on the mausoleum's location and design.

[20] Dio 51. 10. 6–9, Plutarch, *Antony* 76–77, with Pelling (1988), pp.305–308; see also Grant (1972), pp.222–223, and Tyldesley (2009), p.186; Fletcher (2008), pp.309–310 suggests that Cleopatra believed Antony was dead before going to the tomb.

[21] Plutarch, *Antony* 80, Dio 51. 16. 4, with Suetonius, *Augustus* 89. 1, which refers to his association with Areius and other scholars, but also his limited fluency in Greek.

[22] Dio 51. 11. 1–4, and 14. 3 for the eunuch, Plutarch, *Antony* 78–79.

[23] On Antony's funeral see Tyldesley (2009), pp.195–196, and Fletcher (2008), p.312.

[24] Dio 51. 11. 3, 5–13., Plutarch, *Antony* 82–83, with Pelling (1988), pp.313–316, Florus 2. 21. 9–10.

[25] Plutarch, *Antony* 84.

[26] Grant (1972), pp.225–226, argues that it was better for Octavian to let the queen die.

[27] Strabo, *Geog.* 17. 1. 10.

[28] Dio 51. 13. 4–14. 6, Plutarch, *Antony* 84–86, with Pelling (1988), pp.316–322, Velleius Paterculus 2. 87. 1; see also Grant (1972), pp.224–228, Tyldesley (2009), pp.189–195, Fletcher (2008), pp.314–319, E. Rice, *Cleopatra* (1999), pp.86–91, P. Green, *Alexander to Actium: The Historical Evolution of the Hellenistic Age* (1990), pp.679–682, and G. Hölbl, *A History of the Ptolemaic Empire* (trans. T. Saavedra) (2001), pp.248–249.

CONCLUSION: HISTORY AND THE GREAT ROMANCE

[1] Dio 51. 14. 3–4, 15. 1, 16. 3–5, Suetonius, *Augustus* 17. 3–5.

[2] Dio 51. 16. 5–17. 1, 6–8, Plutarch, *Antony* 86, with C. Pelling (ed.), *Plutarch: Life of Antony* (1988), p.323, and G. Goudchaux, 'Cleopatra's Subtle Religious Strategy', in S. Walker & P. Higgs (eds.), *Cleopatra of Egypt: From History to Myth* (2001), pp.128–141, esp. p.140; Pliny, *NH* 9. 121 on the pearl, with E. Gruen, 'Cleopatra in Rome: Fact and Fantasies', in D. Braund & C. Gill (eds.), *Myths, History and Culture in Republican Rome: Studies in Honour of T. P. Wiseman* (2003), pp.257–274, esp. 259.

[3] Velleius Paterculus 2. 86. 1–3, 87. 2–3, R. Syme, *The Roman Revolution* (1960), pp.296–297 and 299–300, and J. Osgood, *Caesar's Legacy: Civil War and the Emergence of the Roman Empire* (2006), pp.276–280.

[4] Dio 51. 15. 5, Plutarch, *Antony* 81.

[5] Plutarch, *Antony* 81, Dio 51. 15. 5–6; quote from Homer, *Iliad* 2. 203–207 (Latimore translation, University of Chicago, 1951).

[6] Dio 51. 21. 5–9, Horace, *Odes* 1. 37, the famous *nunc est bibendum*; see also Osgood (2006), p.385.

[7] Dio 51. 15. 6–7, Plutarch, *Antony* 87.

[8] For example, Appian, *BC* 4. 130, Plutarch, *Antony* 22.

[9] For studies of Cleopatra in later culture see L. Hughes-Hallett, *Cleopatra: Queen, Lover, Legend* (1990, reprinted with new afterword 2006), and M. Hamer, *Signs of Cleopatra: History, Politics, Representation* (1993). For a more specific study of Cleopatra in Roman culture see D. Kleiner, *Cleopatra and Rome* (2005).

INDEX

455

464